1981

GEORGE SAND AND THE VICTORIANS

*Her Influence and Reputation
in Nineteenth-century England*

Patricia Thomson

Columbia University Press
New York   1977

Published in Great Britain in 1977 by
THE MACMILLAN PRESS LTD

Printed in Great Britain

Library of Congress Cataloging in Publication Data

Thomson, Patricia.
  George Sand and the Victorians.

  Bibliography : p.
  Includes index.
  1. Sand, George, pseud. of Mme. Dudevant, 1804–1876—In-
fluence. 2. English literature—19th century—History and criticism.
I. Title.
PQ2419.T5 1977   843'.8   76–30654

ISBN 0–231–04262–0

To Maurice

'Le coeur ne peut pas tromper.'

Contents

Acknowledgements

Some of the research for this book has already been published in article form. Chapter 1 appeared in *Modern Language Review*, vol. 67, no. 3, pp. 501–16. Chapter 3 was first published under the title 'Elizabeth Barrett and George Sand' in the *Durham University Journal*, vol. 33, no. 3, pp. 205–19. Chapter 5 appeared in the *Review of English Studies*, vol. 24, no. 93, pp. 26–37; and chapter 9 in *Nineteenth-Century Fiction*, vol. 18, no. 2, pp. 137–50, © 1963 by the Regents of the University of California, and now reprinted by permission of The Regents.

I am grateful to the editors of these journals for permission to use this material here.

A compensation for the solitary lot of the scholar researching on George Sand in England is that I have very few formal acknowledgements to make. It was very pleasant, however, to be encouraged in correspondence from the other side of the Channel, by M. Georges Lubin, and from across the Atlantic by Professor Ellen Moers. I should also like to thank all my friends and colleagues who, over the past few years, have retrieved for me, from their Victorian reading, specific references to George Sand. I am especially indebted to Beynon John, who was kind enough to read my translations in proof and to make valuable and discriminating suggestions.

Note on the Text

Practically all the Victorians I deal with read George Sand in French and were acutely aware of how much of her distinctive flavour was lost in translation. I have compromised by keeping all the key passages in French, especially those which are dependent for their effect on atmosphere, and have provided translations in the notes. I have translated fairly literally, except where, as in passages from *Lélia*, the result would be ludicrous. Sometimes, too, I have found it useful to leave phrases and sentences in French where the sentiment is so similar to that expressed by an English writer in a parallel extract in the text, that if they were translated it would be difficult to tell the two extracts apart.

Introduction

1

Enough – and more than enough – has been written on George Sand's love-affairs. This is a book about the effect of her novels on England. While it is often very difficult to separate this from her influence as a personality, what is very clear is that her impact on the Victorian reading public and, more importantly, on Victorian writers was enormous and that, although fully recognised at the time, it has now been almost completely forgotten.

And yet reviews, letters, autobiographies, articles of the period all tell the same story. She was read and discussed and argued about up and down the kingdom. Her novels penetrated everywhere; they were as much a source of excitement in Oxford colleges as in drawing-rooms in London or vicarages in Cumberland. Whether or not she was approved of, she was a very significant part of the Victorian conscious-ness and a formative influence on countless young men and women who read her novels. All her English admirers shared in the initial sense of release and liberation that her passionate pages brought them, after which each took from her cornucopia what suited his needs – and what each chose to concentrate on is as revealing of his personality as of her achievement.

As we look back to the period we can scarcely see George Sand for the great, looming bulk of the Victorian novel, which we are so prone to consider as a purely indigenous product, that we tend to ignore any writer who is not deep-rooted in the 'English tradition' as an influence on its growth. But George Sand was read in French in the 1830s and 1840s and, as has been pointed out, critics 'moved at will back and forth across the English Channel',[1] combining major English and French novelists in one line of development. Up to the time of Scott the influence was all one way, from England to France, but after 1830, as we shall see, the situation changed.

When I say that her influence is not known I do not, of course, mean that she is no longer studied by scholars. In fact, it would be true to say that in France of recent years the reverse is the case. There has been a considerable renewal of interest in her novels, as the splendid

Classiques Garnier editions testify; and the great edition of her *Correspondance* is a monument not only to her never-sleeping pen but to the scholarship and dedication of that most distinguished doyen of George Sand studies, Georges Lubin, to whom all George Sandists are indebted. I am sorry that Curtis Cate's lively and scholarly biography of George Sand came out too late for me to make use of it; an English reappraisal was long overdue.

There has been, however, a steady trickle of comparativist studies, focusing attention upon her effect in Russia and America; and I found that my own researches had been to a certain extent forestalled by some thoughtful work upon her relationship with Arnold, Elizabeth Barrett, Clough and Henry James. But there has been no overall picture of 'George Sandism' in Victorian England, although many scholars of the period have been aware of and regretted the lack.[2] I hope that this study, a hundred years after her death, will once again bring to light facts which were so well-known that it would then have seemed inconceivable that they should ever be forgotten.

I am very conscious of the fact that even the most literate readers of this book will have no more than a nodding acquaintance with one or two of George Sand's novels, and often, unfortunately, they are the one or two for which it is difficult to put up a case. I cannot imagine anyone, for instance, who started upon George Sand with *La Comtesse de Rudolstadt* not finishing his exploration that same day. I have tried to avoid giving full accounts of the novels except where one particular tale has been of particular significance for a writer; I leave revaluation of George Sand in the able hands of French literary critics although inevitably, in discussing what her English readers made of her, I have often had to analyse the original text. As her novels are virtually unread in England now, it will probably be helpful to give, at this point, an outline of her literary output and to provide sign-posts to mark the different stages of her career.

2

George Sand was a professional woman of letters all her life, from the time she left Nohant for Paris in 1831, at the age of twenty-seven, until she died in 1876. In these forty-five years she wrote on average two books annually. It is small wonder that critics, when confronted with such a vast quantity of material, have always been tempted to divide it up, chronologically, as neatly as possible into manageable parcels. As soon as one is really familiar with her work, the inadequacy of such labelling becomes obvious, but initially this approach does have the merit of encouraging in the reader a momentary sense of control over her enormous output, by grouping her novels in relation to successive phases of her life. In each case the 'phase' can be shown to be a procrustean bed for her overflowing abundance, but enough of her is contained within it to make the exercise worthwhile.

George Sand's 'first period', then, is distinguished by novels in which the influence of Byron and Rousseau is very evident, novels of personal revolt and passion, turbulent self-expression and feminism. To these early years (1831–7) belong such novels as *Indiana, Valentine, Jacques, Lélia* and *Mauprat*. In them she is exclusively concerned with the relationship between men and women – 'with love – nothing but love', as an outraged English reviewer commented. She attacks not only the marriage laws which make women slaves to their husbands and deprive them of all the rights they had before marriage, but a society which, through its conventions, inhibits truthfulness, spontaneity and passion in women. The law with which she is most concerned in these early romances is the law of the heart – and although she is drawing on her own experiences and wrongs, she feels that she is stating the case for her sex. Indiana, is not simply a heroine; she is '. . . un type; c'est la femme, l'être faible chargé de representer *les passions* comprimées, ou, si vous l'aimez mieux, supprimées par *les lois*; c'est la volonté aux prises avec la nécessité; c'est l'amour heurtant son front aveugle à tous les obstacles de la civilisation'.[3]

The originality and courage of George Sand in challenging pre-conceived and ingrained masculine assumptions about woman's role in society should not be underestimated. When accused of preaching Saint-Simonism she expressed surprise, for she was drawing on her personal experience of an unhappy marriage from which she had just determinedly escaped. *Indiana* not only created a furore; it was generously acclaimed by the critics for its 'boldness of conception'. It was hailed by Balzac as 'a modern novel', a book of which he said 'Je ne connais rien de plus simplement écrit, de plus délicieusement conçu.'[4] There had been nothing quite like *Indiana* before. In comparison with the problems of George Sand's heroine, those of Rousseau's Julie and Madame de Staël's Corinne seemed suddenly out-of-date and irrelevant to la *Jeune France*.

Much the most complex and puzzling of the works of these early years is *Lélia* (1833), which was written by George Sand in a mood of bitter disillusionment and romantic, self-indulgent despair. It is an allegory which at times is ludicrous, fantastic and pretentious, at others moving in its lyrical abandonment and imaginative power. Its heroine, a female Faust or Manfred, who having known satiety is now hopelessly seeking for some escape from the scepticism which is drying up her life-force, is in quite another category from Indiana, whose problems could all be solved by social equality between the sexes. The questions asked in *Lélia* are much more fundamental to nineteenth-century civilisation, and express the *mal du siècle* from which many of George Sand's contemporaries were never wholly to escape, but from which she moved on to the philosophy of optimistic acceptance which became a distinctive feature of her writings.

Even as one describes this early period as that of novels of passion, one also has to remember that her stay in Venice with de Musset at this time, with all its disastrous personal consequences, was an unequivocal good for her literary production, for it led to her using the theme of Italy and the artist in many of her novels, and to making a start upon an undoubted masterpiece, *Lettres d'un Voyageur*. These letters, written after de Musset left, and published at intervals in the *Revue des Deux Mondes*, contain some of her finest, freshest and most lyrically evocative passages, and strike the note of confidential intimacy with her readers which she never from that time lost.

George Sand said herself, of *Indiana*, that she wrote it 'sous l'empire d'une emotion et non d'un système'.[5] She was not however short of 'systèmes' to expound in the next decade, up to the 1848 revolution. This was the period in her life when she was most deeply involved in politics, both theoretically and practically, and her novels reflect her new preoccupation. De Musset, her aristocratic lover, had been followed by the republican lawyer, Michel de Bourges, and it was initially he who directed her gaze outwards to society, away from her own anguish and sufferings. 'Pas tant de sollicitude pour une seule créature!' he said, drawing her attention instead to 'cette humanité qui déroge et qui souffre'.[6] But his ideal society was to come about through militancy and was to be ruled by power, and George Sand, who was, as she said, 'by nature poetic and not legislative', was not won over to his vision of violence. Nor was she long a disciple of the Abbé de Lamennais, who although an idealist, was too austere a moralist and too little a man of action to satisfy her. The prophet who seized her imagination and made a lasting impression on her writings for several years to come, was, instead, Pierre Leroux, to whom, as to Lamennais, she was first introduced by Sainte-Beuve. The critic later regretted her tendency to fall under the spell of prophets who were so vastly inferior to her in talent: 'C'est un écho qui double la voix . . . Et elle faut mieux que doubler leur voix, elle la rend méconnaissable.'[7] But Leroux's gospel of humanity seemed to her then exactly what she had been looking for.

In 1837 she wrote, half-seriously, 'Je tombe dans le Pierre Leroux';[8] by the next year she was his disciple. Leroux had been a Saint-Simonist but had broken with them because of their religious and sexual extravagances. In his socialism he envisaged the gradual and peaceful take-over of government by the proletariat and he preached a form of creative evolution, which stressed the absolute need of co-operation

between men in this life; in the next, theirs would be a collective
immortality. He believed in the sanctity of marriage, but only if the
sexes were considered equal, and he accepted the need in most men for
a religion. As Christianity was defective, the philosophy of Leroux
could fill the gap, with its congenial blend of meliorism and mysticism,
pantheism and reincarnation, egalitarianism and feminism. Leroux's
influence can be seen in many of the novels of George Sand which
followed her initiation into his doctrines; they might indeed have been
especially manufactured for her. The capacious Leroux umbrella
contrived to cover a great many remarkably different novels. His
sentiments can be heard in *Spiridion* (1838–9), a mystic tale set in a
monastery; *Consuelo* (1842–3), which charmed its readers with its *prima
donna* heroine and its recreation of musical circles in the eighteenth
century, but also carried a heavy burden of argument for the sacerdotal
role of the artist in society; *Le Meunier d'Angibault* (1845), which has an
homme du peuple for a hero; and, in varying forms, in many other novels
of the early 1840s, such as *Horace, Le Compagnon du Tour de France, Le
Péché de Monsieur Antoine* and *Jeanne*. And the ghost of his presence can
still be detected in what Sainte-Beuve describes[9] as the 'il faut . . . il
faut . . . il faut' nature of some of her prefaces to the tales, which are
always considered separately in a third group, George Sand's
'bergeries'.

Set in her native Berry countryside, with unlettered peasants for
heroes and heroines, these pastoral stories are remote from politics but
are imbued with democratic humanitarianism. They are realistic in
detail and background but gentle and idealistic in their philosophy.
They have sometimes been considered as George Sand's reaction to the
1848 débacle – a going back to the land in fiction as well as in fact – but
she did actually write the first of them, *La Mare au Diable*, in 1845,
when she was still far from disillusioned with politics. By the time she
wrote *La Petite Fadette* (1848) she was more disposed to consider
these stories as a relief from her involvement in the political scene and
she wrote a charming preface entitled, 'Pourquoi nous revenons à nos
moutons'. The immediate cause of her embarking on this series of
rustic stories was probably a literary one. She made no secret of the
fact that she was revolted by the scenes of horror and filth in Eugène
Sue's *Mystères de Paris* and *Le Juif Errant*, and she also objected to what
she felt was Balzac's biased and cynical presentation of the peasant
mentality in his recent novel, *Les Paysans*. She herself was convinced
that art should ennoble and strengthen, and there seems little doubt
that *La Mare au Diable* was undertaken quite deliberately as 'la
riposte d'un écrivain idéaliste à une littérature surtout préoccupée
d'observer et de peindre la laideur'.[10]

When Chorley, the *Athenaeum* reviewer, talked in 1846 of different 'eras' in George Sand's literary career, Elizabeth Barrett poured scorn on the idea and called it 'infinite trash . . . As if earnestness of aim was not from the beginning . . . a characteristic of George Sand.'[11] And it is true that unifying all her writing in these first two decades is her quality of total commitment. She always cared about what she was attacking or the cause she was espousing; she was often outrageous but never flippant, and in this may lie some of her appeal to the Victorian reader. She is indeed as earnest in her early pleas for justice and freedom within marriage for women as in her pleading in the 1840s for equality and liberty within society for the working classes; but her early novels, written out of a sense of her own sorrows, are still very easily distinguished from those inspired by the teachings of Leroux – and to that extent, at least, they do lend themselves to some sort of meaningful grouping.

But the same cannot be said of the works of her last twenty-five years. It does not help much to call them 'miscellaneous', and yet I suppose it is as good a description as any other. There is only one totally memorable work, her *Histoire de ma Vie* (1855), in which the portraits of her mother and grandmother, the impression she conveys of her father through his letters and her recreation of her own child-hood, are as lively as anything she ever wrote. Or as Henry James put it in typical vein: '. . . as an autobiography of the beginnings and earlier maturities of life it is indeed finer and jollier than anything there is.'[12]

But before that, we have five years of writing for the stage for which, however much the theatre fascinated her, she was not suited, with her fluent expansiveness of style. And in the 1870s, there were such non-fictional works as *Journal d'un Voyageur pendant la Guerre, Impressions et Souvenirs, Questions d'Art et de Littérature*. But on the whole the 'mouton' to which she had returned was novel-making. She wrote for money in order to support her much-loved Nohant establishment of family, friends and dependents. Although she wrote as effortlessly as other women knit – or as she herself said, 'much as another person might garden' – and, once she was seated at her desk, page after page flowed from her pen, her facility should not take away from the sheer self-discipline and professionalism which went into each novel. She followed a rigid routine because she knew that unless she was prepared to shoulder a crushing load of work, Nohant and all it stood for would founder. And so it was that, hot on one another's heels, came *La Daniella, L'Homme de Neige, Valvèdre, Tamaris, Le Marquis de Villemer, Malgrétout, Mademoiselle Merquem* and many, many more, each at first sight more innocuous and moral than the one before, until we reach, in her old age, *Contes d'Une Grandmère*. This is not to say that those who have succumbed to the appeal of George Sand will not find much to please and interest them in these novels. Even Saintsbury, who had no time for her, not only made an exception of *Lucrezia Floriani*, a novel which most of her admirers would have wished unwritten, but admitted grudgingly that 'even at her worst' she is never exactly commonplace.[13] Often these stories surprise by their closeness of observation, wise and thoughtful discussion, and even, in the 1860s, some Flaubertian realism; but on the whole, James's summing up of them as 'charming, improbable romances for initiated persons of the optimistic class' does not do them an injustice. George Sand's earlier passion had now been toned down to a serenely philosophical view of life; the youthful rebel has become la Bonne Dame de Nohant.

It is not surprising, then, that her main impact should have been through the works of her first twenty years, and that those in England who were most vitally influenced by her were, as we shall see, her first generation of readers. Those who made their acquaintance with her novels in the 1840s, when her doctrines were avant-garde and challenging, underwent an experience which was totally different from that of those who read her first in the 1860s and 1870s, however receptive her later public was to her.

But whether it was early George Sand or late George Sand, there was seldom any real correlation between the merits of the novel and its effect on the reader. Even such a book as *Jeanne*, which a normally kindly reviewer condemned as 'feeble', could send Matthew Arnold off to the middle of France to try to meet its author, and provide Clough with ideas for a long poem. What mattered to all her English admirers was that the author raised issues and asked questions which seemed to them to be of supreme contemporary relevance, and that she wrote in a French which enchanted their senses – the last, as will be seen, a point of very great importance.

3

In writing this book it seemed to me essential, first of all, to substantiate my claim that George Sand was not only widely read and reviewed in England in the 1830s and 1840s, but was also very much a talking point in middle-class drawing-rooms. And so the first chapter is a fully documented account of her coverage in reviews and journals, while the second fills in the social background and gives some idea of her effect on literary and radical circles. I then deal with one major Victorian writer after another and, although some warrant much fuller treatment than others, in each case I have attempted first to distinguish the personal response of the writer to George Sand, and then to discuss the literary evidence.

As the century goes on, and her novels and her readers change, there is a place for a further assessment of public attitudes to her, which is gathered from reviews, articles, letters and obituary notices. And finally, I complete the study with a chapter upon the attitude to her of an 'old George Sandist', who was still writing articles on her in the twentieth century – Henry James.

I have guarded against seeming too George Sand-oriented by mentioning as often as I can other writers to whom the Victorians I have singled out are indebted. I am very much aware of how rich a synthesis of source material is drawn upon by most artists, but in a book about George Sand's influence, there is obviously a limit to the amount of space that can be given to others. I make this preliminary caveat in the hope that it will be remembered if, at times, George Sand seems to take over completely and dominate the Victorian age.

But having said this, I am bound to add that there is no great harm in redressing the balance; her influence in England has been neglected for too long. When I began my researches, even though I suspected that the subject would prove very fruitful, I had really no idea that I should find George Sand such a familiar presence in the Victorian age, nor that I should encounter so many writers who not only admired her work but had no hesitation in admitting their indebtedness to her. As I pursued my way through the at times undoubted *longeurs* of George Sand's forgotten novels, one of the minor pleasures of the task has been the sense of following in the tracks of the great Victorians who read her for a different purpose. It is as if all her novels were marked by Victorian pencillings. Two hundred pages into the 900-page novel, *L'Homme de Neige*, nestles the phrase 'cette boisson fade et mélancolique', and as I read it, I know that Arnold has been here before me. For it is the memorable description[14] of tea, as a beverage, of which he made use in his account of his youthful visit to George Sand – even though, with the lapse of thirty years, he attributed the phrase to Balzac.

While I cannot in any sense equal Arnold's long familiarity with the novels, the major pleasure of the work has, of course, been that of getting to know and admire George Sand profoundly through her writings. She certainly wrote much too much, and many of her later novels are simply earlier fictions, either rewritten or turned on their heads. But even though, in the end, there is only a handful of her works to which I shall return, I can honestly say that even from her poorest novels I always took away something of value. Perhaps the only way to do such a writer justice is to read her in bulk, in order to get the benefit of her infinite variety and the genius of her self-expression.

But the major scholarly satisfaction has been that of learning the nature and extent of her influence. As far as nineteenth-century prose fiction is concerned, it has always been difficult to bridge the gap between the achievement of Scott and Jane Austen and that of the Brontës and George Eliot. I see George Sand as the missing link between the earlier nineteenth-century writers and those of the Victorian period, in her introduction of passion as a major theme in the novel. For too long the predominantly English critical tradition has made the Victorians seem more insular, less literary than they were. George Sand, who had learned much from Richardson, Scott and Byron was, in turn, able to influence, with her analysis of passion, her poetry and her generous width of humanity, the later generation of English writers.

1 George Sand and English Reviewers: The First Twenty Years

Of all French writers, George Sand made the most impression in England in the 1830s and 1840s. More than Hugo, much more than Balzac, she stood for English readers as a symbol of the post-revolutionary writing of France. It was in February 1833 that she was first mentioned in English journals. The *Athenaeum*, true to its policy of foreign coverage, gave a largely inaccurate, though picturesque, gossip note on her:

> The writer of *Indiana* and *Valentine*, is now positively known to be Madame Dudevant, a young lady who, some years back, distinguished herself at the age of thirteen by an indomitable wish to escape from her parents and seek out Lord Byron. Frustrated in this, she was subsequently married *à la mode française* to some son of the earth most unlike the poet. Doubtful of the success of her productions, she published under the name of her friend Sand, who thus finds himself loaded with a celebrity which, not having enough talent to support, he has confessed the truth; and the lady thus alone stands answerable for works that do more honour to her genius than her delicacy.[1]

It is typical that rumours of her life should have preceded any account of her works. The *Athenaeum*, however, put that right in subsequent issues with a review of *Indiana* and *Valentine* in March, three columns devoted to *Lélia* in September and an account of *Jacques* in December of the following year – so that, by the end of 1834, its readers should have been up to date with George Sand's output.

These reviews set the tone of admiration, mingled with moral outrage, which becomes very familiar in the next decade. From the start, the reviewer is aware that he is dealing with 'a Phenomenon', with the current French favourite, more read than Balzac, as much talked of in the salons as Rossini – and every disapproving comment is nicely balanced by a tribute. He makes very heavy weather of her name, and cannot leave well alone: 'avowedly Mr George Sands but . . . now known to be Mme Dudevant'; 'The lady (who conceals her odd and harsh sounding name – *Dudevant* – under the pseudonym of George Sand) . . .'; 'This George Sand . . . is no other than Mrs Sand, whose real name is Dudevant.' Each time a new combination is tried. It was, of course, the first, though certainly not the last, masculine pseudonym to trouble English ears. Where George Sand led, Currer Bell and George Eliot were to follow.

The subversive nature of the first novels seems largely to have escaped the reviewer. Indeed much escapes him. Sir Ralph Brown in *Indiana* (also variously referred to by George Sand as M. Rodolphe Brown, Mr Brown, and Sir Brown) was intended to typify a phlegmatic but chivalrous English milord, and his dismissal by the reviewer as an 'absurd Scotchman' does argue a certain cursoriness of reading. He is much more disposed to concentrate on the romantic settings and poetic descriptions. What he marvels at, in particular, is the ability of French readers to enjoy tales which are 'love from beginning to end . . . in England, they would not be tolerated, not only on account of their immoral tendency and licentious descriptions but that, really, two volumes of all love and nothing but love, would be palling to English taste.'[2]

With *Lélia*, the formidable nature of George Sand's challenge to accepted ideas is fully realised: 'We cannot look upon it but as an unreal mockery . . . a bold, brazen paradox born, fostered and nourished . . . in the whirl and turbulence of Parisian politics, manners and questionable morality.' Lélia herself is summed up as 'a monster, a Byronic woman – a woman without hope and without soul'. Her melancholy, perverse philosophy has not been uncommon in French novels but 'no woman has heretofore declared herself as a disciple'. Had this book been written in England it 'would have been pursued by the hue and cry of every critic in the kingdom'.[3]

Equally violent though less patriotic reactions were aroused in France by *Lélia*. What got under the skin of critics on both sides of the Channel was Lélia's total disbelief in progress, her scepticism, her sense of being 'deracinée du présent', and her disbelief in conventional ideas of virtue.

The review of *Jacques*, fifteen months later, is mild in comparison. George Sand is 'undoubtedly the most gifted and most original female writer of her country and times, a sort of female Jean-Jacques Rousseau'. Although her 'perpetual war against the nuptial vow' and 'the highly heated atmosphere of Parisian life must be deplored', she does have 'deep knowledge of the female heart . . . wonderful truth of feeling and observation . . . rapid and burning eloquence'. She is, in fact, 'a woman of genius'.[4]

Other journals, although less systematic in their reviewing than the *Athenaeum* were similarly aware of George Sand's significance; the *Foreign Quarterly Review* in 1834 devoted twenty-six pages[5] to an account of all her novels. There is still considerable uncertainty about the name of the '*soi-disant* George Sand' and some musings about her reputation; 'a lady (as we have been informed, but cannot vouch) of unblemished character . . . a new and radiant, if not perfectly salutiferous star.' Reference is made to the author's own injuries in marriage – 'in the irritation of unhappiness [she] has lost the sensitive pudicity of her sex' – and *Lélia* is deplored as 'decidedly the worst . . . a compound of romance, *ultra*-German transcendentalism, and the coldest irony . . . The poet, ex-galley slave and Lelia herself are all so mystically metaphysical . . . as actually to bewilder a plain English intellect.' *Jacques* is noted as a return to the style of *Indiana* and *Valentine*. Like them, it is concerned with matrimonial miseries and George Sand 'would well deserve to be called the *Anti-Matrimonial Novelist*'. This last quip was one which remained in currency for a long time.

Less barbed, indeed gallant and courtly in tone, showing little critical sense but no ill-will, is an article in the *Monthly Magazine*, entitled 'French Authoresses. No. 1 Madame Sand'. It consists largely of a long extract from *Rose et Blanche*, which the writer strangely prefers to *Indiana*. Owning that he is 'partial to the writings of the gentler sex', he pays tribute to France which 'has been always distinguished for the literary talents of her daughters' and to 'the lady who delights in the unpretending cognomen of G. Sand'. Conscious of being somewhat out of his depth, he attempts, a little helplessly, to define her by what she is not:

> We know of no English authoress whom we could select as a parallel to convey an idea of her peculiar manner. She is not so profoundly Malthusian as Miss Martineau, nor so masculine and philosophical as Miss Edgeworth; neither is she a describer of balls and routs and a puffer of tradesmen, like Mrs Gore. Her style is peculiarly her own.[6]

North of the border, unmindful of the Auld Alliance, *Blackwood's Magazine*[7] and the *Edinburgh Review* were thundering against the moral anarchy, lack of religious convictions, profligate extravagance, and wild flights of imagination of current French fiction, but seemed strangely ill-informed about the novels of George Sand, which they had clearly not read. In fact the *Edinburgh Review* deliberately exempts from censure the tales 'of M. Sand, which are written in a calmer, truer, better spirit than those with which we have been occupied.'[8] As late as

1836, *Blackwood's Magazine* is still so out of touch that, in expressing their indebtedness to an article on Talleyrand by 'Madam Sand, better known by her former name of Madame Dudevant', they describe her as an authoress of 'several very pleasing and successful ro-mances'.[9]

Two months later an embarrassed correction follows. *Blackwood's* had been 'precipitate and . . . credulous . . . touching that highly-gifted but singularly unwomanly, at least unhonest-womanly authoress, Madame Dudevant *alias* George Sand . . . We spoke of this lady and her novels upon report, upon the strength of French praise, without having seen either.' To make amends, they have read no fewer than six of her novels, but their primary concern is to put right their gaffe about her matrimonial status, which they explain in all its intricacies. They do not deny that her books are 'clever . . . very clever', but deplore the fact that she writes, 'if not licentiously yet with an utter recklessness', and proceed to hold up each novel, in turn, to ridicule.[10] Then, having sponged the slate clean in this satisfactory manner, *Blackwood's Magazine* thankfully abandons the subject for a full decade and leaves the vexed question of 'this lady' for other reviews to handle.

1836–1840

The reading public had not long to wait. The very next month, in April 1836, the most notorious attack of the era on the French novel was launched. It was in the best *Quarterly Review* tradition of vitupera-tion and inaccuracy, and its tone recalled the earlier savaging of Keats and Tennyson.

The *Quarterly Review* had already, two years earlier, published a derogatory account of French drama, but the novel article is very much more hostile. In the curious mélange of authors, listed in increasing order of danger to readers – Paul de Kock, Hugo, Dumas, Balzac, Michel Raymond, Michel Masson, and, finally, George Sand – and in the great number of their works to which Croker refers with particu-larity, we can see an all-out effort on the part of the *Quarterly*. It is, as Sainte-Beuve observed with wry mockery, 'une mesure d'hygiène morale, je dirai presque de police locale.'[11]

Quite clearly the contemporary French novel had already made a big impact: Croker would have hesitated to bring this 'mass of profligacy before the eyes of the British public', but 'the novels are seen everywhere . . . they are advertised in a thousand ways over the whole reading world . . . When we see them exhibited even in London in the windows of respectable shops – when they are to be had in circulating libraries . . . nay; ladies' *book-clubs*'[12] the obvious duty is 'to *stigmatise* them with a BRAND'. In fact, he hopes his article will have the same effect as 'labelling vials or packets POISON'.

The source of all the impurity was, of course, Rousseau, the old apostle of disorder, but none of the writers is more tainted than George Sand who is 'a lady – a lady, if not of rank at least of title – of *Madame la Baronne du Devant'*. Croker is comically torn between stressing the discrepancy between George Sand's gentle birth and her views, and disputing her right to a title; and he goes on, in a splendid flight of fancy, to suggest that she has chosen the name of Sand in remembrance of the assassinator of Kotzebue: 'A *German* name can hardly have been chosen at random by a *French* writer.'

But as she has chosen a man's name, he will show her no chivalry. This promise Croker certainly makes good. He presents the plot of each novel in turn in the most ridiculous and distorted light, and lumps them all together in his general condemnation. Sainte-Beuve points out that he speaks, in the same breath, of what is most charming and most open to question in George Sand's novels: 'Indiana et Valentine tombent frappées du même coup que Lélia.' But while it is true that Croker shows no critical sense, he is not unaware that *Lélia* gives him most ammunition:

> We cannot refrain from distinguishing from the impure crowd the revolting romance of *Lélia* of which the heroines – high-born and wealthy heroines, be it observed – are not merely *prostitutes* but *monsters* – the men, convicts, maniacs, and murderers – the incidents such as never before were printed in any book publicly sold – and the work altogether such as in any country in the world but France would be burned by the hangman.

The last clause is blatantly revealing of the Tory distrust and fear of France which underlies the whole review as, apart from a few brief interludes, it had manifested itself in writings throughout the first three decades of the century.

Croker is clearly using the French novel as a stick with which to beat the French nation, but even so the article did George Sand's reputation in England much damage. I cannot agree with Moraud[13] that the abuse was so unrestrained that the article did more good than harm by rousing the hostility of other journals. Much of the mud did stick, and both Mazzini and Lewes were to refer feelingly to the ill-effects of this 'famous-infamous article'. Echoes of its distinctive tone of insular righteousness rumble in many subsequent articles, and as late as 1850 we find the *Dublin University Magazine* still thankful to Croker for having lit the warning beacons: 'It was well for the morality of our higher and middle classes, and especially for the young, that the memorable article on this subject in a leading contemporary scared the public with the mention of some of the grosser abominations in which many of these writers have dealt.'[14]

The immediate response to the article was mixed. The *Examiner* deplored it, not because it disagreed but because it felt that it would serve 'as a catalogue, a complete guide to smutty reading'.[15] The *Westminster Review* briskly described the *Quarterly* as 'a review not famous for the strict honesty of its criticisms',[16] and promised a defence of the French novel in a future issue. The *Athenaeum* in the following year ran a long series by Jules Janin on 'Literature of the Nineteenth Century in France', of which the June article is dedicated to 'that writer without a peer whom your prudish and pedantic England has insulted without knowing . . . George Sand.' This is written in such a bombastic and inflated style that readers must have felt it confirmed their worst fears about the meretricious and hermaphrodite nature of the novelist. There is a great deal of local colour; Janin is concerned to show her as a child of the barricades:

> Shortly after the revolution of July . . . a handsome young man, with quick and penetrating eye, dark hair, and intellectual bearing – lively, laughing, curious and unconstrained – entered Paris. He . . . felt himself, at once, as warmly excited as the young conscript in his first battle. Already was her hand groping in the literary ammunition-box, to find there the baton of a marshal of France . . .
>
> George Sand, in his own home, is, by turns, a capricious young man, of eighteen, and a very pretty woman of from five-and-twenty to thirty, – a youth of eighteen, who smokes and takes snuff with peculiar grace, and a *grande dame* whose brilliancy and fancy at once astonish and humble you.[17]

For seven long *Athenaeum* columns all is exaggerated praise, from the opening 'Who then is *he* – or who is *she*? – man or woman – angel or demon – paradox or truth?' to the final eulogy. It is a strange article and a strange series for the *Athenaeum* to run, although the friendship of Dilke with Janin no doubt goes far to explain it. With Croker as enemy and Janin as sponsor, George Sand's press was not such as any serious novelist would have welcomed.

But in 1838 the *Westminster Review* published its promised article in defence of French fiction. This turned out to be a thoughtful and significant article by 'F.B.',[18] which was the first serious attempt in the 1830s to understand what the French novel had to offer that home produce lacked. What he emphasises, above all, is the vigour and fertility of French literature which 'will and must one day strongly affect ours'. There had been something 'gigantic and exciting in the recent history of France', and this is reflected in French fiction, which

is full of questioning, examining, sifting of all external and internal fact
in the interests of humanity:

> Behind the apparent life, that other unrealized one; a sort of dreamt
> life, which has its pains, its gaiety, its love, its separations, without
> other outward sign than a passing cloud on the brow, a momentary
> light in the eye. This internal poem, which we never read ourselves,
> the novel will repeat to us.[19]

The democratic aspect of the fiction, too, has its attraction. The
heroes 'not only of Sand but of the mere *litterateurs*' are almost always
men of the people, and the social condition of women is one of the many
questions fermenting in the French mind. George Sand is idealistic and
not immoral; she never makes evil agreeable: 'It is against, and not for
license, that Sand is contending; for the right of a woman to belong to
the man she deems worthy, and while she deems him worthy. How
completely is the thing sought always a pure, unselfish, eternal
affection!' In French novels, the manner is as important as the matter:
'And then their style! never, surely, was style carried to a greater
perfection . . . Sand's, for instance, so clear, pure, keen, we seem to
breathe some mountain air, first delightful, then almost trying to our
organs.'

In comparison with all this, what have our writers to offer? Only
'good taste, seated principles and prejudices' which are manifest in the
silver-fork fiction which the *Westminster*[20] had already attacked three
years earlier. What this article makes very clear is that part of the great
effect of George Sand, and even of Balzac, derived from the fact that
English fiction was at a low ebb. With the vogue of Scott past, and that
of Dickens yet to come, the gap was very inadequately filled by the
fashionable and relatively lifeless novels of Bulwer Lytton, Mrs Gore,
Lady Blessington, and the young Disraeli. Polite conversation had
small chance against a *cri de coeur*. An article in the *Dublin University
Magazine*, three months later, makes this point even more convincingly,
because the writer has little good to say for French fiction – except that
it is preferable to English:

> We must confess that in looking over the contemporary trash poured
> forth from the press of Paris, our national pride has reason to be
> anything but exalted at the comparison. The works of our neighbours
> are, indeed, low enough – mean enough – foul enough, perhaps –
> but their homage, however depraved or senseless, is still addressed to
> the human heart . . . they have not yet begun to make for themselves
> idols of silver and gold.[21]

Like 'F.B.', he complains of the 'puppet personages', the 'innumerable
patricians', the stereotyped plots, the stress on 'eating and drinking' –

'the quantity of culinary and cellarly lore which Mr. D'Israeli imparts to us is truly valuable' – in short, the yawning boredom of fashionable novels.

George Sand, in particular, was capable of supplying what the English novel had never had, romantic passion. Scott's brand of the romantic was peculiarly his own; George Sand's was in the great poetic line. Her descriptions recalled Byron, her plea for democracy and sex-equality was Shelleyan (her claim of woman's right to belong to a man, only for as long as she loves him, could have come straight from the notes to *Queen Mab*), and it is obvious that English readers were thrilling to the romantic call.

A review article in the *British and Foreign Review* in 1839 provides, I think, a more representative judgement than either the *Westminster Review* or the *Athenaeum*. In the 1840s H. F. Chorley was one of the most prolific reviewers on the *Athenaeum* staff. The tone of his reviewing has been well summed up by L. A. Marchand;[22] honest and liberal, but soft-centred, Chorley probably mirrored the average opinion of the majority of his readers, and his tendency was to be cautiously favourable to French fiction, while falling back frequently on moral strictures to show his judicial quality. The novels he covers in this review[23] are *André*, *Lettres d'un Voyageur*, *Les Maîtres Mosaïstes*, *Mauprat*, and *Spiridion*, and he is careful to explain why he should be reviewing George Sand at all. He says that the public has become so familiar over the past few years with descriptions of George Sand – of 'the half-sybilline, half-animal countenance poetically rendered by M. Calamatta' – and so interested in the countless tales told of her, that he feels their curiosity should be gratified.

Chorley is really very much more concerned to show that the dangers of reading George Sand have been exaggerated than to do full justice to her powers. He points out that however startling her opinions may be, they are vague, whether she is pleading for freedom in the relations of the sexes or preaching a universal church; and in this vagueness lies the antidote to the 'otherwise fatal mischievousness' of her views. With this skilful, back-handed compliment, Chorley indirectly counters Croker's charge that the novels are 'POISON', and then goes on to over-praise one of the gentlest of her short novels, *André*, clearly because it has so little harm in it. The review is a job of rehabilitation rather than of criticism, but at least it would have alienated no one, and may well have encouraged some to feel it safe to sample a novel by George Sand.

The final significant article of the decade was published in the *Monthly Chronicle* of 1839. It was by Mazzini, long an admirer of George Sand and her democratic principles. It is time to write in praise of her, he says, for 'her novels are sold and read everywhere, not only in

Piccadilly, but we believe even in Albemarle Street.' He considers that 'the anathema hurled against her three years since seems to us singularly to have lost its force'; her latest works are calm, containing 'nothing that can raise a blush in the youngest reader.'[24]

His defence of her is whole-hearted. He stresses her suffering, her struggles, her generosity, her genius. He even defends her smoking: 'Sinners that we are . . . we do not consider a cigar decidedly *immoral*.' He defends her right to a private life – an unheard-of claim. He presents *Indiana* and *Jacques* as powerful lessons in morality and delivers, as in the voice of the author, a long, impassioned homily to the wife-who-is-about-to-err, which sounds more like Dickens than George Sand. He points out that what she, like Goethe, is really attacking is the world of individualism and self-interest. It is a heart-warming, if uncritical, article, because of Mazzini's own sincerity and idealism.

1840–1844

By the 1840s, then, it would have been difficult for any reader not to be aware of what reviewers persisted in calling 'the phenomenon' of George Sand. I have dealt with only the most important review articles, but there were many passing references to her in journals and Bulwer-Lytton,[25] Mrs Trollope[26] and G. W. M. Reynolds[27] had more formally added their praise and Thackeray his censure. It was difficult to tell, however, with Thackeray; like Chorley, he tended to be a trimmer. In his Paris Sketch, 'Madame Sand and the New Apocalypse', he indulges in many cheap gibes at the 'Parisian Pythoness' who, having given her 'notions on morals' in '*Lélia* . . . a regular topsyturvification of morality, a thieves' and prostitutes' apotheosis', had now written *Spiridion*, her 'religious manifesto'. He deplores 'Mrs Sand's . . . philosophical friskiness' and her doubtful reputation but, at the same time as ridiculing *Lélia*, he calls it 'a wonderful book indeed, gorgeous in eloquence, and rich in magnificent poetry'. In fact he praises, almost compulsively, her exuberant imagination, her exquisite style: '. . . she leaves you, at the end of one of her brief rich melancholy sentences with plenty of food for future cogitation. I can't express to you the charm of them; they seem to me like the sound of country bells – provoking I don't know what vein of musing and meditation, and falling sweetly and sadly on the ear.'[28]

In the next two or three years her books continued to be reviewed and referred to steadily, especially in the *Athenaeum*, the *Foreign Quarterly Review* and the *Westminster Review*. There is no particular party line laid down about George Sand in these journals, although the *Westminster* is probably most consistently outspoken about her genius and remarkable qualities. In the *Foreign Quarterly Review* in 1841 there is a hostile article, 'Rousseau and the Modern Littérature Extravagante', designed to bring out what a 'frightful progress in morality has been made since Rousseau'. Most of the blame should be laid upon the doctrine of the equality of the sexes, of which creed George Sand is the apostle:

> An openly avowed hostility to marriage, borne out by a divorce from her husband, the adoption of her male attire, a cigar in her mouth, a whip in her hand, and her conversation with young men carried on in the familiar terms of *tu* and *George*, have invested the talent of Madame Dudevant with a kind of apodectical authority.[29]

But the *Foreign Quarterly* was as full of praise as the *Athenaeum* when *Consuelo* appeared in 1843, and it published its review[30] concurrently with the serialisation of the novel in the *Revue Indépendente*. *Consuelo* was a general favourite; the consensus of opinion was that although the second half of the novel was disappointing, with its Gothic castles and subterranean passages, metempsychosis and trances, dwarves and wandering musicians, the first part amply compensated in truth of characterisation and eloquence. The *Athenaeum* even found much to admire in the latter part: the Canon's household 'is like the best Flemish paintings', and the reviewer especially praises her description of the kitchen garden – the splendour of artichokes and melons, asparagus and courgettes: 'Never, surely, was a kitchen garden represented in such glowing colours, even by the rapturous imagination of a Brillat-Savarin.' Reviewers now feel free to assess her primarily as a novelist: 'Be its views right or wrong, distorted or natural, the aim of this novel is to consider the mutual relations of art and society; and the subject is one of great and increasing interest.'[31]

What of the less open-minded journals? Either there was silence, or the parroting of earlier pronouncements. What does emerge is just how much borrowing, often no doubt unintentional, went on between reviewers. Those hostile to George Sand repeatedly fell back on the phraseology of the 1836 *Quarterly*. An account in the *Dublin Review*[32] of 1840 of a number of French novels is a case in point: the writer gets the same emotional effect: 'disgust', 'depravity', 'moral cholera', 'written by a woman!', 'abominations'; he evokes the same political and national implications,[33] and supplies interesting details of how Belgian publishers reprint Parisian novels at sixpence instead of six shillings and thus propagate the 'moral gangrene' of France in Russia, Spain, Peru, the Brazils and, alas, Britain.

An even more hostile attack in the *Foreign and Colonial Quarterly Review* in 1843 underlined the fact of the popularity of French literature which 'is naturalised in London as soon as it is born in Paris'. The reviewer had done George Sand the honour of plodding through all thirty-three volumes of her collected works in order to slang each novel in turn.

But in case any readers were still ignorant of her life and appearance the writer reiterates the usual malicious account of her liaisons, garb, cigar and pseudonyms – with some additional insults about her 'large hook nose and projecting upper jaw bone'. The article ends with the ominous pronouncement: 'A few George Sands will soon reduce France to the level of the orang-outang or little better, possibly something worse. Let France look to it, her cup may be fuller than she thinks of the wrath of her God.'[34]

The publication of the collected works of George Sand and Balzac occasioned in the following year the most important article that had so far been written on the Frenchwoman. G. H. Lewes was expressing in the *Foreign Quarterly Review* 'serious convictions formed over five years' very intimate acquaintance with her works'. In his impatience with bias and ignorance, Lewes underestimates quite seriously the amount of good criticism and well-balanced analysis that had, in fact, appeared in the columns of the *Westminster Review* and the *Athenaeum*, but he does make the important point that critics had always been acutely conscious of the facts of her life: 'Because she was herself unhappy in marriage, people assumed that she wrote against it; the truth being that she advocated marriage, but not its abuses.'[35]

He makes no mention of his own very substantial article on her two years before in the *Monthly Magazine*,[36] in which he described her as 'the most remarkable writer of the present century'. This is perhaps not only because he, too, had talked a great deal about her life in it, but because he had written it in his sprightly 'Vivian' style, full of exclamation marks and dashes, and he now felt that a more sober, critical article was in order for two such major novelists. In fact, he had made many good points in the earlier article which he now took up and enlarged upon.

His defence of both George Sand and Balzac is in three parts; he considers each as moralist, artist, and entertainer. As moralist, George Sand can be defended because she is earnest. 'She puts forth *convictions* . . . It is incumbent on an author, not that he speak the truth, but what he holds to be the truth.' Unlike Balzac, she does not treat adultery lightly; her heroines are, indeed, singularly chaste. As for her 'social theorising', she is, above all, a democrat and longs for social amelioration; what really manifests itself is her sympathy with greatness of thought and feeling. It is quite extraordinary that the cry of 'immoral' should so often have been raised against George Sand's novels:

Never was there a more notable instance of giving a dog a bad name and hanging him. Madame Sand has been known to travel in androgynous costume; smokes cigars; is separated from her husband, and has been the theme of prolific scandal. The conclusion drawn was, that from such a person nothing but anti-social works could possibly be expected.

Like all George Sand's English enthusiasts, Lewes is enraptured by her style, to which it was allowable to refer with enthusiasm even in otherwise unfavourable notices. It is 'perhaps the most beautiful ever written by a French author.' He goes on to quote at length from *Lélia* which 'we never open . . . at random without feeling as at an open window on a May morn . . . Poetry flows from her pen as water from the rock; she writes as the birds sing: without effort, but with perfect art.' An interesting feature of both articles is close analysis of passages from *Lélia*. After Lewes has given it as his highest praise of her unself-conscious style that 'when reading her works *you are not conscious of reading French*', he goes on to show just how much art there is in it and how its poetic effect depends upon her choice of word and use of a particular tense.

While it is obvious that George Sand excels Balzac in style, each is equally great in characterisation – 'Sand, like a poet, has known and felt life; Balzac has observed it' – but that does not mean that she is not capable of subtle psychological delineation and some remarkable analyses of egotism.

Lewes feels that he has no need to waste time on George Sand and Balzac as entertainers – 'their popularity speaks for them.' What he does want to stress above all (and it is very clear that Lewes's main preoccupation is with George Sand and not with Balzac) is that a great novelist has acquired undeserved odium in England so that 'although her works are largely read (we have a bookseller's authority for the fact), and her genius is recognised by most of our eminent men, it is rare to see any praise of her not qualified by some concession to the prejudices of the day.' What is needed now is 'a calm dispassionate examination' of her works.

1844–1852

Lewes's article was just in time to be still highly relevant as a defence. It is not to underestimate Lewes's very real devotion to George Sand's writing to remember that he was a good journalist, aware of the strategic moment when an issue was a live one – neither too hot to handle nor too cold to revive. In fact, some of the heat was by this time going out of George Sand reviews. This was partly due to increased familiarity with her writings, partly to the nature of the novels themselves. Reviewers felt less threatened by her novels of social reform than by those of passion, although the warning note still had to be sounded about them. The *Edinburgh Review*,[37] pointed out that George Sand had certainly greater genius than the German writer, Mme Hahn-Hahn, but she had a deplorable habit of blaming society for all corruption, whereas the other took up a much healthier attitude to individual responsibility. The 'unfortunate' criminal was a particular delusion of George Sand's. But on the whole the novels did seem to be becoming much less morally impeachable, and the reviews reflected this change.

Indeed, even as George Sand was becoming more respectable, some reviewers were disposed to regret the apparent loss of her old fire. Both the *Foreign Quarterly Review* and the *Athenaeum*, reviewing several of her latest novels in 1846, among them *Jeanne, Isidora, Teverino, Le Péché de M. Antoine*, and *Le Meunier d'Angibault*, could find only in the last any trace of her real genius. In the *Foreign Quarterly*, Lewes dismissed *Jeanne* as a failure which could be 'recommended as a novel which even girls may read' (a former accolade now used as an insult), and commented on the paleness of the colours in which she now wrote:

> We had begun to despair of George Sand. The feebleness of the 'Comtesse de Rudolstadt' and 'Jeanne', – the carelessness and nothingness of 'Isidora' . . . led us to suspect that the cry of 'George Sand has written herself out,' might not be one of envy, but of regret. But there came 'Le Meunier d'Angibault' to overthrow all our conclusions and once more to awaken our enthusiasm.[38]

Like the *Athenaeum* reviewer, though with a less patronising tone than Chorley, he praises the scenes of the Berry countryside and the characterisation of the miller's family, using a favourite Victorian encomium, one used frequently in reviews of George Sand, of Balzac, and later, of George Eliot: 'This is a Dutch painting for life-like effect, with a deeper meaning than any Dutch painter ever cared for.'

Despite a greatly increased number of notices of her books, George Sand is, then, much less of a talking-point for reviewers in the 1840s than she had been in the thirties. She now, of course, faces much more competition from English novelists for the attention of reviewers. There is, however, a very interesting resuscitation of alarm about her in 1847. Several of her novels had already been translated, but a much larger scheme was now envisaged by a handful of her admirers, under the general editorship of a feminist friend of Mazzini's, Matilda Hays. Chorley is fluttered by the fact that George Sand is now being fêted by the ladies, as he calls them. He sees no reason why she should be made available in translation at all. It is all very well for the *cognoscenti* to accept George Sand but, advertised by her admirers as 'the greatest female genius of the day', she could do a great deal of harm to the uninitiated. She is, after all, not a philosopher nor moralist but a woman whose views have been the outcome of her own particular circumstances and, in May 1847, Chorley quotes, in full, his 1839 account of her life, in order to show how inadvisable it would be to accept such a woman as prophet.

Apart from this moral disquiet, he does make two pertinent comments which are also voiced by the *Westminster* reviewer, who, unlike Chorley, welcomes the idea of making available novels always 'less read than talked about by the British public'.[39] There are two things wrong with the translations. Firstly, 'the editors have been so anxious to choose harmless novels, that the choice so far is unrepresentative';[40] and secondly, the standard of translation is very bad and does not in any way capture the magic of George Sand's style. In the event, the project had to be abandoned for lack of support, Miss Hays sadly confessing in a preface that they had overestimated the amount of interest they could depend on; but not before the *Quarterly Review* had been roused from its long and studied silence on the subject of George Sand. Ever since Croker's onslaught of 1836, that journal had ignored her existence, but the revelation that *Le Meunier d'Angibault* was to be translated by a clergyman was too much to tolerate. In the index to the *Quarterly Review* of 1847 appears an entry – 'Sand, infamous novels of' – which directs the reader's attention to a footnote, prompted by a reference to free love: 'See the writings *passim* of that great apostle of pantheism, the "*semivir obscoenus*" of France, George Sand.' The note thunders on in fine excommunicatory vein:

> If we are to believe the newspaper advertisements, an attempt is now making by an English *editrix*, assisted among others by a beneficed clergyman of the English Church, to circulate these productions here in an English translation – *omitting the obscenity*. We denounce this scheme . . . a smuggler's attempt to conceal the real nature of his infamous cargo . . . If there really is such a person as 'the Rev. E. R. Larkin, Chaplain to Lord Monson, and Rector of Burton by Lincoln' the open connexion of his name with 'The Works of George Sand' appears to us a strange phenomenon.[41]

Naturally the Radical *People's Journal* felt very differently towards George Sand. It was started in 1846 as, the advertisement tells us, 'an international publication . . . for every class and condition . . . devoted to the advocacy of the broad principle of Human Brotherhood.' A typical sevenpenny issue consisted of fifty-six pages of letterpress and four engravings; the contributors included John Saunders, the editor, Mary and William Howitt, Mazzini, Harriet Martineau, Thornton Hunt, W. J. Linton[42] and other like-minded progressives, and there was always a selection of Poetry for the People from Ebenezer Elliott and other working-class poets. Articles and poems alike dealt with such acceptable topics as ragged schools, self-culture, social service, the French working classes, and prostitution – the last a theme which roused Mary Howitt to a burst of lyricism:

> God, what a gulph between
> Victoria young and worshipped
> And the suicide Magdalene.[43]

It is obvious that George Sand, the eloquent defender of the heroic role of 'l'homme du peuple', would be looked on with approval in such quarters; and both the *People's Journal* and the short-lived but very interesting *Howitt's Journal*, which broke away from the original paper in 1847 after a quarrel between the editor and the Howitts, are full of tributes to her. There is very little to choose between the two journals. There is a great deal of overlapping of contributors and both, in striking contrast to the *Athenaeum* and the *Quarterly*, enthusiastically welcomed the project of the translation of her novels. An especial favourite of theirs, predictably, was *Le Compagnon du Tour de France* because of its levelling doctrines and its noble idealism. It was important that the novels should be translated because 'Madame Dudevant has penetrated the thousand forms of evil that lie hidden beneath the world's great whited sepulchre.'[44]

In 1847, the two rival journals produced, simultaneously, several reviews of her novels, two full-page engravings of her and two very long articles. It is small wonder that about this time George Sand wrote complacently in a letter '. . . je suis en grande vogue en ce moment, de l'autre côté du détroit.'[45] This optimistic estimate of the changed situation came from Mazzini, who was the author of the *People's Journal* article, handsomely illustrated by W. J. Linton's engraving of David's medallion of her head. His praise of George Sand is as rapturous as it had been eight years earlier, but his peroration strikes a new note in his praise of her womanhood:

> Thanks be to God . . . What she is she is as a *woman*. In the vast and imposing question which is beginning to ferment in men's minds . . . of the emancipation of woman . . . the materials for decision were wanting to us . . . No one has told us before what she has told us about *woman* . . . As a *human being* she has appealed for the equality to which her sex has a right . . . as a woman she has declared to us the secret of her sex, its inward life . . . Her life is in her books.[46]

The other article in *Howitt's Journal* is something of a collector's item, for it is by 'Dr Smiles'. I suppose that, off-hand, one could think of no more unlikely coupling of names than that of George Sand and

Samuel Smiles; and had George Sand known then that the writer of the article was to become the synonym of Victorian respectability through self-help, she would have felt even more strongly that she had conquered England. But these were his younger, radical days. He approved her outspokenness in the exposition of 'Love – the primal necessity of the highest nature and the great business of a woman's life – Such representations as these are generally regarded by us as "immoral"; for we are a marvellously moral people, great worshippers of propriety . . .'[47] wields a sarcastic pen against his fellow-countrymen's hypocrisy, flays the *Quarterly* and gives an admirably inventive account of George Sand's early life. For Smiles is determined to believe no evil of her; all can be explained by her having been married off, as 'simply an article of barter', to an 'old and ill-favoured' soldier. He has clearly taken *Indiana* as literal autobiography and equates the lusty Casimir Dudevant with the decrepit Colonel Delmare, an old soldier at whose voice and 'stern discipline . . . servants, dogs and horses trembled . . . The living body bound side by side to a corpse could scarcely present a more revolting picture.' He is full of sympathy for the 'young and beautiful' wife who 'sought occupation in the relief of the poor of the neighbourhood . . . with food, clothing and medicines'.

He is concerned with all her works, and although his favourites are her recent novels, in which she shows warm sympathy for the masses, he has something good to say for them all. He extols her love and reverence for art as 'a daily dweller in the houses of the industrious and hard-working', and indeed quotes exactly the passage from *André* in praise of poetry which was later to appeal to Hardy. His final accolade is a memorable one, for it enrols George Sand in the vast body of Self-helpers – an incontrovertible truth, when all is said and done: 'She earnestly and eloquently preaches the great gospel of Work.'

Kingsley too, in *Fraser's Magazine*, seizes upon George Sand's democratic appeal, and has the highest praise for her earnestness and forceful simplicity, despite her 'frightful defects'. 'To get a hearing, the people's novelist must succeed in "strong writing". If England ever sees, which Heaven grant she may, a Christian George Sand, this feature of her style must not be watered down into smooth respectability.'[48]

Smiles's confusion of George Sand's life with her heroine's is repeated soon after in a *Blackwood's* review: 'Ignorant of the world she allowed herself to be married to a rough old soldier.'[49] The tone of *Blackwood's* is now kindlier than ten years previously. Many of the stories of her 'swaggering and smoking in man's attire, and brandishing pistol and horsewhip with virile energy and effect' may indeed have been exaggerated. They are still cautious about her but at 'the ripe age of forty-four, we may suppose her sobered down a little' and they speak of her 'sad but serene physiognomy'. The softening process continues into 1849, when approval for *La Petite Fadette* is unequivocal:

> We pass on to a lady of a very different stamp, who does not often obtain commendation at our hands; and yet, in this instance, we know not why we should withold approval from George Sand's last novel, *La Petite Fadette*, one of those seductive trifles which only Madame Dudevant can produce.[50]

These Berry novels, written at the end of the 1840s, completed the acceptance of George Sand by reviewers. The simplicity and rural charm and naturalness of these tales, which are well-punned as 'the Georgics of France', indicated not only that George Sand had mellowed, but that a more responsible attitude to the role of the artist seemed to be arising on the other side of the Channel. In a two-column review of *François le Champi* in 1848, the *Athenaeum* asked: 'Is modern French literature approaching to a new phasis? . . . Are we to . . . be permitted once more to breathe the air of Nature? Is the stimulant literature expiring? . . . George Sand . . . has made a strong effort to recall novelists to a right sense of their office . . . she has made this effort critically and consciously.'[51]

So that when, in the *Westminster Review* of 1852, Lewes discussed the achievements of such a mixed bag of English lady-novelists as Jane Austen, Mrs Gore, Mrs Marsh, Mrs Trollope, Geraldine Jewsbury, Eliza Lynn, Currer Bell and Mrs Gaskell, he felt himself at liberty to use the *Œuvres Complètes de George Sand*, not only as a *point de départ* for his observations, but as an example, throughout the article, of what a woman writer was capable of achieving. His two touchstones for feminine greatness were Jane Austen and George Sand, and he was obviously writing now, as he had not a decade earlier, without fear of contradiction: 'For eloquence, and depth of feeling, no man approaches George Sand.'[52]

In the twenty years since George Sand had first taken away the breath of reviewers, she had attained not only critical respectability, but tacit recognition in England as a great writer and important influence. We shall see now what the attitude was to her in less official circles.

2 'George Sandism' in Cheyne Row

1

'Mrs Buller reads George Sand, like me',[1] Jane Carlyle wrote in a letter of 1842, thereby indicating that someone else was capable of taking a sentimental and romantic view of things. Such a view is not one which we should normally associate with the sharp-eyed, quick-witted, outspoken Mrs Carlyle, and indeed her devotion to the novels of George Sand is probably less immediately understandable than that of other, more idealistic, Victorians. But if we look back to 1821 to a letter to a friend, written when she was twenty, and had just finished reading *La Nouvelle Héloise*, we may find a clue to her later attachment:

> *I do not wish to countenance such irregularities among my female acquaintances* but . . . were any . . . to meet with *such a man*, to struggle . . . to endure . . . to *yield* . . . and to repent . . . I would love (her) better than the chastest, coldest prude between John O'Groats House and Land's End . . . This Book, this fatal Book, has given me an idea of love so *pure* . . . so constant so disinterested, so exalted that no love the men of this world can offer me will ever fill up the picture my imagination has drawn with the help of Rousseau.[2]

This passage, which starts with self-mockery, warms into an avowal of the claims of passion which carries conviction. Even then, before she met Carlyle, her hunger for romance and absolute love is tempered by common sense, and continues to be so increasingly in her life with him. But George Sand touched the same chord as Rousseau, and Jane Carlyle never faltered in her conviction of the genius of the French-woman.

She was, however, constantly aware of the danger of passion and idealism slipping over into self-indulgence and sentimentality, as some of the passing allusions in her letters show. 'George Sandism' was the phrase Carlyle used to convey all he attributed to the novelist – tolerance of immorality, romantic effusiveness, lack of common sense, high-flown sentiments, concentration on love; it is often used by Jane Carlyle also (within quotation marks) as a short hand for qualities that no self-respecting Scot could approve. When she is engaging a servant girl (an undertaking always of enormous interest to her) she discerns the weakness: 'Yesterday I was engaging another – equally refined – *less sensitive* looking but *more sentimental* – with I should say a great tendency to "*George Sandism* and all that sort of thing" . . . But she has a three years character and can cook – especially *fish* her mistress said – "all sorts of fish in all sorts of ways" – pity we never *eat* fish, hardly . . .'3 And when her dog, Nero, goes into a jealous huff and rushes out of the house she comments, 'And yet he had never read George Sand novels that dog, or any sort of Novels!'4 And writing of the fiction of the Gräfin Hahn-Hahn – '(Countess Cock Cock! What a name!) She is a sort of German George Sand *without the genius* – and *en revanche* a good deal more of what we call in Scotland gumtion!'5

But although, for her husband, lack of gumption was an unforgivable sin, Jane Carlyle found too many compensations in George Sand to hold it against her. She read her works steadily, borrowing them from the London Library, from Carlyle's own, well-stocked realm. In January 1843, she writes: '. . . as usual it ended in bringing away French novels – a book of Sand's which I had not before seen and two of – Paul de Kock! Having still however some sense of decency remaining I coolly entered my name in the ledger for these books Erasmus Darwin!'6

It was not so much George Sand whom Mrs Carlyle blushed to own as Paul de Kock, a lightly lascivious novelist whose vogue in prudish England French critics could never understand, and one to whom probably the last literary tribute was paid by Molly Bloom. Jane Carlyle's allegiance to George Sand was always open and acknowledged, and her familiarity with the novels is obvious from her letters. Her closest friends are equated with George Sand characters: thus the faithful Erasmus Darwin 'who is what you know – the type of English gentleman, the "Sir Brown" (Indiana's Ralph) in real life'.7 And Babbie, her beloved cousin, 'so long the comfort of my life', becomes 'my *Consuelo*'8 the year after the book was first published in France.

Through the years Carlyle kept up a rumbling protest, which occasionally erupted into violent condemnation of George Sand's 'erotics'. He felt very strongly indeed about her, and it says much for Mrs Carlyle's strength of mind that she read not one novel the less for his opposition. Indeed, as Espinasse recalls, she challenged him at table, when he was in full flood, saying:

We had small right to throw the first stone at George Sand . . . if we considered what sort of literary ladies might be found in London at present. When one was first told that the strong woman of the Westminster Review (George Eliot) had gone off with a man whom we all knew (Lewes) it was as startling an announcement as if one had heard that a woman of your acquaintance had gone off with the strong man at Astley's.[9]

Carlyle indeed had formidable opposition in his household, with frequent visitors like Mazzini and Geraldine Jewsbury to join in defence of George Sand, but he was capable of out-bellowing them all. He was deeply contemptuous of what he referred to as Jane's 'George Sandish excess of humanity' in condoning the action of 'poor Mrs R.' who had left her unhappy marriage and gone to France with her lover – 'My doctrine on that whole matter, he would have me know, was infamous – and also, my practice in making myself the advocate of W ——s – it behoved me to reform!'[10] – an attack which reduced Jane to tears. In *Latter Day Pamphlets*, Carlyle later fulminated against what he called:

> a strange new religion, named of Universal Love, with Sacraments mainly of Divorce, with Balzac, Sue and Company for Evangelists, and Madame Sand for Virgin . . . a new astonishing Phallus worship . . . with its finer sensibilities of the heart and 'great satisfying loves', with its sacred kiss of peace for scoundrel and hero alike, with its all-embracing Brotherhood and universal Sacrament of Divorce . . .[11]

It is as revealing an onslaught as Jane Carlyle's frequent warnings to young women against a starry-eyed view of marriage. His linking together of Eugène Sue, George Sand and Balzac in their attitudes to marriage shows how little knowledge he had of George Sand's beliefs – and when he actually forced himself to read some of her novels he had to confess as much. Espinasse, that observant young Scotsman, has put Carlyle's grudging retraction on record.

> . . . George Sand he could not away with . . . speaking of her books as distinguished by nothing better than a lax treatment of the sexual relation. The only civil thing I ever heard him say of the Pope and his obsolete creed was, that they might be a sort of barrier against something worse than themselves, George Sandism to wit. Yet . . . he could not help recognising the gifts of that extraordinary woman. George Henry Lewes once told me that he once found Carlyle with some of George Sand's books spread out before him, and confessing that he had broken down in an attempt to indict a scathing invective against her and them. 'There is something Goethian about the woman' he said to Lewes as an excuse for his failure. I was rather surprised when Carlyle spoke to me of her as 'a shrewd woman'. Shrewd undoubtedly she was but that was hardly the characteristic of her to which one expected prominence to be given by Carlyle.[12]

Yet shrewdness would indeed be a quality which Carlyle would have expected to be most conspicuously lacking in her, and one which he felt in honour bound to acknowledge. But her name continued to be anathema to him. When he read her 1848 address to the electors in which she advised them to give their suffrage to none but 'plain honest men, whether uneducated or not, Carlyle warmly approved of the tone and tenor of this address till he found it was by George Sand when he just as warmly condemned it.'[13] Despite his fleeting acknowledgements of her ability, he hated her 'Gospel of Fraternity, Benevolence and a new Heaven on Earth',[14] and dismissed it all as 'George Sandism and the twaddle of a thousand magazines'.[15] Jane Carlyle, equally intolerant of the 'twaddly' – a favourite Cheyne Row pejorative – none the less continued to derive comfort from her pages. And, at the age of fifty-four, in that brief, heart-breaking journal in which she pours out her tormented jealousy and loneliness, she justifies her eloquence painfully with 'George Sand has shrewdly remarked, "rien ne soulage comme la rhetorique." '[16] Perhaps when both Carlyles praised her 'shrewdness' they were really acknowledging not her 'gumption' but her wisdom.

But though Jane Carlyle adhered to her *parti pris* in respect of George Sand, she could not compare with her friend, Geraldine Endsor Jewsbury, whose emotional and passionate nature made her response to the novelist a total one. Ironically, as was so often the case, she was equally bowled over by Carlyle and first visited the household as his disciple, in 1841. His first impression of her as 'one of the most interesting young women he had seen for years – clear, delicate sense and courage looking out of her small sylph-like figure'[17] quickly gave way to a conviction that 'that girl is an incurable fool – and that it is a mercy for her she is so ill-looking!'[18] But her friendship with Jane weathered her gushing, 'tiger-jealousy', and unconventionality, and Jane's embarrassment and distrust; and, though only Geraldine's letters survive, they are full enough of references to George Sand for us to understand Carlyle's disenchantment with his admirer. She writes that she has 'read the "Sept Cordes" at last, and full of genius it is';[19] she enquires anxiously about Carlyle's George Sand article; she mentions that 'when I came back I had my tea and read Mazzini's article on George Sand and was in the most comfortable, innocent sort of spirit';[20] she discusses often and at great length the nature and position of woman and attacks the Mrs Ellis creed; she lends *Lucrezia Floriani* to 'a sober, reputable Scotchman', and is amazed when he writes to express his gratitude 'declaring that he had known many Lucrezias, and that Madame Sand had shown her profound knowledge of the human heart. Pretty well, upon my honour! Codes of morality require revising as well as codes of religion, it seems . . .'[21]

And more striking than all her allusions to George Sand was her attempt to emulate her, as a novelist and in her life-style – in a modified way, of course. Even her very discreet editor, Mrs Ireland, admitted that Miss Jewsbury admired George Sand very much and that it was 'her ambition to become a journalist, to move in the world of letters as a man, a good comrade, "one of the craft." '[22] Her cosy, well-run little house in Manchester, full of talk and good food and cigar smoke,[23] was a meeting place for literary men and women – for Geraldine, like George, had a fondness for cigars. 'The instant I got in I fell foul of my cigars, and I never felt the want of them or the good of them so much. I am sure Providence itself put it into my head to smoke. "It soothes our sorrows, heals our wounds, and wipes away our tears" as one of Dr Watts hymns says. I send you a few of them to comfort you.'[24]

These 'cigaritos' were a weakness of Jane Carlyle's also, which she obviously tried to overcome and indulged in only in privacy. She is amazed at Geraldine's boldness: 'She keeps a regular supply of these little things and smokes them before all the world . . .'[25] And when Geraldine visits her in 1845 she comments that Geraldine had 'brought a good stock of cigaritos with her, which is rather a pity as I had just begun to forget there was such a weed as tobacco in the civilised world'[26] – although, in fact, it was a habit which even her husband seems to have been prepared to condone in her, for Espinasse records Carlyle's commissioning 'a Greek friend to procure as a birthday present for his wife, a little machine for making those cigarettes which at one time she liked to indulge'.[27] Geraldine's smoke-filled salon was commented on by Clough when he visited Manchester, and as we shall see, his description is rather like the Brownings' account of their call upon George Sand:

> Last night I went to a little party chez the Jewsbury and her brother, which was successfully prolonged till 1 a.m. Four men, besides the brother and myself, two mustachios and one beard, a Greek, a Turk, and a French-Englishman. Smoking and I grieve to say in one case spitting, which latter Miss J. did *not* like: the former she more than tolerates.[28]

Geraldine's trip to Paris in 1848, in the company of the Paulets and W. E. Forster ('To get the cobwebs blown out of her brain',[29] wrote Jane Carlyle unkindly), was made in the midst of revolutionary fervour and was no doubt indicative of her desire 'to move in the world of letters as a man'. Emerson and Clough were there already and the visit was a great success, although she did not meet George Sand. Mazzini had already acted as intermediary between them and had given George Sand a copy of Geraldine's first novel *Zoë*, in the hope of extracting from her what Geraldine ardently longed for, an opinion of its merits from the idol herself. But George Sand, a past master at the diplomatic evasion of the demands of her admirers, did not commit herself[30] and, pleading a convenient difficulty with English, postponed their discussion of *Zoë*, which we too shall be looking at later. In the meantime there are many other admirers of George Sand who rate acknowledgement.

2

The Carlyles had a vast circle of friends and acquaintances, and at one time or another most of the literary men and women in London dropped in for tea and talk at 5, Cheyne Row. The range of subjects covered was very wide: tales of domestic disaster, which Jane Carlyle could charge with high drama, of flea-infested mattresses and drunken maidservants, as well as social gossip, political argument and literary chatter; and to single out references to George Sand is to run the risk of drawing out a thread of the rich fabric of discussion and distorting the texture. And yet, partly because most of Jane Carlyle's friends were of a liberal and some of a radical turn of mind, George Sand was a recognised fact of existence, in the 1840s, for most of the intelligent Englishmen and women whom Mrs Carlyle mentions in her diaries. Naturally she impinged on some more than others. When Lady Harriet Baring, for instance, talked to Mazzini with 'the highest commendations of George Sand, expressed the utmost longing to read the new edition of Lélia',[31] Mrs Carlyle's caustic comment that she was playing her cards in order to lure Mazzini into her toils has obviously got some truth in it. But most of the references to George Sand crop up naturally in the letters and memoirs of the period, and I shall make use of only some of the countless allusions to give an idea of her image in a particular social group.

One of her earliest admirers in England was John Stuart Mill who was, according to Carlyle, 'among our chief visitors and social elements' in their first years in London, 'an altogether clear, logical, honest, amicable, affectionate young man . . . though sometimes felt to be rather colourless, even aqueous.'[32] This aqueous young man had definite views, however, on George Sand. In 1842, he wrote to Lewes (about a letter of which there is now no trace):

My dear Lewes,
    I return Sand's letter which it was very pleasant to have an opportunity of reading. I have no right or claim to send any message to her but I should be very willing she should know that there are other admirers of her writings and of herself even in this canting land – among whom I am neither the only nor the best . . .[33]

Her feminism appealed to the Saint-Simonist in him, but he got also from her the sort of solace he received from Wordsworth's poetry: '. . . as a specimen of purely artistic excellence, there is not in all modern literature anything superior to the prose of Madame Sand, whose style acts upon the nervous system like a symphony of Haydn or Mozart.'[34]

The same therapeutic effect was experienced by Mazzini, who was one of Jane Carlyle's most frequent callers, for over ten years from 1837. Mill was instrumental in introducing many French, German and Italian exiles to the Carlyles, and although Mrs Carlyle was almost as sceptical about their revolutionary politics as Carlyle himself, she listened to Mazzini's idealistic outbursts with interest and irritable wonder and something of the friendly pity she extended to many lame dogs, for 'that damned thing called the milk of human kindness is not all drained out of me yet.'[35] He had first read George Sand in the *Revue des Deux Mondes* at a time of crisis and despair in his own life, when he was about to be exiled for the second time. 'I had no longer faith in men; no longer faith in myself.' When he read what he described as this 'confession of a great and noble soul, addressed to all those who suffer and love',[36] he ceased to feel alone in his struggle towards truth. For she had come through her agony to a belief in man's ability to better his existence through constructive action. This woman, whom he persisted in calling 'the best of sisters', had genius and individuality and yet could be the eloquent spokesman for the age: 'There is still as in the sounds of the Aeolian harp an echo of past agony; but the voice of the age preponderates.'[37] *Lettres d'un Voyageur* was Mazzini's favourite book, the one he carried with him everywhere, precisely because for him it marked the transition between George Sand's early phase, with its stress on individual right, and the calm which succeeded it, in which duty took over.

Although he expressed himself in print at length on George Sand on three separate occasions, he was not in correspondence with her until 1843; from then on, until he became disillusioned by her acceptance of the Second Empire, the friendship flourished; he visited Nohant and introduced some of his English friends to her. He saw her as 'an apostle of religious democracy',[38] and the tones in which he refers to her are always romantic and impassioned. For Mazzini, Mrs Carlyle must have softened her abrasive tongue, for he wrote to her after he had 'gone into the valley of Madame Sand',[39] to Nohant itself: 'Madame Sand is all we pictured her and more – the sister of the whole world in her thought. Not a shadow of vanity or pride about her.'[40] Jane Carlyle was no doubt prepared to do so because Mazzini, a man of sorrows, was her confidant and, just as he took her despair seriously when she poured out her torment to him, as she did in the summer of 1846, so was she capable of responding to his high-minded truthfulness.

But much of the time her comments on Mazzini appear to justify Carlyle's shrewd comment that his wife's interest in the exiles who thronged her drawing-room was primarily 'picturesque aesthetic etc'.[41] George Sand and Jane Carlyle were both indefatigable correspondents, and as one turns from the expansive epistles of the one to the witty letters of the other, it is intriguing to find names common to both Nohant and Cheyne Row – Cavaignac, Leroux, Louis Blanc and Mazzini; but the great difference is that George Sand's preoccupation with them was political, while Jane Carlyle's was personal and domestic. She gave her particular exiles hospitality, not only out of kindness, but because she savoured the sense of their foreignness and their links with a world of action and intrigue. At one point her letters are almost as full of European as of Scottish references, and she falls easily into talk about impending revolutions and articles in the *Revue Independente*, the periodical started by Leroux and George Sand to which her beloved Cavaignac contributed. In these letters, Mazzini appears more as a household pet than a freedom fighter, and there is no evidence that he was taken seriously by her at all as a philosophical revolutionary, however many silk purses she worked for his Young Italy bazaars. So that when she found that others did respond to his 'notions', her immediate reaction was to pour scorn on his politically minded new friends.

> Mazzini is pretty well – very busy as usual with his benevolent schemes – not so solitary as he used to be – having got up to the ears in a good twadly family of the name of Ashurst – who have plenty of money – and help 'his things' and toady him till I think it has rather gone to his head. A Miss Eliza Ashurst – who does strange things – made his acquaintance first – by going to his house to drink tea with him all alone, etc. etc!![42]

The sour note of the patron of long standing, bereft of her exclusive rights, can be heard in this dismissal of the 'twaddly family'. Whether deliberately or not, she misrepresents the visit that Eliza Ashurst had made in 1842 to Mazzini in the company of her brother William to express indignation, on their parents' behalf, at the opening of Mazzini's mail by the Post Office – that *cause célèbre* which rocked London. Not that Miss Ashurst would not have gone on her own to visit Mazzini had it occurred to her, for W. H. Ashurst, the radical reformer, had brought up his son and four daughters to believe in the strict equality of the sexes and the virtue of independence. Needless to say, George Sand was favourite family reading. All the girls were remarkable in their different ways, and Mazzini corresponded throughout his life with each one but, at first, it was Eliza especially to whom he wrote because, when they met, she had already translated George Sand's *Spiridion* and sent it to him for his comments. He encouraged her to go on with other translations, and it was as a result of this that the ambitious scheme was launched in 1847 of translating all of George Sand's novels, with Eliza's friend, Matilda Hays, as general editor – an enterprise which, as we have seen, had to end for lack of support. Eliza Ashurst, full of enthusiasm for George Sand's genius, was more successful than Geraldine Jewsbury in having the pathway to Nohant opened for her by Mazzini, but did not find favour in her hostess's eyes. George Sand's letter about her to Mazzini makes amusing reading, for the Frenchwoman, with her vast experience of life and men, was shocked by the naïve outspokenness of her disciple, this emancipated thirty-three year old spinster.

I've seen your friend Eliza. She has come to spend a few days here . . . She is very nice and very clever, she must have fine qualities but she has too good a conceit of herself . . . I'm afraid that reading my novels hasn't done her any good and has helped, to some extent, to make her take off in a direction totally alien to me. *Man* and *Woman* are everything for her and the question of sex . . . wipes out for her the idea of the human being . . . The effect on her of this preoccupation is a sort of state of hysteria of which she is unaware but which lays her open to being taken in by the first rascal who comes along. I believe her behaviour to be proper but not her mind and that is perhaps worse. I'd prefer her to have lovers and not ever speak about them than to have none and go on about them incessantly. In short, a true Englishwoman, a prude without modesty, and also a true Englishman, for the spirit has no gender and every Englishman considers himself the finest fellow in the finest nation in the world.[43]

This harsh judgement, which also reveals George Sand's own settled prejudices about England, was regrettably astute in its prophecy. Whether or not her reading in George Sand had done her harm, as the author feared, Eliza Ashurst did succumb, within months, to 'le premier drôle venu', and married Jean Bardonneau, a second-hand dealer in Paris, against the wishes of her family and Mazzini. George Sand's disapproving comment was 'Dieu veuille . . . qu'il y ait une belle âme sous cette envelope déplaisante.'[44] From this unhappy marriage, which promised, according to Mazzini, only miseries, deception and paltriness, Eliza was rescued in 1850 by her death in childbirth.

George Sand's relationship with the rest of the family, on whom she had set such an indelible stamp, is interesting in that it shows her shying away from the sort of feminism she disapproved of and that her writings, sown in foreign soil, tended to produce. She met three of the four girls and found Emilie, the intrepid traveller and comrade of Mazzini, headstrong and hasty. Only Caroline, the wife of James Stansfeld, appealed to her – partly because of her charm, partly because she shared George Sand's admiration for Louis Blanc and was therefore humanitarian rather than narrowly feminist. When she heard that Emilie had gone to join Mazzini in Geneva in 1849, she wrote 'Qu'elles sont heureuses ces Anglaises, de pouvoir courir où le coeur les pousse!',[45] a comment which comes strangely from the lips of one who had always done exactly the same thing. But what she must have envied in Emilie was her chance to do so without, like herself, becoming 'a phenomenon', because of the enlightened support she received from her family. With the reference to 'ces Anglaises' she is, for the moment, washing her hands of all responsibility for Ashurst behaviour even although, earlier, she had been made fully aware of her influence upon them by Eliza, and had responded with gratitude: 'Je suis heureuse d'être bénie dans votre famille.'[46] The role of a prophet out of her own country can often be very disconcerting.

3

Others in the Carlyle circle – Chorley, Macready, Dickens, Monkton Milnes, for instance – made their contacts with George Sand on a less political and emotionally involved level than Mazzini, but they too have left their records of their meetings with her – or even their glimpses of her. For English visitors to Paris she was one of the sights. Chorley, the critic, who wrote so often about her novels, saw her for the first time in the opposite box at the Théâtre Palais Royal in 1837, and four years later made his memories public:

> The figure was a man's in its habiliments, at least in the frock coat, loose and faced with velvet, which covered its bust. In place of a cravat, however, there was a dubious looking shawl or silk handkerchief: and the throat and chin which rose therefrom had never been visited by a razor . . . There was the rich black hair, parted on the forehead just as M. Calamatta drew it; and there was the Sybilline forehead, and the eyes, melancholy in their sweetness and sublime in their depth, and the gross Satyr-like lips and heavy jaw – the latter a little grosser and heavier than the artist has shown them . . . It was a woman that I saw, 10 minutes afterwards, glide past me in the narrow and stifling lobby, with a hat pushed over her eyes, with the slim waist and long pantaloons – and the whole costume in fact which has so scandalised many an English traveller.[47]

Chorley, himself scandalised but determinedly liberal, is here giving one of the first eyewitness descriptions of George Sand to English readers. But all her life George Sand continued to attract the fascinated gaze of the visiting English, who never forgot the experience. Annie Thackeray was born in the same year that Chorley was peering excitedly at the opposite box, and, in due course, she too was to cast her critical glance on George Sand in a theatre, and to write about it in her old age. She had of course been brought up in the myth, for although her father took a high, contemptuous line about the French writer, the little Thackeray girls were frequent visitors at Mrs Carlyle's, where she comforted them after their cold walk with cups of hot chocolate and friendly conversation. The occasion when Annie Thackeray thought she saw George Sand is in many ways more interesting and revealing than her actual view of her. When she was sixteen, in 1853, they holidayed in a French village and let their imaginations run riot:

> There used to be an odd stout figure walking about Meuney in a workman's blouse and loose trousers, and with a cropped head of black hair and an old casquette. We were told that it was a woman; and a wholly suppositious impression once arose in someone's mind that it might have been George Sand herself. I passed quite close on one occasion, when the mysterious personage looked round and then turned away, and I thrilled from head to foot. How odd these mysterious moments are when nothing seems to be happening but which nevertheless go on all the rest of one's life. I saw a face stolid and sad, giving me an impression of pain and long endurance which comes back still . . . I have now, alas, no doubt that it was *not* George Sand.[48]

Compared to this moment, her sight of George Sand in the flesh was something of a disappointment, although the memory is vivid:

> I saw some figures in the box, two men standing at the back, and a lady in a front seat sitting alone. She was a stout middle-aged woman, dressed in a stiff watered silk dress, with a huge cameo, such as people then wore, at her throat. Her black shiny hair shone like polished ebony, she had a heavy red face, marked brows, great dark eyes; there was something how shall I say it – rather fierce, defiant and set in her appearance; powerful, sulky; she frightened me a little. 'That is George Sand' said Mrs Sartoris, bending her head and making a friendly sign to the lady with her eye-glasses. The figure also bent its head, but I don't remember any smile or change of that fixed expression.[49]

This truthful, girlish recollection, which must surely be one of the most unprepossessing portraits for which George Sand ever sat, is then toned down by Lady Ritchie with a gentle tribute: 'I like better to think of George Sand as I never saw her, with grey hairs and a softened life, outcoming and helpful and living in later years among her plants and her grandchildren and her poor people . . .'[50] This third dimension, of hearsay, added to the other two of imagination and actuality, combine into a fascinating creation – three characters in search of an author. Another theatrical encounter, that of Macready with George Sand, gives yet a different impression.

According to Jane Carlyle, who enjoyed the loyalty of it, Mrs Macready's favourite simile was 'as good as a play'; and her husband's soliloquy in his diary, after reading *Consuelo*, is certainly as good as any play. Macready visited Paris for a Shakespeare season from December 1844 to February 1845 and played *Hamlet*, *Macbeth* and *Othello* with great success. George Sand went to all three plays with her son and daughter, and wrote a graceful letter to Macready expressing her appreciation. Macready called on her twice, got on well with Maurice and Solange, talked about Shakespeare – 'j'ai été enchantée de l'entendre parler sur Shakespeare en homme competent'[51] – and urged her, without much hope of success, to visit England. When he got back he bought her complete works, and later wrote to tell her how much pleasure they were giving him. He also wrote on behalf of her 'young worshipper', Matilda Hays, who wanted to translate the novels. In return he received 'a most charming, most delightful letter'[52] in which she apologised for having been out of town when Miss Hays had called and assured him that whatever pleasure her written word might have given him it was as nothing compared to his acting. 'Combien les choses écrites sont froides et lentes!'[53] And so the courtly correspondence went on. She wrote to him in the summer to acquaint him of Solange's marriage and offered to dedicate her next novel to him; and in his grateful reply, Macready told her of the visit to London of Jenny Lind who could by 'her simplicity, saintliness and fervour of her nature' have posed for her 'divine Consuelo'[54] (a comparison very often made with different visiting opera stars till quite late into the century). The novel *Le Château des Désertes* was delayed in publication till 1851, but duly appeared with the dedication:

A M. W. C. Macready.

Ce petit ouvrage essayant de remuer quelques idées sur l'art dramatique je le mets sous la protection d'un grand nom et d'une honorable amitié.

This account of the acquaintance of Macready and George Sand gives no real indication of the nature of the sympathy between them which was based on her life-long fascination with the stage and with the problems of the professional artist. It was this that caused *Consuelo* to make such a deep impression on him. His *Diaries* reveal Macready as a deeply self-aware actor – always assessing after every performance how the audience has reacted, where he has done well and where fallen short. Consuelo, too, was a professional, and as he read of her dedication to her art and her idealism, his chosen role in life appeared to him transformed. Similar outbursts by Victorians were prompted by death beds in Dickens, but not, I think, to this extent by many other novels:

> July 8, 1846
>
> Read: finished *Consuelo*. It is long since I have been so deeply penetrated by a book. I shall never, during at least the few years left to me of life (and do I wish them to be many? God guide me) forget this book. It is full of genius. My soul has been elevated by its perusal. Thoughts unworthy of me have been driven from my mind. May I keep my mind for ever free from them! Amen! The perusal of *Consuelo* has left a deep impression on me; for which, I trust, I am better. Let no one say it is useless or even weak to suffer and to grieve for fictitious distress; it humanises, softens and purifies the soul. The looser thoughts and more corrupt imaginations that had place in my mind have sunk down into forgetfulness and disappeared before the chastening and elevating influence of sympathy with nobler natures and the contemplation of our mortal condition and its liabilities. Oh God, make me better and wiser and more pure.[55]

Macready's friend, Dickens, took up an altogether less soulful attitude to the Frenchwoman. According to Georges Lubin, he did have correspondence with her, but no letters have been found. He does, however, give a briskly reductive description of her in 1856 when he met her in Paris, at Madame Viardot's, as 'a chubby, matronly, swarthy, black-eyed woman, whom you might suppose to be the Queen's monthly nurse,' adding that she had 'nothing of the blue-stocking about her, except a little, final way of settling all your opinions with hers'.[56] His only literary comment on her which has so far surfaced is simply an expression of indignation that reviewers should complain that the heroes of English novels cannot compare with those of Balzac and Sand, 'too uninteresting – too good – not natural'[57] when it is their hypocrisy and morality which dictate to English writers.

Quite different again is the reaction to Madame Sand of the worldly, polished Richard Monckton Milnes. When 'Milnes' figures in Jane Carlyle's letters he brings the breath of high society with him, and Carlyle questioned in some exasperation whether his sole criterion of excellence should be that a man make a good guest at a breakfast

party. Certainly he gave some very memorable meals. Jane Carlyle did
not forget for a long time the breakfast party he gave in Geraldine
Jewsbury's honour where she found that she and Geraldine were the
only women among eight men – 'the situation would just have suited
Lady Harriet but me it was too *strong* for.'[58] But that was in 1847, the
year before the much stronger situation in which he stage-managed, in
the midst of the Revolution in Paris, his famous luncheon for George
Sand and Prosper Mérimée.

Monckton Milnes had met George Sand first several years before,
and she had mentioned him in an approving postscript to a letter of
1841: 'J'aime beaucoup Mr Milnes, je le crois bon et aussi peu anglais
que possible.'[59] Considering the promising nature of this tribute, the
friendship ripened slowly, although whenever Milnes was in Paris he
made a point of visiting her in her apartment. By 1848 de Toqueville
was able to report that Milnes was 'épris de Madame Sand'[60] but then,
as James Pope-Hennessy has commented, Milnes was always *épris* with
someone, and there is nothing to show that he ever felt anything much
more than friendliness, and a certain enjoyment of her celebrity.

The two sources of information about the luncheon he gave are de
Toqueville's *Souvenirs* and the correspondence of Prosper Mérimée.[61]
George Sand is silent about the event. Milnes had asked an extraordinary assortment of guests, this time three women to nine men, and
de Toqueville's description of the group as 'fort peu homogène' seems
temperate. It consisted of Considérant, who was a Fourierist; Damer,
an English colonel; Charlotte Marliani, George Sand's devoted and
talkative friend; the journalist, F. O. Ward; the historian, Mignet; de
Toqueville; and an unsuspecting English couple, Mr and Mrs
Conyngham. In addition, George Sand had two spectres from her past
to delight her: the poet de Vigny, with whom she had been on frosty
and distant terms ever since their mutual interest in Marie Dorval; and
Prosper Mérimée, with whom she had not exchanged a word since the
fiasco of their affair fifteen years earlier. If we are to believe Mérimée,
he did not at first recognise George Sand in the middle-aged woman
with the magnificent black eyes, and thought she had improved vastly.
They said nothing but kept glancing at each other while de Toqueville,
who had expected to hate George Sand, was disarmed by her naturalness and knowledge of the working classes, and Colonel Damer
gallantly offered her the cigar which Mérimée had just given him. It
says much for Milnes's sang-froid that he carried such an occasion off
and much for George Sand's tolerance that, in referring to him later,
she described him as 'un Anglais qui n'est pas précisément de mes amis,
mais qui m'est sympathique.'[62] Milnes, once *épris*, continued to be
interested in her and as late as August 1864, by which time he had
become Lord Houghton, he stopped in Paris to see Madame Sand who,

he reported to his wife, was 'charming in her grand simplicity'.[63] He may not have been precisely one of her friends, but for quarter of a century, as for so many of his countrymen, she was part of his consciousness.

I have deliberately chosen to concentrate on Mrs Carlyle's friends in this chapter so that I could give some idea of the variety of George Sand's reading public. While it is probably not too much of an exaggeration to say that in the 1840s most of the literary figures in London knew each other, Mrs Carlyle's drawing-room had a much more conventional clientèle than, for instance, John Chapman's multi-purpose house in the Strand. Here he ran his publishing business and, later, the *Westminster Review*; took in paying guests; conducted his *ménage*, permanently *à trois* and occasionally *à quatre*, and kept open house for anyone to drop in. Emerson and other visiting Americans lodged there as did, in turn, Eliza Lynn, Marian Evans and William Hale White; the exiles, Mazzini, Louis Blanc and Pierre Leroux were as welcome there as at Cheyne Row; physicians, scientists, educationalists and political thinkers could be met at the Chapmans' Friday evenings.[64] But the most frequent visitors were connected with his line of business, namely his contributors and authors. It is much less surprising to find George Sand being read by such men and women than by Mrs Carlyle's friend, the elderly, cultured, comfortably-off Mrs Buller, the wife of a retired Indian civil servant. And in the even more bohemian phalanstery in the house of Laurence, the painter, were to be found many more devotees of the French novelist, among writers and artists and well-known public figures of unconventional and socialist views. In her *Reminiscences*,[65] Eliza Lynn mentioned, for instance, Robert Owen, Matilda Hays, Amelia Edwards, the novelist, and Edmund Larken. The latter was the translator of *Le Meunier d'Angibault*, the clergyman whose very existence Croker had doubted and whom Archbishop Whateley had rebuked,[66] but who seems to have been a quite unrepentant radical, perhaps fortified by the security of being not only Lord Monson's chaplain but his son-in-law. He was also one of the chief financial supporters of the *Leader*, the radical critical weekly which Lewes and Thornton Hunt ran, and was considered a dangerous man, not so much because of his approval of George Sand and Fourier, but because he wore a beard, ahead of fashion.[67] As Fourierist theories on marriage were put into practice actively by Lewes and his 'pretty little wife Agnes', and by Thornton Hunt, it can be seen that had I chosen to use Chapman's house or Laurence's phalanstery instead of Jane Carlyle's drawing-room as a focus of George Sand interest, an erroneous impression might have been gained of the nature of her public. The surprising thing about it was that it was, indeed, both representative and respectable.

3 'Through the Prison Bars . . .'

1

The love affair of Elizabeth Barrett with George Sand is much less celebrated than her romance with Browning, but, in its own way, it was as intense, as liberating and as clearly, if not as fully, documented. It was a one-sided devotion, inspired by George Sand's 'long, long books' which the invalid could 'live away into',[1] but was none the less absorbing for that. Elizabeth Barrett had, as she confessed to Miss Mitford, an 'organ of veneration . . . as large as a Welsh mountain' and 'a strong heart . . . for making pilgrimages to certain shrines',[2] and once she had given her allegiance to a writer she was not to be argued out of it.

Indeed, one of her most attractive qualities is the combination of critical shrewdness and generosity which makes her critical observations on her contemporaries both illuminating and warm. As long as she sensed the 'genius' in a writer, she was infinitely tolerant of short-comings. She held fast to what she knew to be good – as is finely manifested in the way she defended Browning's poetry against Miss Mitford's steady carping over the ten years before she met him in person – and she never lost a chance of paying tribute to those whom she thought her benefactors.

Precociously erudite in Greek, Latin, French and Italian literature, and widely read in English writers past and present, she came relatively late to la *Jeune France*. She had certainly read Jules Janin's account of contemporary French literature in the *Athenaeum* of 1837, but it was not until April 1839 that she wrote to Miss Mitford: 'I covet your familiarity with all sorts of French literature . . . a little: but not painfully . . . I am . . . a hundred miles behind everybody as to French literature of the present day.'[3] And when she returned to the topic again in 1842, it was as a mature woman. In the years between she had endured the deepest grief of her life in the death of her brother Edward – a loss which occasioned, in her endless attempts to come to terms with it, some of her finest and most moving poems – and felt herself 'lonely enough and old enough and sad enough and experienced enough in

every sort of good and bad reading, not to be hurt personally by a
French superfluity of bad.' That, at least, was the defence she put up
to Miss Mitford when she wrote to her in November of that year: 'Keep
my secret – but I have been reading lately a good deal of the new
French literature'[4] – although she adds that it might be franker simply
to admit that she read these novels because she was curious about them.
She is very conscious of her daring. She would not let her secret 'loose
in this house for the world, no, nor in any other' but goes on, as she
warms to her subject:

> Do you know much of them? You mentioned Victor Hugo to me;
> and I had held him, long before, for a wonderful genius. So is George
> Sand – shameless as she is sometimes – by which word I mean no
> activity of indignation against herself and her works generally, which
> appear to me unduly decried. For the rest she is eloquent as a fallen
> angel . . . and often free from the taint, and great consistently. A true
> woman of genius! – but of a womanhood tired of itself, and scorned
> by her, while she bears it burning above her head.[5]

George Sand, Sue, Soulié, de Queilhe – she has clearly plunged into
what she describes as the 'conflagration' of French literature, and
emerged exhilarated: 'My whole being aches with the sight of it, – and
when I turn away *home*, there seems nothing to be seen, it is all so
neutral tinted and dull and cold by comparison.' She deplores the want
'of fixed principle', but revels in the power. The ending of the letter is
both tentative and challenging: 'Now tell me, what you think? That
it is very naughty of me to read naughty books – or that you have done
the same?'[6]

Reassured by Miss Mitford that she is almost morally bound to read
this ' "chapter" in the philosophy and literature of our times'[7] in order
to extract the good from it, and learning that, despite Miss Mitford's
great reputation in her circle as an authority on all the latest French
books, she really needs some guidance in this new-found land,
Elizabeth Barrett eagerly considers ways of sending Saunders and
Otley's library books to her at Three Mile Bottom. While agreeing that
Miss Mitford's favourite, Hugo, is splendid, she puts forward her rival
claimant, George Sand:

> Yes! Victor Hugo stands first of all in genius, I think – and I should
> say so distinctly if I could make up my mind to call George Sand
> second to any genius living. He is wonderful – she is wonderful! – he,
> dramatically, and in action and effect – she, in eloquence and
> passion. Why Rousseau is cold lifeless loveless, deaf and dumb to
> her! – and (here is the miserable misfortune!) the worst which is
> offensive in him, is innocent to what is bad in her.[8]

She admits that though a book like *Les Maîtres Mosaïstes* could be read aloud by a governess, *Lélia* had made her blush for George Sand, for her sex and for herself 'in particular, who could hold such a book for five minutes in one hand while a coal-fire burnt within reach of the other.'[9] *Lélia* was the one book of George Sand's that Elizabeth Barrett could not finish and, like so many others, could put up no defence for – 'a serpent-book both for language-color and soul-slime'.[10] The impression given by these letters, however, is that she is exaggerating her reactions of disapproval out of sympathy with her correspondent's viewpoint. For Miss Mitford was not in the least sense a devotee like Elizabeth Barrett. She read French easily and with pleasure and was prepared to be swept along on the wave of her young friend's enthusiasm, occasionally drawing sober inferences upon the state of French society which could produce such works. By December, Elizabeth had not only sent her three novels of Mme Dudevant, but *Père Goriot* as well. She had just discovered Balzac, and was eager to assure her that she believed him to be 'the most powerful writer of the French day next to Victor Hugo and George Sand! – that he completes the *triumvirate*. Pere Goriot is a very painful book – but full of a moody reckless power, dashed with blood and mud.'[11]

She had obviously already devoured many of Balzac's novels and waited impatiently for Miss Mitford's judgement, which seems to have been a hostile one. Later, when Elizabeth Barrett was teasing Miss Mitford about her predilection for Paul de Kock, she succinctly summed up her reaction to the two novelists who offered stronger meat than Miss Mitford was equipped to digest: 'You did not bear Balzac – you did not bear George Sand – the "taint" of both stank in your nostrils.'[12] Miss Mitford's lack of enthusiasm did not in any way change Elizabeth Barrett's own view of these writers: what it did was to make her protest a little too much that she was fully aware of all the 'moral turpitude', 'the sensual tendencies' of George Sand's novels, that she responded to Miss Mitford's 'righteous indignation on the subject of Ma^dme Dudevant . . . from the foundations of my temper and moral economy', but that she was still capable of finding *Indiana*, for instance, 'very brilliant and powerful, and eloquent beyond praising'.[13] She had a tendency to retreat behind the defence of the 'poetry' of George Sand – as did many of her contemporaries whose ears were less responsive than Elizabeth Barrett's to the music of George Sand's style: 'I am very sensitive, – I believe far more than I ought to be . . . to *style* and language. I could read a book upon a walking stick, if it were written eloquently, and delight in the eloquence . . . Now, to my mind and ear too, the bare *french* of that wonderful genius Victor Hugo and of this brilliant monstrous woman Ma^dme Dudevant is french *transfigured* . . .'[14]

A correspondence between Elizabeth Barrett and another worshipper of George Sand, like Lewes, would no doubt have sounded very different. When Miss Mitford praised *André*, a gentle and innocuous tale of Sand's, Elizabeth Barrett replied that she would 'smile to hear that I had not read that work yet. You will think that it isn't naughty enough for me.'[15] She was always aware of the fact that George Sand could give her something totally unneeded by Miss Mitford, something found in those novels which were hardest to defend on conventional moral grounds.

Quite clearly, the impact that a first reading of George Sand had made was extraordinary. Like Aurora Leigh, when she 'chanced upon the poets', Elizabeth Barrett's soul 'sprang up surprised'.[16] Later, she confessed that 'Once, I had a romantic scheme of writing my whole mind to her of her works. That was when I first read them – and I lay awake all night in a vision of her letters anonymous and onymous – but it passed away, and I considered how little good it could do.'[17]

George Sand was all things to all her English admirers, but I know of no other who had such a natural temperamental affinity with her as Elizabeth Barrett. She struck chords in, for example, two people as different from herself as Matthew Arnold and George Eliot; each responded in his own way, but long before Elizabeth Barrett opened a novel by George Sand she had much in common with her. It is true that, although only three years older than Elizabeth Barrett, George Sand was a whole lifetime and world of passionate experience removed from her, but we should not be dazzled by the difference in the life style and scope of the two – of the Frenchwoman, who was herself 'la harpe éolienne de notre temps',[18] and the sheltered invalid, who had had to be content with the strains of the Aeolian harp hung by Mr Barrett in her dusty window. Both were warm, impulsive, emotional; both were Romantics, Byron-worshippers in their youth, radicals, moderate feminists; both were genuinely and effortlessly creative, enthusiastic reformers; and for both, literary creation came first. George Sand spoke of herself as a poet not a reformer,[19] and for Elizabeth Barrett poetry was the truest and highest of all vocations. Both were above all idealists, 'aspiring spirits', to use a favourite term of praise of Elizabeth Barrett's, and it was this quality in George Sand that her English admirer seized on, in the two sonnets she composed to her and published in her 1844 volumes of poetry.

2

No one would claim that these two poems are Elizabeth Barrett at her most distinguished. Clumsy, involuted and laborious, their heartfelt admiration for their subject still comes over powerfully. They are companion pieces – *To George Sand. A Desire*, and *To George Sand. A Recognition*. The 'desire' is that the novelist should be freed from the downward pull of her passions and soar upwards, stainless and sanctified from blame; the 'recognition' is that, however much George Sand appears to 'deny her woman's nature with a manly scorn', she is true woman. This second sonnet ends with the exhortation

> Beat purer, heart, and higher,
> Till God unsex thee on the spirit shore:
> To which alone unsexing, purely aspire.

– a last extraordinary line, which reminds us that the charge of obscurity was not levelled at Browning alone. In 1850, she changed it to the feebler 'Where unincarnate spirits purely aspire!' which, despite its apparent intelligibility, actually means much less than the first version. In both sonnets she makes great play with the man-woman aspect of George Sand.

> Thou large-brained woman and large-hearted man,
> Self-called George Sand! whose soul, amid the lions
> Of thy tumultuous senses, moans defiance,
> And answers roar for roar, as spirits can!

What comes over is not distaste for the lions of the 'tumultuous senses', but for the fact that they are paraded in the public arena – an 'applauded circus'. She longs that others should recognise as she does the nobility of George Sand, and invokes the possibility of a miraculous transformation.

These are interesting poems, though bad ones, because they are so revealing, both of Elizabeth Barrett's own deep involvement and her consciousness of a censorious public, whom she attempts to propitiate with such terms as 'angel', 'pure', 'holier', 'stainless', 'maiden', 'sister', 'nobler'. But despite such mitigating accessories, it was a surprising and courageous gesture for her to publish the sonnets at all. She reported that her cousin Kenyon said that she was ' "a daring person" for the introduction of those sonnets. He had heard an able man say at his table a day or two before, that no modest woman would or *ought* to confess to an acquaintance with the works of George Sand.'[20] And when Chorley wrote to her, praising the sonnets, she replied with gratitude, for 'all my readers have not absolved me equally, I have reason to know. I am more a latitudinarian than it is generally thought expedient for women to be'; but then 'I have . . . admiration for *genius* . . . and if Madame Dudevant is not the first female genius of any country or age, I really do not know who is.'[21]

When Miss Mitford, herself the recipient of a very different sonnet tribute in the same volume, suggested that Elizabeth Barrett should send a copy of her poems to George Sand, an amusing interchange of letters followed. Elizabeth Barrett seized upon the idea with breathless delight: 'Are you in earnest . . . do I understand you rightly? . . . that you advise me to send my book to Madame Dudevant? I am half ashamed to confess how often I have thought of doing it, myself – but every time I shrank back. *Could* I have courage? *Might* I have courage?' She continued to muse wistfully upon the prospect: 'Ah – You tempt me with George Sand! . . . Suppose you send her *Belford Regis* or another work and let me slip mine into the shade of it? Suppose we join *so* in expressing, as two English female writers, our sense of the genius of that distinguished woman? . . . I would give anything to have a letter from her, though it smelt of cigar. And it would, of course!'²²

It is intriguing to consider the disparity between the vision which had been conjured up by Croker in the *Quarterly* of the shameless and sullied women who could contemplate reading a novel by George Sand, and the actuality: the invalid on her sofa, her masculine society restricted to Papa, her brothers and Cousin Kenyon; Miss Mitford, wholesome, hardworking, limited, unromantic; both devoted daughters to tyrannical fathers. And it was between these two women, of un-impeachable purity, that the letters on George Sand were flying back and forth.

But after Elizabeth Barrett's first ecstatic reaction, doubts began to creep in. 'It will never do, I fear.' Papa was the main stumbling block. Mr Barrett knew nothing of Mme Dudevant, and his daughter, not surprisingly, felt disinclined to explain her to him 'as a great genius, and no better than she should be'. He would think she was mad. He had delivered himself of the opinion that 'he could not think highly of the modesty of any woman who could read *Don Juan*!!'; he always kept a canto of *Don Juan* and *La Nouvelle Héloise* locked up, and these books, Elizabeth was well aware, were 'Hanah More and Wilberforce by the side of certain books that we wot of'. Reluctantly the idea is put aside. Perhaps next year when Miss Mitford goes to France . . . in the mean-time they can keep the project dark and if they '*do* send, I won't tell him that the "French authoress" who is to be the recipient, smokes cigars and is discontented with the decencies of life.'²³

There is no doubt at all that, in this discussion, Elizabeth Barrett was the dominating spirit. Miss Mitford's kindly suggestion, perhaps prompted by a desire to please her young friend, has been taken up in a way which must have startled her. Certainly, by 1852, Miss Mitford's memory of the episode was rather different, when she wrote to a friend: 'So entirely do I join with you in condemning George Sand, that I point blank refused Mrs Browning to send her my books with hers some years ago.'²⁴

But for Elizabeth Barrett, George Sand was a lifeline. Years later, in a letter to Mr Kenyon, she wrote: 'When I was a prisoner, my other mania for imaginative literature used to be ministered through the prison bars by Balzac, George Sand, and the like immortal improprieties. They kept the colour in my life to some degree and did good service in their time to me.'[25] And in the letter in which she gave up the project of sending her book to George Sand, we find her attempting to analyse her conflicting feelings about her:

> The dangerous point in George Sand, appears to me to lie in the *irresistible* power she attributes to human passion. The moral of *Jacques* – to apply such a term to the most immoral of lessons . . . is just that Love . . . guilty love, observe . . . cannot be resisted by the strongest will and the most virtuous individuality . . . After all, however, she is great, and capable of noble elevations both intellectual and moral: and I should not be ashamed before the whole world, to confess my sense of this. If I had a reputation like her own, I would do it the next moment.[26]

This last, disarming confession was made before she herself had found Love – indeed in its own way, guilty love – irresistible and, despite the moral tone of the comment, it is clear that the issues raised by George Sand have greatly moved her. A whole new emotional world had been opened up for her by *Indiana, Valentine, Jacques* – even the half-read *Lélia* – which the novels of Jane Austen, so highly recommended by Miss Mitford, were remote from exploring. Passion, in some form, was what Elizabeth Barrett demanded of literature, and no one could deny its presence in the novels of George Sand. Both Balzac and George Sand had brought colour into her life, but the latter's 'good service' must, unknown to him, have extended to Browning also. Her stress on the supremacy of the heart, on the attainability of perfect and ideal love between man and woman, on the emptiness of a life in which love is not all-important, on the need to owe love, and not duty, one's primary allegiance – all these doctrines preached by George Sand's articulate heroines must have made Elizabeth Barrett much less startled by, and even possibly more receptive to, Robert Browning's swift and passionate wooing than she might have been, had she been less well versed in the gospel of George Sand.

3

In the two-year courtship, it was inevitable that Elizabeth Barrett should attempt to convert Browning to her views on George Sand, but her success was only partial. She made some headway and clearly put him through a brief reading course, but Balzac was much more congenial to him. What is interesting is that she speaks to him with far more freedom than to Miss Mitford of her admiration for George Sand. In July 1845, confessing her belief that, on the whole, women really are inferior to men, she makes one exception:

> One woman indeed now alive . . . and only that one down all the ages of the world . . . seems to me to justify for a moment an opposite opinion – that wonderful woman George Sand; who has something monstrous in combination with her genius . . . but whom, in her good and evil together, I regard with infinitely more admiration than all other women of genius who are or have been.[27]

By the next month Browning is groaning his way through *Consuelo*, which wearies him – 'oh wearies – and the fourth volume I have all but stopped at – and Albert wearies too – it seems all false, all writing – (not the first part, though).' He particularly resents the 'easy work these novelists have of it! a Dramatic poet has to *make* you love or admire his men and women . . . but with these novelists, a scrape of the pen – out blurting of a phrase, and the miracle is achieved – "Consuelo possessed to perfection this and the other gift" – what would you more?'[28] Another day or two and he is able to write triumphantly 'There lies *Consuelo* – done with!' and goes on to sum it up insultingly as 'a woman's book, in its merits and defects'. He does not deny George Sand's eloquence, but when he wants her to speak about something important she is silent – ' *"la femme qui parle"* – Ah, that is this all? So I am not George Sand's – she teaches me nothing – I look to her for nothing.'[29]

In Elizabeth Barrett's reply, something of the nature of her addiction to George Sand is revealed. She is unperturbed by Browning's criticism, even agreeing with him about all George Sand's faults, but claims that she is greater than *Consuelo*, not to be classified as a 'femme qui parle' – 'she who is man and woman together.'[30] It is clear that she is prepared calmly to accept a difference in taste between them and will not renege on her idolatry. She is sure of a sympathetic hearing from him anyway, and the half-apologetic strain which crept into her discussions with Miss Mitford is totally absent. When, in April 1846, she has read a review article in the *Athenaeum* on George Sand, written, as she rightly suspects, by Chorley, she explodes wrathfully and at some length to Browning against 'little critics . . . digging and nagging at great reputations'.[31]

It is a diatribe meant only for an understanding ear, and her lover does not fail her: 'Oh yes; that paper is by Chorley, no doubt – I read it, and quite wonder at him. I suppose he follows somebody's "lead".'[32] But George Sand continued to be an author whose appeal for Browning was immeasurably less than for his wife, although, in the letters from Florence, we do get an occasional glimpse of joint George Sand readings going on. In 1848, for instance, Miss Mitford is told 'We have been reading over again *André* and *Leone Leoni*, and Robert is in an enthusiasm about the first.'[33] But the news has a certain suspect quality, for *André* was a favourite of Miss Mitford's and Robert was not, so that the combination of the two may well have been an ingratiatory, artistic touch of Mrs Browning's. She herself went on reading all that George Sand wrote as the novels appeared, and though a certain chill crept in to her references to her around the time of the revolution, when she feared that George Sand was becoming too 'rouge' and writing propaganda for the communists, she melted towards her again when George Sand retired from active politics and went back to Nohant. And when there was at last a chance to meet her idol, she seized it with both hands.

Her elopement with Browning had made many impossibles possible – and her earlier 'romantic dream' of writing to George Sand, which had been so reluctantly laid aside, could now be revived in a more ambitious form. And when she and Browning were themselves in Paris, in the winter of 1851 and spring of 1852, her letters tell of a determined campaign to meet the novelist at last.

In a letter to Miss Mitford in October, she wrote, 'Mazzini is to give us a letter to George Sand. – Come what will, we must have a letter to George Sand.'[34] – but she had heard that George Sand was seldom in Paris, that 'it is most difficult, it appears, to get at her', and people had discouraged them, saying 'She will never see you; you have no chance, I am afraid.'[35] Mrs Browning had not only to reckon with George Sand's reserve but also with Robert's reluctance to co-operate, and on Christmas Eve she wrote disappointedly to Miss Mitford that George Sand had come and gone and that the letter had not been delivered. She had been baffled by a friend who 'did not "*dare*" ' to present their letter and by Robert who would not leave it at the theatre, where a play of George Sand's was staged, in case it got 'mixed up with the love letters of the actresses' or was 'given to the "premier comique" to read aloud'. Robert had been 'a little proud', the friend 'very stupid', and she 'in a furious state of dissent from either . . . Robert tries to smooth down my ruffled plumage now by promising to look out for some other opportunity, but the late one has gone. She is said to have appeared in Paris in a bloom of recovered beauty and brilliancy of eyes . . . A strange, wild, wonderful woman, certainly.'[36]

By February, George Sand was back again in Paris, pleading the cause of her friends with Louis Napoleon, and this time Mrs Browning made sure there was no hitch. The Mazzini letter was sent 'along with a little note signed by both of us, though written by me, as seemed right, being the woman.' Robert was still inclined 'to sit in his chair and be proud a little' but ' "No" said I, "You *shan't* be proud, and I *won't* be proud, and we *will* see her. I won't die, if I can help it, without seeing George Sand".'[37]

The letters elicited an immediate, kindly reply from George Sand and an invitation to visit her. This memorable event took place in the middle of February and the next day Mrs Browning wrote a long account of it to her cousin, John Kenyon, and, thereafter, to Miss Mitford, Mrs Jameson and, no doubt, many other correspondents. Normally she remained incarcerated from autumn to spring, and in February the air was sharp, but she put on her respirator, smothered herself with furs and went in a close carriage after she had represented to Robert that 'one might as well lose one's life as one's peace of mind for ever, and if I lost seeing her I should with difficulty get over it.'[38]

For an occasion so long looked forward to, it was really remarkably successful. Mrs Browning lovingly recounted all her impressions and the scene lives again for us in her animated description – the English-woman, her heart beating fast, stooping to kiss the outstretched hand, and George Sand, preventing her, saying quickly, 'Mais non, je ne veux pas' and kissing her on the lips. Every detail of her dress and appearance is noted – the black, glossy hair, noble eyes and brow, slightly receding chin, somewhat Jewish nose, mobile mouth, the flashing sudden smile, white projecting teeth, full cheeks, deep olive complexion, small, well-shaped hands, simplicity of manners and conversation, low, rapid voice, fashionable grey serge gown and jacket, plain linen collarette and sleeves – the eager and meticulous documentation of one hot for certainty after so many years of dreaming and conjecture. Mrs Browning decided, with surprise, that George Sand could never have been beautiful, although her face had obviously 'great moral as well as intellectual capacities'. But she concluded, with satisfaction, 'I liked her. I did not love her, but I felt the burning soul through all that quietness, and was not disappointed in George Sand. When we rose to go, I could not help saying "C'est pour la dernière fois"; and then she asked us to repeat our visit next Sunday . . . She kissed me again when we went away, and Robert kissed her hand.'[39]

Next Sunday's visit was also put on record, to Mrs Jameson:

> She sat, like a priestess, the other morning, in a circle of eight or nine men, giving no oracles, except with her splendid eyes, sitting at the corner of the fire, and warming her feet quietly, in a general silence of the most profound deference. There was something in the calm disdain of it which pleased me, and struck me as characteristic. She was George Sand, that was enough; you wanted no proof of it. Robert observed that 'if any other mistress of a house had behaved so, he would have walked out of the room' – but, as it was, no sort of incivility was meant. In fact, we hear that she 'likes us very much'

and as we went away she called me 'chère Madame' and kissed me, and desired to see us both again.[40]

That was, however, the last time that Mrs Browning saw her, for she was out on their third and last call. Robert saw her in all six times, giving her his arm the whole length of the Tuileries gardens and reporting to his wife that she was not looking as well as usual – 'a little too "endimanchée" in terrestrial lavenders and super celestial blues'.[41] The reactions of husband and wife are very different – Elizabeth, in her first two accounts of her visits, concentrates almost exclusively on the novelist, while Robert has a wary eye open for the 'riff-raff' who surround her; and by April, when she sums up their visits in a letter to Miss Mitford, she has absorbed some of his prejudices:

[Robert] was really very good and kind to let me go at all after he found the sort of society rampant around her. He didn't like it extremely but, being the prince of husbands he was lenient to my desires and yielded the point. She seems to live in the abomination of desolation as far as regards society – crowds of ill-bred men who adore her *à genoux bas*, betwixt a puff of smoke and an ejection of saliva. Society of the ragged Red diluted with the lower theatrical. She herself so different, so apart, as alone in her melancholy disdain! . . . I did not much mind the Greek in Greek costume who tutoyed her, and kissed her I believe, so Robert said, or the other vulgar man of the theatre who went down on his knees and called her 'sublime'. 'Caprice d'amitié' said she, with her quiet gentle scorn. A noble woman under the mud, be certain.

It is ironic that the presence of Robert, which made the meeting possible, must have diminished the chance of any real relationship between the two women. It is clear that Mrs Browning, while not disappointed in George Sand, felt keenly that she was incapable of impinging on her very much. Her letter continues: I, would kneel down to her, too, if she would leave it all, throw it off, and be herself as God made her. But she would not care for my kneeling; she does not care for me . . . we always felt that we couldn't penetrate – couldn't really *touch* her – it was all vain . . .'[42]

In this letter to Miss Mitford, Mrs Browning strikes unerringly, if instinctively, the note of virtuous ardour that she knows will please her old friend – '*I* would kneel down to her, too, if she would leave it all' – neglecting to mention that she had already bowed down before her at their first meeting, without any such dramatic stipulation. But what does come through, genuinely enough, is a certain bleak and even desolate awareness of how peripheral and unimportant she must seem to this woman, who for ten years had occupied a central place in her own consciousness. On the whole, she was much happier in re-establishing contact with George Sand through her books, and her enthusiasm for them seems to have been little diminished. As each volume of the *Histoire de ma Vie* came out she read it avidly and, in December 1855, she wrote to Mrs Jameson:

> Oh! George Sand. How magnificent that eighteenth volume is; I mean the volume which concludes with the views upon the *sexes*! After all, and through all, if her hands are ever so defiled, that woman has a clean soul . . . I read this book so eagerly and earnestly that I seem to burn it up before me. Really there are great things in it.[43]

And, moreover, she was able to add in triumph: 'Robert quite joins with me at last. He is intensely interested, and full of admiration.' It is pleasant that this glowing tribute to George Sand should be the final one recorded before the publication, in the following year, of *Aurora Leigh*.

4

Aurora Leigh, which expressed, according to its author, her 'highest convictions about Life and Art',[44] was published in 1856 but had been meditated for twelve years, ever since she wrote *Lady Geraldine's Courtship*. This sentimental verse tale about a democratic marriage had been composed by the yard at top speed to fill up her second volume of poems. To her surprise, it was a great success and she determined someday to write 'a novel-poem' exposing 'the Humanity of the age'.[45]

From the moment *Aurora Leigh* was published voices were raised above the immediate acclaim to point out the poem's indebtedness to other writers. Alethea Hayter starts her excellent discussion of *Aurora Leigh*[46] by quoting William Bell Scott's remark – 'It is only a novel à la Jane Eyre, a little tainted by Sand'[47] – and she goes on to point out that source-hunting for the poem has been a favoured diversion ever since. Professor Shackford[48] considered the three main influences on *Aurora Leigh* to be Madame de Staël's *Corinne*, George Sand's *Consuelo* and several of Browning's poems. Although Alethea Hayter's list includes, in addition, Balzac, Soulié, Sue, Carlyle, Stendhal, Charlotte Brontë, Mrs Gaskell, Wordsworth, Byron, Tennyson and Hawthorne, yet she does accept the two Frenchwomen as having exerted the most fundamental influence upon the poem.

The most persuasive and lively case for *Corinne* as a major influence on *Aurora Leigh* – and indeed as a long-lasting myth for Victorians – has been made by Ellen Moers. *Corinne* certainly made an enormous impact on the youthful Elizabeth Barrett, and it is true that Aurora herself perpetuates 'the myth of the famous woman talking, writing, perform-

ing, to the applause of the world'.[49] But I think that for many
Victorians George Sand took over where Madame de Staël left off, and
it was her contemporary who captivated the mature Elizabeth Barrett.
What cannot be denied is that all her life her staple diet was literary
and that whatever she took in to her system, her excellent metabolism
was capable of using and transforming. The list of authors to whom her
poem is indebted could really be prolonged indefinitely, as indeed
could the number of George Sand novels which made themselves felt.
The normal practice of discussing the influence on *Aurora Leigh* of only
one novel, *Consuelo*, simply indicates that critics have been happy to
settle for the most handy source.

The name connection – between George Sand's Christian name of
Aurore and the heroine, Aurora – must strike anyone who is aware of
Mrs Browning's worship of George Sand. It is a pleasing similarity,
but I am less convinced of its significance than Professor Shackford,
considering that Mrs Browning was perfectly prepared to let her poem
go forth under the name of Laura Leigh had she received any
encouragement from her husband and Harriet Hosmer, the sculptor,
with whom she discussed the two names – finally settling on Aurora
Leigh as 'having more backbone'.[50] Alethea Hayter seems to me to be
saying something much more important when she observes that there
is a resemblance between Aurora and George Sand herself.

One of the things that Mrs Browning most admired about George
Sand was the fact that she was a dedicated professional writer who
could hold her own with men and asked for no allowances to be made
for her sex. As we have seen, she considered her not only to be a woman
of genius but the only one she knew of who was not inferior to men.
Aurora Leigh is another such. Just as George Sand came up from
Nohant to Paris, found an attic, five flights up in the quai St Michel,
with a view of roof-tops and sky, river and spires, and started her
literary career, so Aurora came up from the country to London, 'up
three flights of stairs' in Kensington, to a chamber, looking out over
'slant roofs and chimney pots' to 'spires, bridges, streets and squares'.
Here, spurred on by her desire to write a great work, supporting herself
by articles and reviews, working

> with one hand for the booksellers
> While working with the other for myself
> And art   (III, 303–305)

impervious to praise or censure, Aurora gradually becomes a 'lioness'.
Like George Sand, she is 'a man-woman'. She is presented as being an
aspiring spirit, as much of a phenomenon as George Sand had been –
determined to surmount her sex, to write for and of the present-day –

c

> this live throbbing age . . . (V, 203)
> The full-veined, heaving, double-breasted Age (V, 216)

– without mincing her words or images. She converses on equal terms with her male admirers:

> . . . we who have clipt
> The curls before our eyes, may see at least
> As plain as men do. Speak out, man to man (V, 809–812)

It is interesting to see how Browning's dismissal of George Sand as a woman writer and nothing but a 'femme qui parle' has rankled over the years. Romney's discouragement of the young Aurora is couched in almost similar terms when he talks of the praise

> Which men give women when they judge a book.
> Not as mere work but as mere woman's work. (II, 233–234)

and Aurora's whole aim is to prove him wrong. When her masterpiece is published Vincent Carrington praises it as 'a good book, And you a woman!' and Romney eats his humble pie with a will. Aurora looks around at her sex, sees women concerned with women's function, women's mission, women's rights and condemns *them* as the *femmes qui parlent* – 'A woman's function plainly is – to talk.' Only by her works, by doing, by accomplishing, like Aurora – or George Sand, or Mrs Browning herself – will women be able to counter such a charge.

So far the resemblance between Aurora Leigh and George Sand is straightforward. But Aurora is more than a reflection of George Sand; she is all that Mrs Browning had yearned that her idol might be, not only a great writer but a noble, chaste woman. Aurora is the George Sand of the 1844 sonnet, *A Desire*, after the 'miraculous thunder' has sounded and the transformation has taken place. Aurora's soul is not at odds with her feelings, as Elizabeth Barrett had felt George Sand's to be, moaning defiance 'amid the lions Of thy tumultuous senses', as she put it. This lioness, while not lacking passions, has them well under control. *Aurora Leigh* makes the 'Desire' of the sonnet come true and we are shown, in the heroine, a 'pure genius sanctified from blame'. Even the final vision of the sonnet

> Till child and maiden pressed to thy embrace
> To kiss upon thy lips a stainless fame

has its counterpart in the verse-novel, when the blameless Marian and her child drop 'dewy kisses' on Aurora's lips. All that had irked Mrs Browning about her deity – her habit of 'walking in the mud'; her questionable reputation; her monstrous sensuality – all have vanished. For years she had been defending George Sand from the attacks of her respectable friends; now she had the satisfaction of presenting her, in literature, if not in life, 'as God made her' – as a heroine who could claim total respect from the world:

> I am a woman of repute;
> No fly-blow gossip ever specked my life;
> My name is clean and open as this hand. (IX, 264–266)

While there are, of course, resemblances between *Consuelo* and *Aurora Leigh*, it is not the only Sandian source. Consuelo, like Aurora, is an artist, a professional singer; her life is dedicated to her art but, in the end, she decides that however exalted the role of artist 'nul ne peut servir deux maîtres' and the claims of womanhood cannot be denied. Or, as Aurora puts it, as she falls into Romney's arms:

> Art is much, but Love is more.
> O Art, my Art, thou'rt much but Love is more! (IX, 656–657)

On the other hand, if Aurora's endless musings on Art and Life and Art and Nature can be paralleled in *Consuelo* as well as those features mentioned by Professor Shackford – humble life, humanitarianism, justice, individualism, lyrical descriptions of nature – the same can be said for all George Sand's novels. These are major preoccupations of her writing, often treated much more explicitly than in *Consuelo* and with more relevance to the contemporary scene.

For, after all, *Consuelo* is not a picture of this 'modern age' like *Aurora Leigh*, but a deliberate recreation of eighteenth-century Venetian musical society, interspersed with considerably less realistic interludes in the gothic castle of the Rudolstadts. Consuelo herself, is, as has been justly pointed out, a sort of Goethian figure, an angel of consolation. 'Elle passe dans la vie comme un bon chevalier errant, redresseur de toute injustice.'[51] She is very different indeed from the career-woman, Aurora, that strenuous Englishwoman, straining her 'nature at doing something great', always with a rankling sense of having to prove herself as good as a man.

It was not in *Consuelo* but in *Le Compagnon du Tour de France* and *Le Meunier d'Angibault* that George Sand raised the sort of problems that Romney has to face when he attempts to bridge the gap between the classes. In *Le Compagnon*, Pierre, the model workman, sees the hollowness of such utopian visions as Romney's. If he were to marry Iseult, whom he worships, he would automatically become a rich landowner; even if he tried out agricultural experiments on the workers' behalf and founded hospitals and schools he would, by doing so, desert his class. The gap between aristocrat and workman is shown to be unbridgeable in this novel; in *Le Meunier d'Angibault* the marriage shows every sign of being successful, mainly because the heroine has lost all her money.

It was after reading this novel that Elizabeth Barrett commented on the importance for modern fiction, of 'sympathies with the people',[52] and both in her verse-novel and George Sand's 'communist novels' we see evidence of the same homework. Not only Lady Waldemar had read 'half-Fourier-through, Proudhon, Considerant and Louis Blanc'. Mrs Browning can be as idealistic about the poor as George Sand; her drover's daughter, Marian Erle, in her blend of high-minded pride and dog-like devotion recalls another impossibly noble woman of the people, La Savinienne, in *Le Compagnon*; but Romney's 'vain phalanstery' is destroyed by the brutalised and unregenerate recipients of his bounty. Nowhere in George Sand is there a parallel picture to that of the wedding-guests from the slums, in *Aurora Leigh*, who

> clogged the streets, they oozed into the church
> In a dark slow stream, like blood. (IV, 553–554)

the women with

> babies, hanging like a rag
> Forgotten on their mother's neck. (IV, 571–572)

In such scenes of nightmare horror and revulsion, Mrs Browning shakes herself quite free of her affinity with George Sand, and draws closer to Robert Browning.

None the less, in fundamental respects the debt is a real one. From the first, George Sand had attacked what Mrs Browning called 'the squeamishness of this age – this Ostrich age',[53] and it can fairly be said that in these novels she found a precedent and support for doing what her own inclinations would have prompted her towards in any case. The wrongs of women, men's heartlessness in the satisfaction of their appetites, the treatment of women as commodities, conventional hypocrisy and social repression – all are live issues in George Sand's earliest novels, as they are twenty years later in *Aurora Leigh*. Mrs Browning had a great deal of courage and independence, but I doubt if she would have been quite so outspoken without the example of George Sand to hearten her.

On the whole, I would say that she was most in tune with the early romantic novels and such confessional works as *Lettres d'un Voyageur* and *Histoire de ma Vie*, where she felt closest to the warmth and 'noble elevation' of the writer, rather than with her social/political novels in which, she said, 'her hand grows cold'.[54] There are a great many echoes of these early novels in *Aurora Leigh*, and it would be tedious to multiply instances, but I would suggest Sir Ralph in *Indiana*, rather than Count Albert in *Consuelo*, as having much in common with the character of Romney. Sir Ralph, like Romney, befriends his cousin, an orphan child. He is ten years older than she is and loves her, comforts her, teaches her, plays a waiting game – always generous, self-sacrificing, stoical, apparently cold, looking forward to some day making her his bride. This is prevented by *mariages de convenance*, but he continues to act as her protector until the final scene of the book, when, with much use of imagery of the light and darkness to symbolise Indiana's former blindness to his devotion, they voice their love for each other. This scene was undoubtedly buried in Mrs Browning's memory, awaiting resurrection in her own highly-charged *éclaircissement* between Romney and Aurora on the moon-bathed promontory; and it may explain her surprised protest, when she was accused of plagiarising Rochester's calamity from *Jane Eyre*, that Romney's blindness was used symbolically.

But, after all, particular debts are of very little significance compared with the congenial nature of the creed of love which George Sand preached, without faltering, from start to finish. In *Aurora Leigh* the same doctrine is expounded. Aurora's father passes it on to her, in Book I:

> His last word was, 'Love' –
> 'Love, my child, love, love!' (I, 211–212)

and even while Aurora is pursuing her vocation she never denies the supremacy of love. 'I love love' she confesses proudly to the sceptical ear of Lady Waldemar, in Book IV, and in the final Book, in which the word 'love' is mentioned over a hundred times, she is able to make her boast good and give way to her passion. The blend of high-souled fervour, of mysticism and of sensuousness is one which is all too familiar in George Sand's true-life scenes; indeed, also, in George Sand's more detached musings on the relationship of the sexes. The chapter of *Histoire de ma Vie* which Mrs Browning read before finishing her poem, 'so eagerly and earnestly that I seem to burn it up before me', bears a remarkable resemblance to the sentiments expressed in the last book of *Aurora Leigh*. One can see why they should have appealed so much to Mrs Browning. For true consummation, George Sand says, 'Il faut être trois; un homme, une femme et Dieu en eux.' 'Trois' there certainly are in Book Nine of *Aurora Leigh*, which ends in a haze of sanctification, with almost as many references to God as to love. What prevents this climax from being considered as simply an orthodox hymn to married love, like the ending of *In Memoriam*, is, however, the vibrant note of passion which provides a strange counterpoint to the more conventional sentiments. Lines such as

> . . . 'First God's love.'
> 'And next,' he smiled, 'the love of wedded souls
> Which still presents that mystery's counterpart.' (IX, 881–883)

have a very different emotional impact from

> Embrace that was convulsion . . . (IX, 721)

> So close, my very garments crept and thrilled
> With strange electric life . . . (IX, 821–822)

George Sand certainly did not always choose to give a religious aura to earthly love, and Mrs Browning also wrote frankly, and with considerable freedom, of passion. The opening of Book V is a remarkable evocation of Aurora's pent-up longing for love, as she asks whether, in her poetry, she can be in tune

> With spring's delicious trouble in the ground,
> Tormented by the quickened blood of roots,
> And softly pricked by golden crocus-sheaves . . . (V, 8–10)

> . . . with all that strain
> Of sexual passion, which devours the flesh
> In a sacrament of souls . . . (V, 14–16)

It is not surprising that Mrs Browning should have been rebuked by the reviewers. The Brontës alone among Victorian women writers came anywhere near to writing as passionately of love between the sexes as she did, and it should be remembered that not only did the reviewers of Charlotte Brontë reproach her with coarseness, they also compared her power with that of George Sand. It is true that Mrs Browning's lack of inhibition in writing of love could be explained by her own temperament; by her own experience, from having been set free physically and emotionally by her marriage; by the example of Browning as a love-poet. But I think that almost as much of the credit – or perhaps responsibility – must lie with George Sand, with the 'old troubadour of love', herself.

4 'Another Bale of French Books' at Haworth

It seems disproportionately further from Nohant to Haworth than to Wimpole Street but only, I think, because in this century we have tended so much to stress the rugged Yorkshire background of the Brontë sisters and to place them in an exclusively English tradition. This was not an error into which nineteenth-century critics fell and, as late as 1899, Mrs Humphrey Ward was stressing, in her excellent and discerning Prefaces to the Haworth Edition, the European Romantic affinities of the novels of both Charlotte and Emily.

In doing so, although she in no way underrated their Yorkshire environment, Celtic heredity, and their debt to English Romantics, she referred especially to those authors, French and German, who from the beginning of the century to around the 1840s, dominated the Continental literary scene. She claimed that '*Wuthering Heights*' belongs to a particular European moment',[1] and as for *Jane Eyre* 'one may almost say of it . . . that it belongs more to the European than to the special English tradition . . .'[2] Charlotte probably owed much – more I am inclined to believe than has yet been recognised – to the books of French Revolution.'[3] It is certainly true that the shock to the system of *Jane Eyre* is infinitely greater if it is read after, say, *Emma* or Susan Ferrier's *Marriage* or Mrs Trollope's *The Widow Barnaby* than after *Corinne* or *Lélia* or *Consuelo*. Mary Ward was familiar with the works of George Sand, not only because of the partiality of her uncle, Matthew Arnold, but because everyone literary in England till late in the nineteenth century did read her, and she was particularly convinced of Charlotte's link with her: 'That great romantic artist in whom restless imagination went hand-in-hand with a fine and chosen realism, was probably of some true importance in the development of Charlotte Brontë's genius.'[4]

Mrs Ward's prefaces are less well-known than they should be and I read her comments only after I had come to the conclusion myself, through reading George Sand and the Brontës in juxtaposition, that the French influence had indeed extended to the remoteness of Haworth parsonage. In Charlotte's case, there is evidence of her interest in French literature and culture, and pride in her own familiarity with it.

Charlotte's first letter in French was written in 1832, when she was sixteen, to her school and life-time friend, Ellen Nussey, who did not feel up to continuing the correspondence in what Charlotte called 'the universal language'.[5] But the reading, though not the writing, of French was one of the commonest accomplishments of young ladies at that time, and a few years later Charlotte records that she had got 'another bale of French books from Gomersal' [the home of the Taylor sisters] 'containing upwards of forty volumes – I have read about half – they are like the rest – clever, wicked, sophistical and immoral – the best of it is they give me a thorough idea of France and Paris – and are the best substitute for French conversation I have met with.'[6]

This letter was written from Haworth where, in the happy summer of 1840, when all the sisters were at home, French fiction was obviously being swallowed in large gulps. Charlotte's reaction was clearly a mixed one of disapproval and interest – one really very like that of Jane Eyre, as she listens to Mr Rochester's account of his scandalous past in Paris: 'I heard him talk with relish. It was his nature to be communicative – he liked to open to a mind unacquainted with the world glimpses of its scenes and ways (I do not mean its corrupt scenes and wicked ways, but such as derived their interest from the great scale on which they were acted, the strange novelty by which they were characterised) . . .'[7]

Disapproving or not, she did read them – and presumably the earlier bale, too, which had been sent her by the Taylor household, that extraordinary ménage which provided so much interest and stimulus for Charlotte. A houseful of lively, argumentative boys and girls, radical in their politics and non-conformist in their religion, with a strong bias towards feminism – all taking their cue from the father, a well-travelled, cosmopolitan Yorkshireman, whom Charlotte attempted, with only very moderate success, to capture as Hunsden in *The Professor* and Yorke in *Shirley*. It would be very surprising indeed if, among the books sent by the go-ahead Taylor girls to Charlotte, some of George Sand's novels were not included – for her works are mentioned along with Thiers, Goethe, Eugène Sue and Paul de Kock as being seen on Hunsden's 'well-furnished' bookshelves.

This early glimpse, through modern French authors, into other, unknown worlds was no doubt extended in her two-years stay in Brussels, for M. Héger read widely with her among contemporary writers (Victor Hugo is particularly mentioned) and George Sand was still at the peak of her celebrity. We are particularly deprived of literary judgements in Charlotte's correspondence at this time, because all the letters that have survived are addressed to Ellen Nussey, her loyal, limited and unintellectual friend, with whom, she said later, she could never discuss literature. Had her letters to Mary Taylor not been destroyed, the picture of Charlotte in Brussels might have been a less inhibited one, for a remark of Mary Taylor's to Mrs Gaskell, in 1856, when the latter was gathering material for her *Life*, shows a different side of Charlotte. Mary Taylor wrote:

> Of course, artists and authors stood high with Charlotte, and the best thing after their works would have been their company. She used very inconsistently to rail at money and money-getting, and then wish she was able to visit all the large towns in Europe, see all the sights and know all the celebrities. This was her notion of literary fame – a passport to the society of clever people . . .[8]

Here is exactly the same contradiction pointed out by the sharp-eyed Mary Taylor as is evident in Charlotte's works or indeed, in her earlier reaction to the sophisticated French novels – the distinctive blend of puritanical rigidity and romantic yearnings. As intensely aware as Elizabeth Barrett of her narrow confines, passionately longing for a freer, more exciting and rewarding life, she yet sternly condemns the means of attaining it. She is much more divided than Emily, much more drawn to the world and dependent on its approval, and consequently anguished in a way that Emily never was.

We can, then, only conjecture about her reading while at Brussels, but it is clear from later references in letters to Lewes that she had long been familiar with the novels of George Sand. The first reference occurs in the letter which contains her well-known attack upon Jane Austen. This paragraph follows:

> Now I can understand admiration of George Sand; for though I never saw any of her works which I admired throughout (even 'Consuelo' which is the best, or the best that I have read, appears to me to couple strange extravagance with wondrous excellence), yet she has a grasp of mind which, if I cannot fully comprehend, I can very deeply respect: she is sagacious and profound; Miss Austen is only shrewd and observant.[9]

And in her next letter she goes on to explain what she feels the one lacks and the other possesses:

> Can there be a great artist without poetry? What I call – what I will bend to, as a great artist, then – cannot be destitute of the divine gift. But by *poetry*, I am sure, you understand something different to what I do . . . It is *poetry*, as I comprehend the word which elevates that masculine George Sand, and makes out of something coarse something god-like.[10]

And again, in 1850, thanking Lewes for sending her a parcel of books which included some copies of Balzac, who, unlike George Sand, was a new author for her, she wrote:

> Truly – I like George Sand better. Fantastic, fanatical, unpractical enthusiast as she often is – far from truthful as are many of her views of Life – misled as she is apt to be by her feelings – George Sand has a better nature than M. de Balzac – her brain is larger – her heart warmer than his. The 'Lettres d'un Voyageur' are full of the writer's self, and I never felt so strongly as in the perusal of this work – that most of her very faults spring from the excess of her good qualities; it is this excess which has often hurried her into difficulty, which has prepared for her enduring regret. But – I believe – her mind is of that order which disastrous experience teaches – without weakening or too much disheartening, and in that case – the longer she lives the better she will grow.[11]

From such an uncompromising moralist as Charlotte, this is praise indeed. Charlotte has warmed to what she considered to be the indispensable requirements of a novelist – the poetry and the passion – in George Sand, and English reviewers were not slow to find a resemblance between the two writers. It is interesting that both Lewes and George Eliot, one no doubt taking the hint from the other, commented on the fact in 1853, after the publication of *Villette*. George Eliot wrote: 'Yet what passion, what fire in her! Quite as much as in George Sand, only the clothing is less voluptuous';[12] and Lewes, in his review of *Ruth* and *Villette*, said: 'There is no writer of our day, except George Sand, who possesses the glory and the power which light up the writings of Currer Bell.'[13] It was a quite normal analogy; much later, Leslie Stephen also made it: 'Putting aside living writers the only female novelist whom one can distinctly put above her is George Sand.'[14]

One of Charlotte's objections to Jane Austen was that she gave no indication of awareness of the depths of passion involved in the relationship between a man and woman. This could certainly not be objected to in George Sand nor in Charlotte Brontë herself. In fact, as Harriet Martineau said in heavy disapproval in the review of *Villette* which so pained Charlotte: 'All the female characters, in all their thoughts and lives, are full of one thing, or are regarded by the reader in the light of that one thought – love.'[15]

What seems to me George Sand's particular legacy to Charlotte Brontë is her unswerving belief in the truth of the heart's promptings, and her equally firm disbelief in the chances of attaining perfect happiness in the normal marriage. Disenchantment about matrimony and dedication to love is a peculiarly Sandian blend, and as early as 1840, the year in which Charlotte was reading French novels in bulk, she was, as Winifred Gérin says, 'thinking a great deal . . . about a woman's prospects of happiness in marriage'.[16] Her letters to Ellen Nussey are full of warnings:

> . . . as to intense *passion*, I am convinced that that is no desirable feeling. In the first place, it seldom or never meets with a requital; and in the second place, if it did, the feeling would be only temporary; it would last the honeymoon, and then, perhaps, give place to disgust, or indifference, worse perhaps than disgust. Certainly this would be the case on the man's part; and on the woman's – God help her, if she is left to love passionately and alone.[17]

Again, later: 'I hope you will not have the romantic folly to wait for the awakening of what the French call "une grande *passion*" – My good girl "une grande passion" is *une* grande *folie*.'[18]

'*Une grande passion*' – the phrase has taken Charlotte's fancy. She talks of it again to Ellen's stodgy clergyman brother, Henry, and uses it in *Jane Eyre*. It is 'une grande passion' which Mr Rochester has felt for Céline Varens, and which he looks back on with sardonic contempt. It is not a phrase which she uses to describe the emotions of her own heroines, however ardently they love. The wariness of uncontrollable passion, which her letters here reveal, comes both from observation and reading. She refers specifically to the exploitation of the deeply emotional Mary Taylor by Branwell – but she generalises with an authority derived from wider, literary experience. George Sand's endless analysing of the relationships of men and women has surely encouraged Charlotte's own analytical tendencies. In *Lélia*, *ennui*, indifference, and satiety succeed the *grande passion*, and the world-weary heroine preaches detachment to the ardent young poet: 'Vous avez pris pour un besoin du coeur ce qui n'était qu'une fièvre de cerveau.'[19] In *Jacques*, the hero finds after a month or two of marriage that the illusion has gone, that a 'grain de sable' has fallen into the lake of his content and ruffled the smooth surface. Throughout Charlotte's correspondence she maintains a consistently disenchanted attitude to the marriages she sees being made around her. Her attitude has little in common with Jane Austen's lively shrewdness but much with George Sand's sombre awareness of the subjectivity of all conceptions which husbands and wives have of each other. Cold-heartedness, mercenariness, foolishness, vanity – all these she sees as more common in life than a surplus of passion and as stumbling blocks to happiness in marriage – and while Charlotte had much, even in her own narrow circle, to make her muse upon marriage, there can be no doubt that much of what she found 'sagacious and profound' in George Sand related to that topic.

For George Sand was not writing against marriage or even primarily against the legal disabilities of women but against received doctrines in the relationship of the sexes, which forbade to women equality, frankness and a similar intensity of love. When the moment comes, neither Valentine nor Indiana nor Consuelo has any false modesty in declaring her love for the hero; and the convention of reticence which had been adhered to in the English novel is similarly shattered by Charlotte Brontë's heroines. When Jane declares her love for Mr Rochester long before she has any hope of his returning it, this is evidence not only of the pent-up heart overflowing but of the author entering a different and less prudish tradition. The *Dublin University Magazine* immediately seized on Jane's resemblance to a George Sand heroine:

> . . . the little plain-featured, not to say ugly, governess full of passion and feeling, reminds us, in some degree, of the Consuelo of George Sand. There are many points of resemblance between them; both, unpromising infants, improving as they arrived at maturity, with large dark eyes: both governesses, delighting in sombre-coloured wearing apparel – the one loved by her master, the other by the fiancée [*sic*] of her pupil.[20]

And Miss Rigby's famous onslaught, in the *Quarterly Review*,[21] not only on the shamelessness of the heroine but on the dangerously levelling doctrines of the book, the sort of philosophy which had led to the French Revolution, sounds remarkably like Croker's attack upon George Sand. Charlotte Brontë never had to defend herself against charges of immorality as hotly as George Sand, but in the course of her literary life she was charged with being a rebel, a radical, a feminist; with being anti-religious, coarse and masculine; with having written, in Lewes's phrase 'a naughty book'. When she wrote, in the famous preface to the second edition of *Jane Eyre*, 'Conventionality is not morality; self-righteousness is not religion', it might well, indeed, have been George Sand speaking.

In appearance, Jane has very little in common with George Sand's beautiful, romantic heroines, for even Consuelo, the ugly duckling quite soon becomes a swan; but her passion and her outspokenness do not fall short of theirs. While it is Charlotte's own passionate nature which gives veracity to the outpourings of Jane Eyre and Lucy Snowe it is, I think, the literary example of George Sand which has allowed her to be unselfconscious in their revelations. 'Quite as much passion as George Sand only the clothing less voluptuous' was a discerning comment of Marian Evans, for the realism of Charlotte Brontë was, frequently, only skin-deep. The latter wrote 'I hold that a work of fiction ought to be a work of creation; that the *real* should be sparingly introduced in pages dedicated to the *ideal*'[22] – a doctrine which is perfectly in step with George Sand's belief that 'Art is not the study of positive reality but the search for ideal truth.'[23] Romantics both, they were wholly dedicated to the truth of the heart. 'Est-ce un crime de dire tout son chagrin, tout son ennui? Est-ce vertu de le cacher? Peut-être, se taîre, oui: mais mentir! . . .'[24] The rhetorical question asked by George Sand in *Lettres d'un Voyageur* is answered again and again in the negative by the self-revelations of Charlotte Brontë's heroines in their anguish, as their lovers seem to be slipping away from them: Lucy Snowe –

> untamed, tortured, again pacing a solitary room in an unalterable passion of silent desolation . . .[25] I thought he receded. I thought he would go. Pierced deeper than I could endure, made now to feel what defied suppression, I cried – 'My heart will break!' . . .[26] I spoke. All escaped from my lips . . . the whole history, in brief, summoned to his confidence, rushed thither, truthful, literal, ardent, bitter . . . Warm, jealous and haughty, I knew not till now that my nature had such a mood; he gathered me near his heart.[27]

Caroline Helstone glimpses Moore in the distance:

> The apparition had been transient – scarce seen ere gone; but its electric passage left her veins kindled, her soul insurgent. It found her despairing: it left her desperate – two different states. 'Oh! had he but been alone! Had he but seen me!' was her cry, 'He would have said something; he would have given me his hand. He *does*, he *must* love me a little: he would have shown some token of affection; in his eye, on his lips, I should have read comfort: but the chance is lost. The wind – the cloud's shadow does not pass more silently, more emptily than he. I have been mocked, and Heaven is cruel!' Thus, in the utter sickness of longing and disappointment, she went home.[28]

The note of abandonment, of lack of restraint over their grief, is all the more moving in Charlotte Brontë's heroines in contrast to their normal repression of their feelings in public. They are as confirmed idealists as any of George Sand's heroines, despite their very different appearance and circumstances. It is scarcely surprising that George Sand, confident of her charms and rejoicing in her liberty, should have created heroines who bore no outward family resemblance to those of Charlotte Brontë, conscious of her own plainness and chafing hopelessly against her restrictions. And yet in their total dedication to love and their refusal to compromise they are more akin than any other Victorian heroines. We have no doubt at all that whatever flaws they have, Mr Rochester and Gerard Moore and M. Paul are exactly what Jane and Caroline and Lucy have set their hearts on in order to fulfil their deepest needs. Charlotte Brontë was forced to compromise in life, but she does not allow her heroines to do the same – and the ending of *Villette* becomes, not one of realism, but of sombre and tragic romance.

Yet set against these ideal relationships, there is an enormous amount of probing into the nature of marriage and the attitudes of men and women which could have come straight from the pages of *Indiana* or *Jacques* or even George Sand's mildly feminist *Lettres à Marcie*. There was no writer in England in the 1830s and early 1840s expressing such views as George Sand's, but in *The Professor* (1847), Charlotte Brontë's earliest novel, the heroine is not only passionate and independent but has strong views on marriage. When Frances gives her love to Crimsworth, it is with total unselfconsciousness: 'She threw her arms round me and strained me to her heart with passionate earnestness: the energy of her whole being glowed in her dark and then dilated eye, and crimsoned her animated cheek: her look and movement were like inspiration; in one there was such a flash, in the other such a power.'[2]

An embrace which would not have come amiss in *Lélia* ('elle l'entoura de ses bras et le pressa contre elle avec une force surhumaine'[30]) must have come as something of a surprise to the succession of publishers who, in 1847, declined Charlotte Brontë's first novel. And the apparently submissive 'little lace-maker', Frances, had many other unconventional ways. When her husband asks her what she would have done if she had been unhappily married to 'a drunkard, a profligate, a selfish spendthrift, an unjust fool', she replies that she would have left him – and if forced by law to return to him, she would have tried once more; but if she had found no remedy she would have left him again, for

> Monsieur, if a wife's nature loathes that of the man she is wedded to, marriage must be slavery. Against slavery all right thinkers revolt, and though torture be the price of resistance, torture must be dared: though the only road to freedom lie through the gates of death, these gates must be passed; for freedom is indispensable.[31]

Once again, it is the voice of a George Sand heroine – with the difference that when Indiana delivers herself of such sentiments to her husband, the author is careful to undercut the heroics herself, by having Delmare say that her 'high flown novelists' phrases weary him'. This sort of self-preservation against ridicule is something Charlotte Brontë had not yet learned, but in their spirit and content the speeches are identical. Indiana declares

> I know that I am the slave and you are the ruler. The law of this country has made you my master. You can tie me up, bind my hands, control my actions. You have the right of the stronger and the

backing of society; but you cannot command my will, sir. God alone
can bend it and subdue it. Try to find a law, a prison, an instrument
of torture which gives you any hold on it! You might as well try to
grasp the air and snatch at space.[32]

Even in marriage, Frances's independence is dear to her: and she is
resolved not merely to earn a pittance but as much as her husband:

> Think of my marrying you to be kept by you, Monsieur! I could not
> do it; and how dull my days would be! . . . I like an active life
> better; I must act in some way, and act with you. I have taken
> notice, Monsieur, that people who are only in each other's company
> for amusement, never really like each other so well, or esteem each
> other so highly, as those who work together, and perhaps suffer
> together.[33]

Such an observation comes easily to the lips of a George Sand
heroine: Marthe, for instance, in *Horace* (1840), is conscious of a gain
in dignity when she becomes a self-supporting actress, after she has
undergone the humiliation of being Horace's dependent and being
patronised by him. Now, in a new relationship with a worthier man,
she feels the 'doux orgeil' of being the protector as well as the protected.

But it is in *Shirley* above all that marriage, its conditions and conventions, is most closely scrutinised by Charlotte Brontë. Marriage for
money, marriage out of foolishness and vanity, marriage to avoid being
an old maid, all are scathingly dismissed. Caroline and Shirley have no
doubt that marriage to a man who is 'great, good and handsome' is the
best fate imaginable, but they are equally sure that such a man is very
hard to find. It is the novel in which Charlotte Brontë comes closest to
expressing feminist views but, like George Sand, she stops short of
outright feminism. The sentiments expressed by Caroline Helstone as
she faces the prospect of spinsterhood might have been written by
Marcie, the imaginary young woman to whom George Sand addressed
a series of letters in 1837.

The *Lettres à Marcie* were published by Lamennais in his journal,
Le Monde; but although the advice given is very moderate in tone
compared with some of the novels, Lamennais took fright when the
subject of the breakdown of a marriage was about to be broached, and
the series was terminated. Marcie is a beautiful young woman of
twenty-five, clever, respectable, cultivated but poor and, because she
is poor, unmarried and very lonely. Each night she is surprised and
horrified by the prospect stretching before her of empty days and
years, and has been driven to ask for counsel as to how best she may
cope with such a life.

George Sand enters into Marcie's dilemma with so much emotion and sympathy that the least sentimental reader must have warmed to the discussion. 'You are sad, you are wretched; the lack of anything to do preys upon you; you dread the future and are crushed by the present.'[34] It is still possible, she says, even in this unjust and corrupt society, that Marcie may find a husband worthy of her and, if so, that will certainly be the best solution. But if not, will life be impossible? 'It seems to me that nothing is impossible if you have great courage and put your mind to it.' Why not accept the lot of old maid with energy and happiness? Certainly celibacy is much more satisfying than a miserable marriage to a man of inferior intelligence and character, who will be entitled to dominate her.

What then is Marcie to do? She can always become 'artiste', a writer or poet or actress if she has the ability; otherwise there are no jobs available and she will have to summon up all her fortitude, wait patiently and, above all, educate herself. For that is a right of women about which George Sand feels passionately; the great crime of men has been in depriving them of the same education as themselves. Marcie must read serious books and try to understand them; she must educate herself, not in order to become a better companion, but to develop her own potential and to show she is man's equal; what is needed in women is strength, independence, courage and intellect. 'L'avenir est entre leurs mains.'

As can be seen, much of this ground is also the territory of *Shirley*. Masculine complacency and feminine frustration are ever-recurring topics for the two girls. There is a moving passage, very reminiscent of *Lettres à Marcie*, in which Caroline Helstone faces the grey prospect ahead of her of loneliness and a sense of failure as an old maid; as she sits in her 'narrow chamber . . . with the rain on her casement . . . the thin illusion of her own shadow on the wall', she reflects that 'I have to live perhaps till seventy years . . . What was I created for I wonder? Where is my place in the world? . . . Does virtue lie in abnegation of self? I do not believe it. Undue humility makes tyranny; weak concession creates selfishness . . . Each human being has his share of rights.'[35] And after visiting two old maids in the district and admiring their courage, she makes up her mind that she must bestir herself and try to be wise if she cannot be good. Like George Sand, Charlotte Brontë is very well aware that although serious books are no substitute for love, they give a woman not only something to think about but some freedom from dependence upon men for all the significance of her life. Caroline is haunted by the prospect of an existence which will be a 'useless, blank, pale, slow-trailing thing', and although both girls discuss the need for women of 'a profession – a trade', Shirley does not suffer from any of the fears and misgivings of her companion. She is rich, confident and beautiful, and for her the question of woman's equality or inferiority which is of such painful importance to Caroline simply does not arise. 'Shall my left hand dispute for precedence with my right . . . shall my heart quarrel with my pulse?'

But Caroline, sore with being despised by her uncle, will not let the matter rest: 'But are we men's equals or not?' 'Nothing ever charms me more than when I meet my superior,' says Shirley airily; and Caroline asks in surprise, 'Did you ever meet him?'[36]

By the end of the book both girls have married men who seem to make the question of equality irrelevant. When Charlotte Brontë's feminist friend, Mary Taylor, proudly earning her living as a shop-keeper in New Zealand, read *Shirley* she reproached Charlotte for her half-heartedness about women's independence.[37] But Charlotte was no more half-hearted than George Sand, who found herself at odds with a thorough-going feminist like Flora Tristan,[38] because of her dis-missive attitude to women's clubs and suffrage agitations. Both novelists were convinced that woman's real happiness lay in the heart of the family, but both demanded for women the right of choice. It is interesting that when Shirley refuses to marry Sir Philip Nunnely, whom her uncle thinks a very suitable match for her, the reason that she gives is that he is not her superior, that he could never be her *master*, and when asked her intention 'in respect of matrimony' she replies briefly, 'To be quiet – and to do just as I please'; from which her uncle can only conclude that she has been tainted by her reading: 'You read French. Your mind is poisoned with French novels. You have imbibed French principles.'[39]

In 1811, the time at which the book is set, there were no French novels to encourage quite that spirit of masculine independence which Shirley shows here. *Corinne* had certainly made heady reading for young women who aspired to glory; as Ellen Moers points out, she 'stalked untrammelled and unrepressed in the person of Zenobia Percy'[40] in Charlotte Brontë's youthful Angrian tales. But Shirley's terse claim for a life of her own indicates that her creator had in mind, rather, the principles of the many 'advanced' French novels she herself had more recently swallowed which advocated just such freedom of action.

Quite obviously, when a Brontë heroine asks that her lover or husband should be her 'master' – the term that had such a sweet sound for Jane Eyre or Caroline Helstone or Lucy Snowe – she means something very different from 'le maître-esclave' relationship against which George Sand fought so determinedly and vociferously and about which Frances Henry, in *The Professor*, is no less scathing. Even though Rochester and M. Paul are called 'master' to the end, this is not because they have the 'maistrie', but because Jane and Lucy, like Shirley, are glad to have at last met someone they can esteem, after so many false gods. But while there is no sense in Charlotte Brontë's writings of the inferiority of women to men, she is totally lacking in that familiar knowledge of the masculine sex which allows George Sand to present so many erring males in her novels. As Mrs Ward says, 'George Sand, alas! knew too much and knew too well. No schoolroom imaginations are possible to her. The men she creates are handled with a large indulgence, half maternal, half poetic, that may turn to irony or to reproach, never to the mere woman's self-surrender.'[41]

Here, although Mrs Ward captures exactly George Sand's attitude to her 'heroes', she does not do justice to Charlotte Brontë's young women, who are never 'mere'. Although George Sand always 'found herself in the end the better man',[42] she does not allow that unfortunate circumstance to diminish her heroines' idealism or her own theory. She sees men as well as women in a period of transition; the 'right hand', in *Shirley*'s phrase, has to gain strength and sensitivity and skills and freedom of movement before the 'left hand' can hope for the same achievements. She too would be prepared to accept a man as master if, by any unlikely chance, she came across one she could wholly admire: 'It is more difficult to rule than to obey. A distinctive moral force is needed to be the respected head of a family, the master, loved and accepted by a wife.'[43]

Influences from France are apparent, not only in what Charlotte Brontë wrote but in how she wrote. She stays so close to actual experience that it is, of course, necessary to distinguish between what she gained from reading French romantic authors and what from her traumatic two-year stay in Brussels. Despite all her reservations about Continental ways and 'French defects', despite her perfervid anti-Catholicism and the insularity of many of her judgements (in which she is no more prejudiced than George Sand), she was very proud of her French cultural background and no novel is free of it. Even in *Jane Eyre*, the most English of her novels, Mr Rochester's scandalous past in Paris has as its aftermath the small presence of Adèle, which justifies the generous scattering of French phrases throughout.

In all the other novels the foreign strands are much more significant. Both *The Professor* and *Villette* are set in Brussels, so that she is free to use French words not only to give local colour but to express her feelings more accurately. And although she sets *Shirley* in Yorkshire, she still retains the freedom to move back and forth between the two cultures by making the Moores émigrés and Mr Yorke cosmopolitan. Sometimes the effect is laughable, as when Gérard Moore declares 'I have a canine hunger', or quite unjustifiable, as when young Martin Yorke 'paused *interdit* . . . with the true perspicacity "des âmes élites" ', when he might just as well have stopped short, with the perspicacity of a precocious boy – but on the whole the French flavouring blends in naturally. In the little scene by the fireside where Caroline repeats

Chénier's lines from 'La Jeune Captive' in her sweet, tremulous voice to Gérard –

> Mon beau voyage encore est si loin de sa fin! . . .
> Je ne suis qu'au printemps – je veux voir la moisson . . .
> Je veux achever ma journée.[44]

we are given a perfect fusion of the two strands of Charlotte's experience – of literature and life – for here she has placed her heroine in what was for her the ideal situation: the young girl making contact with her pedagogical lover through the medium of romantic lines.

The romantic and the passionate do not always cohere in Charlotte Brontë's writings as they do, on the whole, in George Sand's, partly because so much of the passion comes from her own emotions and even her own deprivations, whereas the romantic conceptions tend to be literary in origin. It is difficult to pinpoint how much Charlotte borrowed from her reading of George Sand. Mrs Ward suggests two passages which may have originated in George Sand – one of which, Shirley's essay, is surely a doubtful blessing, despite Louis Moore's pleasure in the long effusion of his prize pupil, which, by a remarkable feat, he has committed to memory. It is probably true that Charlotte Brontë would not have written it in this style had she not been acquainted with some of the more flowery passages in *Lélia*, and one can only say of it that it almost certainly would have sounded better in French, in which language it was supposed originally to have been written. Rendered as 'Les Noces du Génie et de l'Humanité', it might have been less hard to take, but even so it would have stuck out embarrassingly as a set piece in a way that the wild romantic prose of *Lélia* does not.

Mrs Ward mentions also the letter from Sylvia to her 'brother' in *Jacques*,[45] which she describes as a 'very curious anticipation of the cry of Rochester to Jane'. Sylvia asks whether Jacques is in some terrible danger, for one evening, as she was sitting alone, she had heard his voice distinctly calling to her three or four times, so distinctly that she had gone to search in the thicket to make sure he was not there.

This seems to me to be a case in which there is a likelihood that Charlotte subconsciously stored up an incident in her mind and then adapted it to her own purpose. There are many others which might have stimulated her or given another dimension to her own experience. In *Le Meunier d'Angibault*, for instance, the maniac sister, La Bricoline, who has been disappointed in love, is kept hidden by her parents but breaks out from time to time and howls like a wolf, tears fowls apart with her nails and ends by setting the *château*, chapel and herself on fire and perishing in the flames. While the similarity to *Jane Eyre* is obvious, George Sand was probably indebted in her turn to the maniacal death of Ulrica, in the flaming turret, in *Ivanhoe*. On the other hand, the Creole and whole West Indian episode may owe something to the exotic background of *Indiana*. In *Consuelo*, the fine opening scene between Porpora, the testy, idealistic music master and his frivolous, recalcitrant young lady pupils brings *Villette* to mind, as indeed the relationship between Consuelo, the grave governess-companion and her shallow, vain charge, Amelia, has much in common with that of Lucy Snowe and Ginevra Fanshawe. Jacques, the enigmatic, pipe-smoking hero, with his romantic past of mistresses and his resemblances to a sultan in his flowered silk dressing-gown, may well have added to the picture of Mr Rochester. And it is not, alas, beyond the realms of possibility that some of the supernatural effects like the nun, in *Villette*, may have been inspired by *Consuelo*, which was stagier in this respect than most of George Sand's novels; although it is just as likely that the common source was Mrs Radcliffe.

Rose et Blanche (1831), George Sand's earliest novel, written in collaboration with Jules Sandeau, is a strange and very unequal production which really comes alive only in the scenes in which George Sand is drawing heavily upon the memories of her English convent school in Paris. It was quite a successful novel none the less; it was referred to with some affection by English readers; and the fact that my own copy is a Brussels reprint of 1837 makes it clear that this first joint venture did not sink without trace after George Sand had made her own way to celebrity. If there were only one scene in it which had its parallel in *The Professor* or *Villette*, that could easily be explained by Charlotte Brontë's own experience of a Catholic *pensionnat*. But the presence in *Rose et Blanche* of no fewer than three incidents of marked similarity to passages in the English novel does greatly increase the likelihood that Charlotte Brontë had read this book, either at home or in Brussels.

The first incident is pedestrian enough; it is merely the account of the reactions of Laorens, the visiting art master at the convent, when he finds himself in the midst of a class of young ladies, confronted by sixty young girls, who are for the most part, fresh, mischievous and pretty. Like Crimsworth in *The Professor*, he feels mingled attraction to them, angrily amused by their impudence and coquetry but humiliated by knowing that outside the convent they would despise him and, finally, determined to master them.

> Puis enfin se diriger vers un bruit de rire frais et joyeux . . . entrer dans une classe! Voir autour de soi tout un harem de vièrges qui rougissent, se troublent, se cachent les unes derrières les autres, se rassurent, s'enhardissent . . . avoir le droit de les gronder, être leur surveillant, leur maître, et ne rien oser au-delà; avoir sans cesse

autour de soi une surveillante . . . dont la présence vous glace et
pétrifie; affecter le calme, l'indifférence . . . car les pensionnaires
espiègles et moqueuses veulent vous faire rire . . . imprudentes et
cruelles, elles sont coquettes avec vous.[46]

The other two scenes concern the heroine, Rose, who, as a poor
protégée, feels her loneliness and social inferiority to the rich, snobbish
and aristocratic pupils. At a school fête which is a great occasion there
is a sudden crisis. One of the performers has hurt herself and cannot
go on; the audience consisting, among others, of 'Lady Gillibrand,
Lady Cadogan, Lady Holland, le duc de Montmorency, le prince
Jules de Polignac et l'honorable M. Canning', cannot be disappointed.
Rose is called upon and reacts very much like Lucy Snowe on the
similar occasion when she is forced unexpectedly to take part in the
play through an actor's illness. She is taken aback and feels herself
quite incapable of filling the role; but although afraid, she feels she
cannot be a coward and refuse such an important task. So, with her
head on fire, her hands icy, a ringing in her ears, she rises to the
occasion and sings: 'All at once she sang; for her it was a miracle; to
this day she has not understood how it came about; she could not see;
she trembled; however . . . her voice was strong, sustained, full and
vibrant.' She is an enormous success; even Lady Gillibrand said
several times, 'C'était tres jolé.' But even more like Lucy Snowe, she
has been only briefly transformed, to resume her normal personality as
soon as the magic of self-forgetfulness is over: 'In truth, this was not
Mlle de Beaumont: this was a being created five minutes before who
had to expire five minutes later.'[47]

The final scene brings to mind several different incidents in *Villette*:
the visit to the theatre to hear Rachel; Lucy's desperate wanderings
through the town in the long vacation; and her half-drugged escape
from the pension into the streets in the middle of the night, an episode
of strange unreality which ends in the blaze of lights in the park, which
is *en fête*. Rose, too, makes her escape from the convent into Paris and
wanders through the streets in a delirium, 'une fièvre, une sorte de
délire': 'Everything seemed magical . . . the paving-stones glided away
beneath her feet, no-one paid any attention to her; she joyously took
part in the bustling life of the multitude.'[48] She goes to the theatre and
sees Judith Pasta as Tancred, and is overwhelmed by the magnificence
of the hall, the brilliance of the lights, the crowd of spectators. It is
midnight when she returns through the dark streets to the convent,
gliding along furtively, so much under the spell of the emotion which
had been aroused that she does not know whether it is night or day.

These resemblances have their fascination, but must always remain
not proven. Much more significant is the romantic subjectivism of

natural description which was such a normal feature of English romantic poetry but so unusual in the Victorian novel. It was not, however, absent from the French novel. In *Hiver à Majorque* George Sand, commenting on her own descriptions of wild scenery, said: 'Jean-Jacques Rousseau is the veritable Christopher Columbus of Alpine poetry and, as M. de Chateaubriand has very well remarked, is the father of romance in our language.'[49] Rousseau, Chateaubriand, Senancour – George Sand is indebted to all these writers in her ability to use natural description as a counterpart of the emotions of her characters, and much of her most memorable writing comes into this category. Very often passages in Charlotte Brontë's novels call to mind passages of remarkably similar emotional effect in those of George Sand – not self-conscious essays like Shirley's, but moving descriptions, very different from anything found in the works of her contemporaries, Dickens or Thackeray or Mrs Gaskell. Occasionally a phrase finds its counterpart – for instance, 'oiseaux voyageurs', 'passenger birds' – and Charlotte Brontë's own consciousness that her models in natural description were French comes out when she deliberately chooses the French word in preference to the English. In this passage in *Shirley* for instance: 'A calm day had settled into a crystalline evening; the world wore a North Pole colouring; all its lights and tints looked like the "reflets" of white or violet or pale green gems' – to which she affixes the prosaic footnote: 'Find me an English word as good, Reader, and I will gladly dispense with the French one. "Reflections" won't do.'[50] Or again, when she falls back on 'effleurer' – that verb so loved by the Romantics – when she talks of Caroline's kisses: 'She took those thin fingers between her two little hands – she bent her head "et les effleura de ses lèvres" (I put that in French because the word "effleurer" is an exquisite word).'[51]

But, on the whole, the similarity lies in the ability of both authors to evoke the mood of happiness or desolation or hope rather than in any exact imitation. Swinburne, who admired Charlotte Brontë more than any other Victorian novelist, commented on her 'instinct for the tragic use of landscape' and made the automatic comparison with George Sand: 'No other woman that I know of, not George Sand herself, could have written a prose sentence of such exalted and perfect poetry as this: – "The moon reigns glorious, glad of the gale: as glad as if she gave herself to its fierce caress with love" . . .'[52] The few passages I quote seem to me to show each writer fulfilling perfectly her aim by remarkably similar methods.

Two of the best-known and most moving evocations of mood in *Jane Eyre* are the opening to Chapter 23 and the end of Chapter 26. The first passage, just before Mr Rochester declares his love for Jane, is one of unclouded happiness and contentment.

A splendid Midsummer shone over England; skies so pure, suns so radiant as were then seen in long succession, seldom favour even singly our wave-girt land. It was as if a band of Italian days had come from the South, like a flock of glorious passenger birds, and lighted to rest on the cliffs of Albion. The hay was all got in; the fields round Thornfield were green and shorn; the roads white and baked; the trees were in their dark prime; hedge and wood, full-leaved and deeply tinted, contrasted well with the sunny hue of the cleared meadows between.[53]

A parallel passage, not of fruition, but rather of reviving happiness and expectancy, occurs in *Lettres d'un Voyageur*, when the narrator glimpses the distant mountains:

La campagne n'était pas encore dans toute sa splendeur . . . Mais les amandiers et les pêchers en fleurs entremêlaient ça et là leurs guirlandes roses et blanches aux sombres masses des cypres. Un demi-cercle de collines fertiles . . . faisait un premier cadre au tableau; et les montagnes neigeux, étincelant aux premiers rayons du soleil, formaient au-delà une seconde bordure immense, qui se détachait comme une découpure d'argent sur le bleu solide de l'air . . . De ces cimes lointaines, me disais-je, sont partis mes songes dorés. Ils ont volé jusqu'à moi, comme une troupe d'oiseaux voyageurs . . .[54]

A second memorable passage from *Jane Eyre* is that which brings her short happiness to an end. When, after the interrupted wedding, she has removed her bridal finery and is once more alone in her room, 'a cold, solitary girl again', the mood is of bleak desolation.

A Christmas frost had come at mid-summer; a white December storm had whirled over June; ice glazed the ripe apples, drifts crushed the blowing roses; on hayfield and corn-field lay a frozen shroud: lanes which last night blushed full of flowers, today were pathless with untrodden snow; and the woods, which twelve hours since waved leafy and fragrant as groves between the tropics, now spread, waste, wild and white as pine-forests in wintry Norway. My hopes were all dead – struck with a subtle doom such as in one night fell on all the first-born in the land of Egypt. I looked on my cherished wishes yesterday so blooming and glowing: they lay, stark, chill, livid corpses that could never revive. I looked at my love: that feeling which was my master's – which he had created; it shivered in my heart like a suffering child in a cold cradle.[55]

George Sand similarly uses the summer/winter opposition to great effect. The contrast between the young poet Sténio's blossoming love and Lélia's wintry disillusionment is brought out by Trenmor's terse advice to her: 'Laissez l'enfant croître et vivre, n'étouffez pas la fleur dans son germe. Ne jetez pas votre haleine glacée sur ses belles journées de soleil et de printemps.'[56] And similarly the hopelessness of the Voyageur finds its corollary in the natural scene:

> L'hiver étend ses voiles gris sur la terre attristée, le froid siffle et pleure autour de nos toits . . . Le branchage se dessine en noir dans l'air chargé de gelée blanche . . . Voici le froid, la nuit, la mort. Ce dernier regard du soleil au travers de mes vitres, c'est mon dernier espoir qui brille . . . L'hiver de mon âme est venu, un éternel hiver! Il fut un temps où je ne regardais ni le ciel ni les fleurs, où je ne m'inquiétais pas de l'absence du soleil et ne plaignais pas les moineaux transis sur leurs branche . . . A présent . . . mon âme est veuve.[57]

'Mon âme est veuve' – the despairing cry could as well have come from Jane Eyre or Lucy Snowe. For no matter how different the circumstances and characters of the heroines of the two novelists – and indeed Lélia, rich, surfeited with love, 'flétrie', a solitary by her own choice, could not be more remote from Jane and Lucy, poor, unloved and lonely – when it comes to discussion of their subconscious they speak the same language of dreams, fantasies and hallucinations. It is interesting to see just how much in common the vocabulary and imagery of Lélia's period of seclusion in her deserted mountain châlet has with Lucy Snowe's stifling summer, pent up in the dormitory in the pension in the Rue Fossette. Lucy follows in her imagination the triumphal progress of Ginevra Fanshawe, transformed into a totally unreal figure by her tortured conviction of Dr John's love for her, through enchanted countryside: '. . . these September suns shone for her on fertile plains, where harvest and vintage matured under their yellow beams. The gold and crystal moons rose on her vision over blue horizons waved in mounted lines.'[58] And each night Lélia escapes from herself into fantastic regions:

> Hélas! que d'univers j'ai parcourus dans ces voyages de l'âme! J'ai traversé les steppes blanchies des régions glacées. J'ai jeté mon rapide regard sur les savanes parfumées où la lune se lève si belle et si blanche. J'ai effleuré sur les ailes du sommeil ces vastes mers dont l'immensité épouvante la pensée . . .[59]

Sleeplessness, fever, delirium, torment, nightmares of dead friends, ghastly spectres, pain, anguish, oppressive fears, deaths-heads, monsters, loneliness, moonlight, tombs and sepulchres – there is little to choose in romantic terminology between the two experiences; each is an evocation of a soul in impotent suffering, quite beyond the reach of reason. For each the end of the interlude is despair – Lucy Snowe on her knees in the confessional, Lélia gazing impotently at the pitiless sky.

The imaginative sweep of George Sand is always tethered to a strong consciousness of the personality of the human being who is speaking and suffering. In *Lettres d'un Voyageur* and *Mauprat* there is a first person narrator, and in *Lélia* and *Jacques*, although there is a variety of voices, all speak subjectively. The personal atmosphere was what Charlotte Brontë relished – the quality in her own novels that Virginia Woolf described well as '*I* love – *I* hate – *I* suffer'[60] – and which she responded to more, I think, than anything else in the novels of George Sand. The lack of it was what she could not forgive in Jane Austen. And its presence made her not only overlook the 'strange extravagance', the 'far from truthful . . . views of Life' of the French novelist, but warm to and learn many a lesson from what she described, with sincerity, as George Sand's 'wondrous excellence'.

5 *Wuthering Heights* and *Mauprat*

Charlotte Brontë's description of her sister's novel, in her 1850 preface
to *Wuthering Heights*, as 'hewn in a wild workshop with simple tools out
of homely materials' is not one which can stand up to the evidence
accumulated of late years by Brontë critics. In its sophistication of
technique and design and its multiplicity of echoes of other works, the
novel is clearly as much 'literary' in its inspiration as 'natural'. The
opposition is an artificial one, because whatever Emily Brontë had read
and found congenial she had made her own as certainly as she had
absorbed the sights and sounds of her daily life. My own inclination is
to accept, not only as feasible but as likely, almost all the source
material which has been suggested for *Wuthering Heights*.[1] The Brontës
were avid readers and nothing came amiss to them – from their old
favourite Scott and all the Romantic poets to Gothic fiction, from
Shakespeare and Jacobean drama to articles and reviews in *Blackwood's*
and *Fraser's* magazines. The fact that all these elements are identifiable
simply makes the individual quality of the end product all the more
startling. External evidence about what Emily actually read is as
lacking as it is about what she did or said or thought – as all her
biographers ruefully testify. One can only go on family reading and on
probabilities, and there is little point in adding to the list of possible
sources unless the parallels are striking. This is, I think, the case with
Mauprat, published in 1839, ten years before *Wuthering Heights*, and I
was glad to find that another scholar came to an almost identical
conclusion[2] at the same time as I published my conjectures.

The possibility of any influence from French fiction upon Emily
Brontë has been strangely ignored in favour of German sources,
although according to Mrs Gaskell, Emily, as well as Charlotte, read
French fluently. When the rectory was full of French books in the
summer of 1840, Emily no doubt shared Charlotte's experience of
them; and Winifred Gérin's suggestion[3] that the fluency of phrase and
range of vocabulary exhibited in Emily's early *devoirs* for M. Héger
imply previous knowledge of the language seems reasonable. But even
if she did not read much then, she had plenty of chance to read French
novels later. A knowledge of languages was desirable for governesses but

indispensable if the sisters were going to open their own school and although, in Brussels, Emily was much weaker at conversation and grammar than Charlotte, she was prepared to work like a horse.[4] This unwonted concentration during her nine months' stay abroad and her habit, on her return, of keeping up with French newspapers provide solid backing for Mrs Gaskell's claim.

Charlotte's familiarity with, and even enthusiasm for, the writings of George Sand does, I think, increase the likelihood that Emily also had read some of her novels. It is difficult to imagine Emily ignoring any book that entered the house; like Shirley, Emily was 'tenacious of her book' and not all the stories can be apocryphal. A book is propped up as she bakes the bread; when there are visitors in the sitting room, Emily darts in to retrieve a book; she kneels on the hearth rug, reading; as she is dying, her eyes brighten at the sight of a parcel of books from George Smith. Unlike Anne and Charlotte, Emily was not prepared to write an autobiographical novel, and when she drew upon her imagination, it was upon one enriched by an exotic and varied diet of reading. And the similarities between *Mauprat* and *Wuthering Heights* which surprised me when I first read George Sand's novel incline me to think that this was one of the books which she had absorbed and made part of her imaginative store.

Of all George Sand's novels, *Mauprat* is the one in which the influence of Scott is most clearly seen. In fact, in many respects it is very like one of Scott's historical romances – set back for most of its action (as is the first part of *Wuthering Heights*) to the 1770s. Unlike her earlier novels, there is nothing in it to scandalise readers, unless they were of the sort mentioned by Charlotte who would 'suffer greatly by the introduction . . . of words printed with all their letters, which it had become the custom to represent by the initial and final letter only – a blank line filling the interval.'[5] George Sand – like Emily Brontë, and unlike Scott – was uninhibited in her references to the devil, hell, and damnation, but as her subject in *Mauprat* was the obsessive devotion of one man for a woman, which lasted not only for life but beyond the grave, the novel must have heartened those of her supporters who maintained that her writings were a good influence and were not subversive of monogamy or marriage. *Mauprat* is a well-planned interesting book – in Henry James's phrase, 'a solid, masterly, manly book'[6] – and it is the one of George Sand's which Gosse chose to include in his end-of-the-century collection of well-known French romances. Its debts to Scott are many, though they are irrelevant here. What is more important is that, despite the vigorous action, the well-plotted tale, the evocation of a past era and the realistic portrayal of country characters, the adventure which grips the imagination and lingers in the memory is – as Claude Sicard points out – 'la seule importante, l'aventure intérieure'.[7] It is in the passionate relationship between the hero and heroine that the intensity and strength of the novel lies.

Not only the influence of Scott but of Rousseau is prominent in the novel, for, unlike *Wuthering Heights*, it is essentially a *bildüngsroman* which raises and discusses much more overtly than the later novel the question of natural tendencies and the importance of education and environment. Mauprat is the name of a powerful, land-owning family in the Varenne, which has two branches. The civilised, younger branch whose head is Edmée's father, the Chevalier Hubert de Mauprat, lives on the plain, in the Château de Sainte-Sévère. Six leagues away in a ravine, on a vast moor, in the most thickly wooded and wildest part of the country, is the castle of Roche-Mauprat, in which live the black Mauprats, Tristan and his eight scoundrelly sons, who terrorise the district.

The narrator, Bernard, is now an old man. He tells how, as a child of seven, on the death of his mother he had been seized and brought on the crupper of his grandfather's horse to Roche-Mauprat and thrown to the tender mercies of his hunchback uncle, John. Treated cruelly and bestially, forced to be a nightly witness of the debauchery and oppressions of his uncles, he is in a fair way to being as brutalised as his companions by the time of his grandfather's death almost ten years later. So that when, one night of storm, his beautiful cousin Edmée arrives at Roche-Mauprat after her horse has bolted from a wolf-hunt, and is held captive, his first impulse is to rape her, and he consents to help her to escape only after exacting a vow from her that she will give herself to no one but him. Roche-Mauprat is besieged and set on fire, and most of the Mauprats are killed; but Bernard, this passionate, unlicked cub, escapes with Edmée to the Château of Sainte-Sévère, her luxurious and refined home.

Here he finds that Edmée is already betrothed to a handsome, elegant young man who treats her sullen and savage kinsman with polite curiosity. Tormented by jealousy and humiliation, Bernard refuses to set Edmée free from her secret promise to him – or even to study, in order to become more civilised – and a terrible battle of two strong wills ensues. Edmée has, in fact, fallen in love with her cousin and admits it to her confidant, the abbé, but Bernard overhears only the first part of the conversation, when she says that she would rather kill herself than yield to him. The education and reformation of Bernard is a long process, which involves an absence of six years in America, where he fights in the War of Independence. Even on his return, he has to undergo a further ordeal when he is accused of the attempted murder of Edmée, a crime staged by one of his vengeful uncles. But this is his last trial and at the age of twenty-four,

Bernard ends his probation and starts his life of happiness with Edmée.

It is difficult to do justice to the excellences of a romance in résumé, and *Wuthering Heights*, condensed, would cut as a poor a figure as *Mauprat*. But even in outline, some of the similarities must have emerged.

One of the most striking resemblances is the use of the two houses to represent opposing ways of life, Roche-Mauprat paralleling the primitivism of Wuthering Heights, and the Château of Sainte-Sévère the civilisation of Thrushcross Grange. Roche-Mauprat is even more forbidding than the Heights: used as a fortress by the Mauprats, it has an enormous pile of hunting-weapons, duck-guns, carbines, and blunderbusses on the stone-flagged floor; the rain drives through the small, broken windows; the fires smoke; all is gloomy, damp, and cheerless. Cruelty, brutality, and drunkenness form the texture of daily living. Even when the Chevalier Hubert has taken it over in Bernard's absence and tried to put it in order for him as a farm, and the courtyard is full of cattle and poultry, sheepdogs, and agricultural instruments, the domestication is unsuccessful. Roche-Mauprat retains its evil atmosphere and, in the end, Bernard has the roof taken off and the entrance gate thrown down, and abandons the castle to its ghosts. The country folk, brave enough on the moors during the day, quicken their steps as they pass it at night and swear that they have seen spirits among the ruins. Imagery relating to hell is used consistently in connection with Roche-Mauprat and its inhabitants, although when Bernard first leaves it and finds himself in the luxury of the *château*, he is homesick for it and remembers it as paradise – 'Lorsque j'étais seul, j'avais envie de rugir comme un lion mis en cage, et, la nuit, je faisais des rêves où la mousse des bois, le rideau des arbres de la forêt et jusqu'aux sombres crénaux de la Roche-Mauprat, m'apparaissaient comme le paradis terrestre . . .'[8] – and when he is most miserable he seeks comfort always, out-of-doors, on the grass under the oaks. But later, when he has to pay Roche-Mauprat a visit on his return from abroad, he can scarcely force himself to go – 'It is as if you were driving me out of heaven to send me on a visit to hell.' For Bernard heaven is, finally, the Château de Sainte-Sévère; Roche-Mauprat is hell, and his escape from it has been his redemption.

It can be seen that the attitude to the two houses is more complex in *Wuthering Heights*, although here too a similar profusion of imagery relating to hell – fiends, devils, purgatory, damnation – is used to convey the nature of the devilish events at the Heights. When Heathcliff first looks through the window of Thrushcross Grange he thinks it is heaven, although the behaviour of the children is decidedly unangelic; and Catherine, too, talks of marrying Edgar as entering heaven. But neither Catherine nor Heathcliff are at their ease in heaven – heaven did not seem to be their home – and Catherine is not redeemed by her escape from the Heights and from Heathcliff, but doomed. Unlike Bernard, she never ceases to yearn for her past, and Heathcliff says to Nelly of her life in the Grange, 'I've no doubt she's in hell among you!'⁹ For everyone else in the book, however, Wuthering Heights is, in the end, a prison, a place of damnation. Isabella, for instance, escapes from it like 'a soul escaped from purgatory'. Nelly, however bright and warm and well-scoured her kitchen, is uneasy in the house at night, and even Hareton, once he has been civilised by Cathy, is well content to go with her to the Grange and fulfil his rôle as social, instead of savage, man. Wuthering Heights, like Roche-Mauprat, is in the end abandoned, with only Joseph living on in the kitchen, while the rest of the house is shut up 'for the use of such ghosts as choose to inhabit it'. And on this moorland, too, the country people, as darkness draws in, swear they see ghosts abroad.

The framework of the two novels is thus seen to be remarkably alike, and indeed many aspects of the relationship between Bernard and Edmée are similar to those between Catherine and Heathcliff, and Cathy and Hareton. In Bernard and Edmée, George Sand attempts to show primitive and social traits co-existing in what seems, at times, to be a very unstable compound, whereas Emily Brontë makes no such concession. Her untamed spirits die untamed, and it is left to the next generation to conform. The struggle, none the less, is a very long one for Bernard. Looking back, he says that it has taken him forty or fifty years to 'transform himself from a wolf to a man'. Just as Heathcliff, the patient, sullen foundling, receives the sort of upbringing 'to make a fiend of a saint . . . a pitiless, fierce, wolfish man', so Bernard, the orphan, has his natural tendencies hardened by a regimen of insults, cold, hunger, and beatings. When he comes as a child to Roche-Mauprat, he is already of a violent disposition but his violence 'sullen and suppressed, blind and brutal in anger' and his sense of the injustice of his treatment increases his stubbornness, ferocity, and power to hate. So that when, at seventeen, he falls in love with his beautiful cousin Edmée, George Sand is not unrealistic enough to present him as suddenly transformed into a suitable husband. In fact, marriage is not his concern at all but Edmée's – just as it is Catherine's. In both books, it is the women who are concerned with the social aspect of the relationship, intent on not degrading themselves by marriage; Bernard, like Heathcliff, can see no further than his devouring passion. Edmée loves her cousin because she cannot help herself, but has no illusions about the misery marriage with him, in his present state of savagery, would bring.

One of the points insistently stressed about Edmée and Bernard is their kinship, their feeling of affinity, at times of shared identity. The same turbulent Mauprat blood flows in their veins; they are equally strong-willed, quick-tempered, and imperious. Both Edmée and Catherine, of course, owe something to Di Vernon, but Scott's heroine has nothing of their passion and ruthlessness. In her relations with her father or the abbé or the peasants, Edmée is shown as pure, noble, angelic, unselfish; when she is dealing with Bernard, she can be hard and capricious, with sudden disarming shows of affection and tenderness to compensate for her cruelty. Like Catherine with Heathcliff – but even more like Cathy with Hareton – she taunts Bernard with his stupidity, boorishness, and ignorance in order to get him to read and study. From the moment that she walks into the trap at Roche-Mauprat and the doors are barred behind her, her destiny is linked with Bernard's. She pledges her word to him, in the first instance, in order to escape and rejoin her father. The situation is very close to that of Cathy's enforced stay at the Heights and her promise to marry Linton 'within this hour if I may go to Thrushcross Grange afterwards' to reassure her father. Edmée later recalls that she promised, because 'I wanted to live; above all, I wanted to see my father again and kiss him. To put an end to the anguish that my disappearance was causing him I would have pledged more than my life, I would have pledged my immortal soul.'[10] But having given her word, she finds herself irresistibly drawn to Bernard. Some of the most memorable scenes in the book do not fall short of *Wuthering Heights* in passion, for Bernard, who has no idea of Edmée's strength of feeling for him, is tormented with agonies of angry jealousy and hatred. One such scene is in Chapter 10, when they have quarrelled and Bernard's anger yields to despair: 'Je déscendis au jardin et j'arpentai les allées d'un pas effréné . . . J'allai m'appuyer au hasard contre un mur sombre et, cachant ma tête dans mes mains, j'exhalai des sanglots désespérés. Ma robuste poitrine se brisait, et mes larmes ne la soulagaient pas à mon gré; j'aurais voulu rugir, et je mordais mon mouchoir pour ne pas céder à cette tentation.'[11]

Heathcliff, howling like a savage beast and dashing his head against a knotted tree trunk, must be admitted to have the edge in ferocity and drama over Bernard, stifling his sobs and biting his handkerchief to shreds in order to prevent himself from roaring aloud in anguish as he leans, his breast heaving convulsively, on the gloomy garden wall – but it is obvious that they belong to the same genre of scene. Certainly there are no lovers in English fiction, until *Wuthering Heights*, who are as uninhibited in their behaviour or the expression of their feelings about each other as Bernard and Edmée.

Edmée's open avowal of her love to the abbé parallels Catherine's confession of hers to Nelly, although Emily Brontë puts it to more dramatic use; in each case, the eavesdropper hears only half the speech and is left with the impression that he is despised. It is not until the final pages of the book that the conversation is completed for Bernard by the abbé. He tells him that Edmée had gone on to admit that for Bernard she feels a passion such as she has never known for her gentlemanly suitor, M. de la Marche. She suddenly cries out, defiantly:

> Eh bien! oui, je l'aime! puisque vous voulez le savoir absolument. J'en suis éprise, comme vous dites. Ce n'est pas ma faute, pourquoi en rougirais-je? Je n'y puis rien; cela est venu fatalement. Je n'ai jamais aimé M. de la Marche; je n'ai que de l'amitié pour lui. Et pour Bernard, c'est autre sentiment, un sentiment si fort, si mobile, si rempli d'agitations, de haine, de peur, de pitié, de colère et de tendresses, qu je n'y comprends rien, et que je n'essaie plus d'y rien comprendre . . . Je sais que Bernard est un ours, un blaireau . . . un sauvage, un rustre, quoi encore? Il n'est rien de plus hérissé, de plus épineux, de plus sournois, de plus méchant que Bernard; c'est une brute qui sait à peine signer son nom . . . Voilà le mal, je l'aime! Voilà les symptomes: je ne pense qu'à lui, je ne vois que lui, et je n'ai pas pu dîner aujourd'hui parce qu'il n'était pas rentré. Je le trouve plus beau qu'aucun homme qui existe. Quand il me dit qu'il m'aime, je vois, je sens que c'est vrai; cela me choque et me charme en même temps. M. de la Marche me paraît fade et guindé depuis que je connais Bernard. Bernard seul me semble aussi fier, aussi colère, aussi hardi que moi et aussi faible que moi; car il pleure comme un enfant quand je l'irrite, et voilà que je pleure aussi en songeant à lui.[12]

It is a moving confession and one which has all the impetuosity and fatalism of Catherine's, though it has not its poetry – nor its succinctness: 'My love for Linton is like the foliage in the woods; time will change it, I'm well aware, as winter changes the trees. My love for Heathcliff resembles the eternal rocks beneath; a source of little visible delight but necessary. Nelly, I *am* Heathcliff.'[13]

For Edmée too, Bernard seemed like herself – 'aussi fier, aussi colère . . . Voyez, vous m'êtes nécessaire absolument.'[14] On his side Bernard is equally absolute. In one of their many slanging-matches he threatens her savagely:

> Je ne comprends rien, sinon que je vous aime avec fureur et que je déchirerai avec mes ongles le coeur de celui qui osera vous disputer à moi. Je sais que je vous forcerai à m'aimer, et que, si je ne réussis pas, je ne souffrirai jamais, du moins, que vous apparteniez à un autre, moi vivant. On marchera sur mon corps criblé de blessures et saignant par tous les pores avant de vous passer au doigt un anneau

de mariage; encore vous déshonorerai-je à mon dernier soupir en disant que vous êtes ma maîtresse, et je troublerai ainsi la joie de celui qui triomphera de moi; et, si je puis vois poignarder en expirant, je le ferai, afin que dans la tombe du moins, vous soyez ma femme.[15]

It is after this quarrel that Bernard suddenly leaves the *château* and goes to fight in America. His six years abroad are documented as Heathcliff's three-year absence is not (and it is important, for the effect of the novel, that mystery should hang over this period of Heathcliff's life, as over his origins). But the underlying historical structure of *Wuthering Heights* is very firm, and when Heathcliff returns to Thrush-cross Grange, Nelly immediately asks, 'Have you been for a soldier?' She observes that 'His upright carriage suggested the idea of his having been in the army', and Lockwood queries, as one explanation for Heathcliff's absence, 'Did he escape to America, and earn honours by drawing blood from his foster-country?' The civilising of Bernard, however, not only goes much deeper than that of Heathcliff; more importantly, he returns to find Edmée unmarried.

Even so, the savage man has not been fully replaced by the social, and when Edmée still refuses to give herself to him, he writes her a letter in which throughout his imagery of love and violence and death, the thunder rumbles and lightning flashes. He tells her he is sometimes tempted to kill her to end his suffering:

mais . . . je crains de vous aimer morte avec autant de passion et de ténacité que si vous étiez vivante. Je crains d'être contenu, gouverné, dominé par votre image, comme je le suis par votre personne; et puis il n'y a pas de moyen de destruction dans la main de l'homme, l'être qu'il aime et qu'il redoute existe en lui lorsqu'il a cessé d'exister sur la terre. C'est l'âme d'un amant qui sert de cercueil à sa maîtresse . . . A l'heure où je vous écris, Edmée, le ciel est chargé de nuées plus sombres et plus lourdes que l'airain; le tonnerre gronde, et à la lueur des éclairs semblent flotter les spectres douloureux du purgatoire. Mon âme est sous le poids de l'orage, mon esprit troublé flotte comme ces clartés incertaines qui jaillissent de l'horizon. Il me semble que mon être va éclater comme la tempête . . .[16]

Not only the frenzied tone of the passage – Bernard's anguished awareness that the ghost of Edmée would haunt and dominate him even more ruthlessly than in life – but the way in which the elements are used to reflect and underline his mood have much in common with *Wuthering Heights*. Again and again in *Mauprat* the atmosphere is built up, with that blend of romantic subjectivism and countrywoman's observation of nature which distinguished George Sand's writings,

D

appealed so strongly to English readers, and was rarely found in English fiction before the Brontës. For example, Bernard's sense of foreboding as he approaches his old home is finely conveyed:

> J'arrivai à la Roche-Mauprat, par une soirée brumeuse, aux premiers jours de l'automne; le soleil était voilé, la nature s'assoupissait dans le silence et dans la brume; les plaines étaient désertes, l'air seul etait rempli du mouvement et du bruit des grandes phalanges d'oiseaux de passage; les grues dessinaient dans le ciel des triangles gigantesques, et les cigognes, passant à une hauteur incommensurable, remplissaient les nuées de cris mélancoliques qui planaient sur les campagnes attristées comme le chant funèbre des beaux jours.[17]

Each novel is, of course, deep-rooted in Romanticism and it is important not to overstress resemblances which arise from the nature of the subject-matter. Similar themes imply similar images, and it is not surprising to find animal imagery used lavishly in both books. References to cubs and whelps, foxes and wolves, lions, badgers, vipers, falcons, and kites underline the savagery of Bernard and Heathcliff. Allusions to the tomb and graveyard are almost as frequent in *Mauprat*, where the lovers find their happiness in this life, as in *Wuthering Heights*; and in the fine and private graves of George Sand and Emily Brontë, lovers do indeed embrace. But Heathcliff's unforgettable bribe of the sexton to remove the planks dividing Catherine's coffin from his so that 'by the time Linton gets to us he'll not know which from which' has a stark matter-of-factness about it which makes Bernard's delirious conviction that he is spending his wedding-night with Edmée, shrouded together in the same coffin, sound stagey in comparison. For neither lover does the passage of time make any difference to the intensity of his obsessive love for the dead woman. Heathcliff is haunted all his life by Catherine and dies in the wild exultation of his conviction that he is going to her – 'I am within sight of my heaven'; Bernard, after a lifetime of happiness with Edmée, has been without her for ten years and is waiting impatiently to rejoin her – 'She was the only woman I ever loved . . . Such is my nature; what I love, I love eternally, in the past, in the present, in the future.' But whereas Bernard's passion is made comprehensible and familiar to readers by his own narration of events, the narrative technique of *Wuthering Heights* ensures that Heathcliff is never seen in normal perspective. Interpreters as alien to him as Nelly Dean and Lockwood make certain that this mystery remains unfathomed, and that their moralising goes unheeded.

In her foreword to the 1851 reissue of *Mauprat*, George Sand wrote that her aim was 'de peindre un amour exclusif, éternel, avant, pendant et après le mariage'. In its fashion, this could perhaps serve as a description of *Wuthering Heights* also – but the love of Bernard is eventually controlled and disciplined by education and by social considerations as Heathcliff's never is. The final impression left by *Mauprat* is of the civilising influence of human love; and that is also the message left to us by the second generation in *Wuthering Heights*, by the marriage of Cathy and Hareton. But the only lovers in whom we are interested in Emily Brontë's novel are not concerned with a message at all – nor with anything but each other and their own being. Despite its passion, *Wuthering Heights* is a strangely sexless book in comparison with *Mauprat*; and despite its unconventional attitudes, *Mauprat* seems a very moral and sentimental romance, when set alongside *Wuthering Heights*. Yet none the less, the parallels and connections are there in profusion and I myself have little doubt that *Mauprat* formed part of the literary – and therefore, living – experience on which Emily Brontë drew. The fact that she was able to produce a totally different and much greater book simply emphasises her remarkable powers of assimilation and transformation as well as her originality and creative power.

6 Arnold's 'Days of *Lélia*'

Matthew Arnold was not only an avowed disciple of George Sand in his Oxford days, but continued to be a faithful reader of her novels throughout his life; his French connection has been especially stressed by such critics as Iris Sells, Louis Bonnerot and F. W. Harding, and most editors and Arnold scholars have had something to say about it. But on the whole much more serious attention has been paid to Arnold's links with Senancour, Sainte-Beuve and Renan than with George Sand; while the fact of his early devotion to her is always acknowledged, its significance remains unassessed.

The *Fortnightly Review* essay that Arnold wrote, in 1877, for the first anniversary of George Sand's death pays generous tribute to her and recreates for us the young, impulsive Arnold, long before he was 'past thirty and three parts iced over'. It is full of interest, for he is looking back over three decades to the August of 1846 and reliving his youthful emotions. 'It seems to me but the other day that I saw her',[1] he writes, recalling his sudden resolution to track her down at Nohant. He had been reading *Jeanne* and had got down the big map of France at the Bodleian and, like countless later literary pilgrims, had plotted his route to the *château* of Nohant, two miles from the little town of La Châtre, right in the middle of France. His decision to visit the Berry district, which she had depicted so faithfully and with such charm in her novels, was taken on the spur of the moment, but it must have been in his mind for a long time. For, ever since he went up to Oxford in 1842, he had been reading her works. He and his brother Tom, and Clough and Theodore Walrond had met for Sunday morning breakfasts where they had long literary discussions, and George Sand had been one of their authors. It seems fairly obvious that the young Arnold, foppish and witty, must initially have been drawn to George Sand because she was fashionable and unorthodox reading and a minority cult figure at Oxford. But there were other more positive and admirable reasons for her appeal to him, which Arnold explains in his essay:

> The cry of agony and revolt is in her earlier work only, and passes away in her later . . . as it passed away for Goethe, as it passes away

for their readers likewise. It passes away and does not return; yet those who, amid the agitations, more or less stormy, of their youth betook themselves to the early work of George Sand, may in later life cease to read them, indeed, but they can no more forget them than they can forget Werther. George Sand speaks somewhere of 'her days of *Corinne*'. Days of *Valentine*, many of us may in like manner say, – days of *Valentine*, days of *Lélia*, days never to return! They are gone, we shall read the books no more, and yet how ineffaceable is their impression! How the sentences from George Sand's works of that period still linger in our memory and haunt the ear with their cadences!²

And so it was in a spirit of genuine hero worship – not very different, in fact, from that in which Elizabeth Barrett Browning sought an interview with her divinity – that Arnold approached George Sand. He had a laborious and lengthy journey, by train and two diligences to La Châtre, and after some days of wandering round the district near Boussac, getting the atmosphere and identifying the druid stones of *Jeanne*, he wrote his letter to Madame Sand, conveying to her 'in bad French, the homage of a youthful and enthusiastic foreigner who had read her works with delight.'

George Sand replied kindly, and Arnold presented himself before the midday breakfast was over. 'I entered with some trepidation, as well I might, considering how I had got there', but his hostess put him at his ease and introduced him to her son and daughter and 'Chopin with his wonderful eyes'. He noticed that she was not dressed in man's clothes, that there was 'nothing astonishing' about her dress.

She made me sit by her and poured out for me the insipid and depressing beverage, *boisson fade et mélancholique*, as Balzac called it, for which English people are thought abroad always to be thirsting, – tea. She conversed of the country through which I had been wandering, of the Berry peasants and their mode of life, of Switzerland whither I was going; she touched politely, by a few questions and remarks, upon England and things and persons English, – upon Oxford and Cambridge, Byron, Bulwer. As she spoke her eyes, head, bearing, were all of them striking; but the main impression she made was . . . of *simplicity*, frank, cordial simplicity.³

It was not, unfortunately, until after her death that Arnold was to learn with delight that the impression that he, in his turn, had made upon George Sand was that of 'un Milton, jeune et voyageant'⁴ – an observation relayed to him by John Morley, who had had it from Renan. This was a piece of hearsay so obviously to his taste that it is a pity that he could not have enjoyed it many years earlier. His visit ended after breakfast in the garden where George Sand 'gathered a flower or two and gave them to me, shook hands heartily at the gate, and I saw her no more.'

He could indeed have seen her again in 1859, when he had a letter to her from M. Michelet, but 'a day or two passed before I could call, and when I called, Madame Sand had left Paris and had gone back to Nohant. The impression of 1846 has remained my single impression of her.' Here he is being disingenuous. What he does not say is that by the time he had the chance of seeing her again, she had lost some of her magic for him; he was older, married, a school-inspector on an official fact-finding tour and not a footloose, young Fellow of Oriel on vacation. He remained on the Continent for half that year and though on the point of seeing George Sand at least three times, kept putting his visit off. In August, he was still in two minds about it, and reverted to the project in a letter to his wife, in which he describes a dinner with Sainte-Beuve in the *Restaurant du Quartier*:

> We dined in the cabinet where G. Sand, when she is in Paris, comes and dines every day . . . After dinner he took me back to his own house, where we had tea; and he showed me a number of letters he had had from G. Sand and Alf. de Musset at the time of their love affair, and then again at the time of their rupture. You may imagine how interesting this was after *Elle et Lui*. I will tell you about them when we meet . . . As for G. Sand and him, Sainte Beuve says, '*Tout le mal* qu'ils ont dit l'un de l'autre est vrai.' But de Musset's letters were, I must say, those of a *gentleman* of the very first water. Sainte Beuve rather advised me to go and see George Sand, but I am still disinclined 'to take so long a journey to see such a fat old Muse,' as M. de Circourt says in his funny English. All Sainte Beuve told me of her present proceedings made me less care about seeing her; however, if Berri was nearer, the weather less hot, and French travelling less of a bore, I should go – as it is I shall not.[5]

And so Arnold, in a sentence whose rhythms and sentiments recall *Amours de Voyage* and its hero Claude, another half-hearted admirer, finally evades any closer contact with his former idol. Sainte-Beuve's gossip about her 'present proceedings' and M. de Circourt's ridicule have clinched the matter and Arnold, probably for the first time, fully faces the fact that his days of *Lélia* are decisively behind him. But his visit had been a landmark and memories of it flood back in 1877 as he fulfils, not a critical service to the English people 'who knew her very little and very ill', but a need in himself 'to recall and collect the elements of that powerful total impression which, as a writer, she made upon me . . . What I here attempt is not for the benefit of the indifferent; it is for my own satisfaction, it is for myself.'[6]

It was, above all, as an idealist that she had appealed to him, and the three elements which, he says, remain with him from her writings are her agonised cry of revolt against contemporary society, her delight in natural scenery as a sustaining power and her faith in humanity. He chooses a few words from one of her last publications, *Journal d'un Voyageur* (1870) to sum up her essential message for him: 'Le sentiment de la vie idéale qui n'est autre que la vie normale telle que nous sommes appelés à la connaître' – 'the sentiment of the ideal life, which is none other than man's normal life as we shall some day know it.' This is a sentence which he had quoted more fully in his *Notebooks* and he here omits the important phrase which prefixed it – '*le besoin d'aimer*, le sentiment de la vie idéale . . .'[7] It is a skilful shift of emphasis which presents not an untrue but a rather larger than life George Sand to his readers, one more concerned with mankind than men, with aspiration than the simple need to love and be loved. He deals with each chosen aspect of her in turn, ranging over her works with the ease of long acquaintance. To illustrate her scorn of the arid materialism of society he quotes passage after passage from *Lélia*, from *Jacques*, from *Lettres d'un Voyageur*, from her preface to de Guérin's *Centaure* – each 'grandiose and moving', each sounding a note of impassioned despair and frustrated idealism.

But no despair can be total, as he goes on to point out, when solace can be found in nature. Turning next to the lovely descriptions of the countryside, in *Valentine*, he translates freely and sensitively:

> The winding and deep lanes . . . the great white ox, 'the unfailing dean of these pastures,' staring solemnly at you from the thicket; the farmhouse . . . who, I say, can forget them? And that one lane is especial, the lane where Athénaïs puts her arm out of the side window in the rustic carriage and gathers May from the over-arching hedge, – that lane with its startled blackbirds, and humming insects, and limpid water, and swaying water-plants, and shelving gravel, and yellow wagtails hopping half-pert, half-frightened, on the sand – that land with its rushes, cresses, and mint below, its honeysuckle and traveller's-joy above . . .[8]

In this 'fresh and calm rural world' of George Sand's it is the peasant who is the central figure. This is not only indicative of her delight in the simple life but also of her almost religious belief in social equality, the third important element for Arnold in her novels. Arnold is at one with her, in her opinion of 'poor Jacques Bonhomme', for he considers the peasant to be 'really, so far as I can see, the largest and strongest element of soundness which the body social of any European nation possesses', but he feels less kindly towards Madame Sand's 'Republican friends of the educated classes', whose fanatical eloquence he hastens to distinguish from her tolerant belief in the necessity of eventual organic social change – a belief which Arnold himself now shared.

It is a revealing essay, the tribute of a fifty-five year old public man to one who, for him, has been above all, 'a friend and a power'. As he says, it is not 'a judicial estimate' of her; no one could claim for this essay Arnold's favourite quality of disinterestedness. In his last paragraph he makes it clear that he is aware that her works 'always fresh, always attractive' were poured out too lavishly and rapidly so that 'Posterity, always alarmed at the way in which its literary baggage grows upon it', may well be inclined to leave many of her novels behind. But that is a point that 'I do not care to consider'. All that really concerns him is his certainty that 'the immense vibration of George Sand's voice upon the ear of Europe will not soon die away . . . There will remain of her to mankind the sense of benefit and stimulus from the passage upon earth of that large and pure utterance – *the large utterance of the early gods.*'[9]

It would not be surprising if, after thirty years, Arnold's assessment of the nature of his debt to George Sand had become distorted. But on the whole, it fits in well with what we learn of her impact upon him from his correspondence of the 1840s and from memoirs of the period – although it could be fairly objected that, by placing such emphasis on her as a powerful moral force, he underplays her aesthetic and worldly appeal. His niece Mary Ward, no doubt drawing principally upon her father's reminiscences of Oxford, talks of *Consuelo* and *Wilhelm Meister* as exercising similar 'liberating and enchanting' powers:

> There are many allusions of many dates in the letters of my father and uncle to each other, as to their common Oxford passion for George Sand. *Consuelo* in particular was a revelation to the two young men brought up under the 'earnest' influence of Rugby. It seemed to open to them a world of artistic beauty and joy of which they had never dreamed; and to loosen the bands of an austere conception of life which began to appear to them too narrow for the facts of life.[10]

Arnold's essay does not make much of *Consuelo*; by 1877, it is simply a 'charming story' which shows 'only a portion of what is valuable and significant in George Sand'. But that 'portion' was obviously of significance for the young Arnold, with its insight into the world of music and the stage; soon after, he is a devotee of Rachel, for two months in Paris never missing one of her plays. Clough notes with amusement that 'Matt is full of Parisianism; Theatres in general and Rachel in special: he enters the room with a chanson of Béranger's on his lips – for the sake of the French words almost conscious of tune.' Tom Arnold thought that it was the charm of George Sand's exquisite style which 'made him and long kept him a votary', and Arnold

certainly responded to her eloquent cadences. But he was also concerned with what she was saying, and a letter to Clough in 1845
plunges into discussion of just those moral aspects of George Sand's
novels with which he is still preoccupied thirty years later.

H. F. Lowry thought this letter of Arnold's to Clough 'so important
in what it tells us indirectly about his early thinking' that he printed
the original passages from *Indiana* and *Jacques* in an appendix to his
edition of the letters. Arnold writes:

> . . . You mean INDIANA'S LETTER, without which I think the book not
> pre-eminent among the Author's other novels. 'Believe me', (I quote
> from memory) – 'if a Being so vast deigned to take any Part in our
> miserable Interests, it would be to raise up the weak, and to beat
> down the strong: – it would be to pass his heavy hand over our
> heads, and to level them like the waters of the Sea: – to say to the
> Slave, "throw away thy chain", – and to the Strong, "Bear thy
> Brother's burden: for I have given him strength and wisdom, and
> thou shalt oppress him no longer." ' – And the correspondence of
> Jacques and Sylvia – the Sunday Shoes letter you remember.[12]

We are here breaking into the middle of an animated discussion of
George Sand's philosophy, and the obliqueness of Arnold's references
indicate a long-shared familiarity with the novels. This feminist cry of
Indiana's against male oppression in the name of religion had gone
home to Arnold and Clough as had the 'Sunday-shoes' letter from
Jacques to Sylvia. It is one of the memorable passages in *Jacques*, in
which he deplores the conventional and inadequate education of his
young wife, Fernande, which has made her what she is:

> On ne lui a pas fait, comme à toi, un corps et une âme de fer; on
> lui a parlé de prudence, de raison, de certains calculs pour éviter
> certaines douleurs, et de certaines réflexions pour arriver à un
> certain bien-être que la société permet aux femmes à de certaines
> conditions. On ne lui a pas dit comme à toi: 'Le soleil est âpre et le
> vent est rude; l'homme est fait pour braver la tempête sur la mer,
> la femme pour garder les troupeaux sur la montagne brûlante.
> L'hiver, viennent la neige et la glace, tu iras dans les mêmes lieux,
> et tu tâcheras de te réchauffer à un feu que tu allumeras avec les
> branches sêches de la forêt; si tu ne veux pas le faire tu supporteras
> le froid comme tu pourras. Voici la montagne, voici la mer, voici le
> soleil. Le soleil brûle, la mer engloutit, la montagne fatigue.
> Quelquefois les bêtes sauvages emportent les troupeaux et l'enfant
> qui les garde; tu vivras au milieu de tout cela comme tu pourras; si
> tu es sage et brave, on te donnera des souliers pour te parer le
> dimanche.[13]

What I think appealed so much to Arnold about this letter is not the fact that it is advocating real equality of the sexes – Arnold never showed any interest in feminist issues – but that George Sand is expressing, in prose whose rhythms seize the heart and imagination, a sort of stoicism which was entirely congenial to him. In returning to first principles she is in harmony with the teaching of Carlyle, who was then Arnold's other sage, but she does not rule out the possibility of happiness. As Kenneth Allott points out, in one of his many wise footnotes to 'Empedocles on Etna', Arnold, too, unlike Carlyle, 'thinks happiness a proper aim for man, but with the Stoics and Spinoza he holds that his direct aim should be to live in conformity with nature and so contentedly.'[14] Man has indeed the 'thirst for bliss', but this is born in him –

> Nor is the thirst to blame.
> Man errs not that he deems
> His welfare his true aim.
> He errs because he dreams
> The world does but exist that welfare to bestow.

Even as Arnold responds to George Sand's heartfelt convictions, he is a little worried by the fact that she is 'a strong-minded writer' and consequently open to being made a cult of and distorted and systematised by followers: 'Rightly considered a Code-G-Sand would make G. Sands impossible.' He is prepared to 'believe in the Universality of Passion as Passion' but not as doctrine – and George Sand's appeal for him lies as much in her individuality and spontaneity as in the truth of anything she says. From the start he is aware of her as a 'great nature' and, despite her failings, he never demotes her from his élite band. This is a courtesy that he does not extend to other female celebrities, such as Harriet Martineau ('what an unpleasant life and unpleasant nature');[15] Margaret Fuller ('that partly brazen female . . . my G-d what rot did she and the other female dogs of Boston talk about Greek mythology!'); Charlotte Brontë ('a fire without aliment – one of the most distressing barren sights one can witness'). He is especially scathing about *Villette*:

Miss Brontë has written a hideous undelightful convulsed constricted novel . . . It is one of the most utterly disagreeable novels I ever read – and having seen her makes it more so . . . It gives you an insight into the *heaven-born* character of Waverley and Indiana and such-like when you read the undeniably powerful but most un-heaven-born productions of the present people – Thackeray – the woman Stowe etc. The woman Stowe by her picture must be a Gorgon . . .[16]

Apart from the reference to Harriet Martineau, all these comments occur in a single letter to Clough of 1853. It is a virtuoso display of Arnold's prejudices, even to his final unworthy gibe at Mrs Stowe's unoffending countenance. It is ironic that many of these phrases – 'unpleasant life', 'brazen female', 'utterly disagreeable novel' – had been applied by reviewers in the past to George Sand, but for Arnold even such a novel as *Indiana*, which he admits is far from her best, has a 'heaven-born' quality about it which shields its author and makes all her goings graces.

In fact, it is not really as a novelist at all that Arnold is judging George Sand. Compared with most of his contemporaries, Arnold was no novel addict, as the reading lists in his *Notebooks* show. Although some tried favourites do crop up from time to time, along with the occasional new title such as *Nana* or *Anna Karenina*, the only novelist who appears with predictable regularity is George Sand. Even *The Mill on the Floss* was not read till nine years after it came out, and *Scenes of Clerical Life* had to wait for twenty-five years before being placed on Arnold's list for 1881. Even then he made heavy going with them and *Janet's Repentance* was entered in both 1882 and 1883, before being finally scored off as read. Philosophy, history, theology, drama, poetry – all these take precedence over the novel for Arnold. If it had not been that he found qualities in George Sand which distinguished her from all other novelists, she would no doubt have suffered the same fate as Balzac, whose *Illusions Perdues* appears on six consecutive New Year lists from 1881 onwards, is taken with him to America and back in 1883 and is not struck off as read till 1886. The *Notebooks* are of great interest because they allow us to see, from the extracts Arnold chose, just what nourishment he was able to extract from George Sand, even from her feeblest potboilers, until the end of his days – and we shall look at them more closely later. But as he did not start these jottings till 1853, they tell us nothing of her initial impact. If she were as great an influence as Arnold himself acknowledged her to have been in a letter to his mother in 1869 on Sainte-Beuve's death – 'When George Sand and Newman go, there will be no writers left from whom I have received a strong influence; they will have all departed'[17] – then the evidence should surely be found in her early novels and in his early poetry. For these poems of 1849 are the product of his Oxford years, the outcome of his 'days of *Lélia*'.

2

It should be stressed that *Lélia* existed for Arnold not merely as a stepping-stone to Senancour's *Obermann*, which is how most critics have chosen to regard it, but as a work in its own right, pondered by him, probably three or four years before he read Senancour around 1847. The critic who has discussed *Lélia* most fully, in relation to Arnold, is Iris Sells in *Arnold and France* (1935). Although her major preoccupation is Senancour, she devotes two chapters to George Sand, in the first of which she concentrates upon *Lélia*, while the second gives a highly coloured account of Arnold's visit to Nohant. It is a pity that she chose to indulge, in Bonnerot's phrase, in 'biographie romancée', to fabricate an unauthenticated conversation about Sainte-Beuve, the Guérins and above all, Senancour, and to despatch Arnold hot-foot on the latter's tracks to Geneva via Lyons, where 'we assume, he took care to acquire, among a parcel of other books, a copy of Madame Sand's edition of *Obermann*.'[18] For these flights of fancy (uncorrected in the recent second edition) make some of her genuine exploratory insights in the preceding chapter unfairly suspect. It is indeed, as she says, very likely that *Lélia* was 'the first instance Matthew Arnold had yet encountered of a type of character which was to fascinate him henceforth,' the embodiment of the *maladie du siècle*, of *ennui* and despair. And when Louis Bonnerot redresses the balance of Mrs Sell's enthusiasm by commenting that the influence of George Sand on Arnold, of all others, 'servit plus à révéler sa nature profonde qu'à la modifier',[19] the distinction he is making seems to me a difficult and perhaps meaningless one; any writer who can reveal the nature of the reader to himself is profoundly affecting him. There is some truth in Mrs Sell's claim that 'In *Lélia* lies the clue to those profound and far reaching influences which were to modify the whole of Matthew Arnold's literary career'; *Lélia* did make an ineffaceable impression upon Arnold, and even when he found a surrogate for it in *Obermann*, scenes, moods, passages of lyrical prose, even characters remained with him to reappear, transformed but still recognisable, in his poetry.

When Arnold scholars refer to *Lélia*, the normal reference given is to the 1833 edition, but it was certainly the 1839 version from which he quoted in his essay on George Sand. The impressive dying outburst of Lélia, from the chapter 'Délire', part of which Arnold translated, does not occur in the first version. I make this point not wholly out of pedantry: the aim of the two versions was completely different. It was the 1833 *Lélia* which so horrified its readers, a book written at a time of utter and untypical despair for George Sand. It could well be subtitled, as Pierre Reboul suggests, *La Pensée de George Sand en 1833*.[20] Much of the book could also quite fairly be called *La Pensée de Senancour*, for she had just been reading *Obermann* at the instigation of Sainte-Beuve, who had revived interest in this earlier work. Although, as George Sand herself commented, Senancour had been a misfit in 1804, when the stress was on war, glory and action, he seemed to express perfectly the mood of the 1830s in his *ennui*, doubt and gloom – and also George Sand's own personal sense of impotence and meaninglessness in the midst of her exhausted love affair and her foundering marriage.

And so she wrote *Lélia*, which was immediately recognised as the cry of 'un Obermann féminisé'; 'une âme flétrie'. Lélia is a solitary, beautiful woman, disillusioned by her experience of love, whose frigidity contrasts with the passion and naïve idealism of her young lover, Sténio. Her vision is of a nightmare universe: 'L'homme a l'impuissance du mollusque avec les appétits du tigre; la misère et la nécessité l'emprisonnent dans une écaille de tortue.'[21] With all its faults and excesses, the 1833 *Lélia* has the great virtue of coherence of mood, of despairing lucidity. The work is ambitious in form, consisting for the most part of long monologues of self-revelation by the five characters, who counter each others' arguments and gradually move the narrative onwards. Each character carries a heavy burden of symbolism. Sténio is not only Lélia's lover, but represents poetry, youth, idealism, credulity, unbridled passion; while Trenmor, the ex-convict, represents age, wisdom, reason, calm stoicism. Lélia herself is midway between the two extremes. Unlike Sténio, she no longer sees any reason for living, but is still torn by doubt and resentment and has not attained Trenmor's acceptance of suffering.

It was not, however, this text which most later Victorians knew as *Lélia*, but the revised version of 1839 – an incomparably poorer work, which it is even more difficult to take seriously and which was unenthusiastically received in France. The fine *Classiques Garnier* edition of 1960 makes it very easy to see just how George Sand hacked about at *Lélia* in order to bring it into line with her changed circumstances and philosophy. In the intervening years Nodier and Senancour had been replaced as mentors by Pierre Leroux and Michel de Bourges. She tampered with her original conception in order to convey her new serenity and progressivist tendencies, her belief in humanity and social and political engagement. Intent on changing, as she put it, a poison into a cure,[22] she brings about two highly unlikely metamorphoses. Trenmor, the passive stoic, develops into a man of action, leading an underground movement, and Lélia becomes the highly efficient abbess of the monastery of the Camaldules, an eventual martyr to the Church rather than the victim of a lust-crazed monk, as in the first version. There is an absurd amount of whitewashing of the heroine and denigration of Sténio in the 1839 *Lélia*, and if it is difficult to understand, as Trilling suggests, how Arnold, with his humour and urbanity, could have given *Obermann* so important a place in his life, it is even harder to see how he could have tolerated the second *Lélia* at all.

Arnold may well have known both versions, but since about four-fifths of the original text remained unaltered, even the 1839 *Lélia* exposed him to what must have seemed then a startling dose of Senancour-like sentiments. Lélia's alienation, impotence and doubt, her disgust with contemporary civilisation, her turning for solace to Nature, even the Rousseau-ish nocturnal outings on the lake – all these are features of *Obermann* and of both *Lélia*s. That Arnold outgrew *Lélia* is due largely, I think, to the fact that when he read Senancour he felt he had reached the source and had no further need of the tributaries. When he wrote 'Senancour has a gravity and severity which distinguish him from all other writers of the sentimental school. The world is with him in his solitude far less than it is with them; of all writers he is the most perfectly isolated and the least attitudinising',[23] there can be no doubt that he had *Lélia*'s histrionics in mind. In 1877, Arnold includes not *Lélia* but *Lettres d'un Voyageur* in his brief list of works of George Sand which would give an idea of her essential quality to someone who had never read her. F. W. Harding[24] takes Arnold to task as a critic for including the *Lettres* because George Sand had admitted that 'Jamais ouvrage, si ouvrage il y a, n'a été moins raisonné et moins travaillé que ces deux volumes.' But Arnold was right to do so. The tone of the *Lettres*, begun the year after *Lélia*, is no longer heightened, sybilline and self-justifying. The conversational opening 'J'étais arrivé à Bassano à neuf heures du soir, par un temps froid et humide. Je m'étais couché, triste et fatigué . . .'[25] exactly catches the nonchalant directness with which Obermann opens his second letter. 'J'arrivai de nuit à Genève; j'y logeai dans une assez triste auberge, où mes fenêtres donnaient sur une cour; je n'en fus point fâché.'[26] And while this tone must have appealed to Arnold, the authentic note of George Sand is also heard in the *Lettres*. As well as despair, anger, frustration and introspection there is gaiety, lyricism and warmth – a sense of the world outside her own being. No one who has felt the strength of George Sand would omit the *Lettres* from a selection of her works, and Arnold, by including it, shows that he had learned that what she had to offer him was quite distinct from what he got from Senancour.

3

Arnold would have been the last man to deny the importance of literary influences. In the recognition of affinities and debts, however, the danger lies in over-simplification, and when Bonnerot defends what he feels is Arnold's own vein of Romanticism against Mrs Sell's claim that it is largely derived from his reading of Senancour, he is right to show the complexity of the issue. Before Arnold wrote a line he was well read in English Romantic poets, and such poems as 'Dejection: an Ode' or 'Ode to the Nightingale' display almost as fully the qualities of isolation, sadness, stoicism, *ennui* and disenchantment as any that Senancour or Arnold ever wrote. On the other hand, Bonnerot's counter-claim[27] that Arnold's distinctive Romanticism is anterior to *all* influence from Senancour because it is found in his early poems before he read Senancour when he was twenty-five, is unconvincing when we remember the dose of 'Obermann-ism' to which he had been exposed in *Lélia*, three or four years earlier.

One of the earliest of his poems, 'To a Gypsy Child by the Sea-shore', probably written *c.* 1843, has puzzled many critics, as indeed it puzzled Arnold's own family. Allott quotes Tom Arnold's recollection of the incident in Douglas, Isle of Man, which prompted the poem. He and his brother were 'watching the passengers landed from the Liverpool steamer. There was a crowd and just in front of them stood a poor woman: she might have been a gypsy . . . and the child in her arms was looking backwards over her shoulder. Its pitiful wan face and sad dark eyes rested on Matthew for some time without change of expression.'[28] As Arnold looked at the child he became 'completely abstracted'. Of the resulting poem, his sister Mary commented: 'Some [of his poems] are perfect riddles to me such as that to the Child at Douglas, which is surely more poetical than true.'[29] What strikes the reader, as Bonnerot points out, is that the pessimism expressed is greatly in excess of the objective correlative, the babe in arms, and seems to be a melancholy emanation from the poet himself:

> Who lent thee, child, this meditative guise?
> Who massed, round that slight brow, these clouds of doom? . . .

> With eyes which sought thine eyes thou didst converse,
> And that soul-searching vision fell on me.

> Glooms that go deep as thine I have not known:
> Moods of fantastic sadness, nothing worth.
> Thy sorrow and thy calmness are thine own:
> Scorns that enhance and glorify this earth . . .

> Is the calm thine of stoic souls, who weigh
> Life well, and find it wanting, nor deplore;
> But in disdainful silence turn away,
> Stand mute, self-centred, stern, and dream no more?

To the question 'Who massed, round that slight brow, these clouds of doom?' Bonnerot suggests that the reader should reply 'the poet'.[30] But not, I think, the poet unstimulated and unsustained by some literary memories. The infantine gaze is certainly not sufficient in itself to carry the weight of sophisticated, romantic pessimism of the poem. But if we once accept the possibility that the penetrating gaze of the sad, dark eyes, set in the pale face, started off in Arnold's mind a train of recent literary associations, then the poem becomes more comprehensible. It is interesting that Kenneth Allott noted a parallel between the surprising final couplet:

> Ere the long evening close, thou shalt return,
> And wear this majesty of grief again.

and the description of Lélia, 'la majesté pleine de tristesse qui entourait Lélia comme d'une auréole', but he did not elaborate upon the connection. It comes, however, from a purple passage of *Lélia* – one of the most memorable scenes of the book, at the costume ball of the rich musician, Spuelo.[31] It is a passage which was commented upon appreciatively and quoted in full by Lewes in his 1842 article on George Sand. The attention of Trenmor and Sténio is suddenly seized by the brooding presence of Lélia, as she stands on the flight of steps isolated from the noise of the throng of dancers; she is a striking figure, her cloak only less black and velvety than her large eyes in her white face, her gaze searching and profound. Her contempt for life is expressed in both a 'défiance haineuse' and a silent rejection of its pleasures. She is without hope and expectation and, like Arnold's gypsy child, bears a 'funereal aspect'. Sténio is suddenly repelled by her silence and coldness, as if she had come from the tomb. And indeed, the theme of pre-existence and pre-natal memories, of the difference between 'old' and 'young' souls, which Arnold touches on in his poem, runs through *Lélia*: 'Il y a des souvenirs qui viennent au jour avec des douleurs qu'on dirait contractées dans la tombe, car l'homme quitte peut-être le froid du cerceuil pour rentrer dans le duvet du berceau.'[32]

Sténio talks of Lélia as an angel, exiled from God, and when she makes a desperate attempt to find happiness in loving the young poet, Trenmor comments, 'La dernière plume de votre aile n'est pas encore tombée.'[33] He rebukes her for her attempt to return on her tracks – 'Songez-vous au siècles qui vous séparent de lui' – while admitting that she is less advanced than he is: 'Il vous reste quelques réminiscences des temps passées.'[34]

It can be seen that Arnold's poem is full of echoes of these themes and scenes:

> Some exile's, mindful how the past was glad?
> Some angel's, in an alien planet born?
> – No exile's dream was ever half so sad,
> Nor any angel's sorrow so forlorn . . .

Ere the long night, whose stillness brooks no star,
Match that funereal aspect with her pall,
I think thou wilt have fathomed life too far,
Have known too much – or else forgotten all . . .

Ah! not the nectarous poppy lovers use,
Not daily labour's dull, Lethean spring,
Oblivion in lost angels can infuse
Of the soiled glory and the trailing wing.

What comes over in Arnold's poem is a certain 'positive pessimism', in Allott's phrase, which is not found in Keats or Coleridge. There is no question of these melancholy souls, these *âmes flétries*, glutting their sorrow on a morning rose. That is the recourse of the young soul; the old soul, whether Lélia or the gypsy child, has nothing to learn and is totally solipsistic. It is their stoical glooms which 'enhance and glorify the earth', and theirs is the 'majesty of grief'. What George Sand offered Arnold in *Lélia* was her own distinctive blend of Byron and Senancour – more drama than *Obermann*, more *ennui* than 'Lara' – and Arnold strikes the same note of romantic stoicism in his early poems. In 'Mycerinus' – in which another hero challenges an indifferent universe – a memorable little vignette recalls either the scene in which Lélia surveys the revelling dancers with disdain, or a later episode, in the Bambucci palace, where again she is detached from the other guests, remote and icy in her apathy – 'muette et glacée'. Hers is the 'unmoved eye' and 'frozen apathy' of Mycerinus.

Seems it so light a thing, then, austere Powers,
To spurn man's common lure, life's pleasant things?
Seems there no joy in dances crowned with flowers,
Love, free to range, and regal banquetings?
Bend ye on these, indeed, an unmoved eye,
Not Gods but ghosts, in frozen apathy?

One of the poems about whose source there can be no doubt is 'The New Sirens'. Arnold wrote this about the same time as 'To a Gypsy Child', worked over it for a long time and, after publication in 1849, deprecatingly agreed with Clough's judgement that it was 'a mumble'. He did not reprint it until 1876, probably, as Allott suggests, as a tribute to George Sand who had died earlier that year – at the same time commenting, ironically, 'I don't thoroughly understand it myself but I believe it is very fine and Rossetti and his school say it is the best thing I have done.' Allott notes:

The germ of Arnold's distinction between the old and the new sirens was probably the debate in G. Sand's *Lélia* (1833) . . . between

Pulchèrie (sensuality) and Lélia (alternating between romantic passion and ennui); and the scene of the debate the Villa Bambucci with its 'pavillon d'Aphrodise' is perhaps recalled in A's setting.[35]

Allott is certainly right to stress the indebtedness to George Sand: his note misleads only in directing attention to a simple opposition between romantic passion and sensuality. The whole of *Lélia* is an extended verbal duel between concepts, and the different characters can be considered, as George Sand herself said, as various sides of the heroine – each a differing 'moi'. What seems to have most interested Arnold is the battle which goes on between Sténio, the young poet and romantic lover, and Lélia, who, although she appears romantic when contrasted with her courtesan sister, Pulcheria, is the spokesman for stoicism and renunciation in reply to Sténio's unbounded claims for feeling.

It is not surprising that the poet Arnold should have found the arguments of Sténio particularly relevant to his own situation, 'by the dragon-wardered fountain,/Where the springs of knowledge are.' Sténio is young, handsome, an idealist devoted to the raptures of his senses – 'Only what we feel, we know'. Yet he is deluded by Lélia when she substitutes her courtesan sister for herself, not recognising the difference between woman and woman until he is disillusioned in the cold dawn, and in his reaction from ecstacy to despair gives himself over to debauchery and loses all his youthful glory in surfeit and premature age. The parallel between Sténio's downward path and that of the poets lured by the New Sirens is obvious, and Arnold makes it even clearer in the explanatory 'argument'[36] which he sent to Clough (an exposition not unlike that which George Sand felt constrained to offer for *Lélia*). He describes his speaker as 'one of a band of poets' who is torn between the 'vehement emotional life of passion' of the New Sirens and his own 'conscientious regrets after the spiritual life'. He asks himself 'whether this *alternation* of ennui and excitement is worth much,' whether in the end nothing will be left but weariness – a question which exactly sums up the pervading atmosphere of Lélia's life of sensations, from which she finally escapes into the calm of the cloister.

It is not difficult to see why the poem should have failed to satisfy Arnold and seemed to him a bit of a 'a mumble', because he had based it on a very complex and confusing model, a very real 'dialogue of the mind with itself'. As such, it was, like 'Empedocles', liable to omission from later collections of Arnold's poetry. And there are times, indeed, when the confusion of the poem for Arnold, who had read *Lélia*, must have seemed even greater than for those who had not. It is impossible, for instance, to read the description of the disillusioned Sirens without instantly visualising Lélia herself.

> With a sad, majestic motion,
> With a stately, slow surprise,
> From their earthward-bound devotion
> Lifting up your languid eyes –
> Would you freeze my too loud boldness,
> Dumbly smiling as you go,
> One faint frown of distant coldness
> Flitting fast across each marble brow?

The actual settings of the poem are simpler echoes of *Lélia*, of the high life scenes, not only at the ball, but at the fete of the prince Bambucci and at the courtesan's palace in Book 5.

> Les façades et les cours de la villa étincelaient de lumières. Mais les jardins n'étaient éclairés que par le reflet des appartements. A mesure qu'on s'éloignait on pouvait s'ensevelir dans une molle et mystérieuse obscurité et se reposer du mouvement et du bruit au fond de ces ombrages où les sons de l'orchestre arrivaient doux et faibles, interrompus souvent par les bouffées d'un vent, chargé de parfums.[37]

All the exotic descriptions of the revels and music and scent and flowers had obviously impressed Arnold – the palace and courtyards brilliantly illuminated, the gardens and grassy glades and statued alleys where the lovers stray, unlit except by the lights from the windows.

> Scent, and song, and light, and flowers!
> Gust on gust, the harsh winds blow . . .
> From your dazzled windows streaming,
> From your humming festal room,
> Deep and far, a broken gleaming
> Reels and shivers on the ruffled gloom.

The 'unlovely dawning' of the New Sirens is experienced twice by Sténio. First,[38] when he is awakened by the song of the birds and the fresh morning breeze on his brow and looks out. He sees the lights paling in the palace and Lélia passing beneath his window, and realises that he has been incapable of distinguishing sensuality from romantic love. The second memorable dawn[39] comes after his year of libertinism with Pulchérie. Trenmor enters the lamplit palace, from out of the morning air, again filled with bird-song and the scent of flowers, and surveys the joyless scene after the courtesans have withdrawn from a long night of rose-decked revelry. The once-radiant poet and lover is now pale, dull-eyed, aged and debauched, his fine hair tumbling in loose locks on his shoulders

> And those warm locks men were praising,
> Drooped, unbraided, on your listless arms . . .

> Come, loose hands! The wingèd fleetness
> Of immortal feet is gone;
> And your scents have shed their sweetness,
> And your flowers are overblown.
> And your jewelled gauds surrender
> Half their glories to the day;
> Freely did they flash their splendour,
> Freely gave it – but it dies away.
>
> In the pines the thrush is waking –
> Lo, yon orient hill in flames!
> Scores of true love-knots are breaking
> At divorce which it proclaims.
> When the lamps are paled at morning,
> Heart quits heart and hand quits hand.
> Cold in that unlovely dawning,
> Loveless, rayless, joyless you shall stand!

The figure of the young Romantic poet is one which haunts these early poems of Arnold's. Bonnerot rightly remarks that 'Callicles has a family resemblance to the hero of "The New Sirens" and "The Strayed Reveller" ';[40] Callicles is entirely Arnold's own conception – there is no authority for him in Karsten's account of Empedocles – but his resemblance to the prelapsarian Sténio is very marked. Arnold contrasts Callicles' innocence and hedonism with the stoicism and disillusionment of Empedocles, just as George Sand opposes the same qualities in Sténio, the young soul, with those of the old souls of Trenmor and Lélia.

Any edition of 'Empedocles' is bound to give Senancour as the source of many of the protagonist's philosophical comments, but it would be difficult to be categorical as to whether Arnold was influenced directly by Senancour or by George Sand, for in almost every case the equivalent passage can be found in her pages. There are occasions when George Sand has borrowed a scene or mood and has so developed it that it overpowers the original. Kenneth Allott does full justice to the variety of Arnold's sources – Empedocles, Lucretius, Epictetus, Marcus Aurelius, Carlyle and Senancour – and picks his way discriminatingly among them. When he points out that Empedocles' death on the summit of Etna formally resembles Manfred's, but that 'Arnold's main debt is probably to *Obermann*',[41] one can agree while still pointing to the plethora of Alpine suicides that George Sand went in for. And while again no one would quarrel with Allott's mention[42] of Carlyle's 'famous recipe for content . . . lessening your Denominator' as a source for Empedocles' prayer, 'Make us not fly to dreams but moderate desire', who is to say that Arnold had *Sartor* in mind rather than *Obermann* or *Lélia*? Senancour's counter-argument to suicide: 'Arrêtez vos désirs, bornez ces besoins trop avides';[43] George Sand: 'Je n'ai pas demandé à la vie plus qu'elle ne pouvait me donner. J'ai reduit tous mes ambitions à savoir jouir de ce qui est.'[44] It is a wise annotator who knows his definitive source, and most richly-textured poetry defies precise attribution. In Arnold's case it is fair to assume that all the concepts congenial to him in books he had read and brooded over contributed to his own formulation of them. But the figure of Callicles does, I think, owe much to Arnold's memories of *Lélia*.

Book 2 of *Lélia* opens, like 'Empedocles', with some fine pastoral description. The young poet is coming down from the wooded slopes of Monte Rosa in the first light, after having spent the night, as he frequently did, wrapped in his cloak on the grass by the side of a clear stream, listening to the varying sounds of the torrent, gazing at the moon and dreaming of his love. The vine-covered slopes, dark with firs and cypresses and pines scenting the air are a traditional setting for the poet, whether Sténio or Callicles. In lyrical interludes Sténio plays his harp to Lélia, and sings sweet hymns in her praise and to the glory of God and life and the natural world and love. These are strange regressions to traditional pastoral in the contemporary world of *Lélia*. When Lélia appears to be near death, and her despair is overwhelming, she tells Sténio to play to her: 'Hélas, Trenmor, où sommes-nous? Où en est le siècle? Le savant nie, le prêtre doute. Voyons si le poète existe encore. Sténio, prends ta harpe et chante-moi les vers de Faust, où bien ouvre tes livres et redis-moi les souffrances d'Obermann, les transports de Saint-Preux.'[45]

Lélia is obsessed with what Arnold in his 1853 Preface, speaking of Empedocles' preoccupations, describes as 'modern problems . . . we hear already the doubts, we witness the discouragement of Hamlet and of Faust.' But Sténio, as he sings, has a brief victory over her doubts – brief because the distance between youth and maturity, innocence and experience can never wholly be bridged.

This is a point which is made again in a different way in an episode which George Sand added to Part 2 of the revised *Lélia*. As Sténio leaves Monte Rosa he meets his friend, Edméo. Sténio had known him as a student of philosophy, but now Edméo is setting out to join the ranks of Trenmor, to work in the service of ungrateful and unworthy humanity, and to win his 'laurels of martyrdom'.[46] The conversation between the youths – one dedicated to stoical renunciation and death, the other wholly given over to the life of the senses – underlines the irrevocable gap between them. Some time after they have parted, the farewell song that Edméo had promised, comes to Sténio's ears on the rocky mountainside. 'Sténio had remained seated on a rock. It was a clear, cold night, the ground was dry and the air vibrant. Edméo's strong voice chanting this hymn came distinctly to his friend's ears.'[47] It is a hymn to Sirius, the fixed immutable star in the firmament, the brightest of all heaven's torches – and it is as lyrical and as alien to Sténio as any of Callicles' songs are to Empedocles.

> in these solitudes,
> In this clear mountain-air, a voice will rise,
> Though from afar, distinctly; . . .

And like Callicles' disembodied songs it has no power to affect its hearer's resolution, for Sténio's eyes are fixed on Venus, not on Sirius, and his fate is decided. Two figures on a mountainside, each 'on his own strict line', with a song helpless to unite them – the picture is a memorable one which may well have remained in Arnold's memory.

Despite all its attitudinising and its egocentric outpourings, *Lélia* had, then, a great deal to give Arnold in 'the agitations more or less strong' of his youth. The whole book is after all, a debate between irreconcilables, expressing forcefully what his own poetry returns to again and again, the loss involved in the wholehearted pursuit of one extreme or the other, and the impossibility of their reconcilement. One has to be resolute, to 'take up ones assiètte' – and yet repining is inevitable. Arnold was as aware of the contradictions of his nature as any critic since, and when, in a letter of 1849, he begged his sister not to try to make a coherent whole of the fragmented personality illustrated by his poetry, he was admitting to the same turmoil in himself as in Lélia, in her painful midway state between the idealism and passion of poetic youth and the rational stoicism of age. At every moment the reader is made aware of the strong tug of oppositions; and the enigmatic Lélia herself, with the 'soul of ice or fire',[48] the dazzling exterior and the despairing heart, solitary in the midst of society, 'hiding within herself in order to laugh at life',[49] is only a more romanticised and less ironically observed paradox than that of which Arnold was keenly aware in himself – the discrepancy between his outer, social gaiety and his inner melancholy. As it can scarcely have been the originality of Lélia's unanswerable query – 'Alas, why has it pleased God to make such a disproportion between man's illusions and the reality?' – which impressed Arnold, it must have been her particular disenchanted tone. The question runs like a sombre thread through Arnold's poetry:

> Why each is striving, from of old,
> To love more deeply than he can?
> Still would be true, yet still grows cold?
> – Ask of the Powers that sport with man!

They yoked in him, for endless strife,
A heart of ice, a soul of fire;
And hurled him on the Field of Life,
An aimless unallayed Desire.

4

When we think of Arnold's poetry it is not normally 'The New Sirens'
or even 'Empedocles' which come to mind. But if we turn to poems
which are much more distinctive of him we shall find that three of his
intrinsic themes – youth and age, the nature of love and the *Zeitgeist* –
were absorbing topics for George Sand also.

It has been frequently noted how very much aware, for a young man,
Arnold was of the passing of youth. Had this been shown in a *carpe diem*
philosophy, or a Keatsian sense of the transience of life and the
imminence of death, it would be easy to ascribe it to his father's early
death and his sense of his own vulnerability. But only in 'Mycerinus'
does anything of this attitude come over. What concerns Arnold much
more is the nature of youth and the total disavowal of its values by age.
He had certainly before his eyes, in Wordsworth, living proof of how
a poet could 'burn to the socket' and gutter away into a cold flicker
of what he had been – but the lesson must also have been driven home
by his early, attentive reading of George Sand. For the contrast between
youth and age, innocence and experience, the 'coeur d'enfant' and the
'coeur flétri' is there on every page of *Lélia*. It is not that Lélia is simply
contrasted with Sténio; she has *been* Sténio. She has known his ardour
and poetic idealism and warmth – but now she is as icily devoid of
emotion as if she were indeed another person. And it is this terrible
metamorphosis which Arnold fears and harps on, continually. Lélia is
at the half-way stage; she still has memories of her youth and is torn
by regret at its passing; she can still pray for 'la force de vivre'; desire
still has its appeal.

When I shall be divorced, some ten years hence,
From this poor present self which I am now; . . .

Then I shall wish its agitations back,
And all its thwarting currents of desire; . . . ('Youth's Agitations')

Her vision of experience is a double one. She sees Trenmor sometimes
as cold and inimical in his renunciation of passion, sometimes as the
desired end of humanity in his wisdom and self-forgetfulness – a state
of beatitude summed up by the word 'calm'. In Book 1 of *Lélia*, the
scene on the lake, with youth at the oars and age at the prow, is the
most persuasive discussion in the book of the wisdom of quiet resigna-

tion; in it man is seen as the note of discordant doubt in the harmony of nature. This passage was a favourite with Victorian readers and was analysed appreciatively by Lewes in one of his reviews. The simple opening, 'The lake was calm that night' brings another more familiar opening to mind, and was no doubt one of the sentences which lingered in Arnold's memory to 'haunt the ear with their cadences'.

Le lac etait calme ce-soir là; calme comme les derniers jours de l'automne, alors que le vent d'hiver n'ose pas encore troubler les flots muets et que les glaïeuls roses de la rive dorment à peine, bercés par de molles ondulations. De pâles vapeurs mangèrent insensiblement les contours anguleux de la montagne et, se laissant tomber sur les eaux, semblèrent reculer l'horizon, qu'elles finirent par faire entièrement disparaître. Alors la surface du lac sembla devenir aussi vaste que celle de la mer . . . La rêverie devint solennelle et profonde, vague comme le lac brumeux, immense comme le ciel sans bornes. Il n'y avait plus dans la nature que les cieux et l'homme, que l'âme et le doute . . .

'Le calme!' dit Trenmor en levant vers le ciel son regard sublime; 'c'est le calme, c'est le plus grand bienfait de la Divinité, c'est l'avenir où tend sans cesse l'âme immortelle, c'est la béatitude! le calme, c'est Dieu!'[50]

And calm can be for Arnold, too, the wished-for state – the time when man is no longer 'Time's chafing prisoner' but has achieved, through resignation, a 'sad lucidity of soul'.

> Weary of myself, and sick of asking
> What I am, and what I ought to be,
> At this vessel's prow I stand, which bears me
> Forwards, forwards o'er the starlit sea.
>
> And a look of passionate desire
> O'er the sea and to the stars I send:
> Ye whom from my childhood up have calmed me,
> Calm me, ah, compose me to the end! . . .
>
> O air borne voice! long since, severely clear,
> A cry like thine in mine own heart I hear:
> 'Resolve to be thyself; and know that he,
> Who finds himself, loses his misery!' ('Self-Dependence')

The calm of self-knowledge, of detachment from the time-stream and from the torment of 'the old unquiet breast', these are the desirable aspects of age. But even as Arnold begs for calm, he fears the loss of intense feeling:

> Calm, calm me more! nor let me die
> Before I have begun to live. ('Lines written in
>   Kensington Gardens')

Always present is the fear of petrifaction, of the narrowing of all the emotional arteries. Lélia has this nightmare awareness: 'Mes yeux sont plus secs que les déserts de sable où la rosée ne tombe jamais et mon coeur est plus sec que mes yeux . . . Tout s'épuise pour moi, tout s'en va . . .'[51] And from one poem to the next Arnold displays the same dual reaction to the loss of youth as George Sand. Images of dryness and sterility which convey age alternate with calm moonlight or still seas, which also represent the answer of experience to tempestuous youth. Old age has impaired Empedocles' 'spirit's strength/And dried its self-sufficing power of joy'. Arnold's old men can be a sorry lot:

> And they remember,
> With piercing, untold anguish,
> The proud boasting of their youth.
> And they feel how Nature was fair.
> And the mists of delusion,
> And the scales of habit,
> Fall away from their eyes;
> And they see for a moment,
> Stretching out, like the desert
> In its weary, unprofitable length,
> Their faded, ignoble lives. ('The Youth of Man')

On 'life's arid mount' it is only youth who can divine the poetic spring. The old man 'rakes among the stones' and finds 'the channel dry'. And just as Lélia, at her most dazzling and apparently successful, has ice at her heart and is like a spectre at life's feast so, in the terrible last stanza of 'Growing Old', Arnold's middle-aged public men sense their alienation from the world and from their former selves:

> It is – last stage of all –
> When we are frozen up within, and quite
> The phantom of ourselves,
> To hear the world applaud the hollow ghost
> Which blamed the living man. ('Growing Old')

And even if such a fate is avoided and the hoped-for calm is achieved, Arnold still bleakly sees how far short it falls of earlier expectations.

Calm's not life's crown, though calm is well
Tis all perhaps which man acquires,
But 'tis not what our youth desires. ('Youth and Calm')

In love, as in life, Arnold's vision is one of unfulfilment and forced compromise, as it also is, strangely enough, in the early novels of George Sand. Strangely, because the strength of her optimism and her profound faith in progress and the ability of man eventually to surmount all obstacles is indeed the dominant impression she has left behind – and is the feature of her writings from which Arnold was later to draw comfort. But in her early works, those first pondered by her young Oxford admirers, human love, though analysed with the tirelessness due to a force of such significance, repeatedly fails to satisfy or to surmount worldly strains. Indeed, *Jacques* had the effect on Tom Arnold of totally depressing him about the possibility of ever achieving a perfect union in this world[52] – an indication of how respectfully receptive these undergraduates were to the teachings of a French-woman of experience. Of the importance and supremacy of love George Sand never had any doubt, and she preached its gospel from her first novel to her last. But its attainment this side of the grave was another matter. Jacques, even as he flings himself into his glacier abyss, is not only a betrayed husband but a disappointed idealist; the dream of love has brought home to him his isolation. Again, in *Lélia*, the question is asked how far it is possible for any lover to distinguish truth from illusion. When Sténio awakens after his night in Pulchérie's arms and hears Lélia's voice below the window, he says 'Je vous vois double. Je vous vois et je vous entends ici près de moi; et je vous entends et je vous vois encore là-bas.'[53] The doubleness of his vision is simply a cruel confirmation of the sombre earlier warning of Lélia, that the lover transforms the object of his adoration to satisfy his own needs.

Nous refusons à Dieu le sentiment de l'adoration . . . Nous le reportons sur un être incomplet et faible, qui devient le dieu de notre culte idolâtre . . . Aussi quand tombe le voile divin et que la créature se montre, chétive et imparfaite, derrière ces nuages d'encens, derrière cette auréole d'amour, nous sommes effrayés de notre illusion, nous en rougissons, nous renversons l'idole et nous la foulons aux pieds.
Et puis nous en cherchons une autre! car il nous faut aimer . . .[54]

The absolute necessity for love and at the same time an awareness of its illusory quality, its 'mimic raptures', are both strong elements in Arnold's poetry. Bonnerot, in commenting upon Arnold's pessimistic denial of the possibility of the union on earth of souls, says 'Love appeared to him more than anything else as a tragic mystery, a source of doubts and infinite torment, as a mystery which becomes confused with, because it reflects, that of life itself.'[55] The poet is aware of the difference between himself and 'happier men'.

>   – for they, at least,
> Have *dreamed* two human hearts might blend
> In one and were through faith released
> From isolation without end
> Prolonged; nor knew, although not less
> Alone than thou, their loneliness. ('Isolation. To Marguerite')

But he is all too aware of the reality:

> We mortal millions live *alone* . . .
> Who ordered, that their longing's fire
> Should be, as soon as kindled, cooled?
> Who renders vain their deep desire? –
> A God, a God their severance ruled!

He is appalled by the way in which one idol can so easily replace another, when the first has disappointed – 'quand . . . nous sommes effrayés de notre illusion . . . nous en cherchons une autre! car il nous faut aimer . . .'

> In this fair stranger's eyes of grey
> Thine eyes, my love! I see.
> I shiver; for the passing day
> Had borne me far from thee. ('Absence')

Arnold's love poems tell of his anguished awareness of the otherness of the beloved, of the lack of real communion:

> Light flows our war of mocking words and yet
> Behold, with tears mine eyes are wet! . . .
> Alas! is even love too weak
> To unlock the heart, and let it speak?
> Are even lovers powerless to reveal
> To one another what indeed they feel? . . .
> Ah! well for us, if even we,
> Even for a moment, can get free
> Our heart, and have our lips unchained; ('The Buried Life')

And yet, despite all its deficiencies and all its illusions, love is still the 'one thing needful'. 'Il n'est qu'un bonheur au monde, c'est l'amour . . . tout marche au gré de ce sentiment qu'on appelle avec raison l'âme du monde . . . mais quand il s'éteint, toute la nudité de la vie réelle reparaît.'⁵⁶ However desperate the clutch – 'Ah, love, let us be true/To one another' – it is the only way, however momentarily, to reach the buried self.

Only – but this is rare –
When a belovèd hand is laid in ours . . .
A bolt is shot back somewhere in our breast,
And a lost pulse of feeling stirs again.
The eye sinks inward, and the heart lies plain,
And what we mean, we say, and what we would, we know.
A man becomes aware of his life's flow,
And hears its winding murmur; and he sees
The meadows where it glides, the sun, the breeze. ('The Buried Life')

The vision of the world from which love provides a temporary respite and defence is similar in both writers. It is also, certainly, the vision of many others – of Stendhal and Carlyle and Balzac, for example – but none of these are concerned like Arnold and George Sand to oppose the aridity of their waste lands with the oasis of human love. What Arnold calls, 'the modern situation in its true *blankness* and *barrenness* and *unpoetrylessness*'⁵⁷ is analysed by George Sand in *Lélia* and *Jacques*. Her mood is one of revulsion from an 'arid and terrible' civilisation which has nothing to commend it. It is, above all, an age of prose; Lélia is described as having 'the profound gaze of a young poet of times gone by, of a poetic age when poetry was not jostled in the throng'.⁵⁸ Whatever achievements are being made in the arts, industry and science are simply a showy way of dissembling the essential spiritual and mental poverty of these unpoetic times. The cry of revolt in the last letters of *Jacques* is against 'the heartless and aimless crowds which vegetate without living'⁵⁹ – all strictures on the *Zeitgeist* which are in tune with Arnold's prose criticism. The final chapter of the revised *Lélia*, 'Délire', which Arnold quotes in his essay, provides a more impassioned, and less localised, cry of despair and impotent suffering. Lélia's vision of the world in its total hopelessness, compares with that of Arnold's of the 'turbid ebb and flow of human misery' in 'Dover Beach'.

J'ai tout cherché, tout souffert, tout cru, tout accepté . . . J'ai demandé à l'amour ses joies, à la foi ses mystères, à la douleur ses mérites . . . Vérité! Vérité! tu ne t'es pas révélée, depuis dix mille ans je te cherche et je ne t'ai pas trouvée!

Et depuis dix mille ans, pour toute réponse à mes cris, pour tout soulagement à mon agonie, j'entends planer sur cette terre maudite le sanglot désespéré du désir impuissant!⁶⁰

These last lines Arnold translated: 'And for ten thousand years, as the sole answer to my cries, as the sole comfort in my agony, I hear astir, over this earth accurst, the despairing sob of impotent agony.' Her poetic vision here is, like his, of a world which has

> neither joy, nor love, nor light,
> Nor certitude, nor peace, nor help for pain;

It is one which moved him deeply and which he never forgot.

5

In the 1840s Arnold was free to pursue his intellectual and cultural enthusiasms and to indulge in his own style of detached mockery. But when, in the next decade, he submerged himself in marriage, domesticity and an amazingly uncongenial career of drudgery, he needed high spirits and resolve of a very different order to sustain him. It would not have been surprising if he had jettisoned authors whom he had relished in his days of irresponsibility. But, in fact, both Senancour and George Sand had too firm a grip on him for that. He never lost his sense of grateful affection and reverence for Senancour, as his biographical note of 1868 to 'Obermann once more' shows. At the same time, it is impossible not to agree with Sainte-Beuve that this is 'un Obermann transfiguré' – delivering a changed message for a changed Arnold. Gone is the icy despair and the *ennui*. Arnold's letter to his sister in 1856 makes it clear that it would have been quite impossible for him to retain his earlier involvement in *Obermann*'s pessimism and still tread his chosen path: 'To make a habitual war on depression and low spirits, which in one's early youth one is apt to indulge and be somewhat interested in is one of the things one learns as one gets older. They are noxious alike to body and mind, and already partake of the nature of death.'[61]

Good health, in body and mind, was indispensable for Arnold to survive his crowded days in the grim buildings of council schools, examining pupils and pupil teachers, meeting headmasters, munching a bun or 'a biscuit which a charitable lady gave me' for lunch, trudging through Battersea mud to his next appointment or snatching a half-hour between trains on a station platform to scribble a letter or read a report, marking piles of grammar papers, which unless he resolutely marked at the rate of twenty-five a day mounted up with terrifying speed to eighty or ninety a day and swamped his Christmas break. To endure such an existence Obermannism had to be put on one side and eventually restated in a less debilitating form.

He does not, however, have to rewrite George Sand, for she too left her days of *Lélia* behind and passed through different phases until she achieved serenity, faith in meliorism and her own form of undogmatic religion. Unlike Senancour, she is not a one-book writer, and Arnold continued to read her, as his *Notebooks* show, at the rate of at least one a year throughout the 1850s and 1860s. One gets the impression that he remained a faithful reader of everything she wrote, however mediocre, and that often he took a novel of hers away on holiday with him to Fox How, but that she did not impinge actively and strongly upon his consciousness again until her death. There are many old favourites but no *new* quotations entered from her novels in his *Notebooks* in the 1860s. One side of him may well have felt her to be outdated – 'a fat old Muse' – but the other side of him, which prompted him to go on reading her, still felt drawn to her personality.

As is well known, these *Notebooks* consist of fragments that Arnold shored up against his backsliding and faltering – or, more positively, they are a storehouse of odd lines and passages which had struck him in his reading and which he felt he could use and return to. His mild rebuke to a working man at Bedford who wrote to him in 1872 about 'useful knowledge' is relevant to the nature of the *Notebooks'* utility: 'And as to useful knowledge a single line of poetry working in the mind may produce more thoughts and lead to more light, which is what man wants, than the fullest acquaintance (to take your own instance) with the processes of digestion.'[62]

The quotations are taken from works written in seven different languages and spanning 3,000 years, and the vast majority of them are from philosophical or religious writings. Over 500 different authors have been quarried, and it is strange to find a romantic novelist in such prominence. The Bible, St Thomas à Kempis and Goethe are far ahead of the field – but then come Sainte-Beuve, Renan and George Sand representing France, out-distancing by many lengths Plato and Epictetus and Cicero. When one investigates more closely the sentiments which Arnold has most often jotted down – each repetition obviously increasing the significance for him – they are often seen to be confirmations of a position or attitude or resolve that Arnold has already taken rather than new directives. When, at the age of thirty-eight, Arnold read *La Daniella*, he extracted several sentences from it but the phrase which he pounced on and wrote in his *Notebooks* six more times in the years that followed was a very simple one: 'les saines habitudes de la maturité'. He placed this phrase on the January page of several of the *Notebooks* that followed, in the company of other equally bracing exhortations such as 'Rien n'augmente autant le découragement que l'oisiveté' (Joubert); 'Rien ne sauve dans cette vie-ci que l'occupation et le travail' (Bonstatten); 'Semper aliquid certi proponendum est' (St Thomas). This shows not only that he derived comfort from the fact that George Sand, the preceptor of his youth, could give him different rules for his middle-age, but that he used her to spur his flagging spirits. Nothing could be more sharply opposed to the mood of Pater than the temper of Arnold which comes through in his *Notebooks*. When Pater suggests that it is a sign of failure in man if he forms habits, he is undermining the mid-Victorian sense of ordered purpose which Arnold so deliberately cultivated. It is indeed open to question how healthy the habits of Arnold's maturity were, when they constrained him so often to enter in his *Notebooks* such a determined little resolution as this: 'up before 7 & Greek daily. no sleeping. to put down each day's work before hand before dinner arrange for things after',[63] but it is obvious that Arnold needed all the fortifying he could get, whether from George Sand or the Psalms, in his daily conduct, his 'three fourths of life'. His admiration for her as a worker as well as an artist is touching. 'She continued at work till she died. For forty-five years she was writing and publishing and filled Europe with her name.'[64] George Sand's strict writing routine, her relentless night work which drove de Musset to desperation and incurred the scorn of the de Goncourts certainly would not have impressed Arnold adversely. A long extract which he made in 1860 from *L'Homme de Neige* was simply homely counsel against being too easily discouraged by a sense of having wasted time in the past. 'You're still young enough' the message ran 'to recover lost ground. Anyone who's not feeble and ailing can work twelve hours a day.'[65]

When George Sand died, Arnold's immediate feeling was one of loss, and a sense that he must pay her tribute. He wrote to his sister: 'Her death has been much in my mind; she was the greatest spirit in our European world from the time that Goethe departed. With all her faults and her Frenchism, she was this. I must write a few pages about her.'[66] Thirty years earlier 'Frenchism' had been a positive asset; now it was something to be condoned. A year later the article was still not completed, but she had begun to work her spell on him again: 'G. Sand is beginning to weigh upon me greatly, though she also interests me very much; the old feeling of liking for her and refreshment from her, in spite of her faults, comes back.'[67] And from then till his death eleven years later his reading lists show his reawakened interest in her works.

The publication of F. W. Myers's long article on George Sand in *The Nineteenth Century* in April 1877 may well have spurred Arnold on not only to write as full an assessment of his debt to her as possible, but to take her really seriously again. For Myers certainly did so, and Arnold solemnly summarised in his *Notebooks* what Myers felt had been George Sand's main preoccupations:

Religious aspiration and unselfish love should form the spirit of life; its substance is best filled out by practical devotion to some impersonal ideal; the scientific or meditative observation of nature, the improvement of the conditions of the people or the realisation of our visionary conceptions in a sincere and noble art.[68]

These heavy features do not make for a very recognisable George Sand – some of her more worldly and unregenerate aspects seem to be missing – but quite obviously it was a face which was congenial to Arnold, and if one looks closely at it one sees that each part, though not perhaps in the usual place, does indeed belong to her.

It is interesting that in his essay Arnold agrees with Myers's surprisingly high estimate of *Valvèdre* (1861), a novel which he had mentioned nowhere else. This book is really *Jacques* thirty years after. The disastrous marriage this time is between a romantic, demanding young wife and her distinguished, scientist husband. He is one of George Sand's reasonable, wise older men who opposes the self-indulgent passion of his wife and her equally romantic lover and who has no intention, unlike Jacques, of committing suicide for love. It is easy to see what must have appealed in the book to Arnold.

In the first place the narrator is looking back over twenty years, as Arnold could also, to his youthful love-affair in Switzerland, 'son drâme intérieur', in its Alpine surroundings, and is placing in perspective the *maladie du siècle* of youth – the *ennui*, the doubts, the arrogance. He and the young wife had been caught up in an 'orage de délices', and in their romantic exaltation had been impervious to reason or conscience. The entire novel is a warning against man making himself and his emotional life the centre of his universe; 'sortir de soi' is George Sand's message. Disinterested knowledge, through intellectual analysis and introspection, and not the over-subtilising of the human spirit, is man's primary need. Such a plea for detached objectivity was bound to strike Arnold favourably. In fact he might have written the following sentence from *Valvèdre* himself: 'Les calmes et saintes puissances de l'étude sont nécessaires à notre équilibre, à notre raison, permettez-moi de le dire aussi, à notre moralité.'[69] An Arnoldian version might have been: 'The strength of study is that it makes for those qualities of righteousness and calm which are essential for our disinterestedness, our reason, and if I may say so, also for our morality.' And certainly what does come through strongly in his 1877 article, apart from his emotional bond with George Sand, is a renewed sense of her relevance to the interests of his later years. Trilling sums up the essay well:

> If with this sentiment [idealism] George Sand had fired Arnold's youth, with it she also fortified his age. Her passionate idealism, her concern 'not with death but with life', her devotion to bringing about a social new-birth, her belief that only by the principle of association could man live, her faith in the Revolution, her certainty that social

change was a religious duty: these affirmations Arnold found on the occasion of her death as valid as they ever had been; they were, he said, 'the large utterances of the early gods'.[70]

In the years that followed, extracts in his *Notebooks* with the familiar initials G.S. occur very frequently. All are marked by the qualities he most appreciated in her – her lack of acrimony, her faith in goodness and her ability to detach herself – and all the most frequently-quoted advocate virtues that he himself tried to inculcate. 'Rien ne s'arrangera plus en ce monde que par la raison et l'équité, la patience, le savoir, le dévouement et la modestie';[71] 'En toutes choses, il n'y a pas à dire, il faut s'arranger pour voir de haut';[72] 'Ce qu'il m'apprit de plus précieux fut de m'habituer à me connaître moi-même et à réfléchir sur mes impressions.'[73] Perhaps the most convincing evidence of Arnold's revived addiction to George Sand was his reading – possibly even re-reading – of *Spiridion* in 1882 and entering no fewer than thirty-two extracts in his *Notebooks*, the greatest number from one book in any single year. This mystical work of 1839, written under the powerful influence of Lamennais, is one which makes even devotees flinch. Myers had singled it out in his essay as being 'almost unreadable except by religious enquirers', and when it first came out Thackeray had mocked it in his article, 'Madame Sand and the New Apocalypse'. The *Westminster Review*, always kindly towards intellectual effort, had praised it as containing within the form of a novel, 'a review of the principal speculations, religious and metaphysical which have extensively influenced the civilised world since the advent of Christianity.'[74] It is an allegory of the soul in search of the true faith which has long ago been revealed to Spiridion, the founder of the monastery, and which lies buried in his tomb in a small parchment manuscript. This manuscript – dismissed by Thackeray as 'of all dull, vague, windy documents that mortals ever set eyes on this is the dullest'[75] – expresses the belief, at some length, that man is born to martyrdom but is gradually evolving to a better state. A wicked quotation in the *Quarterly Review* article of 1877 conveys something of the quality of inflated earnestness of this book 'about priests, monks and the well-being of the soul'.[76]

' "So father," said I, "we are no longer Catholics?" "Nor Christians" he said, in a firm voice; "no, nor Protestants" he added, as he clasped my hand "nor philosophers like Voltaire, Helvetius and Diderot; we are not even Socialists like Jean Jacques and for all that we are neither pagans nor Theists!" "What are we then, Father Alexis?" I asked . . .'[77] And so does the bewildered reader without getting any satisfactory reply.

But perhaps because Arnold was a 'religious enquirer' as well as an admirer of George Sand, and possessed of a life-long interest in monasteries and cloisters, he managed to pick his way through the maze of mysticism and extract from the book a remarkably large number of sound, sensible warnings and exhortations which he jotted down, – warnings against laziness, indifference, worldliness, the desire for too rapid results, whether in education or social change, and exhortations to justice, love, purity of heart, faith in poetry and the arts, equality, some sort of religious belief and above all hope. Earlier he had quoted approvingly George Sand's point that 'the philosopher underlies any artist of real value', and by the end of his days the philosopher in George Sand had for him almost completely taken over from the artist. So much so that one surprising *Notebooks* entry is 'G.S. and Epict. on happiness'.[78]

In 1888, before his sudden death, he was reading and enjoying one volume after another of her correspondence, reading her 'Tales of a Grandmother', planning an article on 'The Old Age of George Sand' and speaking to his niece of his wish to make a small volume, 'such a little one', of George Sand's best letters. From first to last, apart perhaps from a brief hesitation around 1859, George Sand had been magically exempt from any moral disapproval from Arnold; from any taint of French 'lubricity'. There is a revealing inscription, in his own handwriting, on the fly-leaf of his copy of *Impressions et Souvenirs*. It is a quotation from the first chapter of *Mauprat*: 'Dans l'impression qu'elle m'a faite il se mêle quelque chose de si consolant . . . et de si sain à l'âme.'[79] It is not often in research that a voice speaks from the grave quite so helpfully. It is only telling us what Arnold's public tributes to George Sand, and his choice of quotations from her works also tell us but it is a touching, private assessment, in his maturity, of the nature of his debt to her. George Sand, who had the tendency all her life to turn her admirers into her children, to give them solace instead of passion, seems to have contrived the same feat with Arnold.

7 'Citizen Clough'

1

If Clough's letters to Matthew Arnold had survived, there would have been a more substantial record of his feelings about George Sand than is now available. But the hints in Arnold's letters as well as the extant references to novels in Clough's correspondence add up to an impressive list – *André, Indiana, Valentine, Jacques, Mauprat, Consuelo, Jeanne, Le Meunier, La Mare, François le Champi*, and *Teverino*. There is no mention of *Lélia* or *Lettres d'un Voyageur*, but the fact that Clough was able to answer a query from his sister about 'the suitability' of *Le Sécretaire Intime*, that early, fantastic tale, adds substance to Veyriras's claim[1] that Clough had probably read almost all George Sand had written before 1848. Most advanced young men at Oxford read her novels, and Froude, looking back on his relationship with Clough, comments 'We had read Rousseau and Louis Blanc and George Sand';[2] but Matthew and Tom Arnold were especial enthusiasts.

When Tom Arnold decided in 1847 to emigrate to New Zealand, he whiled away the tedium of the long sea voyage by writing a sort of *apologia pro exitus suus*. In the so-called *Equator Letters* he attempted to justify to his friends his decision to emigrate and to give some account of his spiritual history up to that time. Letter 3, which is headed *At Sea. The John Wycliffe, Jan 11, 1848*, is extraordinarily revealing: he comments that one of the really important events in his life has been his acquaintance with her writings; he had never seen her but he must 'ever revere and love her with a more than filial affection. For she who brings light to the soul and, in making it see its duty gives peace to the troubled conscience – what love does not she deserve – what sacrifice may not she exact?'

He goes on to record that it was his brother Matthew who admired her first and that he himself had been slower to appreciate her, as he was too much of an admirer of Coleridge and German thought to give sufficient attention to French writers. He had enjoyed *Mauprat* but had disliked *Horace*; it was when he read *Indiana* first that it began to dawn on him that

. . . here was genius indeed: that a great and noble heart was here breathing out its cry of agony. Yet . . . it was not till I read *Jacques* that my interest was completely excited both in the book and the writer. There was something in the divine stoicism of Jacques which was perhaps congenial to my nature, and the fate of his love impressed me with sad forebodings . . . In the age in which we live and in the society in which we move there is a curse on love and marriage for those who will not bow the knee to the world's laws; those who have resolved to put away illusions and to live for truth.

Gradually, thanks be to God and George Sand, the interpreter of His truth, I found that this misery . . . was altogether an outrage and an offence in the sight of God . . . that man had done it, by force of iniquitous laws and social customs, but chiefly through the absence of the spirit of Love. With inexpressible joy I read and pondered upon the sacred symbol, 'Freedom, Equality, Brotherhood'.[3]

Clough's response to George Sand is nearer to the earnestness of Tom than the aestheticism of Matthew. Her views on socialism and feminism, on religion and sex, were not only liberating and challenging for him at the time but continued to ferment in his 'speculating brain' throughout the decade. His reading of her did not even end, as so many things did, with his marriage, for in 1855 he is recommending, if somewhat tepidly, her latest book, *Histoire de ma Vie*, to Emerson.[4]

It can, I think, very fairly be said of Clough that he *approved* of George Sand much less than he did of Carlyle and Emerson, the other two idols of the group – although even this may be going too far, for it is difficult ever to detect an absolutely consistent stance in Clough. Only in *Amours de Voyage* do we have a sense of a total, sophisticated control of his vision – both of his hero and of society. But for the most part irreconcilables stay irreconciled for Clough, and in no sphere is this truer than in his attitude to sex. It was Clough's peculiar accomplishment, as his exasperated friends so often testified, to be able to approve and disapprove, affirm and deny simultaneously – and George Sand provided him with much to exercise his talents upon. Socialism and religion were topics on which he found himself largely in agreement with her; in sexual matters his reaction was much more complex.

George Sand was an idealist about love all her life. Even the *ennui* and despair of *Lélia* are the reaction of a disappointed idealist. Love, by which she means affection and tenderness as well as physical passion, is for her the transforming force of life and the only surety. At the same time, she is tolerant of the frailties of men and women and never, in all her century of romances, makes an emotional crisis out of a straightforward lapse.

Both her idealism and her tolerance had, as we shall see, a very definite appeal for Clough, although he was capable of reacting with puritanical self-righteousness when confronted by hedonism and the flesh in actual life. When he is travelling in Scotland in 1845 and meets first Walrond's two sisters and then Shairp's five, his comments on them are repressively priggish:

I like the whole family very fairly, and they are extremely kind and hospitable. The hours are disgracefully late and they dance and play to excess, it would seem.[5]

I . . . like the sisterhood considerably. But their gaieties perpetual must be very pernicious; and I wonder that they are not worse than they are with them.[6]

He is taken by the Shairp family to see Taglioni and writes: '. . . may I never be carried again to the ballet! It is really strange that matrons and maidens delicately nurtured, not to speak of daughter-delighting-in papas should patronise such sights . . .'[7]

Clough's disapproval of Taglioni's professional display of her calves – 'this *callida surarum ostentatrix*' – contrasts with his rollicking enjoyment of the flesh in *The Bothie of Tober-na-Vuolich*, in which the nether regions of Clough's healthy young men and women are constantly on display – the high-kilted lasses of Dundee:

Petticoats up to their knees, or even it might be above them
Matching their lily-white legs with the clothes they trod in the
    wash-tub: (II. 110–11)

Lindsay, 'Hyperion of calves':

Hobbes, briefest kilted of heroes . . .
Him see I frisking and whisking and ever at swifter gyration
Under brief curtain revealing broad acres – not of broad cloth:
    (IV. 89–93)

or, Hobbes again, going for a bathe:

. . . in heavy pea-coat his trouserless trunk enfolding,
. . . under coat overbrief those lusty legs displaying. (V. 17–18)

What can be relished in literature, of course, is not always palatable in life, and even Geraldine Jewsbury, who was much more unconventional than Clough, commented to Jane Carlyle that 'When brothers and friends are in question, how differently one sees things to what one does in abstract cases of "George Sandism."' '[8] Prim about his friends' sisters, Clough was prepared to be judicious and tolerant about George

Sand: 'What one has heard of the actual life of Mad. Dudevant is certainly so far as it goes, agst. her in this respect [purity]. Howbeit I encline to think her a Socrates amongst the Sophists.'[9]

Despite his misgivings, he is prepared to ignore George Sand's private life because in her novels, she is, like Socrates, asking fundamental questions – some of which were concerned with sex, which was, after all, an important preoccupation of Clough's poetry. However much Clough repressed his sexual instincts in his daily life, a poem like 'Natura Naturans' affirms as frankly as any passage in the pages of George Sand the kindling of sexual awareness between a young man and woman. The stirrings of passion, the vibrations which pass between two people who a moment before were strangers – these were harmonies which the 'troubadour of love' herself had made use of, time without number: Valentine, for instance, sits close by Benedict without exchanging a word, but each is alive to the other's presence:

> Valentine . . . resta ainsi, sous le charme de ce fluide eléctrique qui à son âge et à celui de Benedict . . . a tant de puissance et de magie! Ils ne se dirent rien, ils n'osèrent échanger ni un sourire ni un mot. Valentine resta fascinée à sa place, Benedict s'oublia dans la sensation d'un bonheur impétueux . . .[10]

But Clough describes the brief encounter – or, to use a favourite word of his, juxtaposition – in the second class railway carriage with much more humour than George Sand would ever have brought to bear on the subject:

> Beside me in the car she sat
> She spake not, no, nor looked to me:
> From her to me from me to her
> What passed so subtly, stealthily?

Clough has no inclination to answer his question with 'the mystic name of Love'. What both are feeling is 'desire' and, with bravura imagery and light-hearted alliteration, he describes the invasion of their bodies 'fused in one' by the forces of the natural kingdom. They are aware of 'the feeblest stir of the lichen' – the strange sensation of the lily growing to pendant head 'in me and her' – and the glad movements of the animal world

> Flashed flickering forth fantastic flies,
> Big bees their burly bodies swung,
> Rooks roused with civic din the elms,
> And lark its wild reveillez rung.
> In Libyan dell, the light gazelle,
> The leopard lithe in Indian glade,

And dolphin, brightening tropic seas,
In us were living, leapt and played.

Clough's debt in this poem is a complex one – to Spinoza, to
Emerson's pantheism, and to recent evolutionary theories[11] – but what
gives it life and strength is his acknowledgement not only of his own
sexuality, but of that of the young woman whose body has come into
unwitting contact with his, and his ability to invest the moment with
a touch of fantastic comedy. It is no wonder that Clough's wife,
Blanche, hated the poem, tried to suppress it and did not feel that it
was 'necessary to an understanding of his mind'.[12] It was certainly not
necessary to an understanding of Clough's later domesticity, but it does
show the side of him which his reading of George Sand must have
helped to liberate in his Oriel years.

The same preoccupation with the rights of the flesh is shown in an
interesting Latin dialogue of his Oxford days to which R. K. Biswas
draws attention. It is *Addenda ad Apocalypsin Secundum Interpretationem
Vulgatam* and is a 500-word addition by Clough to the Book of
Revelations, in the form of a dream. The dreamer is introduced by 'the
Spirit' to her sister, Pandemia, who, unlike herself, has 'body and flesh
and limbs and substance', and he is told 'Come take her and lie with
her for it is not possible to lie with me'. And in the Babylonian streets
the dreamer calls out to Pandemia to come to him, and he sees standing
before him a tall, well-developed woman, about thirty years of age,
who tells him: 'Blessed are those who lie with me . . . I am the life and
the way and the truth. He who has me does not walk in darkness; he
who is without me is wholly in darkness and dares neither to do good
nor evil.' But the dreamer protests, weeping, that he is spirit and cannot
lie with flesh. To which Pandemia answers 'Come and try and see'. But
the dreamer, in anguish, calls on God for help. And there was a silence
in heaven and earth and after the space of a day, in the evening, the
dreamer saw a woman in white raiment who came up to him and took
his hand and said ' "I am your fellow servant" . . . And I looked in her
face and said, "Are you not Pandemia whom I called on and with
whom I talked?" And she said, "I am your fellow-servant, the servant
of the most high, creator of everything . . . Come let us serve together
. . ." And the Spirit and the Virgin said Come.'[13]

It is an intriguing document, partly because there are so many
echoes of the Apocalypse, partly because of the debt to the *Symposium*
in the two Aphrodites, the heavenly Aphrodite and the common Eros
Pandemos, but also because it is reminiscent of the climactic scene in
Lélia in which the earthly, sensual Pulchéria is introduced to the bed
of the idealistic young poet in the pavilion of Aphrodite by her un-
attainable sister. Sténio too protests vehemently that he is spiritual and

not physical, and there is the same aura of sanctification surrounding Lélia and the confusing blending and merging of the sisters. The resolution of the dialogue, representing human love as fellow-service, is in accord with George Sand's humanitarian philosophy, which appealed to Clough very much. I would disagree with Biswas's interpretation of the dialogue as 'semi-facetious'; it shows the sort of earnest sexuality and reverence for the claims of the flesh which is found in both Kingsley and Coventry Patmore, and can be seen as an answer both to the stress of Revelations on the abominations of fornication and the disillusionment with physical love of *Lélia*.

Clough could be as healthily distrustful as George Sand of over-emotionalism about sexual shortcomings in women. He thought Mrs Gaskell's *Ruth*, the story of an unmarried mother, 'rather cowardly and "pokey" in its views . . . She has not got the whole truth – I do not think that such an overpowering humiliation should be the result in the soul of the not really guilty though misguided girl any more than it should be, justly, in the judgement of the world.'[14] This is the sort of advanced view that George Eliot also expressed in reading the book – but it was a far from common reaction. Mrs Gaskell was either vilified or lauded, and feelings ran high. 'Not really guilty though misguided' – Clough's verdict is very much the same as that passed by George Sand's heroine, Jeanne, on her friend and fellow-servant, Claudie, who had succumbed to her lover's seductions, and has been deserted by him. Jeanne is pure herself and determined to remain so, but she consoles Claudie, with her matter-of-fact acceptance of her loss of chastity:

> You must cheer up, Claudie . . . All that doesn't prevent you from being a good girl, who works well and who can still be loved by a respectable man. Your misfortune is one which has happened to many others and it's not such a great wrong when it's been done through good nature and affection.[15]

It was of this book that Clough wrote to Burbridge:

> I have found time in the last three days to read 'Jeanne par George Sand', the most cleanly French novel I ever read, and not cleanly only but pure . . . If I knew French well enough and was not a college tutor I would translate it; and I believe it would take, – for one thing the hero is an Englishman, and by no means a common but a very veritable kind of hero.[16]

We shall look more closely at the novel later to see just what elements in it so appealed to Clough that he would have contemplated translating it, had he not had his reputation and responsibility as an Oxford tutor to think of, but its blend of romantic idealism and common sense where love was concerned was bound to appeal to him. What was always totally lacking in George Sand's treatment of sexual relationships was the sense of guilt or sin, which infinitely complicated Clough's own emotional responses. R. K. Biswas has summed up his position well:

> Clough's dilemma, as a thinker, as a man, lies in his inability to reject either of the contrary logics which grew out of his self-scrutiny . . . His predicament . . . is that of a man who asserts the goodness of man, of nature, of the flesh and the world, and in the same tortured breath confesses their contaminating corruptness.[17]

His vision of the relationship of men and women can suddenly become reductive: 'And as I go on my way I behold them consorting and coupling' – or deliberately magnified: 'Through the great sinful streets of Naples as I passed.' He can convey the neurotic guilt of the self-tormenting lover: 'No, Great Unjust God! she is purity; I am the lost one'; or the exaggerated masochism of the unfaithful husband:

The lamps appeared to fling a baleful glare,
A brazen heat was heavy in the air;
And it was hell, and he some unblest wanderer there. ('Mari Magno')

And, quite unexpectedly, his idealism will be undermined by cynicism and disillusionment, as in 'Dipsychus':

> O pretty girl who tripst along,
> Come to my bed – it isn't wrong.
> Uncork the bottle, sing the song . . .
> Speak, outraged maiden, in thy wrong
> Did terror bring no secret bliss?
> Were boys' shy lips worth half a song
> Compared to the hot soldier's kiss? . . .

Clough's guilty vision of gas-lit street scenes in which 'dressy girls slithering-by upon pavements give sign for accosting' is so alien to that of George Sand that in some moods he must have turned to her pages as an escape from his own dark imaginings. For she was the actual 'sinner', with the serene and clear conscience, who never cast herself in the role of the evil doer, who believed in the holiness of the heart's and body's affections and who could write a book which was not only 'cleanly' but 'cleanly and pure'. These reiterations throw more light on Clough himself indeed than on the novel.

2

'A novel ought to make you think'[18] wrote Clough to his sister Anne in 1847, in one of the many letters of advice and literary talk which passed between them. Involved in the 1830s and 1840s in all the philanthropic and educational pursuits which marked the tentative beginnings of feminism for young girls, Anne Clough talked a great deal with her brother on the topics which made *him* think – religion, woman's role, social inequality – and as these were all to be found developed in the novels of George Sand, she read what he read: not, of course, without first asking his advice. His reply to her query about *Le Sécretaire Intime* is typical of his dilemma about womanhood: '. . . I dare say it will do no harm to your morals or anyone else's; but I never know what exactly to say; men are obliged to go through the mud, while women may keep the causeway.'[19] But later he has obviously given her the free run of his library: 'Haven't you unpacked my boxes? The George Sand is [in] one of them . . .'[20]

Clough was not drawn to books which held forth, like *Corinne*, on the 'high beauty-beatification line, Italy and Art and love à L'Aesthetique'.[21] He longed for a 'genuine live-and-act story' and George Sand's socialist novels of the 1840s, while still carrying a heavy weight of romantic idealism, expounded doctrines congenial to him which he could certainly have recommended to his sister with less hesitation than the meretricious and fantastic tale, *Le Sécretaire Intime*. For what, quite apart from her uninhibited views on love, seized the imagination of George Sand's Oxford admirers was her heart-warming belief in democracy, in the dignity of labour, in the equality of landowner and peasant, in a religion free from all dogma, superstition, priests and miracles, in man and woman as fellow-labourers in the cause of humanity, equal in intellect and opportunity but still retaining their own strengths and virtues.

This outline of George Sand's doctrines is equally a résumé of Clough's most cherished ideas. These are concerns which have little to do with the Clough of *Amours de Voyage*, but they have a great deal to do with the Clough who gave up his post at Oxford, mainly because of conscientious scruples, but no doubt also because Oxford was so palpably not of the progressive, reforming world; who argued the case for the equality of peasants with lords and ladies at the Decade, the Oxford debating society, and in a pamphlet questioned the conception of property as an 'inalienably personal, individual thing'; who rejected, with some violence, his betrothed's sentimental belief in 'Love is everything' as 'fond foolishness' and asked her in Lawrentian terms to be, in reality, his 'help-mate' – 'I will ask no one to put off her individuality for me; nor will I, weak and yielding as I am, if I can help it, put off mine for anyone';[22] and the 'Citizen Clough, Oriel Lyceum, Oxford', as Arnold addressed him, who went off to Paris for five weeks in 1848 to see the revolution at close quarters. All these sides of Clough are catered for in George Sand's writings. This is not to say that he was not sensitive to every breath that blew on him – to Dr Arnold and Carlyle and Emerson and Goethe and Strauss and Spinoza, to name only a few of his masters. But what is interesting about George Sand as a source and stimulus for Clough is that she impinges upon his preoccupations at so many points, and had the entrée to his emotional life in a way that none of the others had, except possibly Goethe.

Perhaps because one side of Clough was sentimental and romantic he shared, in a way Arnold did not, George Sand's faith in 'the people'. In March 1848, Arnold wrote testily to Clough of George Sand's *Lettres au Peuple*: 'I have G. Sand's Letter – do you want it? I do not like it as well as at first. For my soul I cannot *understand* this violent praise of the people. I praise a faggot where-of the several twigs are nought; but a people?'[23]

The 1848 revolution was, in fact, something of a tourist attraction for France's English well-wishers. In April, Jowett, Palgrave, Stanley and Forster visited Paris, and in May Clough crossed the Channel and found that his visit coincided with that of Emerson, Monckton Milnes, Geraldine Jewsbury – 'fidgety-feverish' – and the Paulets. Clough's letters give a sharp and dispassionate picture of the last few confused weeks of a failed revolution. After a fortnight of enthusiasm he became detached, like Claude in Rome, pottering 'about under the Tuileries Chestnuts and here and there about bridges and under streets, pour savourer la République',[24] reading all about it in his halfpenny newspaper in the cafés, and casting an ironic eye on the spectacle of political expediency, bourgeois cunning and revolutionary greed. The scene provided little nourishment for his own utopianism and radical- ism as he saw 'Liberty, Equality and Fraternity, driven back by the shop-keeping bayonet.' He was not the only disappointed idealist. He wrote to Stanley: 'George Sand has gone into the country: she says that the air of Paris seemed lourde to her after hearing the *à-bas* of the Nat. Guard, and after the arrests of so many generous-minded men . . .'[25] And he wrote to Tom Arnold, who he knew would be interested, that her paper, *La Vraie République*, had been suppressed but that he had read three articles she had written on 'the religion, dogma and worship of France', the views in which were obviously more congenial to him than Emerson's:

The dogma very boldly eliminating everything miraculous from the Gospel History, leaving personality with prophetic and exalted physical power to Xt. Yet retaining a Liberty-Equality-Fraternity Gospel as Xty. Emerson is unequivocally pagan but dislikes con- troversy. His most pure disciple is a certain Mrs. Paulet (friend to Mrs. Carlyle and to Miss Jewsbury, her of Zoë).[26]

Despite his disillusionment with the Revolution, Clough studied the newspapers well and pondered the reports, not only on workmen's pay and unemployment benefit but on the radical divorce bill, which suggested divorce for incompatibility of temper 'if the man be above 25, the woman above 21 and under 45.' He also attended a meeting of the *Club des Femmes* which was to discuss the projected bill, and was disgusted by the 'unpolitesse of Frenchmen . . . or say beasts' to the chairwoman:

Occupying the seats reserved for women – laughing and shouting – greedily seizing and creating doubles-entendres etc. etc. However Mad. Niboyer is a woman of considerable power and patience, and she works through it: though to what effect I don't know. Perhaps it may be useful for Frenchmen to see a woman face them and present herself before them *not* for purposes of flirtation.[27]

His discussions over dinner with Emerson often touched upon the state of women and, Emerson commented, Clough talked 'so considerately of the grisette estate' that he impressed him as 'the best pièce de résistance and tough adherence that one could desire'.[28]

Three months later, Clough's blend of chivalry and feminism, of democratic radicalism and romantic idealism found its expression in *The Bothie of Tober-na-Vuolich*.

For much of the inspiration of *The Bothie* one need, of course, look no further than Clough's immediate background and the many reading parties he had taken as tutor, either to the Lake District or the Highlands of Scotland. The atmosphere of the whole of this 'modern poem' is one of easy familiarity and enjoyment; the in-jokes, the slang, the academic banter between the undergraduates, the early morning bathes in the nearby river, the dinner after the Highland games, the reels and skirling of the pipes at the inn – Clough's letters are full of similar details. His friends could recognise their own features in those of the characters, and it is quite possible that the Elspie love-affair was based on his own experience. For not only do his letters of 1846 to his sister hint that he may marry and give a glimpse of a shy, modest girl, but in *Mari Magno*, in the last year of his life, he gives another version of a Highland love affair; only this time it is between a tutor and Scots girl, not an undergraduate, and it does not end happily. Even the lochs, glens and mountains figure as dramatically in his correspondence as in the poem: 'Here, in Badenoch, here in Lochaber anon, in Lochiel, in/Knoydart, Moydart, Morrer, Ardgower and Ardnamurchan/Here I see him and here . . .' (IV. 15–17). This *envoi* to Oxford, spontaneous and sensuous in its hexameters, welcomed by his peers for (in Emerson's words) 'this wealth of expression, this wealth of imagery, this joyful heart of youth',[29] is first and foremost a poem arising out of Clough's own history.

But having said that, it is also undeniable that there is a very real literary inspiration also. George Sand's *Jeanne* is the source most often referred to because of Clough's enthusiasm for it – but its philosophy of social levelling is found in most of her novels of the 1840s, and even a novel as early as *André* (1835) expresses very democratic ideas about marriage.

She was concerned in *André*, she said, with 'la poésie des humbles' and this book, like *The Bothie*, is a blend of sentimentality and energetic realism. The main thread is the love affair between Geneviève, a tender, loving, studious little *grisette*, and André, the son of a prosperous estate owner, the Marquis de Moreau. He first catches sight of her gathering flowers for her trade in the meadows, for she makes artificial flowers. This sweet idyll, which has Perdita overtones and leads inevitably to much discussion on art and nature, is conducted against a background of determined class feuding between the other young workwomen, who are bold, flirtatious and gossiping, and the Marquis, who is feudal and maddened by their assumption of equality with him. The atmosphere of the district and its customs, with cabals of *grisettes* going from one big house to the next, spending weeks doing all the sewing jobs required, then moving on, carrying with them all the scandal, comes over well – as does the vigorous account of a clandestine outing arranged for all the *grisettes* by André in his father's *char-à-banc*. After it is over, they rampage over the Marquis's flower borders, break branches off his fruit trees and steal his fruit – while he revenges himself on them by lying down on the sofa, crushing their finery with his muddy boots and locking up the *char-à-banc* so that they have to walk home. Without this background of class warfare, the tale would be one of feeble idealism, although it was through its sentiment that it made its appeal to most of its English readers, and even gained a word of grudging praise from Croker.

Ten years later, in *Jeanne*, George Sand's socialism is much more decisive, for she makes her hero not a romantic, rather spineless, youth but a mature man. Her 'very veritable hero', as Clough called him, is Sir Arthur Harley, a real English milord, who from his first appearance expresses the views of a radical humanitarian. As he and his friends survey the uncultivated moorland, in which the superstitious country folk believe treasure is buried, he comments, in his laconic French, which always amuses the others, that there is indeed treasure in the earth but that:

. . . il faut un autre trésor pour l'en retirer.
'Oui, des capitaux!' dit Marsillat.

'Et des paysans!' ajouta Guillaume. 'Cette terre est dépeuplée.'

'*Des hommes et puis des hommes,*' reprit l'Anglais.

'Comprends pas,' dit Guillaume en souriant, à Marsillat.

'Pas de maîtres et pas de'esclaves; des hommes et des hommes,' reprit Sir Arthur, étonné de n'avoir pas été compris, lui qui croyait parler clair.

'Est-ce qu'il y a des esclaves en France?' s'écria Marsillat en haussant les épaules.

'Oui, et en Angleterre aussi,' répondit l'Anglais sans se déconcerter.

'La philosophie m'ennuie' reprit à demi-voix Marsillat en s'addressant à son jeune compatriote 'votre Anglais me dégouterait d'être libéral.'[30]

What Sir Arthur says in Chapter 1 has become even the superstitious Jeanne's conviction by the last chapter, and her dying message is the same as his: the riches of the earth are there for the taking if men will labour together and cultivate the barren places. If this doctrine had been all that the novel had to offer, Clough would have been as well served by *Past and Present*, with its moving picture of the wealth of England, the golden harvests ungathered by workers denied the right to labour. But Carlyle's 'Am I not a man and brother?' was not to be taken literally as a gospel of equality; all it meant was that he was convinced of the dignity of physical labour for those whose lot in life it was to labour. George Sand, like Morris later, was idealistic about physical labour for everyone and her form of communism, or rather, communionism, was at the other political pole from Carlyle's beliefs. Echoes of her sentiments are heard again and again in the letters of Tom Arnold, that utopian enthusiast, as well as in the poetry of Clough, and are certainly not such as Carlyle would ever have accepted. Her hero, Sir Arthur, not only admires Jeanne, the ignorant country girl, who is as strong, strapping and hard-working as she is beautiful and good, but he immediately annihilates all class distinction by asking her to marry him and, when she refuses him, settles down to a long and patient courtship.

In the preface to *Jeanne*, which George Sand added in 1852 in order to describe the genesis of the tale, she says that she had wanted to depict 'a country girl, a dreamer, austere and simple: a soul of infinite candour . . . but where are we to find this primitive woman in modern society? From the moment she knows how to read and write she is no doubt none the worse for it, but she is different.' In other words, it is essential for her purposes that her heroine should be unlettered in order to be as near nature as possible. So that although George Sand's debt to Scott, throughout the novel, is very marked and, in her common sense, Jeanne is reminiscent of Jeannie Deans, it is Wordsworth's conception of the peasant that dominates. And the same romantic primitivism can be heard in the attempt of Clough's hero to persuade his Highland girl that learning is unnecessary for her:

> Women must read – as if they didn't know all beforehand . . .
> Weary and sick of our books, we come to repose in your eye-light
> As to the woodland and water, the freshness and beauty of Nature.
>   (VIII. 114; 117–18)

But in Elspie's no-nonsense reply can be heard a more modern, feminist timbre:

> What, she said, and if I have let you become my sweetheart,
> I am to read no books! but you may go your ways then,
> And I will read, she said, with my father at home as I used to.
> If you must have it, he said, I myself will read them to you.
> Well, she said, but no, I will read to myself, when I choose it.
>   (VIII. 120–4)

This sounds much more like George Sand herself than her heroine, who was indeed 'primitive', and therefore of little interest to Clough compared with the progressive hero. It is clear from his comments that it was the masculine point of view that appealed to him, but what must have first taken his interest is the excellent prologue to *Jeanne*, with its picture of three friends, two of them students, on a vacation hunting-party in the mountains. The moorland scenery, the quick-witted *badinage* between the young men and the shouted boasts and wagers as they scramble up the rocks must have put him in mind of the sort of masculine cameraderie he was so accustomed to on reading parties in the wilds. And in his poem he was able to make good use of the dominant traits of two of the three young men, who all fall in love with Jeanne after their fashion – of Sir Arthur Harley, the admirable Englishman, and Guillaume de Bossac, a romantic young baron. Of the third, Marsillat, the witty and licentious lawyer, Clough made no use at all. Actual libertinism was allowed to play no part in Clough's long vacation pastoral.

The principal debt of *The Bothie* to *Jeanne* lies in the conception of a man from the upper classes, of avowedly extreme socialist views, putting his theories into practice by marriage with a peasant girl. George Sand later came to view as a weakness the fact that she mingled in her novel country types with figures from high society and did not sufficiently trust her rustics to sustain the full interest on their own, and she put this right in her later pastoral tales. But it was precisely this contrast which intrigued Clough, and he heightened the already considerable opposition between the way of life of an Oxford undergraduate and a peasant girl by his hero's interlude at the castle with Lady Maria, a picture of aristocratic luxury which has a certain parallel with the background of *château* life, to which the action of *Jeanne* moves less than half-way through the book. Clough is fascinated by all the visible signs which distinguish the life of a peasant girl from a lady. They are all there in George Sand, but Clough makes even greater play with them: the simple cotton dresses, the bare feet and bare legs, the nicely rounded elbow, revealed by the sleeve neatly turned up for butter-churning or cheese-making; the milking of the cattle in the fields, fetching water from the pump, building the stooks, laying the washing out to dry or bleach on the grass: all evidence, as has been said by Biswas, of 'the theorist's insistence that labour is attractive'. What George Sand, as a countrywoman, takes in her stride, Clough dwells on frenetically, so that instead of a picture of Jeanne sitting knitting quietly by the riverside as she listens to Sir Arthur's proposal, we have, in *The Bothie*, 'unwavering attention in the love-scenes to the shifting fortunes of Elspie Mackay's knitting – when she took it up, when she laid it in her lap, when she put it on the bench.'[31] But although Clough may make heavy weather of the commonplace he does avoid with aggressive energy George Sand's tendency to prettify.

George Sand's hero, Sir Arthur Harley, made such an impression on Clough that his principal features are reproduced in the character of Arthur Audley as well as in the idealistic radicalism of the hero, Philip Hewson. Sir Arthur is deliberately given one or two slightly comic touches by George Sand – his dogged French with the marked English accent, which becomes ungrammatical under stress, and his habit of reacting to startling situations monosyllabically: ' "Ho!" . . . dit M. Harley avec l'accent indéfinissable de surprise flegmatique que les Anglais mettent dans cette exclamation.'[32]

But these are only in order to make her paragon human. Sir Arthur is indeed the soul of nobility, the touchstone of all around him. He has 'un esprit sérieux, une âme passionnée, un caractère génereux'; he is wise, kindly, chivalrous and temperate; always the peacemaker in quarrels, the moderator of passions around him. Under his imperturbable exterior, we are told, lie great spontaneity and great tenacity in his affections, not only for Jeanne but for his impulsive young friend, Guillaume. He is tall and handsome, physically strong and tireless, capable of great athletic feats. He has an affinity with Jeanne's natural graces in his gravity and truthfulness, his loyalty and patience.

The Arthur of *The Bothie* tends to be remembered principally for that form of athleticism which was particularly dear to Clough's heart –

Arthur, the bather of bathers, *par excellence*, Audley by
surname . . . (I. 33)
Arthur the shapely, the brave the unboasting, the Glory of
headers . . . (III. 81)

But he is also, even more significantly,

the light giving orb of the household,
Arthur, the shapely, the tranquil, the-strength-and-contentment-
diffusing
In the pure presence of whom none could quarrel long, nor be
pettish. (III. 85–7)

The bond between him and Adam, the tutor, and Philip Hewson, the
hot-headed radical young poet, is particularly strong. In Canto 1 the
three leave the festivities early and walk home together while the others
remain behind; it is Arthur who constantly corrects and moderates the
Piper's highly coloured tale of Philip's philanderings with Katie; and
most important it is Arthur to whom Adam refers at length (in the 1848
edition) as being the possessor of grace as opposed to 'wisdom bought
for a price in the market':

There are exceptional beings . . .
. . . most loving yet most withholding;
Least unfeeling though calm, self-contained yet most unselfish;
Renders help and accepts it, a man among men that are brothers,
Views, not plucks the beauty, adores and demands no embrac-
ing . . .
No, I do not set Philip herein on the level of Arthur.
No, I do not compare still tarn with furious torrent,
Yet will the tarn overflow, assuaged in the lake be the torrent.
(IV. 183–212)

Sir Arthur's unselfishness had shown itself in *Jeanne* in his long and
patient wooing of her, content to 'view not pluck the beauty', and in
his immediate departure from the *château* when he found out that his
friend Guillaume was suffering for love of Jeanne. Guillaume is a poet,
a romantic, who has preconceived ideas of country life and country
maidens – 'il rêvait tout un poème champêtre' – and lacking a heroine
for his poem has seized passionately on the idea of Jeanne. Guillaume's
infatuation resembles Philip's when, in his first phase – his courtship of
Katie – he is suddenly startled by the lust which underlies his romantic
feelings about her, and is overcome by guilt and shame at his unworthiness and the harm he has done her. The stagey episode in *The
Bothie* in which Philip takes to the hills and contemplates darkly and
unrelentingly the damage he might have done Katie, is the counterpart

of 'le drâme inquiet et sombre de Guillaume' as opposed to 'le poème calme et pastoral dont Sir Arthur était le héros'.[33] The contrast between the self-deluding and self-indulgent romanticism of Guillaume and the true, self-forgetful radicalism of Sir Arthur has clearly been pondered by Clough, and he shows both aspects in the development of his own hero. Philip is eventually made to realise the impractical and dangerous nature of his dreaming by one straight look from Elspie, as she passes by – and at the end of the poem he has achieved something of the wisdom of Arthur Audley; through knowledge, if not grace, the tarn and the torrent have become one. And he and Elspie are able to go forth and achieve the emigrants' dream of cultivating (with the suitably symbolic wedding gift of Arthur's plough) their own land, as fellow labourers in the cause of radicalism and chivalrous feminism.

It was a prospect which Sir Arthur, too, had contemplated hopefully but which was denied him by Jeanne's death. George Sand's hero did not, like Clough's, wax lyrical over the beauty of forking potatoes with 'a capless and bonnetless maiden'. But he did fork hay with her and imagined their future together on the farm once he had made her his wife. The happiest scene in the book is at hay-making time when Sir Arthur, a handsome figure in his blue peasant blouse and straw hat and ruddy complexion, showed off his muscles and dreamed of becoming

> propriétaire d'une bonne ferme de la Marche ou de Berri vivant à sa guise en bon campagnard loin du monde dont il était las; serrant lui-même ses récoltes, travaillant comme un homme, avec ses métayers, enrichissant ses colons, faisant le bonheur de sa commune, et goûtant lui-même la plus grande félicité auprès de sa belle et robuste compagne. Voilà la vie que j'ai toujours revée, pensait-il . . . Arthur, le front baigné de sueur, et les yeux brillants d'espérance, échangeait avec Jeanne des regards bienveillants, des paroles enjouées et de grandes fourchées de foin . . .[34]

Even although Clough had to give up his first idea of translating *Jeanne*, it can be seen that in a way he did translate all that appealed to him in it into his own highly individual and original poem.

8 Georgy Sandon

Most of the men and women in this chapter are now forgotten as novelists, however much they may be remembered in other spheres. In each case, the influence of George Sand is visible in their writings; at times, one might add, all too visible.

It may be well to start with the best critic and the worst novelist of the lot, G. H. Lewes. As we have seen, he was an outspoken champion of George Sand from the time he started reading her in 1839, at the age of twenty-two. He was in correspondence with her, sent her at least one article, and tried more than once to meet her. A letter of his of 1847 has survived, though not her reply. The year before, she had described him to a friend who was about to visit London, as someone who would be useful to him:

> He knows many eminent people and is himself distinguished. He is the author of a book on philosophy which has been very successful, of poetry, criticism etc. You've seen him, he's very nice and more French than English in character. He has my work by heart and knows the *Lettres d'un Voyageur* much better than I do.[1]

In his letter, accompanying the George Sand article, which he described as 'a feeble expression of my admiration for your genius', he goes on:

> I am here only for a few days, and need not tell you how pleased I should be if your engagements would allow you to see me for half an hour. That you have no time for visits of curiosity I am aware; but you too well know my sentiments towards you, not to be assured that whatever curiosity I may have to see the *femme célèbre*, my great desire is to press the hand and hear the voice of one whom I have long considered a friend.[2]

Whether Lewes met her or not, he continued to praise her in public until she had no more need of his defence and he had become involved instead in the encouragement of an English novelist who might rival her. As far as his own fiction was concerned, he seems to have been incapable of doing more than adapting and imitating; when I say that he was the worst of the minor novelists discussed in this chapter, I mean that in relation to his high intelligence and critical ability he is by far the most disappointing.

He first translated and bowdlerised a short novel of hers, *Le Sécretaire Intime*, for *Fraser's Magazine* which was published in 1844 in two undistinguished parts as *The State Murder* and was prefaced by the assurance that this 'charming novel is not defaced by any of those faults usually so offensive to English tastes.'[3] It was a strange choice; a fantasy, based by George Sand on a tale of Hoffmann, and written in 1833, about the same time as de Musset's *Fantasio*. Indeed there is scarcely a scene in *Fantasio* which cannot be found in *Le Sécretaire Intime*, and the reader is alerted to the connection between the two works by the presence in both of a character with the unexpected name of Spark.

What the readers of *Fraser's* made of this version by Lewes it is difficult to imagine. It is the tale of Saint-Julien, a poor young Count, who as he walks along a dusty road one day, is given a lift in the carriage of a beautiful, extraordinarily learned and fascinating princess, Quintillia, and becomes her private secretary in her exotic palace. It is a fairy tale, 'sans rime, ni raison' as George Sand confessed, with an overtone of decadence and rich splendour to remind us that it is of the same era as *Lélia*. One of the most memorable scenes in the original is a fancy-dress ball, an entomological fantasy, to which all the guests come dressed as every imaginable species of insect and butterfly, grasshopper and stag-beetle, wasp and owl-moth, praying mantis and cockchafer.

The vision of his new employer which met Saint-Julien's startled gaze at the beginning of Chapter 5, gives some idea of the side of George Sand which appealed to Ouida later:

> Quintillia was reclining on a sumptuous ottoman, smoking latakié in a long *chibouque* covered with precious stones. She was dressed in the Greek costume, which she preferred above all others, and looked most ravishing in it. Rich Indian stuffs with flowers exquisitely woven on a white ground, were bordered with precious stones; and diamonds sparkled on the shoulders and arms. Her little cap was of blue velvet, embroidered with rare pearls, and was placed jauntily upon her raven hair. A rich poniard glittered at her side.

There is very little connection between Lewes's novel of 1848, *Rose Blanche and Violet*, and George Sand's *Rose et Blanche* except the title. While this was not a book which George Sand looked back upon with any pride, it can safely be said that Lewes's was much, much worse. Mrs Carlyle did not let her friendly feelings for Lewes blunt her sharp tongue. For once, she and Lady Baring were in unison in condemning the book as 'Execrable . . . I could not have believed the Ape possible of writing anything so silly.'[4] It is an extraordinary hotch-potch of romance and crude pseudo-realism with a wicked young stepmother as a central character. The opening paragraphs sound not unpromising, for in them the narrator discusses what lies behind the apparently calm façade of the high street of some small country town. To the eye of the stranger everything was dull and lifeless but 'every house was really the theatre of some comedy or some grotesque tragedy – the well-known scene of some humble heroism or ridiculous pretension.' This is, however, much nearer to Balzac than George Sand, and the first favourable impression is dispelled by the stagey, bad-Dickensian dialogue which follows – 'Dead! Dead! Good God! So young, so young – Dead! So beautiful and good! – Dead!'[5]

The Apprenticeship of Life was a piece of fictional hackwork, serialised in the *Leader*, and was no doubt run up by Lewes to fill a gap between March and June 1850. The hero, Armand, disinherited by his rich infidel uncle because he is a convert to Christianity, spends three years of soul-searching in Paris; then once again, just like the Sécretaire Intime, walking along a dusty road, exhausted and half-starved, he is rescued by a beautiful woman in a travelling carriage. She turns out to be his cousin, Hortense, who is older than Armand – thirty-three – with a 'full ripe figure . . . dimpled arms . . . heavy beauty . . . a warm brown face . . . large eyes'. She is an estate owner, democratic in her ideas, accustomed to living among her peasantry; a widow with Saint-Simonist ideas about marriage, who proceeds to take a maternal interest in Armand, which is followed by a mutual love. Edgar Hirshberg[6] suggests temperately that Hortense may be a projection of George Sand – of which there can surely be little doubt. Set over ten years, the story becomes infinitely complicated, with politics and pre-revolutionary conspiracies competing for the reader's interest with Hortense's 'encroaching *embonpoint*' and 'loss of *moral* influence' over Armand; it peters out indecisively in the June issue, with vague promises of continuation later, to be replaced by a novel by Mrs Crowe. Fortunately Lewes never fulfilled these promises, and we can only be thankful, in view of his influence over George Eliot, that his critical theory was so much superior to his fictional practice.

In his article of 1852, 'The Lady Novelists', Lewes wrote of 'Geraldine Jewsbury and Eliza Lynn, two writers in whom the influence of George Sand is traceable.' He discussed the former's first novel, '*Zoë*, in which the impetuous passionate style clearly betrays the influence of George Sand' and the next, *The Half Sisters* 'in which the style is toned down to a more truthful pitch'.

When Jane Carlyle saw the first draft of *Zoë* in 1842, three years before it was published and ten years before Lewes's article, she thought it 'an extraordinary jumble of sense and nonsense' but admitted 'I do not believe there is a woman alive at the present day, not even George Sand herself, that could have written some of the best passages in the book';[7] and two years later, in 1844, she was even more enthusiastic: 'I have all Geraldine's MS. now and by the powers it is a wonderful book! Decidedly the cleverest Englishwoman's book I ever remember to have read.'[8]

It was certainly such a book as no well-bred Englishwoman had written before; as remote as possible from Fanny Burney, Maria Edgeworth, Jane Austen, Susan Ferrier, Mary Russell Mitford and Harriet Martineau, to mention some of Geraldine Jewsbury's predecessors, who were well within the English tradition of domestic realism. Jane Carlyle's first reaction – 'a jumble of sense and nonsense' – is probably that of the modern reader also; and yet this book had a *succès de scandale*, and even the publisher's reader confessed that he 'was taken hold of . . . with a grasp of iron' by this 'philosophical novel'. Although the book is called *Zoë*, it is sub-titled *The History of Two Lives*. The other life is that of Everhard, a priest who has doubts, loses his religion, becomes a social worker among ignorant savages in a Welsh village and is routed by the Methodist revival which has more appeal in its faith than all his good works. This thread of the story, which is taken up every few chapters like a dropped stitch, has the distinction of being, as Espinasse claims, 'the first novel in which the hero's career is made dependent on the victory of modern scepticism over ancient belief';[10] and, by being the precursor of *The Nemesis of Faith* (1848) and *Robert Elsmere* (1889), underlines the truth of Wilde's comment that the latter novel 'heralded a dawn which had broken forty years before.'

But it was not for its theological arguments, nor even for the conversations about 'woman's genius and equality', that *Zoë* took the fancy of the circulating libraries and became a best-seller, while its author found herself in flattering demand at dinner parties in London. It was for its passion – passion always just stopping short of actual immorality, but far more uncontrolled and electrifying than anything produced before by a middle-class Englishwoman for a middle-class market. When the two lives of Everhard and Zoë converge, and the priest is exposed to the allurements of Zoë, with her 'tropical organisation . . . and the strong passions lying latent within her', the pages sizzle: Everhard presses 'burning kisses upon her face, her lips, her bosom: but kisses are too weak to express the passion that was within him. It was madness like hatred . . . beads of sweat stood thick on his forehead – his breath came in gasps.'[11] But Everhard is still a priest at this point, and Zoë is married, and both are capable of sublimating their love since (and here the voice of George Sand comes through) 'Love, rightly conceived in its highest manifestations, ceases to be a mere passion; it becomes a worship, a religion; it regenerates the whole soul; till a man has found an object to love, his faculties are un-developed . . . True love and high morality are the same.'[12]

But though Everhard escapes, Zoë has still to undergo another passionate experience with Mirabeau, her distinguished suitor. (Geraldine Jewsbury also followed George Sand in setting her novel, like *Consuelo*, back in the eighteenth century and in providing a far more private life for historical personages than Scott ever created.) It would have been inconceivable for Miss Jewsbury to have imagined the Mirabeau love-scenes without her reading of George Sand, and it seems to me very likely that this may be a case in which the indirect influence of the French writer may have been exerted through the pages of Zoë on Charlotte Brontë. Geraldine Jewsbury's Mirabeau was, after 1845, a very well-known hero indeed, and bears a striking resemblance, especially in his proposal scene, to Mr Rochester.[13] He can be dominating, passionate, angry and bitter, but when he 'lifts Zoë in his arms like a child' he is tender and gentle. When the proposal for which Zoë is waiting comes, it is not that she should marry him but become his mistress:

Mirabeau smiled bitterly and tossed back his long, shaggy locks. 'Why' said he sternly, 'do you mention Wife to me? Why do you speak to me of that cursed one? . . . Yes, my wife was a fool but she spoiled and ruined my existence . . . We are divorced, it is true; but with us divorce does not allow either party to contract new ties; till that woman dies you cannot be my wife . . .[14]

And he continues to urge Zoë to prefer love to conventionality:

I love you, Zoë, with all the force of my soul; you possess me like a demon and you shall be mine. You shall not drive me mad, and remain yourself in your cold, selfish safety – your whole being shall be molten into mine, – you are worthy to be a portion of me, Zoë. I do not ask for soft, honeyed words; I love you like hatred – and hatred it will be if you oppose me . . . I shall never forget you but I shall remember you with bitterness and curses, as one of those who made my life a howling wilderness, as one who had the power to save me, and would not stretch out a hand, preferring to dwell in worldly respectability without me . . . if you fail me now, all hope of good is over for me . . . Oh, Zoë! no man ever loved a woman as I love you: will you save your reputation at the cost of my happiness? Will you sacrifice me at the shrine of a word that has no substance – for a formula?[15]

Even in the throes of her passion, Zoë, like Jane Eyre, is conscious of the fact that if she once gives in to Mirabeau and becomes his mistress she will soon lose her power over him, a utilitarian scruple which would never occur to a George Sand heroine. But in the end, the decisive factor for each sorely-tempted heroine is duty; in Zoë's case duty to her children, in Jane's duty to herself and her religion. And the outcome of each crisis is the same: the heroine unyielding, deaf to the reproaches of the 'terrible and savage voice' of her lover, and finally 'stiff and senseless on the floor'.

It was this novel which made Geraldine Jewsbury a minor literary celebrity. She was now received everywhere, Jane Carlyle comments,

> because she has put her cleverness into a *book* – above all a book accused of immorality (quite a new sort of distinction for a young Englishwoman) . . . Even Miss Wilson to whom I dared to lend it – tho' she confessed to never having 'ventured on reading a line of George Sand in her life' brought it back to me with *a certain* equanimity. 'It is avowedly the book of an audacious *esprit fort*, and so of course you did not expect *me* to *approve* of it, nor do I, but I think it very clever and amusing' – voilà tout! While old and young roués of the Reform Club almost go off in hysterics over its *indecency* . . .[16]

Through many letters, Jane marvels at the way in which her friends take Geraldine's 'improper novel' in their stride: Erasmus Darwin, 'the type of English gentleman', is a warm admirer of *Zoë* and also Arthur Helps, 'a man of the *deadly sensible* sort, moral to the fingertips'.[17] Strangely enough, it was Geraldine's next novel which Jane herself repudiated, although it was an immeasurably better book. She deplored its 'actresses and hysteric seizures and all that sort of thing'[18] and did not relish its dedication to her – while Carlyle forbade her to assist with the proof-correcting. *The Half-Sisters* was certainly a much more feminist book than *Zoë*, but it was no more passionate and Lewes was right to stress 'its more truthful pitch'.

As all the reviewers pointed out, *The Half-Sisters* was much indebted to *Consuelo* (and to a lesser extent *Corinne*) for the conception of the heroine, Bianca, a beautiful, destitute young Italian, with blue-black hair, large grey eyes and the usual 'simple, black silk dress' to set off her charms. She is the protégée of a Cambridge student, Conrad Percy, and becomes a celebrated professional artist on the London stage. Geraldine Jewsbury's friendship with the actress, Charlotte Cushman, no doubt added verisimilitude to the novel, but Bianca's discussions of art and the need of women to have a worthwhile and creative outlet for their talents and energies come straight from *Consuelo* and the *Lettres à Marcie*. In her devotion to her profession, Bianca is an appealing and far more credible heroine than Zoë. Acting gives significance to her life: when she is 'resting' in the luxury of a country house and a letter arrives with an offer of a part, it is 'like the sound of a trumpet to a war-horse'. Love is important for her, but because of her profession it is not the be-all and end-all of her life; and when Conrad gives her up, disgusted with the theatrical, with 'the French-novel style of woman', she is capable of surviving the blow. *The Half-Sisters*, especially in the seventeen-page discussion between Conrad and Lord Melton on acting as a career,[19] is like a crude foretaste of *The Tragic Muse*; but of course there are similar discussions in *Consuelo*. Just as Porpora counsels Consuelo about the need for dedication, so an old actor is always at hand to remind Bianca of her duty: 'You must consider your genius as a sacred deposit entrusted to you . . . must make the profession what it has never been made yet . . . The stage has had no priests.'[20] And, Bianca, unrepentant when reproached for not pursuing a normal, domestic, ladylike life, counterattacks disarmingly: 'I have often wondered how women, who were *not* actresses, contrived to pass their time.'[22]

Geraldine Jewsbury does go to great pains to present her heroine as a really professional woman – and yet at the end of the novel Bianca is content to leave the stage and dwindle into Lord Melton's wife. This dénouement posed a problem for the *Athenaeum* reviewer, Chorley. He obviously had sympathy with the common view that art should not be the main business of a woman's life, but was shocked by the startling inconsistency of the ending of *The Half-Sisters*, and commented that 'Madame Dudevant was more true to her text in making her Countess of Rudolstadt (Consuelo) never quit the arena in which the exercise of her talents became a duty.'[23] A strange situation when George Sand is praised by Chorley for her consistency to an unwomanly ideal – but, in this review, the moralist and critic were at war. It must indeed have been one of the few times in her life that Geraldine Jewsbury was blamed for not going far enough.

Eliza Lynn Linton is remembered today, if at all, as a confirmed anti-feminist, a prolific writing woman ('Good for anything', noted Dickens approvingly) and the author, in 1867, of 'The Girl of the Period', the *Saturday Review* series of vitriolic essays directed against the modern young woman whom she described as fast, mercenary and bold. But she herself, twenty years earlier, had been, as she confessed, 'as much of an insurgent as the rest',[24] and had moved in progressive circles in London. She is an interesting testimony to the unlikely soil in which George Sandism could flourish.

Eliza Lynn was a clergyman's daughter, the youngest of a huge and motherless family in Cumberland, where she educated herself with the purposefulness peculiar to so many underprivileged, middle-class Victorian young women, read omnivorously and learned Latin and Greek and a smattering of several other languages. In 1845, at the age of twenty-three, she was allowed to leave home for a year in order to prove her literary abilities by writing a novel and, after intensive research, did indeed produce a work of awesome erudition called *Azeth the Egyptian*, which though now practically unreadable, and wisely unread, earned her the accolade of *The Times* and, from more irreverent readers, the title of 'Miss Sennacherib', after one of its characters. Although the author tried hard to brighten up what she admitted to be an 'intractable subject', with dwarves, dancing girls and a High Priest, who, we are often told, is burning with passion, the novel has been well summed up as 'the dry fruit of the year in the British Museum'.[24] It did mean, however, that she gained the freedom of literary circles, both at the Chapmans and at the Laurence phalanstery, and she was able to savour a sense of independence and of intellectual equality with men. She was exposed to much talk by Lewes and Thornton Hunt of free love and marriage without bondage; it all came as a shock to the embarrassed Eliza Lynn, fresh from the vicarage and the Reading Room, and she was to describe Lewes feelingly, in her old age, as 'the first of the audacious men of my existence'.[25]

It was no doubt then that she read George Sand's works, perhaps for the first time. Certainly, her next novel, *Amymone*, although it is also a work of formidable scholarship, set this time in the age of Pericles, is not only much more readable but expresses many startling and unorthodox opinions. This novel, and her next, *Realities*, which had the distinction of being turned down by Chapman as too sensual for his readers, are the only two works of Eliza Lynn which I propose to discuss, although many of her later novels are considerably better. My reason is that at this point she had had no chance to benefit from the example of the Brontës or Mrs Gaskell or, of course, George Eliot, all of whom were such potent influences on minor women novelists later in the century.

Despite the impressive cast list of *Amymone*, which reads like a page from a classical encyclopaedia and includes Pericles, Socrates, Thucydides, Sophocles, Euripides, Pheidias and Alcibiades among many others, and despite the 'thees' and 'thous' which implacably remind the reader that he is in a past age, the author's intention, as she makes clear from the start, is to clothe 'in Grecian form, the spirit of modern England'.

The title of the novel might reasonably lead one to expect that the heroine will be called Amymone, but this is not the case. Aspasia, the beautiful and celebrated mistress of Pericles, whose house was the meeting place of the best literary and philosophical society in Athens, and was frequented even by Socrates, is the object of Miss Lynn's admiration. A learned lady herself, she could appreciate that Aspasia's 'salon' was certainly more highpowered than any she attended either at the Chapmans or the Laurences but, none the less, she was aware that she was mixing with some of the brightest and most progressive men and women in London, and she warmed to Aspasia's unorthodoxy.

For her novel, she tones down the courtesan background of Aspasia, and concentrates on her as the devoted help-mate and intellectual equal of Pericles who compels admiration and love by her strength, independence, enlightened views and generous humanity. Amymone, her enemy, also has an active intellect but her fierce passions, her mercenary nature, her desire to dominate her weak lover, her unscrupulousness in using her sexual charms to get her way sound remarkably like a preview of the qualities of 'The Girl of the Period' twenty years later, for these were all features of womanhood which Eliza Lynn despised. Aspasia is her ideal: one who had 'endeavoured to rescue philosophy, learning and art from the purposes of seduction' (the cultured *heterai*) and had striven 'to establish the truth of an equal love between the sexes'. It may well be that Amymone is as she is because of her illegitimacy, which has perverted her – and here Miss Lynn swats, in passing, Victorian hypocrisy: 'Society was lenient to the infidelity of men, where it covered the frail fair maid with undying opprobrium.' But, whatever the reason, the product is unpleasing and has to be brought to a bad end, while Aspasia triumphs. In the midst of all the Athenian paraphernalia it is comical to hear the voice of George Sand ring out once again: 'The bond of marriage is love . . . When this is dead, the true tie is broken. A marriage without affection, solemnize it as ye may, is guilt . . . What, does love require man's sanction to make it holy? Oh no! Its truth is its own sanctification . . .'[27] And when, in Volume 3, Aspasia stands accused, the itemising of her sins could well pass as a rather more moderate version of Croker's attack on George Sand:

> Thou deniest the gods; thou wouldst subvert our social laws; thou opposest the existing state of things and education and custom thou namest of no value; thou companionest with the men who come to visit thy husband . . . thou wouldst teach the arts hitherto reserved for the hetairai to the modest maiden; thou wouldst that women should be seen in the men's peculiar places, at the games and at the comedy; thou talkest of strange things, equality, the right of private judgment, the divinity of common sense.[28]

Amymone is a curiosity and, after reading it, many of the points made by Lewes in his article 'The Lady Novelists' seem clearer, especially his opening paragraph in which he defends learning in women; for none of the other women writers with whom he deals, not even George Sand, was as eager a student as Eliza Lynn. And though no doubt he also had the assistant editor of the *Westminster Review*, Marian Evans, in mind, her début as a novelist lay four years ahead. Miss Lynn was often referred to, in terms that he uses, as a bluestocking and literary lady, and even more frequently as 'a strong-minded woman'; and when he talks of the awkwardness of hearing 'a woman venture on Greek when you don't know Greek', or quoting 'from a philosophical treatise', and when he admits that 'literary women are not *always* the most charming of their sex', there can be no doubt that Eliza Lynn, intellectual and plain, has contributed to his sketch.

Later, in his long essay, he devotes a paragraph completely to Miss Lynn and her 'strange and defiant standpoint'. What he objects to in her third novel, *Realities,* in which she abandoned the past for the contemporary scene, is 'the *unreality* of this passionate and exaggerated protest against conventions . . . She is lacking in Observation . . . She feels deeply . . . but she sees dimly.'[29] As Lewes himself had supplied her with much of the theatrical background for her novel, he was in a good position to judge her deficiency in actual experience.

In her foreword to *Realities,* Eliza Lynn said that her friends thought of this novel as a 'species of literary Caliban'. It did arouse very strong feelings in readers. Many of the episodes have a blunt crudeness and passionate abandon such as only an outspoken and unwordly young woman would have ventured to express. Even the 'improper' Geraldine Jewsbury was startled by it: 'Have you seen a wonderful book by Miss Lynn called "Realities"? O good gracious! good gracious! that any woman should have ever been given over to such bad taste!'[30] And a scene of high comedy was played between Eliza Lynn and Chapman, who took a strong moral stance, supported by his wife, his mistress and Marian Evans, about 'some objectionable passages . . . [which] excite the sensual nature and were therefore injurious.' As G. S. Haight points out, 'Though he refused to publish a novel containing an objectionable love scene, he maintained in the heart of mid-Victorian London a household no novelist would then have dared to describe.'[31]

What remains in the modern reader's mind, as no doubt it did in Chapman's, is the way in which the tempestuous, frank and un-inhibited heroine, Claire, who has run away from an unloving home to the theatre, contrives to live for many chapters as the near-mistress of 'Vasty Vaughan', the libidinous manager, generating intense passion but retaining her chastity. This liaison is set against a garish theatrical background and sordid scenes of the poverty and prostitution to which Vasty's wife has sunk. Claire also resists the advances of a fanatically religious young man who tries to save her, and she finally marries Percival, who throughout the three volumes has been waiting in the wings for her to feel 'mature love' for him.

This blast against Victorian hypocrisy and complacency – so different from George Sand in its rawness and naïvety – was courageous as well as laughable in the year of the Great Exhibition, when middle-class conventionality was in the ascendant. Eliza Lynn was herself an indomitably respectable woman (as became the daughter of a vicar, the granddaughter of a bishop and the niece of a dean) who, when the incompatibility of her marriage to W. J. Linton became evident to them both, happily pursued a separate and self-sufficient career. Her attitude to the union of George Eliot and Lewes was interesting. Like Jane Carlyle and Mrs Oliphant, she resented the aura of sanctity which gradually surrounded the pair, and said briskly that they were 'perfectly justified in their union – perfectly', but that they were not justified in their assumption of special sacredness. And in common with others she found it impossible to forgive the marriage of George Eliot to Cross, feeling badly let down by what she considered to be an act of treachery to a union of love.[32] She had to pay George Eliot tribute, however unwilling, as a writer, but she got her own back when she discussed her 'unreal life': 'She was the very antithesis of George Sand whose impulsive, large and loving nature never became artificialised by her fame, never grew to be self-conscious by excess of intellect as was the case with George Eliot. It was nature and art once more, as so often before.'[33]

And in this novel, in however crude and inept a way, she is striking a blow for sexual honesty, and challenging the masculine stereotype of the angel in the house. So that, although *Realities* is indeed something of a deformed and monstrous offspring, it must still be considered as owing its existence to the doctrines and example of George Sand.

In the year 1849, a dramatic scene took place in Exeter College, Oxford. The Reverend William Sewell, a professor of that college, fervently denounced *The Nemesis of Faith*, a novel which had just been published, and, on finding that a student possessed a copy, dashed it into the hall fire. As has been pointed out, it was the only book to be 'piously burned at Oxford in the nineteenth century'.[34] It was certainly a very different book from the gentle High Church novels written by William Sewell's sister, Elizabeth, to which he was pleased to write the forewords. The author was J. A. Froude, a Fellow of Exeter, who proceeded to resign his fellowship, without any protest from the university, shortly before Clough also left Oriel.

Though now remembered as a historian and Carlyle's biographer, Froude did write other novels, but none that attracted the notoriety of *The Nemesis of Faith*. Its hero, Markham, is a clergyman who, after struggling with his doubts, gives up his charge. This resolution takes up almost three-quarters of the novel; it is only the last quarter which reveals that the hero's religious heterodoxy was not the only cause of Sewell's wrath. Without this section of the novel, the claim, which has been made by Halévy,[35] that *The Nemesis of Faith* was directly influenced by the reading of George Sand would be meaningless, for

Froude was sufficiently involved in the Newman controversy himself
not to need any additional spur to his scepticism. But once Markham
has turned to nature for solace and gone abroad to Lake Como to spend
the winter, the effect of Froude's early Oxford reading of George Sand
becomes visible.

In this romantic setting he is thrown into the company of Helen
Leonard by her pleasant, though not very compatible, husband, who
is happy to leave Markham to entertain his wife. They gradually fall
in love, and although Markham makes gallant efforts to get the
husband to see the danger he is too complaisant to return. At this stage
it is Rousseau, rather than George Sand, whose presence is obvious.
The quotation 'Ils commençaient à dire *nous*. Ah, qu'il est touchant, ce
"nous" prononcé par l'amour',³⁶ followed by an idyllic episode on the
lake, is a clear indication that an unhappy ending must follow.
Markham's fervent declaration of his love is the last stage in a very
articulate wooing, which has succeeded in persuading Helen of the
essential rightness of the heart's affections, and she too admits her
passion, although, like Zoë, she refuses to leave her child. But their
neglect of the child does, in fact, bring about her death.

The contrast between the reactions of Markham and Helen to this
tragedy is startling. Markham is brought to a shocked realisation that
he has only been infatuated, and is in guilty despair. By a strange
coincidence, the Newman figure, 'Frederick Mornington', happens to
be 'passing through Como on the 10th on his way to Rome', and after
a talk with him, Markham 'saw more clearly or thought he saw'; he
repents his loss of faith, goes over to Rome and enters a monastery.
Helen, on the other hand, believes that the death of her daughter is a
punishment, not for loving Markham, but for her loveless marriage. She
dies, after two years, unreconciled with the Church: 'With singular
persistency, she declared to the last that her sin had been in her
marriage, not in her love.'³⁷

Unlike Helen, the 'unpardoned sinner' who 'passed tranquilly away
to God', Markham, in his solitary cell, finds that his new faith is once
again sapped by doubt and his final emotion is 'remorse, not for what
he had done, but for what he had not done'.

As can be seen, by the end of this novel, which, despite its manipulation of the characters, is heartfelt and powerfully expressed, George
Sand has taken over from Rousseau. What might have been a conventional ending is transformed by the note of defiance expressed by Helen
and the sombre presentation of Markham, who has attempted in vain
to find a solution to his moral problem in subduing his reason to
ecclesiastical authority. The book was published by Chapman and
enthusiastically reviewed by all progressive journals, and even by some
not so advanced; for the Coventry *Herald* had a notice describing it as

'a true product of genius'[38] written by the unknown Mary Ann Evans, who at that stage had translated Strauss and had as idols both Rousseau and George Sand, and so, as we shall see, was better equipped than most to respond to Froude's novel.

Not all of George Sand's avowed followers, however, wrote shocking books. Matilda Hays, for example, whose novel, *Helen Stanley* (1846), was sent to George Sand by Mazzini but was received in merciful silence, was well within the bounds of propriety. It is an innocuous and romantic tale, prefixed by two epigraphs from Carlyle, which is in essence an extended attack on mercenary 'unsanctified' marriages. Much more interesting, because of the equivocal attitude of its author towards George Sand, is a novel of 1854 called *A Lost Love*.

Its author was Ashford Owen (Ann Charlotte Ogle, 1832–1918), another vicar's daughter, this time from Northumberland. She too came from a large family of brothers and sisters, but was timid and retiring. Her main resources were reading and music, and she wrote the novel, she said, in the 'despair of youth' for, like her heroine, her life was passing, 'a bit of gray blotting paper might best tell how'.[39] Her story, which she said later gave a true picture of herself, had as its heroine a young girl, Georgy Sandon. Hers is a drab, lonely life: 'Georgy had had no youth – none.' She has been engaged for three years to a dull man who is overseas, and, unable to face the prospect of marrying him, she breaks off the engagement and leaves home. She then falls deeply in love with a distant cousin, James Erskine, and has the courage to end that engagement also when she realises that he is in love with someone else – with Constance, who is much more charming and fascinating than Georgy. She herself marries her first suitor and after her eventual death, James Erskine has second thoughts about the wisdom of his choice; he has a feeling of remorse and unfulfilment at the memory of Georgy; an epilogue which clearly gave Ashford Owen some satisfaction to write.

This quiet novel was, surprisingly, a best-seller. It was translated into French and appeared as 'Un Amour Perdu' in the *Revue des Deux Mondes* and later, in 1860, was one of the stories in a collection for the Bibliothèque des Chemins de Fer, which carried the title *Le Rose et le Gris: Scènes de la Vie Anglaise*. It was pirated in America, under the title *Georgy*, which was what the author had wanted to call it in England, and was still in demand when the second edition came out in 1890. After its publication, Ashford Owen's circle widened and she became friendly with the Brownings,[40] Swinburne, Tennyson, the Carlyles, Thackeray and the Brookfields, but she never wrote another novel and looked back at it deprecatingly. It is a very unequal book, with much gaucherie and inconsistency in most of the characterisation, except for the heroine. The influence of Jane Austen and Charlotte Brontë seems more marked than that of any other authors; the scene in which the heroine arrives in London could be straight from the pages of *Villette*, and Georgy herself, however autobiographical, is constantly reminiscent of Lucy Snowe in her repressions, her self-despising and her passion. Where then, apart from the name of the heroine, is the connection with the French novelist?

Quite clearly Ashford Owen was widely read in foreign novels and, while fascinated by them, found that the solution they offered of following where the heart led inadequate in her own situation or, she suspected, in any normal life. 'French novels' are mentioned so frequently in the course of the book, at times every few pages, that the opposition between the true (Georgy's unfulfilled romance) and the sentimental and self-indulgent (the lot of a George Sand heroine) is always being implicitly invoked. One character after another 'indulges' in French novels; Constance is 'very like one of Madame Hahn-Hahn's heroines' and in her room are 'all the French books'; there are countless references to 'sentimental French novels', to 'the pleasure of assuming a man's name' and going in for 'womanly writing among masculine touches', to the opposition between doing one's duty and 'taking the comfort which sentiment and the French books might perhaps suggest'. When a frivolous woman, Mrs Lucas, dips into a French novel, the disillusioned heroine comments that both the reader and the book were

> an exquisite satire upon reality . . . The empty headed, empty-hearted woman, with her jargon of sentiment and her familiar use of words; words of which she never knew, could never learn, the true meaning; and the book, which was as much beyond her, as it lay far from Georgy, then. It was one of those stories in which French literature stands pre-eminent. A wonderful analysis of passion, such as it were better perhaps had never been written and never felt.
>
> To have written that book, the feeling must have been past, and (as the phrase is) the author's experiences had been *exploitées* for that work. The book in its cold-blooded consciousness and the lady in her unconsciousness, were both equally repulsive to Georgy.[41]

This is a touching passage, for it reveals both the young author's response to George Sand and her sense of the gulf between the sort of mastery over life and passion that the French writer revealed and her own vulnerability to experience. The book is not short of passion, nor of awareness of the failed marriage, where no one can be blamed: 'Love once gone in marriage is gone for good – yet it is no one's fault particularly'; nor of the sense of sexual desirability which Georgy is aware she lacks: 'The Frenchman's praise of the woman he loved has seldom been surpassed: "Elle était mieux femme que les autres." ' In fact, Georgy's passion for James is so strong that 'it excludes her from

thoughts of heaven where there is no marrying and giving in marriage.'
But in the end, because she is English and has no part in a French novel
of sentiment, she buries her love and looks at it no more; she does what
she conceives to be her duty, and consoles herself with the thought that
'Passion cannot last for ever'. It is an interesting, thoughtful and deeply
personal response to the novels of George Sand by a lonely and
disillusioned girl; one which verges on satire but which just falls short
because, in fact, she has been deeply moved by the revelation of a world
of emotional fulfilment which she is sure is neither true nor attainable
by her and which none the less can make reality seem, in comparison,
like a 'bit of gray blotting paper'.

F

9 The Two Georges

1

In 1876, the year that George Sand died, George Eliot published *Daniel Deronda*. In his review of the book,[1] Sidney Colvin discussed the writings of both at some length and described them as 'sisters in greatness'. He would have found few readers to disagree with this estimate of them, for most literary-minded Victorians had long found some comparison between the two women irresistible. Not only was each the most distinguished female novelist of her age and country, but certain similarities intrigued them, which even a century later still seem remarkable. Apart from their choice of pseudonym, there was the fact that each, in her own way, had not only flouted the marriage bond but had then proceeded to assume the role of moralist. This was a point which, after Marian Evans's union with Lewes and her disclosure as George Eliot, Jane Welsh Carlyle was not slow to make. What really surprised her, she commented tartly, was that 'the partners in the adventure had set up as moralists . . . To renounce George Sand as a teacher of morals was right enough but it was scarcely consistent with making so much of our own George in that capacity.'[2] But, eventually, both Georges were able to impose their chosen way of life on society, and if we observe the two writers only in the late 1860s and 1870s, when they were serenely queening it in almost bourgeois respectability over their circles at Nohant and the Priory, we see coeval national institutions. They even seemed to have grown to look alike.

With the passing of the years, when George Sand's beauty had faded and her features appeared more massive, when she had long since abandoned what Lewes called her 'androgynous garments', more than one caller at Hampstead noted the resemblance between them.[3] It is easy to forget – and made easier by the fact that George Eliot outlived George Sand by only five years – that the two women were of different generations, that George Sand had been an established novelist for twenty-five years before George Eliot produced her first work of fiction and that initially, at least, the Englishwoman was George Sand's disciple.

This is something that a Victorian such as Gosse was much more aware of than a modern critic. In looking back at George Eliot from 'the gay world' of 1922, he comments that everyone has now forgotten 'what a solemn, what a portentous thing was the contemporary fame of George Eliot', and goes on:

> If I had time and space it would be very interesting to study George Eliot's attitude towards that mighty woman, the full-bosomed caryatid of romantic literature, who had by a few years preceded her. When George Eliot was at the outset of her own literary career, which as we know was much belated, George Sand had already bewitched and thrilled and scandalised Europe for a generation. The impact of the Frenchwoman's mind on that of her English contemporary produced sparks or flashes of starry enthusiasm.[4]

And if we look back to Coventry in the 1840s, the picture is indeed one of contrast, between George Sand, the beautiful, notorious writer, the 'most talked of woman in Europe', and Marian Evans, plain, obscure, provincial and full of 'self-despisings'. There are frequent references to George Sand in her letters from 1845 onwards, references which show that she was not only familiar with the novels but prepared to defend them against the strictures of her friends, the Brays and Sara Hennell, who for all their emancipation, did not share her new enthusiasm: 'Dear Cara, your husband desired me to send you the newspaper paragraph about George Sand and I obey – but if you disapprove, utter none of your blasphemies to me . . .[5] Beware there are not too many blasphemies against my divinity . . .'[6]

The tone is jocular, but there is no doubt that George Sand had gained another proselyte. It is not difficult to see why, at this stage of her life, Marian Evans should have felt so much attracted to George Sand's writings. Her first emancipation a few years earlier had been an intellectual one. But the immediate sense of relief which followed her liberation from 'the wretched giant's bed of dogmas' was succeeded by consciousness that intellectual truth was not an absolute, that only upon the '*truth of feeling*' could she depend. In her own life, however, instinct and intellect, desire and duty were constantly at war. Through all the 'soul stupefying' labour of translating Strauss she was tortured by his relentless intellectual dissection of 'myths', to the beauty and truth of which her heart still responded. As she groaned under the task, she looked forward to its end, to her 'butterfly days' when she could spread her wings. But no sooner was she free of Strauss than she found herself chained by duty and self-sacrifice to her father, through the long dragging anxiety of his illness until his death in 1849. It was small wonder, then, that with physical freedom denied her, she turned for emotional emancipation to works of the imagination – a complete re-reading of Shakespeare first, followed by a large and varied selection of other writers, old and new, English and foreign, who could give her solace and stimulus. In May 1847, she writes in a letter that if she sounds impious, it is because she has been 'guano-ing' her mind with French novels. But two years later the note she strikes is serious when, writing to Sara Hennell, she classes George Sand as a formative influence upon her, with Jean-Jacques Rousseau, whose *Confessions* she had recently admitted to Emerson to be the first book to awaken her to deep reflection. It is a lengthy and significant passage:

> I wish you thoroughly to understand that the writers who have most profoundly influenced me – who have rolled away the waters from their bed raised new mountains and spread delicious valleys for me – are not in the least oracles to me. It is just possible that I may not embrace one of their opinions, that I may wish my life to be shaped quite differently from theirs . . . it would not be the less true that Rousseau's genius has sent that electric thrill through my intellectual and moral frame which has awakened me to new perceptions, which has made man and nature a fresh world of thought and feeling to me – and this not by teaching me any new belief . . . It is thus with G. Sand. I should never dream of going to her writings as a moral code or text-book. I don't care whether I agree with her about marriage or not – whether I think the design of her plot correct or that she had no precise design at all but began to write as the spirit moved her and trusted to Providence for the catastrophe, which I think the more probable case – it is sufficient for me as a reason for bowing before her in eternal gratitude to that 'great power of God' manifested in her – that I cannot read six pages of hers without feeling that it is given to her to delineate human passion and its results (and I must say in spite of your judgment) some of the moral instincts and their tendencies – with such truthfulness such nicety of discrimination such tragic power and withal such loving gentle humour that one might live a century with nothing but one's own dull faculties and not know so much as these six pages will suggest.[7]

Indiana, Mauprat, Consuelo, Lélia, Lettres d'un Voyageur, Jacques, Spiridion, Le Meunier d'Angibault – we know that Marian Evans read these works of George Sand, written before 1847, from actual references to them in her letters. But it is unlikely, in view of her thoroughness and her tendency to become an *afficianado*, that any of the novels slipped through her net. Unlike most other readers she seems not to have been dismayed by *Lélia*, and the self-revelation in *Lettres d'un Voyageur* appealed to her very much.

She picks out for especial attention the passage in Chapter 4 in which

George Sand, in defending *Lélia*, says that nothing can be immoral which is really true to human experience. Moral platitudes soon lose their relevance for later generations but what is written from the heart will always find receptive readers – 'ceux-là seuls qui, souffrant des mêmes angoisses l'ont ecouté comme une plainte entrecoupée, mêlée de fièvre, de sanglots, de rires lugubres et de jurements, l'ont fort bien compris, et ceux-là l'aiment sans l'approuver.' As Marian consigned the extract to the less receptive Sara Hennell, she commented soberly: 'It has a very deep meaning to my apprehension.'

She was in sympathy not only with George Sand's *cris de coeur* but with her note of stoic acceptance of whatever life brought – the note which she herself was to sound so often in her novels. George Sand, too, had had to learn to do without an orthodox creed, without 'the crutches of superstition'. In a letter to John Sibree, George Eliot quotes (again from *Lettres d'un Voyageur*) a verse which she describes as 'almost the ultimatum in human wisdom, on the question of human sorrow'.

> Le bonheur et le malheur
> Nous viennent du même auteur
> Voilà la ressemblance.
> Le bonheur nous rend heureux
> Et le malheur malheureux
> Voilà la différence.

and then goes on appreciatively to give George Sand's comment: 'Sais-tu bien que tout est dit devant Dieu et devant les hommes quand l'homme infortuné demande compte de ses maux et qu'il obtienne cette résponse. Qu'y-a-t-il de plus? Rien.'[8]

She certainly needed all the stoicism she could muster in her 'doleful prison of stupidity and barrenness with a yawning trapdoor ready to let me down into utter fatuity', and her old favourite, Carlyle, is as vital a presence in her letters at this time as her more recent saviour, George Sand – an alliance which neither would have relished. But despite all her anguish and frustrations a new note of vitality persists: 'Poor pebble as I am left entangled among the slimy weeds – I can yet hear from afar the rushing of the blessed torrent.'[9] Her fight against 'shrinking into that mathematical abstraction, a point' is a vigorous one, and she makes no attempt to disguise from her friends her fluctuations of mood – gaiety, despair, gloom, cynicism, faith, *ennui* – that *Lélia* word which would never have crossed the lips of the Evangelical Mary Ann a few years earlier. The uninhibited, informal tone is no doubt due to many things: the end of her 'Strauss-sickness', the stimulus given her by her lively young correspondent, John Sibree, but also, I think, to 'new perceptions' at work and the example of an accomplished letter writer, who was never afraid to unbosom herself, who always wrote 'de tout son coeur'.

Even if we did not have Marian Evans's own testimony, there are plenty of superficial traces in the correspondence to guide us. There is now a spattering of French words and phrases; she falls into the easy address of 'mon ami' to her two male correspondents, Charles Bray and John Sibree; she has been 'turning over Lavater's queer sketches of physiognomies and still queerer judgments upon them'[10] (most of Chapter 7 of *Lettres d'un Voyageur* is given over to a discussion of Lavater, although it should also be said that *The Peoples Journal* took him up about this time, too). Immediately after expressing her admiration of George Sand, she mentions that she has at last got an *Imitation of Christ* – 'one breathes a cool air as of cloisters'[11] – the book which, above all others, Lélia found of most comfort and inspiration 'au fond de mon cloître'; in 1848 she is full of revolutionary ardour and deplores 'our little humbug of a queen';[12] she cries out to John Sibree (who has finally lost his faith and is bound for Germany), 'Oh, the bliss of having a very high attic in a romantic Continental town!'[13] Her letters are full of throw-away allusions to characters in George Sand's novels: 'You are ever with me as Spiridion was with Alexis and Angel'[14] she writes to Sara Hennell – or again (quoting the catch-phrase of the avaricious farmer in *Le Meunier d'Angibault*) 'aujour d'aujour d'hui as M. Bricolin says'.[15] These are straws in the wind which all point the same way – towards George Sand. The French novelist was exerting an influence upon her in a variety of ways, not simply as a 'guano', but as a leaven. These, more than any others, were her George Sand years. She continued to read her but it was in this period, when she was most receptive to works of the imagination, and most in need of solace and stimulus, that George Sand got into her system. And what she absorbed then from a writer to whom she responded so instinctively, was there to be drawn upon, a few years later, when she herself started to write fiction at the prompting of yet another George, George Henry Lewes.

2

Lewes, as we have already seen, had been a most consistent and committed admirer of George Sand for over a decade before his work for the *Westminster Review* had brought together him and its new assistant editor, Marian Evans, in 1851. Lewes's perfect woman novelist was undoubtedly a sort of amalgam of the best aspects of George Sand and Jane Austen – two women whom anyone less mercurial and imaginative than Lewes might have despaired of reconciling. There can be little doubt that this is what he worked towards in the 1850s with

George Eliot, in their leisurely evenings of reading aloud of Jane Austen and of thoughtful discussion, and that, equally, he eventually felt that in her he had achieved his ideal . . . but this is to run ahead. In 1854, when Marian Evans made her extraordinarily courageous decision and left for Weimar with Lewes, passion and not decorum, sensibility rather than sense, George Sand and not Jane Austen was in the ascendant – and George Eliot had not yet been born.

Marcel Moraud long ago suggested that Marian Evans's decision to live with Lewes would not have been possible for her nad she not been emboldened and strengthened by the example of George Sand. It is certainly true that Marie d'Agoult was encouraged by it in her resolve to live with Liszt, and though I would hesitate to attribute every other daring Victorian runaway union to an excess of George Sandism – Elizabeth Barrett and Robert Browning, Marian Evans and Lewes – there is, I think, enough truth in the suggestion for it to be treated with respect.

Marian Evans might have been unsure 'whether I agree with her about marriage or not', but there is no doubt that she had, in Moraud's phrase, 'acquired a whole wardrobe of romantic ideas'[16] from George Sand. For anyone who had responded so wholeheartedly to the passionate self-revelations of George Sand, who had translated Feuerbach – 'Love is God himself and apart from it there is no God'[17] – the momentous decision to go away with Lewes was virtually made when he confessed his love and need of her. Despite her sober sessions with Charles Bray and John Chapman, in which they assessed the social and utilitarian consequences of the contemplated step, she was doing no more than paying lip-service to reason. Like any George Sand heroine, like George Sand herself, she was declaring her right to follow openly the promptings of her heart. And although she herself was not fundamentally changed by her decisive move, her way of life was instantly, startlingly, affected. A few months later, in Weimar, when she found herself in distinguished cosmopolitan society, in conversation with Liszt, there is a note of wonder and satisfaction in her comment, as she writes to Sara Hennell: 'When I read George Sand's letter to Franz Liszt in her *Lettres d'un Voyageur* I little thought that I should ever be seated tête-à-tête with him for an hour, as I was yesterday and telling him my ideas and feelings . . .'[18] Quite suddenly – as had happened also in the case of Elizabeth Barrett – the immense gap between the two women has narrowed.

Although the courage of Marian Evans in affronting society by her extra-marital union with Lewes has often and rightly been stressed, very much less has been said about the bravado of her choice of pseudonym. There is no reason to disbelieve her when she says that she chose 'George' because it was Lewes's name, while Eliot seemed 'a good mouth-filling easily-pronounced word'. On the other hand, she cannot have been unaware of the fact that such a pseudonym would invite comparison with George Sand. Although the latter was no longer, in 1856, the talking point that she had been in the 1830s and 1840s, she was still the leading French woman writer and a figure of perennial interest. Her autobiography, *Histoire de ma Vie*, had been published in 1855 and was widely read and reviewed in England – reviewed in the *Westminster* by Marian Evans herself. George Sand, in choosing her masculine pseudonym, had taken her lover's name and George Eliot, thus paying tribute to her 'husband', was laying herself open to the charge of likeness to the other George. The comparison was not one that she herself ever made and, in fact, the references to George Sand in her letters after her union with Lewes are strikingly few. This could be explained by the fact that her 'days of *Lélia*' were now so definitely behind her. But it can also be understood as George Eliot's reluctance, having once taken her unorthodox step, to say or write anything which would tend towards her being grouped with George Sand as a rebel against society rather than an unwilling victim of its legal anomalies. She was indeed deeply conservative and traditional by heredity and upbringing, and (as her eventual marriage to Cross shows) placed infinitely greater stress than George Sand on the form of marriage.

It is ironic that the relationship with Lewes, which liberated her into creativity, should at the same time have been so socially isolating and inhibiting that much of her former self-consciousness returned. When Mark Rutherford complained,[19] after the publication of Cross's *Life and Letters*, that the woman revealed by them was not the Marian Evans he had known from 1852–4, when they were fellow-boarders at John Chapman's, his complaint was justified. It was justified, however, not simply because Cross had bowdlerised many of the livelier passages, but also because 'Mrs Lewes' was indeed a different woman from the 'free spirit' he had known and later sketched, unforgettably, as Theresa, in the last chapter of the *Autobiography of Mark Rutherford*. The price that she had to pay for her new-found private happiness was an increased feeling of responsibility as a possible example to the public; and, as the years went on, the extraordinary respectability of her union meant that there was less and less temptation to draw parallels between the two Georges. When, in 1876, Sidney Colvin informed John Morley that he intended to do so, in reviewing *Daniel Deronda*, Morley told him 'You can say what you like about George Sand. But you will, of course, spare George Eliot's feelings as much as critical honesty will permit'[20] – a directive which was in accord with the reticence that had been observed for many years.

The comparison between George Sand and George Eliot as novelists, then, began to be made openly in the 1870s, and there are many interesting discussions of similarities between the two writers, without any definite suggestion of indebtedness and influence. Sometimes indeed they are treated as coevals, or as if George Eliot had written first. Writing in 1876, Andrew Lang makes George Sand's novels sound remarkably like George Eliot's:

> Thus, in almost every one of George Sand's stories we find the high souled being, *justissimus unus* or more often, *justissima una*, tolerant and yet impassioned, unselfish, devoted to the happiness of others. This noble creature is always in contrast with the smallness and selfishness and *personnalité* of some other man or woman. As a rule George Sand prefers to select some such man as Raymon in *Indiana* or Anzoleto in *Consuelo* or Horace in the novel of that name to display the qualities she most despises. She has a perfect gallery of men who remind us of Tito and of Arthur Donnithorne in their pleasant and successful selfishness, their weakness and their need of approval and esteem. These despised men are her successful lovers.[21]

The *Quarterly* reviewer was writing for a generation to whom the names of Raymon and Anzoleto still meant something, and this continued to be the case for the next twenty-five years. The opening chapter of Mathilde Blind's *George Eliot* (1883), the first full length study of the novelist after her death, is devoted to a discussion of their resemblances and differences; and in 1901 Leslie Stephen was confident that his discussion of the affinity between the two writers would go home to a reading-public still familiar with the works of both novelists.[22] But from then on, each writer was allowed to go her separate way; in each case, in fact, downwards into relative neglect and unpopularity. Leslie Stephen's daughter was one of the first to sound the trumpet for the resurrection of George Eliot, but she rose from the grave alone, as an English writer 'for grown-up people',[23] whereas her French predecessor continued to suffer the ignominy of being read only as a school-room text, for her 'bergeries'. The coralling and branding of George Eliot in more recent years into an exclusively English Great Tradition of novelists has contributed to contemporary unawareness of her debt to foreign influences, but even in the 1890s the tendency to treat the two writers as totally independent was being commented on drily by Jules Lemaître in the *Revue de Deux Mondes*. His article entitled 'De l'Influence Récente des Littératures du Nord' is significant in view of later critical insularity, even though he could fairly be accused of chauvinism himself.

His main thesis is that there is a tendency in France to take up writers from other countries and to treat them as phoenixes – such writers as George Eliot, Tolstoi, Ibsen and Strindberg – and to prefer them to home products. Is it not possible, he asks, that much of what

French critics admire in them can already be found in France, and especially in the second period of romanticism? He points to the resemblances between Ibsen's Norah and George Sand's Indiana and Valentine and, as for George Eliot, for whom there had been a positive cult in France around 1880 – surely her constant moral preoccupation and sympathy with the mediocre and ordinary things in human life are there in 'le George français' as much as in 'le George d'outremanche'? But what Frenchmen find original about these writers is not their ideas but a new *accent*. What, for instance, George Eliot has done is to return to France the substance of its own literature of forty years back 'modifiée, renouvelée, enrichée de son passage dans des esprits notablement différent du nôtre.'[24]

Lemaître is right to stress both the indebtedness and the distinctiveness of George Eliot, for it seems to me indisputable not only that she was deeply and intimately influenced by George Sand, from her first novel to her last, but that she was capable of writing individual and very much greater works.

3

It may, perhaps, be best to begin with the heroines – or what has often loosely been described as the 'autobiographical' element in George Eliot's heroines. There has been an assumption, sometimes tacit, sometimes very explicit, that the girlhood of Maggie Tulliver and Dorothea Brooke, their frustrations, yearnings, their avid desire for knowledge, can all be traced back to Marian Evans's own youth. In the case of *The Mill on The Floss*, much of the work is indeed autobiographical – in everything to do with Maggie's childhood, and especially with the brother-sister relationship which was so important to George Eliot that she allowed it to overweight the book and ensure an immature and sentimental ending. But when Maggie leaves childhood behind her she becomes a very different young woman from the Evangelical and strait-laced Mary Ann Evans, sententious, severe, disapproving of anything 'not consistent with millennial holiness'. This puritanical period of Marian Evans's life, which lasted from the time she was fifteen until she was twenty has, apart from certain renunciatory tendencies in her heroines, no counterpart in the novels. As Gordon Haight rightly says 'the experience of George Eliot's heroines provides not even hypothetical parallels . . . When trouble came to her [Maggie] it was economic not spiritual; she found her solace not in evangelical tracts but in Thomas à Kempis's *Imitation of Christ*.'[25]

If George Eliot did not use her own youthful experiences as copy, if she did not turn back to the girl whom she later recognised to have 'gone about like an owl', intolerant, humourless and repressive – a young woman, moreover, painfully felt by her to be devoid of beauty and charm – on whom, if anyone, are her heroines modelled? They are certainly a very different breed from anything that had gone before in the English novel. Their like is not to be found in Fielding or Richardson, Jane Austen or Scott, Dickens or Thackeray, the Brontës or Mrs Gaskell. I do not, of course, refer to the line of worldly young women – Hetty, Esther, Rosamond – who have the potentiality for causing such havoc in the lives of good men, and whom George Eliot became surer and surer at handling until the final triumph of Gwendolen was achieved. It is rather Maggie, Romola, Dorothea who come to mind when we talk of the George Eliot heroine. On them the creator has certainly stamped some of her own characteristics of emotionalism, a desire for learning, a passionate need for affection – but, in addition, these beautiful, ardent, trustful, high-souled young women bear a considerable family resemblance, not just to the heroines of George Sand, but much more significantly to George Sand's own account of herself as a girl, to the young Aurore Dupin, revealed to us in *Histoire de ma Vie*, and, in glimpses, in *Lélia* and *Lettres d'un Voyageur*. It is an account which merits some attention.

Like Mary Ann Evans, but much more like Maggie Tulliver, Aurore underwent a sudden conversion at the age of fifteen. At the time, Aurore was in Paris, at the Convent of the Dames Augustines Anglaises – a rebellious tomboy, always in mischief, avid for affection, very little concerned with religion, and eager to learn but impatient of discipline. Then one day she opened a book she had been lent and started reading it at random; it was a *Life of the Saints*. As she read, the stoicism and faith of the martyrs touched a responsive chord in her heart and mind, and later in church she thought she heard a voice in her ear, murmuring the words which St Augustine had heard in his miraculous conversion: *Tolle, lege*. And in that moment, for the first time, she felt in direct ecstatic communion with God: 'Je voyais un chemin vaste, immense, sans bornes, s'ouvrir devant moi; je brûlais de m'y élancer.'[26]

And she did rush into self-sacrifice with all the ardour, dedication, self-mortification and renunciation at her command. From that day she was transformed, thinking only of how she could devote herself to others. She seriously contemplated entering the order, dramatically envisaging herself drudging at only the most humble tasks. 'Je brûlais littéralement comme sainte Thérèse . . . Je me condamnais à des austérités qui étaient sans mérite puisque je n'avais plus rien à immoler, à changer ou à détruire en moi.'[27] If there had been a hair-shirt available she would have worn it, but had to make do instead with a filigree necklace which rubbed a sore on her neck. Her companions and the sisters marvelled at the change in her. Aglow with self-sacrifice, 'j'étais devenue sage, obéissante et laborieuse', although both Sister Alicia and her father confessor were aware of the element of egoism and pride in her excessive renunciation of self and warned her against her 'morbid scrupulosity'.

At the age of seventeen, back at Nohant, with her beloved grandmother dying by inches, she was entirely her own mistress and free, in the intervals of sitting by the invalid's bed, to roam the country on horseback and to recover her taste for serious reading of books other than the Bible and *The Imitation of Christ*, which had for so long been her guide. It was ironic that it was *Le Génie du Christianisme*, a work lent her by the local *curé*, which first raised serious doubts in her mind. The romantic beauty of the descriptions, both of the splendour of nature and of earthly love, took her by storm. This was the opposite of the renunciation of the world that St Thomas à Kempis had enjoined upon her, and she felt herself caught up in a terrible struggle between the two protagonists of religion – the one voice urging her to annihilate all desires, all awareness of self, the other to glorify God by accepting all his gifts; the one saying 'Soyons boue et poussière', the other 'Soyons flamme et lumière'; the one urging total unthinking acceptance, the other insisting on the importance of questioning.

In her torment, she turned again to her well-thumbed *Imitation of Christ*, her name written on its fly-leaf by Sister Alicia, and listened to the voice of the saint, whose eloquence and simplicity had so charmed and persuaded her. She knew it by heart and in *Histoire de ma Vie*, in George Sand's account of the young Aurore's struggles, there follow two pages in which one maxim after another is recalled. 'Qu'est-ce que ceci ou cela vous regarde? Pour vous, suivez-moi – Quitte-toi toi-même, et tu me trouveras – Donne tout pour tout – Tu auras la liberté du coeur et les ténèbres ne t'offusqueront plus – Quitte-toi, résigne-toi –'[28] But as the well-remembered phrases passed through her mind they had lost their magic, and seemed like the creed of the cloister.

It was, however, a conflict which was not to be easily resolved, for the doctrines of the *Imitation* had become so much part of her way of life that even as she read and doubted, she was reproaching herself for having ever strayed from the straight and well-defined path of renunciation. She appealed for help once again to her father confessor, asking whether she should try to subdue her thirst for study, her instinctive longing for poetry and philosophy. And yielding to his affectionate mockery of her fears, she launched herself upon an assortment of the authors she had been yearning to read with all the urgency of one who felt that it was a matter of life or death, that from her reading she would be able to understand whether indeed she were heading for the life of the world or the voluntary death of the cloister. First she read all the philosophers (whose pages her grandmother had marked, so that she would know which passages to omit), then the poets and moralists; and when, at last, she came to Rousseau, she was totally enslaved. For the young Aurore he was what Voltaire had been for her grandmother – the apogee of all her admiration, a 'life-changer', as he was also, most notably, for George Eliot.

I have given this detailed account of Aurore Dupin's adolescence because it seems to me to offer striking evidence of George Eliot's indebtedness to literary precedent rather than to autobiography or imagination. As Maggie passed from a childhood – many of whose incidents are well authenticated from George Eliot's own past – to young womanhood, her transition period is given a feeling of authenticity by being largely modelled on a real but more romantic girl than Marian Evans ever was. The resemblances are much too striking to be merely coincidence. Like Aurore, Maggie takes up at random a Thomas à Kempis left her by Bob Jakin. 'She took up the little, old, clumsy book with some curiosity; it had the corners turned down in many places, and some hand, now for ever quiet, had made at certain passages strong pen-and-ink marks, long since browned by time.' Like Aurore, Maggie goes from one maxim of renunciation to another, seeking guidance and comfort:

> If thou seekest this or that, and wouldst be here or there to enjoy thy own will and pleasure thou shalt never be quiet nor free from care . . . Why dost thou here gaze about since this is not the place of thy rest? . . . If a man should give all his substance yet it is as nothing . . . Forsake thyself, resign thyself, and thou shalt enjoy much inward peace.

There is a similar suddenness in Maggie's vision of renunciation, in her feeling of frustration before reading and her sense of having found the key to living when the lesson of self-annihilation has been understood: 'A strange thrill of awe passed through Maggie while she read, as if she had been wakened in the night by a strain of solemn music, telling of beings whose souls had been astir while hers was in stupor.' There is the same quality of pride and egotism in her abnegation, but at the same time a new consideration for others. ' "From what you know of her, you will not be surprised that she threw some exaggeration and wilfulness, some pride and impetuosity, even into her self-renunciation . . . [But] that new inward life of hers, notwithstanding some volcanic upheavings of imprisoned passion, yet shone out of her face with a tender soft light . . ." '[29] There is also the intrusion into her life of a contrary viewpoint; many of the arguments used by Philip – even the very phrases – are there in *Histoire de ma Vie* in the case made by Aurore herself, after reading Chateaubriand, and by her confessor:

You will not always be shut up in your present lot; why should you starve your mind in that way? It is narrow asceticism – I don't like to see you persisting in it, Maggie. Poetry and art and knowledge are sacred and pure . . . Joy and peace are not resignation; and it is stupefaction to remain in ignorance – to shut up all the avenues by which the life of your fellow-men might become known to you.[30]

And even when she succumbs to Philip's arguments and enjoys his course of reading and music and art (which includes French novels – *Corinne* is particularly mentioned) she is still torn by the conflict between what she sees as alternate goods and what Philip sees as the choice between life and death.

The parallels are all there between this section of *Histoire de ma Vie* and *The Mill on the Floss*; and much of what I have said about Maggie Tulliver holds for both Romola and Dorothea – two other young Saint Theresas who painfully learn the lesson of sacrifice and achieve nobility and compassion in the process. What indeed are Maggie or Dorothea or Romola if not, in the words of the *Quarterly Review* on George Sand's heroines, '*justissima una*, tolerant and yet impassioned, unselfish, devoted to the happiness of others'? Few of George Sand's heroines, it should be said, emulate her own advanced behaviour; and those who do are so idealistic and trustful and noble that the reader who ventures to pass moral judgements on them is made to feel worldly and unworthy. As Henry James commented with some asperity, 'George Sand never accepts a weakness as a weakness; she always dresses it up as a virtue; and if her heroines abandon their lovers and lie to their husbands, you may be sure it is from motives of the highest morality.'[31]

But one heroine in particular, who won the hearts of English readers and whose purity was unquestionable, was Consuelo – Bertha Thomas's observation in 1883, 'Upon so well-known a work lengthened comment would be superfluous',[32] gives some idea of the extent of the run that Consuelo had in England, and of the size of her reading public which even included Queen Victoria, who found the book '*dreadfully* interesting'.[33] Most of its popularity was undoubtedly due to the character of the heroine, the small gipsy-like waif with the short thick black hair, who has a wonderful voice and eventually becomes a beautiful prima donna, whose singing and greatness of soul and sweetness of disposition win all hearts. Hers is not, however, a sentimental virtue; she has spirit and courage and good sense to assist her in her solitary destiny. The novel does, I think, have considerable relevance not only to *The Mill on the Floss* in particular, but to the entire corpus of George Eliot's novels.

Even from this brief description it is obvious that Consuelo and the young Maggie have some points in common – the ugly duckling who becomes a cygnet, the little sparrow who turns into a lark; Maggie, the 'little gypsy' with the brown complexion and the recalcitrant black mop is more like Consuelo than she is like the young Mary Ann with her light brown hair, blue eyes and fair skin. And as Consuelo and Maggie mature and grow beautiful the resemblances are equally marked; each with magnificent, long, dark gleaming hair, each impervious to fashion, always dressed in – and outshining others in – 'a simple black dress'. All these are superficial echoes and are only of interest in that they again show George Eliot drawing on literary rather than auto-biographical sources. What is of much more significance in any comparison of the two books is the handling of the love interest.

A review of *The Mill on the Floss* which appeared in 1860 commented disapprovingly that the author showed

> one or two unfortunate modern tendencies like Miss Brontë, and her way of treating the passion of love is even more questionable. Currer Bell, George Eliot and, we may add, George Sand all like to dwell on love as a strange overmastering force which through the senses captivates and enthralls the soul. They linger on the description of physical sensations that accompany the meetings of hearts in love.[34]

The reviewer, as is common, has added the name of George Sand as if she were a contemporary rather than an author to whom both the other novelists had, in some respects at least, gone to school. The point he is making surprises a twentieth-century reader. Even someone as relatively guarded in his treatment of sex as Henry James spoke of the 'singular austerity' with which George Eliot treated love, commenting that *Middlemarch* and *Daniel Deronda* 'seem to foreign readers probably like vast cold commodious respectable rooms (looking out on a snow-covered landscape) – across whose acres of sober-hued carpet one looks in vain for a fireplace or a fire.'[35] He does, however, exempt Maggie Tulliver from his charge that George Eliot's men and women are lacking in passion,[36] and certainly *The Mill on the Floss* is from this point of view her least inhibited work. The river idyll of Stephen and Maggie may have owed something to the love-scenes of Julie and Saint-Preux on the lake, but it seems more likely that her real literary educator in love between the sexes was George Sand. For, unlike Rousseau, George Sand respected women and their independent potentialities, and makes it clear that her heroines need more from life than simply to worship or be worshipped.

What then *is* George Eliot's 'way of treating the passion of love' in *The Mill on the Floss*? She does indeed linger, as not even the Brontës had, on the 'physical sensations that accompany the meetings of hearts'. Stephen and Maggie from the first are oppressively conscious of each other:

> Maggie had no distinct thought . . . only the sense of a presence like that of a closely-hovering broad-winged bird in the darkness . . . Maggie bent her arm a little upward towards the large half-opened rose that had attracted her . . . A mad impulse seized on Stephen; he darted towards the arm, and showered kisses on it, clasping the wrist . . . She darted from him into the adjoining room, and threw herself on the sofa, panting and trembling . . . [Stephen] leaned back against the framework of the conservatory, dizzy with the conflict of passions – love, rage and confused despair.[37]

The effects come rather closer to Lawrence in the scene at Aunt Moss's when Stephen rides out to confront Maggie on 'a tall bay horse; and the flanks and the neck of the horse were streaked black with fast riding. Maggie felt a beating at heart and head – horrible as the sudden leaping to life of a savage enemy who had feigned death.'[38] And in the meeting before the final river episode all the stops are full out from the moment of Stephen's unexpected arrival:

> Maggie had started up and sat down again with her heart beating violently . . . she trembled visibly . . . He was looking into her deep, deep eyes – far-off and mysterious as the starlit blackness . . . Maggie sat perfectly still . . . until the helpless trembling had ceased and there was a warm glow on her cheek . . . They glided rapidly along . . . between the silent sunny fields and pastures, which seemed filled with a natural joy that had no reproach for theirs. The breath of the young unwearied day, the delicious rhythmic dip of the oars, the fragmentary song of a passing bird heard now and then . . . all helped to bring her into more complete subjection to that strong, mysterious charm which made a last parting from Stephen seem the death of all joy . . .[39]

The emotional impact of such passages need be compared with only one, very typical extract from *Consuelo* for us to see the family resemblance:

> Consuelo . . . sortit du salon et alla dans le jardin . . . Elle tremblait, comme si elle eût senti son courage l'abandonner dans la crise la plus dangeureuse de sa vie; et, pour la première fois, elle ne retrouvait en elle cette droiture de premier mouvement, cette sainte confiance dans ses intentions, qui l'avaient toujours soutenue dans ses épreuves. Elle avait quitté le salon pour se dérober à la fascination qu'Anzoleto exerçait sur elle, et elle avait éprouvé en même temps, comme un vague désir d'être suivie par lui . . . et, prête à fuir, n'osant

se retourner, elle restait enchainée à sa place par une puissance magique . . .

Consternée comme quelqu'un qui se sent rouler dans un precipice, et qui voit se briser une à une les faibles branches qu'il voulait saisir pour arrêter sa chute, elle regardait le fond de l'abîme et le vertige bourdonnait dans son cerveau . . . Anzoleto était près d'elle . . . il recontrait ses mains, et les retenait dans les siennes pendant une seconde; mais cette rapide et brûlante pression résumait tout un siècle de volupté. Il lui disait à la dérobée de ces mots qui étouffent, il lui lançait de ces regards qui dévorent . . .

Toujours ce sentiment double, faux, insurmontable, tourmentait sa pensée, et mettait son coeur aux prises avec sa conscience. Jamais elle ne s'était sentie si malheureuse, si exposée, si seule sur la terre . . .[40]

What Consuelo is here trying to escape from is a triangular situation which has much in common with that of Maggie, Philip and Stephen. On the face of it, the young prima donna's dilemma, torn between her affection and pity for Count Albert and her love for Anzoleto, seems at a very far remove from the trials of Maggie in St Ogg's. But the underlying tensions are very similar, as are the authors' admiration of the 'droiture de premier mouvement' of their heroines – the rightness of instinct and purity of intention which sustains them, when put to the test. It is noteworthy that Sara Hennell, George Eliot's tactless and truthful friend, wrote her in these terms after she had read *The Mill on the Floss*: 'Go on! – write once more, and give us something as much better than this, as this, if finished, would be better (in moral tone) than *Consuelo*. For *Consuelo* is the only thing to compare with it.'[41]

The resemblance is especially striking in the drawing-room music scenes in both novels. Consuelo has transformed the isolated life of Albert who, though noble, generous, intellectual and artistic is, none the less, a misfit. His infirmity, which manifests itself in trances, has cut him off from normal living. He confesses to Consuelo his overpowering devotion for her, and reassures her about how little he expects in return. Consuelo is aware that her feelings for Albert, despite the attraction of a life of service and self-forgetfulness, are very different from her love for Anzoleto. She wanders through the *château*'s labyrinth of passages and is conscious of its chill and gloom, a prison 'which the sun itself seemed afraid to penetrate'.[42] Whenever she thinks of her future with Albert, of entering his 'région des idées abstraites', an austere imagery of cold and darkness prevails. She is conscious of it as a denial of life, such as Dorothea finds her marriage with Casaubon to be. This formula of conflict between idealism and the flesh was to be a favourite one with George Eliot, and in every case the worldly lover breaks in upon the incarceration of the heroine like a shaft of warm sunshine. When Anzoleto turns up again, it is as if Consuelo has been given a sudden glimpse of freedom and normal life; she cannot help feeling his physical attraction, his masculine energy and gaiety. And when, in the salon after dinner, Anzoleto lifts up his voice in happy, lively songs which bring a whole other carefree world to mind, her delight in the music seizes her against her will and she joins her voice to his, until Anzoleto finally steals a passionate kiss. Only the watchful Albert intercepts Anzoleto's glances and interprets them accurately. He suddenly realises that Anzoleto is not, as he pretends to be, Consuelo's brother, but 'un amant audacieux, acharné et dangereux'[43] – just as Philip, watching Stephen and Maggie keenly, suspects the state of affairs between them and recognises a rival, 'a dangerous and persevering lover'. The scene is really very similar; both Consuelo and Maggie are aware of their weakness and determined not to give in – and in each case the music works its spell and all their good intentions are lost in the overpowering emotion it induces. Consuelo's conflict is sharp and brief. She thinks of binding herself to Albert to fortify her opposition to Anzoleto, but instead chooses to return to her professional life of independence in the hope of regaining her former self-respect. She leaves the *château*, after surviving, alone in her bedroom, a crisis of temptation, despair and loneliness as passionate as Maggie's on the receipt of Stephen's letter. She holds out hope to Albert that she may yet love him, when this 'hideous dream' is over, and Albert's confidence in her remains unshaken. 'Elle est pure', he tells his father, 'elle veut m'aimer. Elle sent que mon amour est vrai et ma foi inébranlable.'[44]

The sentiments expressed by Albert for Consuelo, with her 'grandeur d'âme', and by Philip for the 'great-souled' Maggie are indeed remarkably interchangeable. Each is convinced of the unworthiness of the rival, the truth and fidelity of his beloved and each, cut off from normal living by infirmity, feels nothing but gratitude for the relationship:

> Quant à m'affliger, cela n'est pas en ton pouvoir, Consuelo. Je ne me suis point fait d'illusions; je suis habitué aux plus atroces douleurs; je sais que ma vie est devouée aux sacrifices les plus cuisants . . . Il me suffit de te regarder pour que mon âme vivifiée monte vers le ciel comme un hymne de reconnaissance et un encens de purification.[45]

What Albert says, Philip writes: 'I want you to put aside all grief because of the grief you have caused me. I was nurtured in the sense of privation. I never expected happiness and in knowing you, in loving you, I have had, and still have, what reconciles me to life.'[46] Each goes through a similar period of anguish, when he thinks himself betrayed: 'J'ai cru à votre abandon, et je me suis laissé frapper par le désèspoir;

mais . . . j'ai recouvré ma raison . . . J'ai su enfin que tu avais été fidèle
à ton serment, Consuelo; que tu avais fait ton possible pour m'aimer;
que tu m'avais aimé véritablement durant quelques heures.'[47] Or, in
Philip's words:

> I know you tried to keep faith to me . . . The night after I last parted
> from you I suffered torments. I had seen what convinced me that you
> were not free . . . but through all the suggestions – almost murderous
> suggestions – of rage and jealousy, my mind made its way to believe
> in your truthfulness.[48]

These parallels show, I think, that the presentation of the relationship
between Stephen, Maggie and Philip, is not simply, as F. R. Leavis
suggested, indicative of the immediate presence of the author. While it
is true that George Eliot would not have leant on George Sand if the
latter's emotionalism had not been extremely congenial to her,
Maggie's resemblance to both Consuelo and Aurore Dupin should
finally scotch the belief that 'Maggie Tulliver is essentially identical
with the young Mary Ann Evans.'[49] The source is at least as literary
as it is autobiographical – if not more so. And it may well be that
George Eliot is writing with considerable confidence in these parts
because of her knowledge of the enormous popularity of *Consuelo*.

Not only in *Consuelo*, but throughout George Sand's novels, music is
used as a test of greatness of soul. In this belief George Sand is true to
her romantic inheritance. The real artist is not simply the skilful
performer, but the man or woman whose soul can be made to vibrate
with all the passion and intensity and self-forgetfulness that great music
demands. The shallow or showy executant is held up to scorn by both
authors, in a significantly different way from Jane Austen or even Mme
de Staël. In *Consuelo*, Corilla and Anzoleto and Amelia, because they
lack these admirable qualities, do not pass the test – any more than
does Rosamond with her tinkling piano-playing or Gwendolen with
her amateur vocal flourishes, though the latter does have 'fullness of
nature' enough to respond to the power of Klesmer's playing, a sure
sign that she is redeemable. It is in a very early story, in *Scenes of
Clerical Life*, that we find her first trying out the theme; Caterina, in
'Mr Gilfil's Love Story', is another heroine who comes very close
indeed to the young Consuelo.

Like her, Caterina is a passionate, artless little Italian waif, black-
eyed, black-haired, the orphaned daughter of an impoverished singer.
She is brought up by her benefactor, Sir Christopher, in a great house
in England, where her extraordinary musical gift is cherished, and
where eventually she has her heart broken by Sir Christopher's self-
indulgent, handsome nephew, Anthony. The terms in which George
Eliot describes Caterina's magical transformation are identical with the

many descriptions of Consuelo's response to music – or Maggie Tulliver's, if it comes to that. 'The vibration rushed through Caterina like an electric shock; it seemed as if, at that instant, a new soul were entering in to her and filling her with a deeper, more significant life.'[50] As it is a life which only the dedicated artist or the great of soul can enter, it is one from which Beatrice, Anthony's statuesque betrothed, is excluded – for although she 'doats on it', she has no ear for music.

The problems of the artist, which George Sand discusses so often, find their fullest exposition by George Eliot in *Daniel Deronda*. It is here that – through Klesmer – she conveys something of what it means to be a professional. Gwendolen's 'sinking of heart at the sudden width of horizon opened round her own small musical performance',[51] is very like the sensation of the frivolous Amelia when she listens to Consuelo's singing. She began fretfully to be aware of her own lack of musical talent: 'Elle comprenait enfin qu'elle ne savait rien, et peut-être qu'elle ne pourrait jamais rien apprendre.'[52] Klesmer speaks of a life of arduous, unceasing work '. . . for natures framed to love perfection and to labour for it.'[53] Daniel Deronda's mother is a prima donna who has never ceased to repent her apostacy from her chosen role: 'You may try – but you can never imagine what it is like to have a man's force of genius in you, and yet to suffer the slavery of being a girl.'[54] Against this vain and ruthless professional George Eliot sets Mirah, whose sweet voice will never fill a concert-hall but whose nobility of nature ensures that her life will not be a lonely one, and that her music will be used for the solace of others. George Eliot is ultimately much more divided in her mind about professionalism than George Sand ever was, and much less convinced that the human sacrifice involved is worth it. None the less, many of the responses of her heroines to musical stimuli echo in a fascinating way similar scenes in George Sand. A minor but interesting instance is that well-known reference in *Middlemarch* to Dorothea's sensibility; she reminds her uncle, 'When we listened to the great organ at Freiburg it made me sob.'[55] It had also moved to tears Liszt's mistress, Marie d'Agoult, when he played the great organ at Freiburg, and the account of the incident in *Lettres d'un Voyageur*[56] had been deeply pondered and appreciated by George Eliot. So that if we find ourselves in sympathy with Mr Brooke's comment on Dorothea's emotion – 'Not healthy that in a young girl' – it is, I fear, counter to the author's intention.

4

So far, then, George Sand seems rather to have fostered the emotional, idealistic side of George Eliot's writing, to have intensified tendencies which cannot really be considered as strengths in her as a novelist. But this is to give an incomplete picture of her indebtedness. Why, for instance, should a novel like *Jacques* have so moved Marian Evans when she read it in 1846? The 'six pages' she referred to in the letter to Sara Hennell, which she said delineated 'human passion and its results with such truthfulness, such nicety of discrimination, such tragic power and withal such loving gentle humour', were from *Jacques*. At first reading, it appears so remote from her most heartfelt convictions about self-control and duty that it seems difficult to understand its appeal for her.

The theme of this epistolary novel is simple. Jacques, a disillusioned man of thirty-five marries Fernande, an innocent girl of seventeen (it is, he admits, 'the only way of getting her'). He believes that at last he has found happiness, although he soon realises that Fernande's love for him is really veneration, that she wishes to love him not as an equal but 'as a slave feels for his master'. Fernande, in her turn, finds the strain of living up to Jacques's ideals too much and falls in love with Octave, who is 'enfant comme lui'. The world-weary Jacques nobly sacrifices himself for their happiness and stages a fatal accident for himself on a glacier.

The faults of this novel are very obvious: the excess of sensibility and heroics and the lovers' lack of any sense of proportion, as well as the at times comically self-indulgent introspection of all the characters. It is indeed a novel 'all about love'. 'Il n'est qu'un bonheur au monde, c'est l'amour.'[57] Balzac punctured very neatly the emotional afflatus in his dry observation[58] that Mme Dudevant's latest novel was a word of advice to husbands who were in their wives' way to kill themselves and so leave their partners free.

And yet there is no suspicion of a similar want of sympathy in George Eliot's reaction. She shows herself aware of the lack of plot and the loose construction, and dissociates herself from George Sand's views on marriage ('une des plus barbares institutions'). What is more important for her is that when she reads George Sand she feels, in Lewes's phrase, in the presence of 'the forlorn splendour of a life of passionate experience' and conscious of new worlds of feeling. But although the résumé of *Jacques* seems very unlike anything George Eliot ever wrote or was interested in, the questions asked in it and in George Sand's other early novels about the relationship of men and women were those which continued to be asked by George Eliot in all her own writings.

Jacques is, above all, the anatomy of a marriage. It is not a study of the gradual wearing-away of the freshness of love by the exigencies of domesticity and finance and family cares and social pressures, but of the loss of illusion in the early days of marriage. With her usual ability to generalise from the particular case, George Eliot saw past the

Romantic trappings and decided that 'the psychological anatomy of
Jacques and Fernande in the early days of their marriage seems quite
preternaturally true – I mean that her power of describing it is
preternatural. Fernande and Jacques are merely the masculine and the
feminine nature and their early married life an everyday tragedy.' It
had not been, however, an 'everyday tragedy' in the English novel,
which had dealt not with marriage but the quest of a man for a wife.
Lewes was very much aware of this difference between French and
English novels and, while deploring the stress laid by French writers on
adultery, saw that their interest in the husband-wife relationship
allowed for greater psychological complexity. And already we find
George Eliot singling out for praise George Sand's treatment of those
problems which she herself, for the first time in the English novel, was
to treat with maturity and subtlety.

The 'everyday tragedy' of Fernande and Jacques is a marriage of
incompatibility – incompatibility in age, in experience, in education
for life. Jacques and Fernande love each other, yet within months they
have made each other miserable. Jacques expects nothing of life and
knows all about love; Fernande expects everything of life and mistakes
her hero-worship of Jacques for love. George Sand conveys, with
remarkable sensitivity, the powerlessness of the couple to arrest the
deterioration of their relationship as one illusion goes after another – as
Jacques finds that his charming young wife is possessive, emotional and
irrational, as Fernande grows resentful of the qualities she had admired
in him before marriage, his self-sufficiency, his experience, and his inner
resources. While George Sand gives the heroic rôle to Jacques, she
blames, not Fernande, but Fernande's education – and here it might be
George Eliot speaking. The differences between the 'masculine and
feminine nature' are intensified by the false and shallow preparation for
life given to young girls like Fernande. She had been sheltered from the
realities of life and was living in a world of illusion. This passage went
home to George Eliot as it had to Matthew and Tom Arnold:

> On lui a parlé de prudence, de raison, de certains calculs pour éviter
> certaines douleurs et de certaines réflexions pour arriver à un certain
> bienêtre que la société permet aux femmes à de certaines conditions
> ... Nul n'eût la sagesse de lui dire: la vie est aride et terrible, le repos
> est une chimère, la prudence est inutile: la raison seule ne sert qu'à
> dessécher le coeur; il n'y a qu'une vertu, l'éternel sacrifice de
> soi-même.[59]

Here George Sand is touching upon a theme to which George Eliot
returned again and again in her novels. She is, of course, fascinated by
the early months of marriage, 'the door-sill of marriage once crossed',

by the spectacle of a husband or wife awakening to the loss of illusion. Dorothea and Mr Casaubon: 'but was not Mr Casaubon just as learned as before? The light had changed and you cannot find the pearly dawn at mid-day';[60] Rosamond and Lydgate: 'It was as if a fracture in delicate crystal had begun and he was afraid of any movement that might make it fatal';[61] Gwendolen, her brief fancy of mastery gone; Romola, deluded no longer as to Tito's worth.

But what interests her even more is the terrible propensity of the 'feminine nature' to hold a man back from fulfilling his destiny or even his normal potentialities. In the perfect marriage there is no room for egoism. Fernande's failure is summed up by George Sand: 'Un peu d'égoisme a paralysé son amour.' The egoism, too, which made a 'creeping paralysis' of the Lydgate marriage, which brought tragedy to Hetty, which made Gwendolen 'mount the chariot where another held the reins,' which would have caused Esther to ruin Felix Holt's life had he not first warned her off and then reformed her: 'I can't bear to see you going the way of the foolish women who spoil men's lives. Men can't help loving them, and so they make themselves slaves to the petty desires of petty creatures . . . That's what makes women a curse; all life is stunted to suit their littleness.'[62]

What women must cultivate is not only a larger vision but resources of their own. In 1870 George Eliot wrote: 'We women are always in danger of living too exclusively in the affections; and though our affections are perhaps the best gifts we have, we ought also to have our share of the independent life – some joy in things for their own sake.'[63] Fernande lives 'exclusively in the affections', and glories in doing so. She says deprecatingly of Jacques, to her lover: 'Il y'a dans sa vie autre chose que l'amour. La solitude, les voyages, l'étude, la réflexion, il aime tout cela: et nous, nous n'aimons que nous.'[64]

Fernande is understandably vague about the nature of Jacques's other interests which we have to take on trust, but George Eliot was to enlarge upon this theme and to give reality and significance to the 'other things besides love' which can claim a husband's attention; most memorably in her unsparing, compassionate treatment of the incompatibility of Rosamond and Lydgate. 'Poor Lydgate! or shall I say, Poor Rosamond! Each lived in a world of which the other knew nothing.'[65]

This is the same fairness towards both partners in an incompatible marriage which George Sand shows in *Jacques* – 'Ce n'est ni sa faute ni la mienne'[66] – and also, even earlier, in *Indiana*, in which a noble, impulsive young girl is ill-matched with the elderly, retired soldier, a dry stick of a man, who can give nothing to the marriage, whose only arbiter of action is public opinion and 'the done thing'. There are many long, thoughtful discussions of the relationship between them – the sort of sensitive brooding over the lack of absolute rights and wrongs which so enriches the presentation of the marriage of Dorothea to Casaubon. Like the latter, M. Delmare is made miserable by his idealistic young wife – 'Une femme encore enfant l'avait donc rendu malheureux!' – and George Sand writes of these two ill-assorted beings 'En vérité, je ne sais lequel etait plus malheureux d'elle ou de lui.'[67] As in *Jacques*, the nature of egoism is considered at some length and each character is shown to have his share of it, for, in the end, what is egoism but 'un besoin de bonheur qui nous dévore?'[68]

There was certainly no English author to whom George Eliot could turn for comparable treatment of these themes. Not only was George Sand making the point that in a marriage of incompatibility 'no villain need be'; in her novels she was also describing a new sort of villain – one not positively bad, but causing enormous unhappiness and even tragedy through his weakness and irresponsibility. As Andrew Lang pointed out, Raymon or Anzoleto – or, an even more extreme case, Horace – are remarkably similar to many handsome, self-indulgent young men in the novels of George Eliot. There is a long procession of them – Anthony Wybrow, Arthur Donnithorne, Stephen Guest, Godfrey Cass, Fred Vincy, Tito Melema – whose actions are marked by thoughtlessness and vanity, weakness and egotism in varying degrees. Their pursuit of the immediate pleasure is what brings about disaster.

George Sand broaches the type in *Indiana*. Raymon, a rich dashing young gentleman who lives on the nearby country estate, falls in love with Noun, Indiana's attractive maid-servant. They meet, first at the village fête and later in the summer-house in the grounds; he seduces her and when she becomes pregnant and is aware that he is no longer interested in her, she drowns herself in the millstream. The actual theme brings *Adam Bede* to mind, but what is much more striking is the similarity of the character of Raymon to Arthur Donnithorne. Raymon is full of good intentions, for he likes to think of himself as a good fellow and 'le jour où il triompha de ce coeur facile, il rentra chez lui, effrayé de sa victoire et se frappant le front, il se dit "Pourvu qu'elle ne m'aime pas!"'[69] When he is most in love with her, he even thinks seriously of marrying her – but the difference between their stations in life, and the prospect of family opposition is enough to jolt him back to reality, and all he can finally think of is making it up to her, somehow, with money. Just as, for Arthur Donnithorne, 'other men's opinion was like a native climate' so Raymon is 'envieux de l'estime de tous'; each is a universal favourite, affectionate and vain; each lavishes kindness on others but gives in without too much of a struggle to his desires. George Sand's analysis of Raymon's character and motivation in the few pages which open Chapter 4 of *Indiana*, is almost identical with George Eliot's of her likeable, self-indulgent young squire – even to her trick of involving the reader in ironical moral judgements on his course of action: 'Non, vous conviendrez avec lui que ce n'était pas possible . . . qu'on ne lutte point ainsi contre la société.' Raymon is described as being of high principle when he argues with himself, but carried by his strong passions beyond the bounds of his theories, so that he avoids bringing himself to the tribunal of his own conscience. 'L'homme de la veille s'efforçait de tromper celui de lendemain' – just as the good resolutions made by Arthur the night before fade over next day's breakfast with Mr Irwine. Noun is handled more sympathetically than Hetty, but both writers are at pains to stress the resemblances between the thought processes and passions of a lady's maid and a lady – and also the difference between the consequences of their action. For a poor girl's loss of reputation means not only the loss of the husband she might have had but may, as in the case of both Noun and Hetty, mean eventual death.

George Eliot's firm belief that 'our deeds determine us as much as we determine our deeds' means that Arthur's self-indulgence inevitably starts a hardening process in him which is only reversed in the end by his full acceptance of responsibility for the tragedy. Raymon has far less positive idealism in him than Arthur; his deterioration has no point of return and is much less dramatically treated. After he has gained Indiana's love, his underlying hardness grows more like that of Tito Melema. Each of these lovers find it too much of a strain to live up to the expectations of a noble, high-souled young woman; their love is succeeded by embarrassment and impatience at the unworldliness and emotionalism of Indiana and Romola; each feels the desire, first to dominate and hurt, next to get free. The emotions and expressions are very similar in the following passages: firstly, Raymon's thoughts:

De ce moment il ne l'aima plus. Elle avait froissé son amour-propre; elle avait déçu l'espoir d'un de ses triomphes, déjoué l'attente d'un de ses plaisirs . . . Cet amour avait déjà arrivé pour lui au dernier degré de dégout, à l'ennui . . . Il jura qu'il serait son maître, ne fut-ce qu'un jour, et qu'ensuite il l'abondonnerait . . .[70] Indiana eut peur. Un bon ange étendit ses ailes sur cette âme chancelante et troublée.[71]

Lorsqu'il éveilla, un sentiment de bien-être inonda son âme; . . . depuis longtemps il avait prévu qu'un instant viendrait le mettre aux prises avec cet amour de femme, qu'il faudrait défendre sa liberté contre les exigences d'une passion romanesque et il s'encourageait d'avance à combattre de telles prétentions . . . Il se sentait enfin redevenir libre, et il se livrait entièrement à de béates meditations sur ce précieux état.[72]

In Tito, good-humoured acquiescence and easy-going self-interest
have hardened, and Romola's exaggerated expectations of him bring
him to a point of crisis:

> She looked like his good angel pleading with him, as she bent her
> face towards him with dilated eyes, and laid her hand upon his arm.
> But Romola's hand and glance no longer stirred any fibre of tender-
> ness in her husband. Tito . . . felt himself becoming strangely
> hard . . . Romola had an energy of her own which thwarted his, and
> no man, who is not exceptionally feeble, will endure being thwarted
> by his wife. Marriage must be a relation either of sympathy or
> conquest . . . There was now for the first time . . . a desire to be free
> from Romola and to leave her behind him. She had ceased to belong
> to the desirable furniture of his life.[73]

Both writers are concerned to bring home the enormous gap between
the shallow nature and the unworldly one and the insensible day-by-
day hardening process which goes on even in an amiable human being
who puts his own comfort and advancement above all other considerations. But more than that, they are concerned with the widespread effects of selfishness and self-indulgence upon others, and the
significance of the moment of choice which comes to everyone. In
Valvèdre, Francis, the lover, is conscious that he has reached this point
but that his passion does not allow him to heed the warning voice: 'Il
est des moments dans les plus fatales destinées ou la Providence nous
tend la planche de salut et semble nous dire: "Prends-la ou tu es
perdu." '[74] It is a crisis which brings to mind many in George Eliot,
perhaps most notably Gwendolen's moment of decision when Grand-
court is drowning, or Tito's, when he falters and then turns away from
Baldassare: '. . . there are moments when our passions speak and decide
for us, and we seem to stand by and wonder.'[75]

In the novels of George Sand the consequences are seldom as
irrevocably tragic as in George Eliot; her vision is both more optimistic
and less doctrinaire. She did not share the conviction, which Lord
Acton believed to be fundamental to George Eliot, that 'the wages of
sin are paid in ready money.'[76] Raymon's punishment is considerably
less than Arthur's; nemesis for him consists of marriage to a cold-
hearted and dominating young woman, Laure. But, none the less, his
past relationships have determined his unsatisfactory future, and it is
interesting to note that in the 'Belles Lettres' section of the *Westminster
Review* of October 1855, the reviewer of *Histoire de ma Vie* comments
particularly upon the fact that 'George Sand lays great stress on her
conviction that all existences are *solidaires, les unes des autres.*' That
reviewer was George Eliot and it is obvious that once again she is
singling out for comment that aspect of George Sand which most

appealed to her own philosophy of life and which she herself was to make the central theme of her fiction.

5

Not only the early romantic novels and the confessional, discursive writings of George Sand appealed to George Eliot. The former's output in the 1840s was extremely varied but, as we have seen, her predominant interest was socialist in the broadest sense. Her faith was 'in the people', no matter how much she inveighed from time to time against the narrow-mindedness and stupidity of the Berry peasants, and her pastorals were written as a deliberate riposte to 'realistic' contemporary fiction. Her reply was her own blend of idealism and truthful observation in *La Mare au Diable*, *François le Champi* and *La Petite Fadette*, in which she attempted something that, though not new in poetry, was new in the novel, English as well as French.

What she aims at and achieves in her three stories is eloquence of the heart, with very little authorial intrusion upon the rustic idylls. Idyllic they certainly are, for even although there are plenty of shrewd sketches of country avarice and close-fistedness, superstition and jealousy, vanity and malice, they serve only to throw into relief the qualities of unaffected gentleness and sweetness, generosity and patience displayed by the central characters. The theme they all have in common is the transforming power of love which, by the last pages, has accomplished its magic. The narrator's response at the end of *François le Champi* to the query 'L'histoire est donc vraie de tous points?' is George Sand's defiant answer to 'realism' – 'Si elle ne l'est pas, elle le pourrait être.'

As has more than once been pointed out, it is in *Silas Marner* that George Eliot comes closest to the atmosphere of these stories. She was being very guarded when she wrote of her novel to John Blackwood:

> I should not have believed that anyone would have been interested in it but myself (since William Wordsworth is dead) . . . It came to me first of all quite suddenly as a sort of legendary tale, suggested by my recollection of having once, in early childhood, seen a linen-weaver with a bag on his back.[77]

A reference to George Sand would certainly have been as relevant as to Wordsworth; there are many details in *Silas Marner* which have parallels in the Berry tales. Gold coins are a symbolic motif in *Jeanne*; legends of the district abound in the tales and as addenda to them; the mother of little Fadette, like Silas, cures the villagers of their ailments with herbs and berries and is feared as a witch – and keeps a store of gold in a hole, which she has made by displacing bricks in her cellar. But such similarities as these are, however, of much less significance than resemblances in tone. Mathilde Blind, the first biographer of George Eliot, had no doubt of the influence. Her gushing style should not devalue for us the truth of the comment:

> The exquisite picture of Eppie's childhood, the dance she leads her soft-hearted foster-father are things to read not to describe, unless one could quote whole pages of this delightful idyll, which for gracious charm and limpid purity of description recalls those pearls among prose-poems George Sand's *François le Champi* and *La Mare au Diable*.[78]

Silas Marner, like George Sand's pastorals, is George Eliot's glimpse of life as it could be if love were allowed to work its transforming powers unhindered. But for her, unlike her predecessor, it is a rare and untypical vision, for in this tale, as she herself commented, 'the Nemesis is a very mild one.'

In discussing the fairy tale quality of these stories of George Sand's, I have not done sufficient justice to the force with which she comes over in them as a deliberate apologist of the apparently humdrum. It was her firm belief that every life, if only observed closely enough, had something to offer the novelist. In Chapter 2 of *La Mare au Diable* George Sand, as narrator, is watching a peasant and his little son in the fields and musing upon their restricted lot. She claims that their tale is none the less worth the telling: 'Je savais leur histoire – car ils avaient une histoire, tout le monde a la sienne, et chacun pourrait intéresser au roman de sa propre vie, s'il l'avait compris.' She then embarks on a series of tales which is to underline the poetry in everyday events and characters. This is what Jules Lemaître was referring to when he said that George Eliot was doing nothing new in finding tragic potential in 'mediocrity', in 'the veriest earthworms', in Blackwood's deprecating phrase. And although to strengthen his thesis he underplayed the discrepancy between the two writers' treatment of their themes, there can be little doubt that George Eliot benefited by her predecessor's purposeful handling of material, which was apparently unsuitable for serious fictional treatment.

But George Eliot's well-known homily in *Amos Barton* on 'the poetry and the pathos, the tragedy and the comedy, lying in the experience of a human soul that looks out through dull grey eyes and that speaks in a voice of quite ordinary tones'[79] comes quite close to one of George Sand's prefaces. In the foreword to *François le Champi*, for instance, she says that her aim is truth, which will be found in neither a hideous realism nor an embellished idealism but only in allowing the chosen characters – in this case simple country people – to speak for themselves. She admits that she is aware of the limitations of the peasant in powers of reflection and intelligence which may make him fall short of being a wholly tragic figure, for he does not have 'la connaissance de son sentiment'. But what she does claim for him is that he may be nobler than the man in whom knowledge has stifled the ability to feel. This claim of George Sand's, made with the full weight of Rousseau, Wordsworth and Scott behind her, is much less daring than George Eliot's for her snuffling, insignificant curate Amos Barton, but, in the event, it is a more acceptable one. Without George Eliot's constant nudging, no reader would be aware of Amos as a potentially tragic figure, for if ever anyone lacks full self-awareness it is he – but with him George Eliot has made a clumsy start upon her own sort of ordinary tragedy, which starts from the same compassionate assumption that everyone's story, *once understood*, is worthy of attention.

Novels which were also, I think, of significance for George Eliot, though of less real value, were those which featured as heroes admirable, high-minded, intelligent working-men. These carpenters, millers and farmers who appear in *Le Compagnon du Tour de France* (1840) and *Le Meunier d'Angibault* (1843) have much in common with Adam Bede or Felix Holt. *Le Compagnon* is one of George Sand's dullest and most doctrinaire novels, but, none the less, in it she breaks significantly new ground for the novel by having as hero a model workman, Pierre Hugenin. He belongs to one of the guilds of 'compagnages' which were at that time (for it is set back in the 1820s) generating new, revolutionary ideas of human brotherhood. The Tour de France was not then as now a matter of bicycles but 'un apprentissage ambulant', and when the novel opens Pierre has been on the move for several years and is now a highly skilled carpenter. Like Adam Bede he is the idealised and articulate artisan with an undeveloped potential for learning. He has exactingly high standards for himself and is intolerant of the shoddy job or the hastily downed tools. He holds strongly democratic views but is no fanatic and preaches patience. As seems inevitable where a virtuous carpenter is concerned, there are at times, again as in *Adam Bede*, strong religious overtones and even some Christ imagery.

A comparable figure is Jean, in *Le Péché de M. Antoine* (1845) – who is also a meticulous carpenter, independent, sturdy, incorruptible, quick-tempered and prepared to work day and night to finish a job he is proud of. There is an interesting flash-back in this novel; Jean's wife has had a child by his closest friend and Jean, after going through a period of hatred and resentment of them both, has eventually been capable of forgiveness. The wife, the cause of the estrangement, is now dead and the two men's friendship has endured. These similarities to *Adam Bede* should not be overstressed but they are enough, I think, to discourage the practice of simply turning to George Eliot's own life for models for her characters. It was a habit which she deplored in her own lifetime but which is still going indomitably on – for example, in the claim that 'Adam Bede is an idealised portrait of Robert Evans, George Eliot's father.'[80] George Eliot's own comment on her method of creation was a wise one. 'I could never have written *Adam Bede* if I had not learned something of my father's early experience but no one who knew my father could call Adam a portrait of him . . . *everything* is a combination from widely sundered elements of experience.'[81]

Le Meunier d'Angibault is one of the books from which George Eliot quotes with enjoyment in her letters, and indeed the grasping farmer, M. Bricolin, and his wife – penny-pinching, hard-hearted, on the make – in their 'new *château*', a large farmhouse with monster heaps of dung in the yard and hens walking in and out of the sitting rooms, might well have come from her own pages, or from Scott's or Galt's. But more relevant to *Felix Holt* is the relationship between the idealistic, socialistic hero, Henri Leroux, and Marcelle de Blanchemont, a young, rich widow. Henri refuses to bring her down to his poverty and Marcelle, who has never given these matters much thought before, begins seriously to ponder his radical ideas. The possibility of a different attitude to life suddenly strikes her, as it does Esther when Felix tells her of 'the force there would be in one beautiful woman whose mind was as noble as her face was beautiful – who made a man's passion for her rush in one current with all the great aims of his life.'[82] Henri Lemor is as wooden a young man as Felix without his solidity and bluntness; the real vitality of the novel comes from the miller himself, and all the scenes on the Bricolin estate. There is no tension in the relationship between him and Marcelle because she is an immediate convert and eventually becomes almost poor enough to satisfy his scruples. Like Felix, he has given up his patrimony because of what he considers the dishonest scoundrelly business methods of his father, and has apprenticed himself to a trade as mechanic; and, like Felix, he holds forth on his duty as a man of this generation and on his abhorrence of riches, without even the Reform Bill background to give some justification for his speech-making. If indeed George Eliot got the germ of an idea for *Felix Holt* from *Le Meunier d'Angibault*, she chose the least effective part of the book to develop.

But it was no doubt one which appealed to her own form of idealistic and basically conservative radicalism. For all of these men-of-the-people preach patience, a gradual meliorism, individual self-sacrifice and non-violence. However involved George Sand was in revolutionary activities – and her active participation in the 1848 revolution contrasts very greatly with George Eliot's sideline position throughout her life – none the less, her *Lettres au Peuple* in 1848, especially her second one, bears an amusing resemblance to the *Address to Working Men, by*

Felix Holt, which George Eliot wrote at Blackwood's instigation for his magazine in 1867; *festina lente* is the directive which each gives. The real difference between them is that George Eliot's article was designed for the predominantly middle-class readers of *Blackwood's*, but her political gesture may seem a little less surprising, when we remember that she must have had George Sand's precedent in mind.

Throughout George Eliot's writings, then, there are many, many echoes of George Sand – far too many for them to be dismissed as irrelevant, and equally far too numerous to recount in further detail. Leslie Stephen long ago pointed out that George Eliot's memory was 'very retentive of the novels – George Sand's for example – that she had read in her youth.'[83] Many incidents were stored away, and emerged later, when the need arose, for the impression had been made indelibly and unconsciously at a formative time. Such, for instance, might be the relationship between the ending of *The Mill on the Floss*, and a memorable scene in *Le Péché de M. Antoine*, when the hero is marooned by a flooded mill-stream, sees great pieces of timber hurtling towards him and is threatened by the breaking loose of a huge piece of machinery. It is the same sort of recall as George Sand herself must have had of the well-loved novels of Scott; so that in *Jeanne*, the attempted rape of the heroine in the high tower parallels with striking closeness the attack on Rebecca in *Ivanhoe*.

These comparisons are of some interest, but just as it is more valuable to contemplate the influence which Scott exerted on George Sand in his realism and his own brand of feudal democracy, so is it more important to be aware of the integral influence of George Sand upon the actual way that George Eliot *thought* – especially about the relationship between men and women. Before George Eliot started writing novels, she paid tribute, in an essay of 1854, to the contribution which had been made to fiction by French women writers. The long list of distinguished names culminated in that of George Sand: 'They alone have had a vital influence on the development of literature. For in France alone the mind of women has passed like an electric current through the language making crisp and definite what is elsewhere heavy and blurred.'[84] Like Lewes, George Eliot believed that what the woman writer had to offer was quite different from a man and that French women had excelled because they had, in Mathilde Blind's phrase, 'the courage of their sex'. Certainly no one could deny this courage to either George Sand or George Eliot, but there is irony in the fact that the highest praise the English writer's contemporaries could ever give her was the accolade that 'it may be doubted whether . . . any man could have done better.'

If we now return to the article of Sidney Colvin with which I began this chapter, we shall see that he was reluctant to award the crown to the 'philosophical' rather than the 'poetical' novelist. Indeed, he quoted wickedly from the opening of Book 8 of *Daniel Deronda* to show how George Eliot labours her points. He gives the paragraph in full:

> Extension we know is a very imperfect measure of things; and the length of the sun's journeying can no more tell us how far life has advanced than the acreage of a field can tell us what growths may be active within it. A man may go south, and, stumbling over a bone, may meditate upon it till he has found a new starting-point for anatomy; or eastward, and discover a new key to language, telling a new story of races; or he may head an expedition that opens new continental pathways, get himself maimed in body, and go through a whole heroic poem of resolve and endurance; and at the end of a few months he may come back to find his neighbours grumbling at the same parish grievance as before, or to see the same elderly gentleman treading the pavement in discourse with himself, shaking his head after the same percussive butcher's boy, and pausing at the same shop-window to look at the same prints. If the swiftest thinking has about the pace of a greyhound, the slowest must be supposed to move, like the limpet, by an apparent sticking, which after a good while is discerned to be a slight progression. Such differences are manifest in the variable intensity which we call human experience, from the revolutionary rush of change which marked a new inner and outer life, to the quiet recurrence of the familiar which has no other epochs than those of hunger and the heavens.

He then asks the reader to compare 'this with the form in which another writer, also a novelist and a woman, expresses . . . the same general idea':

> Yes, quiet life is short. In the slumber of the spirit fifty years pass like a day; but the life of emotions and events can gather into a day whole centuries of trouble and endurance.

'What a difference is here! How flowingly the French writer makes her reflections and passes on! How the English writer elaborates hers and what a quantity of things she gives us to think about and pause over, insisting that we shall see all the contents and bearings of the idea.'

He quotes, too, the parting between Deronda and Gwendolen which he feels George Sand would have handled better: 'There is force and noble passion but in the attitudes, the picture, there is something wrong, a commonness.' And although he heaps generous praise upon the English writer, he has obviously responded to the ardour of the other.

I do not know that any one of the many and noble lessons of George Eliot is brought home to us so perfectly as that one which George Sand had at heart – the lesson that a woman must begin her own emancipation by ceasing to hold herself a slave and cheap: that she must become a free, responsible, individual human being, recognising her own sacredness, being no more ready to give herself in carelessness to the first asker than to sell herself in infancy to the first bidder but putting devotion to the proof, judging before she chooses, living her own life and valuing her own soul.[85]

In the long run, George Eliot has easily outdistanced the other George to whom she was indebted for so many insights and such a great enlargement of her horizons. It is not simply that the idealist, optimist and romantic has less of value to communicate than the writer with a deep and realistic sense of the irony and tragedy of life – although for modern readers this is surely a vital distinction. Nor is it just, as Jules Lemaître suggested, that English readers respond to the Protestantism of George Eliot, to her stress on individual man's responsibility for the consequences of his actions and his duty to control his passions and desires – although it is undeniable that in this she does differ markedly from George Sand, who took very literally the advice given her by her confessor to trust her heart: 'N'ayez pas jamais d'effroi quand c'est votre coeur qui vous conseille; le coeur *ne peut pas tromper.*' Nor is it even that nowhere in George Sand do we get the calibre of wise and compassionate comedy that we find, at its finest, in the presentation of the Dodsons in *The Mill on the Floss.* What, quite apart from all questions of relative weight, has made George Eliot wear better than George Sand, is that she was more of a conscious artist. James's description of how George Sand gathered impressions all day and then 'at night she would give all this forth as a sort of emanation' does less than justice to the amount of preparatory research and imaginative historical reconstruction which went in to such works as *Consuelo* or *Les Maîtres Mosaïstes* – the latter a brief masterpiece of fifteenth-century Venetian life which is one lesson from which the leaden-footed *Romola* could well have profited. But none the less, it is largely true that George Sand did have a fatal facility, which has been her undoing for posterity. The long pondering, the extensive gestation period, the hard labour and the birth pangs which left George Eliot exhausted and empty after each novel compares instructively with the insouciance with which George Sand once completed a novel in the watches of the night, put it in the mail for her publisher and started another. The story comes from Gautier via those malicious diarists, the Goncourts, but is certainly not unbelievable: 'Elle retravaille à minuit jusqu'a quatre heures . . . Enfin vous savez ce qui est arrivé. Quelque chose de monstrueux. Un jour, elle finit un roman à une heure du matin et elle en recommence un autre dans la nuit . . . La copie est un fonction chez Mme Sand.'[86]

So that while, as James said, we are invariably struck in reading George Sand by 'the generosity of her genius', in the end we have to agree with him that her novels are 'the easy writing which makes hard reading – twice'.[87] That this is so is sad, because if she has not George Eliot's weight she does have much wisdom: 'Every novel she wrote made for charity – for a better acquaintance with our neighbour's woes and our own egoism'.[88] And, in addition, she was never afflicted, as John Blackwood somewhat regretfully observed George Eliot to be, by 'the sense of what a great author should do for mankind'.[89] She was never self-conscious – she 'wrote as the bird sings' – and it is when we feel the fullest impact of her rich and tolerant personality that we get most from her still. The hard-won artistic objectivity of George Eliot's achievement was something beyond her reach.

10 Wessex and the Vallée Noire

In 1912 Henry Newbolt and Yeats travelled to Max Gate to make the award of the Royal Society of Literature's gold medal to Hardy. In his speech acknowledging the honour, the seventy-two-year-old author spoke of the enduring nature of poetry and quoted from a minor novel of George Sand's to substantiate his claims:

> I cannot do better than wind up these rambling remarks with some of her words on the question:
> 'Poesy cannot die. Should she find for refuge but the brain of a single man she would yet have centuries of life, for she would leap out of it like the lava of Vesuvius and mark out a way for herself among the most prosaic realities. Despite her overturned temples and the false gods adored among their ruins, she is immortal as the perfume of the flowers and the splendour of the skies.'[1]

As it is highly unlikely that *André* (1835) was Hardy's current reading for the year – when even such a life-long partisan as Henry James was admitting that George Sand 'is a fictionist too superannuated and rococo at the present time'[2] – his choice of quotation must surely bear out Arnold's assertion of the lingering effect of the French writer on all those who had read her novels in their youth.

The yoking together of George Sand, the largely serene optimist, unquenchably vital, undoctrinally religious, and the small, weary figure of Hardy, the realist who 'waits in unhope', disenchanted and sceptical, may well seem an improbable metaphysical conceit. The evidence for Hardy's having read and been influenced by her works is largely internal – unlike that for most of the other writers with whom I have dealt. This is perhaps not surprising in that he was never very ready to admit indebtedness, even to George Eliot, where the influence is manifest. But there is the further point that even although again and again in reading George Sand, incidents and characters in Hardy come to mind, it may well seem a futile enterprise to go source hunting in French novels for what is so obviously personal and, in the best sense, provincial. Hardy's own rich background of folk-lore and local gossip, his well-authenticated Dorset topography, his close observations of country matters, appear entirely self-sufficient. None the less, although often the resemblance between George Sand and Hardy may be merely a matter of affinity and of a similar country background, at other times it seems to go further than that.

Because Hardy lived so long and strikes us as modern in so many of his attitudes, it is hard to remember that he was born in 1840 and that in the 1850s, when George Sand was still very much of a name, he was reading everything he could lay his hands on, including French and Latin classics. We know that he had private French lessons when he was fifteen and later, in London, went to French classes at King's College; but by then there were a good many translations of George Sand available, so that it was not necessary for him to read her in the original. A letter written to him by Leslie Stephen in 1867 is enlightening about the scope of his interests and Stephen's editorial caution:

> You say you have been reading some French novels lately. I am much given to that amusement, though I have never read de Musset. By the way, I don't quite agree with your praise of them. Of course, it is true that English writers – Thackeray conspicuously so – are injured by being cramped as to love in its various manifestations. Still, I doubt whether the French gain much by the opposite system . . . much as I like reading them and specially Balzac and Sand.[3]

Carl Weber has suggested that Hardy's 'predilection for romantic tales of fair ladies and moonlight meetings, mysterious horsemen and secret marriages, Gothic casements and unlucky accidents'[4] may have been a taste encouraged by his early reading of Saint-Pierre and Dumas, Grant, James and Ainsworth. To this list could certainly be added the name of George Sand, not only because she wrote many romantic novels, most of which had what Hardy approved of – a story 'striking enough to be worth the telling' – but because a poem of Hardy's tells us so. The poem is 'An Ancient to Ancients',[5] and its fourth verse is as follows:

> This season's paintings do not please,
>   Gentlemen,
> Like Etty, Mulready, Maclise;
> Throbbing romance has waned and wanned;
> No wizard wields the witching pen
> Of Bulwer, Scott, Dumas and Sand,
>   Gentlemen.

The only other overt reference that Hardy seems to have made to George Sand was dragged out of him by a questionnaire in 1899, posed by *Le Gaulois du Dimanche* – 'Which French authors now dead best represented in their works the distinctive genius of France?'. Hardy, while confessing that his reading in French literature had not been extensive, drew up a first team of ten which included George Sand, and even though he then lost his head and suggested a supplementary three – and finally, desperately, another possible nine who might also join the immortals – it is significant that he did not scruple to give George Sand a distinguished place at a time when her reputation was ebbing fast.[6]

Under the Greenwood Tree was the nearest thing to a rustic idyll that Hardy ever wrote, and even as late as 1883 Havelock Ellis was drawing the comparison between it and George Sand's pastorals: 'It is a sketch, short and slight, of rural life, but a sketch of the freshest and most delightful order, only comparable, if at all, with the best of George Sand's rural studies, with *La Mare au Diable*.'[7] But this resemblance had been noted by the very first reader of the book, before its publication. John Morley was asked by Macmillans to read the manuscript and his report was sent on to Hardy. He commented favourably on the harmony of the construction and the treatment of the 'simple and uneventful sketch of a rural courtship', and went on: 'The writer is wanting in the fine poetic breath which gives such a charm to George Sand's work in the same kind, but he has evidently a true artistic feeling, if it is somewhat in excess of the feeling of a realist.' Then after suggesting that the opening scenes should be shortened and praising the delicacy of the work he made three positive recommendations:

The writer would do well
1. To study George Sand's best work.
2. To shut his ears to the fooleries of critics, as his letter to you proves he does not do.
3. To beware of letting realism grow out of proportion to his fancy.[8]

What is interesting about this letter is not only John Morley's insistence on the fact that Hardy is working in the same genre as George Sand, but the omission in the *Early Life*, when Morley's comments are quoted, of all reference to George Sand. What are mentioned as 'the chief points' are the praise of the style, the construction and the delicacy of the idea and also the counsel to pay no attention to critics (this last a piece of advice which Hardy signally failed to follow in the next twenty years). There can be several reasons why Hardy chose to forget – or not to record – Morley's stress on George Sand as an example to be followed, but two in particular are feasible. One is that at the time – 1874 – as a young writer, he had felt insulted by being told to devote his days and nights to the study of an out-of-date novelist, one who, unlike Balzac, seemed to belong to another age. And the other, and I think much more likely reason, could be that he had already read and absorbed enough of George Sand to know that he had got what she had to give him and that Morley's advice was therefore superfluous. It was advice given him also by Leslie Stephen in an equally tactless letter in 1876:

> If you were seriously to ask me what critical books I recommend, I can only say I recommend none . . . If I were in the vein, I think I should exhort you above all to read George Sand, whose country stories seem to me perfect, and have a certain affinity to yours. The last I read was the 'Maîtres Sonneurs' which (if you don't know it) I commend to you as well nigh perfect. You could do something of the same kind, though I won't flatter you by saying that I think you could equal her in her own level. I don't think anyone could. But the harmony and grace, even if strictly inimitable, are good to aim at.[9]

However he reacted to such unflattering comparisons, Hardy was bound to feel the appeal of George Sand's serious and intimate pre-occupation with country people and country ways. It is true that both writers owed an enormous debt to Scott in their interest in folk-lore and antiquarianism, in ballads and, to a certain extent, dialect, but the tone of their treatment of the peasantry is entirely different from his. The element of class consciousness which underlies Scott's genial democracy is quite lacking in their treatment of their country lovers, – of Germain the farm labourer who loves little Marie, and Dick, the tranter's son, who loves Fancy Day. Although Havelock Ellis's comparison with *La Mare au Diable* is right in that the latter is indeed also 'a simple and uneventful sketch of a rural courtship', depending for its interest entirely upon the country characters and scenes, in many ways the texture of Hardy's story is more like the book Stephen mentions, *Les Maîtres Sonneurs*, which is as preoccupied with rural music-making and its rivalries as with the love interest. Hardy is as eager as George Sand to record, while they are still within living memory, all the details of a past way of life – a fact which his original title, *The Mellstock Quire*, would have underlined. But Hardy, always unnervingly accom-modating in these matters, entitled his work *Under the Greenwood Tree*, 'because titles from poetry were in fashion just then',[10] and thus transferred the main stress to the lovers.

This easy awareness of his contemporaries that Hardy was not an innovator in his peasant tales is not found in twentieth-century critics. In his book *Thomas Hardy and Rural England*, Merryn Williams discusses Hardy's English predecessors in the genre – Scott, Harriet Martineau, Kingsley, the Brontës, Mrs Gaskell, the Howitts and George Eliot – in order to bring out the originality of Hardy's own approach. And in an essay, 'The Traditional Basis of Hardy's Fiction' (1963), Donald

Davidson writes: 'Hardy is the only specimen of his genius in modern English literature and I do not know how to account for him. He has no immediate predecessor . . .'[11]

While I would certainly not claim to 'account for him', Hardy does have, in some respects at least, an immediate predecessor – but in France, and not England. As a novelist of a much-loved and intimately known region, George Sand has more in common with Hardy than any English writer – and, in addition, was capable in descriptions founded on close and accurate observations, of presenting nature as Hardy felt it should be seen – not only as a beauty but as a mystery. Hardy's development led him far away from the serenity of *Under the Greenwood Tree*, and it would be difficult to imagine any novel which has less in common with George Sand, even in her early despair, than *Jude the Obscure*. But what I think he may have got from his reading of her novels in his youth was something to start from and to build on – many suggestions as to the literary possibilities of the country experience and material which was common to them both, many discussions of the differences between the psychology of the peasant and the city dweller to stimulate his own reflections. The reviewers of Hardy's early works praised him for doing something quite new in the English novel by concentrating entirely on the life of an agricultural district and characters who are 'children of the soil – unsophisticated country folk'. But this was what George Sand had also done, and she too had been praised as an innovator, 'opening up the life of a region before almost unknown'.

For just as Hardy was a real countryman, so was George Sand a real countrywoman,[12] in a way that George Eliot was not. As Haight has pointed out,[13] her ideal view was of farm land, preferably well-managed – not surprising in a land agent's daughter. Primitive and untamed nature had very little appeal for her, and her countrymen, seldom inarticulate even if ignorant, exist well within a social structure; poverty as the ineluctable and dominating feature of their existence is never seriously considered. Primitive heath-dwellers such as George Sand describes in *Jeanne* or Hardy in *The Return of the Native* are outside George Eliot's sphere of knowledge and interest. Hardy's surprise when *Under the Greenwood Tree* was ascribed to George Eliot seems to have been genuine enough. He commented that

> so far as he had read that great thinker – one of the greatest living, he thought, though not a born story-teller by any means – she had never touched the life of the fields: her country-people having seemed to him, too, more like small townsfolk than rustics; and as evidencing a woman's wit cast in country dialogue rather than real country humour.[14]

George Sand, who, whatever else she was not, was certainly a born story-teller, 'touched the life of the fields' in a great number of her novels – and just as Hardy saw in Tess Durbeyfield not only a girl with her own personal tragedy but 'part and parcel of ordinary nature . . . a field woman' who is 'a portion of the field',[15] so George Sand alternates between individualising her peasant heroes and heroines and then imperceptibly allowing their surroundings and occupations to dominate the reader's impression of them. Both writers convey an emotional reciprocity between man and nature which is totally different from anything found in the pages of George Eliot. Prone as George Sand was to idealise her heroes and heroines, she can be unsentimental about her ordinary countrymen:

L'habitant de ces montagnes, attaché à un pays aride, et habitué à une sobriété parcimonieuse, est le plus âpre au gain au monde. Il est actif et industrieux comme tous ceux qu'une nature marâtre dresse au joug de la nécessité. Il aime ce sol ingrat qui ne le nourrit pas, et quand il a fait la vie de maquignon ou de maçon bohemien dans sa jeunesse, il revient mourir de la fièvre sous son toit de chaume . . .[16]

'Il aime ce sol ingrat qui ne le nourrit pas.' The emotion is primitive, and one which Hardy and George Sand wholly understand.

Within a realistic and faithfully observed natural setting, George Sand's country lovers support, in their honesty and courage, their loving natures and simple hearts, her well-known riposte to Balzac: 'Vous voulez et vous savez peindre *l'homme tel qu'il est*, soit. Moi, je me sens portée à le peindre tel que *je souhaite qu'il soit, tel que je crois qu'il doit être*.'[17] Her staunch heroes – Germain, François, Landry and Grand Louis – and her pure and frank heroines – Jeanne, Marie, Fadette – are idealised, without a doubt, but in relation to the temperament of the author, Hardy's equally admirable countryfolk come as much more of a surprise. How better could one describe Gabriel Oak, Diggory Venn, Giles Winterbourne, Marty Southwood and even Tess Durbeyfield (had she not had the pollution of Sixth Standard learning in her veins) than as 'l'homme tel que je crois qu'il doit être'? The great difference between the two writers is not in their belief in the possibility of the existence of such generosity and innocent passion in these untutored human beings but in their expectations of what life holds for them – which, in Hardy's case, becomes less and less with the passing years and the encroachments of civilisation.

These are their exceptional peasants. When it comes to the other country characters, neither author is disposed to idealise. When, in *Jeanne*, Guillaume de Boussac 'courait après la poésie' in the mountainous district of Toull, hoping to find Wordsworthian peasants, grave, simple and austere, he encountered, instead, rudeness and avarice and gossiping tongues, and had to lodge in a dreary cottage smelling of cheese and washing. This sort of realism in such writers as Crabbe or Scott or Galt or Balzac or George Sand or Hardy is quite obviously not so much a literary convention as the result of observation – but it is the more startling in the last two novelists in its juxtaposition with so much that is romantic and idealistic. Both are aware of the fact of a peasant psychology – credulous, suspicious of change, superstitious and unreasoning – while insisting on the need to recognise the country-man's individuality. When George Sand raised her eyes from the Holbein engraving of the old labourer at the plough, his horses lashed on by the skeletal figure of death prancing beside them, and saw the handsome, strong figure of Germain, the ploughman, driving his straight furrow across the rich Berry land, she felt the impulse to challenge the prototype of the wretched countryman by telling Germain's own particular story – the story of *le fin laboureur* – one 'aussi droite et aussi peu ornée que le sillon qu'il traçait avec sa charrue.'[18] And Hardy puts into the mouth of Angel Clare what he himself had earlier remarked, in an interview, that 'At close quarters no Hodge was to be seen . . . The typical and unvarying Hodge ceased to exist. He had been disintegrated into a number of varied fellow-creatures . . . men everyone of whom walked in his own individual way the road to dusty death.'[19] There is indeed a striking similarity in the way in which both authors make lives governed by the seasons, by seed-time and harvest, by pasturing and milking, by cock-crow and sunset, contrive to have both a rich monotony and an individual movement.

Although Scott, Balzac, Trollope and Emily Brontë could all, to some extent, be described as regional novelists, only George Sand and Hardy use their countryside in exactly the same way. The Berry countryside had provided the background for half a dozen of the novels before *Jeanne*, but in the group of tales which followed, George Sand made her reading public thoroughly familiar with her own favourite region, which she had called the Vallée Noire, because of the darkness of its woods – a name which, like Wessex, caught on immediately and has stayed in currency. She used the landmarks of these 120 square miles faithfully – its rich pastures with the great white oxen, the meandering tributaries of the Indre, the wooded hills, the smallholdings, the grotesque shapes of the brutally pollarded trees by the roadside, the little villages, the ruined castles, the narrow roads criss-crossing each other, the inns, the mills. When the action demanded a more austere background she went out of the immediate area into the moorlands and mountainous regions of the Creuse area to the south, with its druid stones and Roman remains. But wherever she set her story she drew on her local knowledge, and although some of the names of villages and towns are fictional – and she sometimes went to considerable trouble to cover her tracks because she was so often reproved by locals who thought they recognised themselves in her pages – the itineraries of all her characters can be accurately traced by her commentators. What comes over very well is the distinctive quality of each small area, for the Berry district is varied and for its inhabitants the next district is 'another country' to be looked on with distrust. When Marie is hired out to a farmer five miles away in *La Mare au Diable* she leaves the rich farmlands and Germain says to her 'Tu vas vivre loin de tes parents et dans un vilain pays de landes et de marécages, où tu attraperas les fièvres d'automne, où les bêtes à laine ne profitent pas, ce qui chagrine toujours une bergère qui a bonne intention.'[20] As the narrative point of view is from within the region, we have the distinctive blend, with which we are so familiar in Hardy, of geographical exactitude and infinitely expanding space. Just as in reading *The Return of the Native* we are never tempted to consider that Egdon Heath is actually only eight miles long and two miles deep, so, in *La Mare*, once Germain and Marie have left the road at Corlay, three miles from Belair and four miles from their destination, Fourche, and have taken the wrong path across the moorland and lost themselves in the woods in the autumn mists, the sense of mystery and the inability of man to reduce nature to intelligible measurements takes over. The observation 'C'est très loin de chez nous, c'est au moins à quatre grandes lieues' which is made by a peasant in *Le Meunier d'Angibault*, simply shows in that context the rooted quality of the *berrichon* peasant. But in *La Mare* when, in much less than 'quatre lieues', within a few hundred metres of leaving the security of the inn, Germain and Marie have lost their bearings, the distances and surroundings take on symbolic qualities. Their environment becomes to them what they bring to it. It is not in itself inimical – the point which Hardy makes so often about Egdon Heath – but Germain, the superstitious, feels the loneliness of the moorland and his inadequacy much more than the practical and philosophical Marie who, like Thomasin, takes the heath very much for granted.

Arnold was, I suppose, the first notable Englishman to succumb to the fascination of 'getting down the big map of France' and to feel the excitement of locating on it all the villages and mountains and rivers and tors with which under real or assumed names George Sand's fictional Berry was studded. And he was certainly the first Englishman then to pursue his researches to the district itself and to spend several days in visiting the places. Only Hardy's Wessex can provide as pleasant and active a literary pilgrimage as the Vallée Noire, with identifiable landmarks every few hundred yards and the sense at the end of it that although the flesh is there the spirit is so entirely dependent on the creative imagination of the author that the exercise has been only one of harmless topography. Hardy went further than George

Sand in actually supplying a map of his Wessex in his later editions –
although her commentators have made up for this deficiency – but in
every other respect he was following, though literally in 'another
country', in her footsteps.

Although much attention has been paid to those passages of description in Hardy which are heavily charged with symbolism, it should
not be forgotten how often, as a matter of course, the changing scene
of the countryside is commented on – frequently by an observer placed
at a vantage point. Sometimes the passages are brief – sometimes only
a line or two – but their effect, as in George Sand also, is to build up
not only the impression of the density of the rural life and background
which is independent of the central action but also to place human
affairs in perspective, 'to give ballast to the mind adrift on change'.[21]
After a fine description of the scene below Guillaume, as he stands on
the mountainside, George Sand goes on:

> C'est un coup d'oeuil magnifique, mais impossible à soutenir
> longtemps. Cet infini vous donne des vertiges . . . Il me semble que
> sur tous les sommets isolés, à voir ainsi le cercle entier de l'horizon,
> on a la perception sensible de la rondeur du globe et on s'imagine
> avoir aussi celle du mouvement rapide qui le précipite dans sa
> rotation éternelle. On croit se sentir entraîné dans cette course
> inévitable à travers les abîmes du ciel et on cherche en vain au-dessus
> de soi une branche pour se retenir.[22]

Hardy, too, is partial to such observations:

> To persons standing alone on a hill during a clear midnight such as
> this, the roll of the world eastward is almost a palpable movement.
> The sensation may be caused by the panoramic glide of the stars past
> earthly objects, which is perceptible in a few minutes of stillness or
> by the better outlook upon space that a hill affords, or by the wind,
> or by the solitude; but whatever be its origin, the impression of
> riding along is vivid and abiding.[23]

The emotion generated by each passage is very different – Hardy's
calm philosophising is remote from George Sand's vertiginous excitement – but what is important technically is each writer's tendency to
glide easily from close description of the countryside into cosmic
comment and back again.

As in Wordsworth, such philosophising is the more effective in that
the writers have already proved themselves Nature's familiars. But
although they both resemble the Romantic poet in their ability to shed
a strange and new light on the apparently ordinary features of their
surroundings, they are concerned, as he never was, with the customs,
legends, speech forms, history, dress, work of the peasant – in short with

everything that gives their regions their individuality. But without the poetic eye and ear, the accuracy of detail could become arid anti-quarianism – as sometimes in Scott – and the descriptions that are most memorable in both Hardy and George Sand are those in which the sharp observation is touched with emotion. Those are the passages which never grow stale with repetition. No reader of Hardy, for instance, can forget 'the worn whisper dry and papery . . . of the mummied heath bells of the past summer', which formed an accompaniment to the 'lengthened sighing' of Eustacia, alone on the heath;[24] the curious microscopic life of Clym in which 'strange amber coloured butterflies which Egdon produced . . . quivered on the breath of his lips . . . and tribes of emerald green grasshoppers leaped over his feet, falling awkwardly on their backs like unskilful acrobats';[25] the 'warm November rain which floated down like meal and lay in a powdery form on the naps of hats and coats'[26] at Henchard's re-marriage; the hoar frost which covered every twig 'with a white nap as of fur grown from the rind during the night, giving it four times its usual dimension' in the stealthy winter at Talbothays;[27] Giles's 'marvellous power of making trees grow . . . Winterborne's fingers were endowed with a gentle conjuror's touch in spreading the roots of each little tree, resulting in a sort of caress under which the delicate fibres all laid themselves out in their proper direction for growth.'[28] All these are details such as Sainte-Beuve admired in George Sand's rural scenes. He wrote of the little episode in *La Mare au Diable* in which the old mare, La Grise, hears her filly passing by on the road, comes up to the hedge and whinnies after her 'inquiète, le nez au vent, la bouche pleine d'herbes qu'elle ne songeait plus à manger'[29] – 'On n'a pas affaire ici à un peintre amateur qui a traversé les champs pour y prendre des points de vue; le peintre y a véçu, y a habité des années; il en connaît toute chose et en sait l'âme.'[30]

As in Hardy, the choice of haunting descriptions is unlimited, but Arnold had good reason to remember the little grass-grown lanes in *Valentine*, 'les traînes', cool and silent in the burning midday sun (p. 93, above). George Sand is especially sensitive to 'les petits bruits de la nature' such as Jeanne hears with delight as she is hurrying back over the moorland to her old home. 'L'insecte des prés et la grenouille du marécage interrompaient à peine leur oraison monotone et aussitôt après ils recommencaient avec une nouvelle ferveur cette mystérieuse psalmodie que la nuit leur inspire.'[31] Or the unexpected and strange country sounds which are the epiphany of autumn, in the extended description that Henri de Latouche said he would gladly have given his remaining years to have written; the raucous groans of a phalanx of emigrant cranes passing by, high up in the clouds, when the exhausted leader has gone off course and lost the wind and has to be replaced by another – 'que de cris, que de reproches, que de rémontrances, que de malédictions . . . dans la nuit sonore' – and in the orchards, the creaking of fruit-laden branches:

> La cueille de fruits n'est pas encore faite et mille crépitations inusitées font ressembler les arbres à des êtres animées, une branche grince, en se courbant, sous un poids arrivé tout à coup, à son dernier degré de développement; où bien, une pomme se détache et tombe à vos pieds avec un son mat sur la terre humide. Alors vous entendez fuir, en frôlant les branches et les herbes un être que vous ne voyez pas; c'est le chien du paysan, ce rodeur curieux, inquiet, à la fois insolent et poltron, qui se glisse partout, qui ne dort jamais, qui cherche toujours on ne sait quoi, qui vous épie, cache dans les broussailles, et prend la fuite au bruit de la pomme tombée, croyant que vous lui lancez une pierre.[32]

Enough has been quoted, I hope, to make it clear that when Morley and Stephen advised Hardy to study George Sand, the counsel would not have been distasteful to him on the ground of diversity of interests or technique. How far indeed he had more than an affinity with her, how far he was actually influenced by her can only be a matter of conjecture. But if we turn to *André*, the book that we certainly know that Hardy had read and appreciated, we shall find at least one scene, which bears a striking resemblance to one of the best-known interludes in *Tess* – that in which Tess and her small brother are in the country lanes in the waggon, gazing up at the stars. The conversation is too familiar to quote in full – Abraham's childish prattle and Tess's replies are engraved on the memories of all readers of Hardy:

> 'Did you say the stars were worlds, Tess?'
> 'Yes.'
> 'All like ours?'
> 'I don't know; but I think so. They sometimes seem to be like the apples on our stubbard-tree. Most of them splendid and sound – a few blighted.'
> 'Which do we live on – a splendid one or a blighted one?'
> 'A blighted one.'[33]

The relevant scene in *André* takes place after the débâcle of the *grisettes* dinner-party, when the *char-à-banc* has been locked up and they all have to walk home. André, Geneviève and Justine are walking along the quiet lanes behind the rest, under the stars, and Justine, who is an educated young lady, unlike the unlettered though pure and charming heroine, Geneviève, comments 'A quoi ne pense-t-on pas en regardant ces milliers de mondes au près desquels le nôtre n'est qu'une tache lumineuse dans l'espace?' André replies suitably, but Geneviève is startled and after a pause asks André why Justine has talked of thousands of worlds. André is, in turn, shocked by her ignorance – 'Est-ce-que tu ne sais pas . . . que toutes ces lumières comme tu les appelles, sont autant de soleils et de mondes?' – and proceeds to explain the system of the universe to her. When she asks him innocently if he really believes it, he replies: 'Oui, je crois que notre monde n'est qu'un lieu de passage et d'épreuve et qu'il y a parmi tous ceux que vous voyez au ciel, quelque monde meilleur où les âmes qui s'entendent peuvent se réunir et s'appartenir mutuellement.' For, as he goes on to explain, there is not a great deal to be said for the present world 'Je ne sais pas où Dieu a caché le bonheur qu'il fait espérer aux hommes.'[34]

What is fascinating about the two scenes is their similarity and their unlikeness. Through this one, no matter what André says about the unsatisfactory nature of existence on this planet, the irrepressibly optimistic voice of George Sand comes through – and on the other, Hardy has set his own stamp of unhope and disillusionment. But the scenes themselves are too close to be a coincidence; and indeed Geneviève's tragedy – that of a pure, young, country girl, whose strength of character is greater than that of her conventional and well-born lover – bears a certain resemblance to that of Tess, although the latter's superstition and fatalism has more in common with Jeanne. I think it very likely that Hardy got many hints from his reading of George Sand, not only how to use the material for fiction which lay close to his hand, but also for characters and incidents.

One particular scene in *Valentine*, for instance, has marked associations with an episode in *Tess*. It takes place on a midsummer day of intense heat when Benedict, the young hero, has gone out from the farm on a fishing party to the banks of the Indre with his betrothed, the farmer's daughter, Athénaïs, with Valentine and her sister, Louise. The three women scatter themselves, in their pretty dresses, over the bright green grass by the river while Benedict fishes for trout and adroitly leaps the stream, showing off his skills to the admiring girls. Although Benedict is in peasant blouse he has returned to the land from Paris where he had studied art and science but, like Angel Clare, had preferred study for its own sake and had shied away from adopting a profession. His air of remoteness, his pallor, his tranquillity, his learning mark him off from the other countrymen so that, we are told, no woman can view him with indifference. As Valentine gazes at him she finds that she is in love with him – as indeed is Louise already, and Athénaïs also. The scorching air is full of 'magnetic emanations', and Benedict gradually becomes aware of how much he loves Valentine as she broods over him with tender solicitude. And the other two girls sense his inclination, so that the atmosphere becomes charged not only with yearning but with jealousy, suffering and compassion. The scene is not without comedy as Benedict feels gratified self-esteem at being the focus of so much passionate concern, but the total effect is of warmth, throbbing sexual desire and the rich fertility of the natural surrounding which complements the emotional situation – emotions which persist in the sleepless bed-chamber that night: 'There was no sleep for anyone at the farm on the night following that day.'[35]

The parallel in *Tess* is, of course, the incident one hot Sunday, in the rich farmlands, when Angel Clare carries Izzy and Marian and Retty and Tess, the four dairymaids in their bright dresses, across the overflow from the river and makes his preference for Tess clear – and that night 'the air of the sleeping chamber seemed to palpitate with the hopeless passion of the girls.'[36] There is enough resemblance in the analysis of the sensations of the girls to warrant the assumption that this scene had stuck in Hardy's memory – and also to suggest that when we call the overtones of a Hardy scene Lawrentian, it might be more accurate to describe them as Sandian.

But it is *Jeanne*, of all George Sand's novels, which most frequently calls Hardy to mind. The novel is set outside the Vallée Noire, out of the agricultural belt, in wild moorland – although, once again, the action of the story covers only a few miles, to the south of Boussac. The prologue immediately sets the tone with its description of the great druid stones 'in the midst of the most barren, melancholy and lonely scenery in France'.[37] For thirty centuries these gigantic altars have stood there, the wind moaning mysteriously through their arches, reminders of barbarian gods and bloody sacrifices. It is in the middle of the biggest group of all – Les Pierres Jaumâtres – that three young men, out on a hunting expedition, are surprised by the sight of a young peasant girl, Jeanne, innocently asleep. As they bend over her they marvel at finding such beauty and fairness (explained by George Sand as the result of centuries of in-breeding) in such a place – 'sinister, neither beautiful nor grand, but full of a sense of desolation'.[38]

Throughout the book the stress is laid (as in *The Return of the Native* and *Tess of the D'Urbervilles*) on the active presence of the past and its effect on the lives and attitudes of the heath-dwellers and villagers. The entire district is superstition-ridden, and legends of 'les fades' – who are more powerful than witches, more like Fates, always to be propitiated – mingle with Christian practices. History lies heavily upon them, for the villagers are always digging up Roman medallions or coins and have the vague sense of infinite riches there for the taking, under the gorse and heather. Prehistoric antiquities, mounds, druid stones and tors, are everywhere around – 'prehistoric stones rising up in these solitudes like the protest of the old, idolatrous world against the progress of civilisation'.[39] The countrymen are suspicious of strangers, opposed to change, fatalistic, avaricious and ignorant – although the young girls

who seek employment at the seasonal hiring fairs and become farm
servants in the neighbouring provinces are more adaptable. The
heroine – a Jeanne d'Arc figure – is as deeply superstitious as the other
peasants, and indeed much of her strength of character comes from her
fatalism; but despite her rooted beliefs she has peasant common sense.
She has not, like Tess, been half-educated into ideas of social convention, she has no 'moral hobgoblins' – and her matter-of-fact acceptance
of Claudie's seduction by the young lawyer, Marsillat (which was noted
earlier), is a more admirable rendering of Joan Durbeyfield's 'Tis
nater'; nearer in fact to Hardy's own comment.[40]

Marsillat is in many ways an Alec D'Urberville figure – although
much less stagey and more credibly analysed. He cuts a dash with the
peasant girls as he rides along the narrow lanes on his big horse, and
he has often surprised one asleep in the shelter of the rocks, or in the
lonely spinneys, and left her, in Hardy's phrase, a 'maiden no more'.
Jeanne distrusts his advances and, again like Tess, always refuses to
ride on his crupper until a moment of crisis, when, by a ruse, he
prevails on her to ride with him and carries her off to an attempted
seduction which ends in violence. On her death bed Jeanne recom-
mends her foster-sister Marie to Sir Arthur as a suitable wife – in much
the same way as Tess ensures Angel's future nuptials with Liza-Lu –
and George Sand's final comment on the survivors is that their ideas
and generous actions are a century in advance of the miserable and
doomed times in which we live: a sentiment less characteristic of her
than of Hardy, who always had a weakness for 'a man of the future'
like Jude or Clym.

Despite the great drawback of its impossibly untouchable heroine,
Jeanne makes its impact by what Balzac rightly described as its superb
country background.[41] One of the most striking scenes occurs in
Chapter 7 before Jeanne leaves the district to go as a dairymaid to the
de Boussac family. Her mother has died, and late in the evening their
hovel of a cottage catches fire. Jeanne risks her life to carry the body
of her mother from the flames and, looking like a druidess, with the
stiff corpse in her strong arms, she lays it on the flat table-like stone of
Ep-Nell. Through the long night watch she refuses to be parted from
her mother, and Guillaume stays near her, watching over her lovingly,
till the dawn. It is a memorable and dramatic episode, with sudden
spurts of flame from the dying fire lighting up the figures from time to
time and giving the corpse the appearance of life. An all-night vigil in
the shelter of druid stones, the grotesque effects of flames from a
bonfire – surely this is what we are accustomed to thinking of as Hardy
machinery, and it comes as something of a shock to find it used by
George Sand almost half a century earlier. Stonehenge and fifth of
November bonfires are part of Hardy's own background, and one need

look no further than his own creative imagination for what use he put them to. But what literature can do is to reveal possibilities to an artist, and just as George Sand was indebted to other writers – to Rousseau, to Chateaubriand, to Scott – in the way she reacted to her beloved Berry so, I feel certain, was Hardy to George Sand. And even if there were nothing else to link them, the fact that, as far as I know, among nineteenth-century novelists only George Sand also has a hero with the extraordinary name of Angel[42] provides a final, eccentric connection.

11 The Late Madame Sand

1

By the time both the century and George Sand had advanced into their sixties and seventies, she had ceased to be a controversial figure. In fact, in 1864, Justin M'Carthy claimed in the *Westminster Review* that 'What English people used to think Madame Sand very wicked years ago for saying, newspapers and books and even sermons not uncommonly say now. It is discovered that throughout English social life immorality is a much more general institution than successful and satisfactory marriage.'[1]

This observation has to be qualified. Immorality as an institution had never been advocated by Madame Sand, and although there was now more open discussion of the shortcomings of marriage, such emancipation was much less widespread than M'Carthy, a radical writer contributing to a radical journal, would imply. It is difficult to imagine even the most innocuous of George Sand's later romances in the hands of Georgina Podsnap, for the author suffered the disadvantage of being not only not moral but 'not English', and insularity had kept apace with national prosperity. None the less, it certainly is true that the English reading public, whatever might be true of the 'English people', had grown so accustomed to George Sand over thirty years or so that she was generally accepted as a great writer, and one still widely read, even by a much younger generation.

One should also, presumably, not take as gospel M'Carthy's declaration, in an article in *Galaxy* in 1870, that not a single 'revolutionary' idea for the last twenty years was not due immediately to the influence of George Sand and her unhappy marriage; but, if we believe even half of what he affirms, then her accountability is great indeed. He goes on to say that she has been felt as a power in every country of the world, as a great disorganising force; thousands of protests have been uttered in America and Europe by people who never saw a volume of George Sand and yet are only echoing her sentiments and even repeating her words, for she was assuredly the greatest champion of women's rights the world has ever seen, the first woman to speak out for herself as powerfully as a man. It is just as well, M'Carthy adds circumspectly, that very little was actually known about George Sand in the early days, for what would have been said had people really known the extravagances into which a passionate soul had hurried? But as these escapades had remained obscure, even the world of English Philistinism had soon ceased to regard George Sand as a monster and had felt her influence.[2]

Apart from the criticism of Henry James, which will be looked at in the next chapter, the comments made upon George Sand by later readers add very little to earlier appreciations of her; it is remarkable enough that she still had a public in the great days of the Victorian novel – although one must at the same time remember the Victorians' insatiable appetite for fiction of almost any kind. It is still of interest, however, that at a time when she was receiving only few and lukewarm reviews in the journals, numbers of men of letters were still reading her earlier novels in particular, and responding to them enthusiastically. The situation was very different in France, where Zola, while admitting that George Sand herself was capable of moving him profoundly,[3] was crying out against the dead hand of her imitators, whose old-fashioned idealism monopolised the pages of the *Revue des Deux Mondes*. Despite her greatness, the truth should be told: she did not exist any more for the present generation: 'George Sand représente une formule morte, voilà tout. C'est la science, c'est l'esprit moderne qu'elle a contre elle et qui, peu à peu, fait pâlir ces oeuvres.'[4]

For English readers of all ages her works still held plenty of colour and, as always, each took what he needed. Meredith's *Emilia in England* came out in 1864, and the resemblance of the heroine to Consuelo was noted. It then would have been very difficult to miss it, for Emilia is the charming, honest, artless Italian girl – whom we have met so often – with the black hair and eyes and the wonderful voice, who is taken from her Bohemian background by her patrons and eventually becomes a prima donna. Like Consuelo, she falls passionately and transparently in love with an amiable but unworthy young man, is comforted in her disillusionment by her dedication to her art, and is hectored by her patron, Mr Patrocles, much as Consuelo is by Porpora. The dark, riverside scene of her rescue from suicide by a faithful admirer recalls that of Indiana by Ralph, and points forward to the succour of Mirah by Deronda. Meredith refers to George Sand in his letters only a couple of times but his romantic, passionate moralising side, which forms a counterpoint to his satirical, witty realism, brings her often to mind, and never more so than in the nightingale-haunted scenes in which the full-throated song of Emilia blends with the magic of the moonlight. Such scenes, allied with the element of Italian patriotic fervour, the figure of Marini (Mazzini) and the novelist's friendship, at the time of writing, with the two Ashurst daughters,

Emily Venturi and Caroline Stansfeld, combine to give both this book and *Vittoria* its sequel, a distinct ambiance of George Sand and her intimates.

Perhaps the most efficient and economical exploitation of any work of George Sand's was achieved by Charles Reade, who in 1851 adapted her play *Claudie*, which had had a great success in Paris. Its heroine is a beautiful country girl who has been tricked into a false marriage – and has had a child who has died – and who, despite the disgrace, is happily married to the farmer's son by the end of the play. Claudie's pride and innocence and also the authentic rural background, with its sense of isolation from 'another country' a few miles off, are very like Hardy. Indeed it must have been difficult for anyone at the time not to be familiar with the story, for Reade adapted it first as a play, *A Village Tale* (1852) and, when that was a failure, he re-wrote it as a story, *Clouds and Sunshine* (1855), in which he stuck very closely to the original text, except for the introduction of an extra character, an entomologist, who, with that hobby, could have very well come from a George Sand story. Then in 1874, he had a final go at it, gave it a new title – *Rachel the Reaper* – and a new cast, and put it on at the Queen's Theatre. In the quarter of a century since the last version of the play, the fashion had changed to naturalism and Reade, as opportunist as ever, responded to the new demands. Ellen Terry tells of his innovations – 'real pigs, real sheep, a real goat, and a real dog. Real litter was strewn all over the stage' –[6] but even all these accessories could not turn the play into a hit like the original. Compared with Reade's wholesale takeover, Robert Lytton's plagiarism of an early tale of George Sand's, *Lavinia*, in his poem 'Lucille' (1860) was very small-scale borrowing; but, unlike Reade's, it was unacknowledged. His father, Bulwer Lytton, deliberately advised him against making any reference to his debt in the preface and his *post hoc* letter to Robert, when a law suit was threatened, is a masterpiece of lofty equivocation.[7]

On the whole, however, the benefits derived from reading George Sand were much less practical. For many, it was still her idealism that constituted her chief appeal. This was true certainly of Ruskin, of Frederick Harrison and of John Morley, all of whom found her optimism more appealing than George Eliot's unsparing sense of nemesis. Ruskin's diaries tell of reading George Sand when he was in France in 1856, and again in 1868. The early entries indicate his turning to her as a relief from his moods, as much as anything:

Sept. 13. Paris. Reading *La Petite Fadette* all day and able to think of nothing else. Nothing learned today but the finish and passion of George Sand among French writers and her sense of goodness among general thinkers.

Sept. 17. . . . very sad and sulky all day. Reading *Le Péché de Monsieur Antoine*, diluted and romantic, not good.

Sept. 20. Nothing but going to the Louvre and reading George Sand. Note in the Péché, first Emile and the Carpenter lying when it suits them; then Carpenter so angry at the blow of cane and shouting at his work.

It would be difficult to tell from this last observation whether Ruskin is admiring the author's attention to detail or deploring the fact that the two characters fall so far short of model behaviour, if we did not know that his approach to fiction was unswervingly moral. He found the pastoral tales pure enough to read aloud to his mother and did so, in Calais:

Sept. 25. Reading *François le Champi* all day to my mother: a beautiful tale, and these three women, Madeleine, Fanchon Fadette and la Petite Marie are enough to justify all Mrs Browning's love of George Sand.[8]

This concentration on the French writer's innocent heroines allowed him to use her against George Eliot in his vehement denunciation of the ugliness of the dénouement of the *Mill on the Floss*[9] – like Swinburne, who considered the last third of the book as 'a gangrene in the very flesh' of a novel which had started so well, whose 'first two volumes have all the intensity and all the perfection of George Sand's best work.'[10] A letter of John Morley's of 1872 underlines the almost schoolboyish fervour with which these mature English disciples of George Sand regarded her. He records, of Frederick Harrison, that he is 'back from the continent full of George Sand and her wonderful writings which he contrasted with the sad anatomical novels of George Eliot' and declares:

Oct. 8. I feel that my life is imperfect until I have spent a day with that wonderful woman and I mean to do so before I am much older . . . George Eliot is great and profound but I certainly agree with you as to the superiority of George Sand qua artist . . . G.S. seems to me simply the loveliest prose-writer that ever lived. I have been reading her sedulously, partly to prevent myself from falling asleep before bedtime, partly to try and soften out some of the crudities of my own prose.[11]

The familiarity with her novels of this generation – all men, except for Ruskin and Reade, born several years after her first impact on England – is very striking. When John Addington Symonds goes to

Il Trovatore in 1859, he comments on the prima donna's likeness to George Sand's best loved heroine:

> Mlle Tietjens is *just* what I have ever imagined Consuelo. Tall, svelte . . . her hair . . . floating out in broad undulations, dark as night and lustrous as ye morning . . . her face intellectual, fine forehead, eyes and mouth . . . I thought of Consuelo all along and whenever she came before ye curtain, ye resemblance was still more striking . . .[12]

On holiday the following year, he reads the novel yet again: 'Raining despairingly for some time . . . Consuelo and Molière are a great blessing. I have read the former, and Puller is now doing the same, I for about the 6th, he for the 1st time.'[13]

When he is in the Alps in 1866, he talks of 'the monarchs of the human soul' as being Goethe, Milton, Shakespeare, Dante, Virgil and Beethoven. But 'There are others too – Shelley, Mendelssohn and George Sand – less great but not less true and fresh, who chime in whispers with the grass and flowers of the field.'[14] There are many other references in Symond's diaries; it is obvious that some of his delight comes from the charm of the unfamiliar idiom as well as from her 'description steeped in sentiment'. More than once he quotes the same phrase appreciatively – ' "J'ai fait de ma vie une vraie école buissonnière" I might say with George Sand' – and for him, as had always been the case with her English admirers, the sound of her words contributed to her spell.

Thackeray's daughter, Lady Ritchie, went further than Symonds and said 'I really and actually come upon bits of Beethoven in George Sand. George Eliot is only Mendelssohn (*Romola* is Kalkbrenner's exercises).'[15] She also comments on how pleasant it is to read her books in France: 'It seems a charming natural accompaniment to George Sand's books and letters to be reading them among the very scenes she describes to the pleasant echoes of the friendly French voices'[16] – an experience which many other English readers had savoured and recorded in the preceding years. For this last observation was not made by Lady Ritchie until 1901, when she wrote her idyllic description of the place which 'is a household word to many of us', Nohant, and was able to satisfy at least part of an earlier unfulfilled ambition. The wail of disappointment in a letter of 1876, just after George Sand's death, recalls a similar emotional outburst long before from Elizabeth Barrett: 'I *should* like to write something about George Sand. I wish I had sent the letter I wrote her once (which I burnt) so as to have crossed pens with her once.'[17] Lady Ritchie's romantic feelings about George Sand co-exist with admiration, as a fellow-writer, of her professionalism and also critical awareness of her tendency to dash off in a week a 'stupid, stupid novel' – 'I do envy George Sand and George Eliot so when they strike up and begin to tune their instruments, especially George Sand, who seems to me to boom an echo all through her prefaces, and sweep one into her stupid books so that it doesn't matter how stupid they are.'[18] But, on the whole, it is the hero-worship that predominates and we find her, like the rest, going on pilgrimage, not only to Nohant but to the apartment *below* the one that George Sand used in her last years in Paris, in 5 rue Gay-Lussac, in order at least to get an idea of the layout of the rooms and to gaze upon and to be allowed to sit on Madame Sand's sofa, which had made its way downstairs, 'the biggest sofa I ever saw, with a corner to it and leather buttons all along'.[19]

Swinburne, though highly appreciative of George Sand, 'the glorious mistress of all forms and powers of imaginative prose', adopts a less reverent tone in his letters. Writing to Monckton Milnes in 1863, he plays with the idea of having himself passed off 'upon Madame Sand as the typical *miss anglaise émancipée* and holding the most ultra views';[20] and he is very much aware of her private life: 'Mrs Manners (who as you know is something of a prude – as Balzac said of George Sand!!!!!)'[21] He tries to cheer up his friend, Mrs Lynn Linton, when she shows signs of flagging, at the age of fifty-nine, with a calculation which is not only flattering, but which he knew would appeal to her: 'Aug. 30. 1883. George Sand had plenty of good work before her at an age when, I suppose her daughter would have been about *your* age.'[22]

By younger writers, for whom no moral problems were involved, George Sand could simply be enjoyed as a story-teller of great virtuosity. In 1873 R.L.S. wrote: 'I have found a new friend, to whom I grow daily more devoted – George Sand. I go on from one novel to another and think the last I have read the most sympathetic and friendly in tone, until I have read another. It is a life in dreamland.'[23] And Gissing, also in his early twenties, spent his time in 1876 in the library in Boston just reading one George Sand novel after another. Even later, when he was writing *Thyrza*, 'He had extravagant praise for his old favourite, George Sand.'[24] It is curious to think of those two young men – one to be a writer of romantic adventures, the other a rigorously realistic novelist – swallowing George Sand in large gulps and retaining what best suited their systems: in the case of Stevenson, no doubt, her ability to hold the reader's interest in a tale of action; in that of Gissing, her social conscience and compassion.

The persistence with which George Sand's name continues to crop up, even late into the century, in memoirs, letters and journals prompts the suspicion that there is a strange lack of negative instances. But although of course the general reading public was totally unaffected by George Sand, I think that very few literate Victorians were unacquainted with at least one or two of her works. It is certainly difficult to find anyone before the end of the century denying all knowledge of her, so that George Moore makes a refreshing exception in his categorical avowal to his publisher in 1896, that he is totally ignorant of her novels: 'Regarding George Sand I regret to say I have never read a word by her. She was not of my time but it is possible she may be going up in the world again. I know she wrote 80 novels or nearly. Do you propose to issue translations of them all?'[25]

In this respect, however, as in so many others, he was fashionably eccentric even in his circle; other aesthetes were familiar with George Sand's works. Pater wrote approvingly of her more than once, and in his essay on Wordsworth linked the two writers together in their depiction of 'this strange new passionate pastoral world of which he first raised the image, and the reflection of which some of our best modern fiction has caught from him.'[26] Though it is doubtful how far George Sand was indebted to Wordsworth (Scott is the writer whom she mentions most frequently), there is no doubt that Pater was right to sense their affinity. Wilde, Pater's admirer, admired her too, despite her belief in Art for Life's Sake. In a review of a novel by Ouida in 1889, he pointed out that, although she belonged to 'the school of Bulwer Lytton and George Sand' she lacked 'the learning of the one and the sincerity of the other'.[27] There was in fact little doubt that Ouida had read George Sand and also had read all about her, and that she occasionally sounded like a pastiche of the French writer's more fashionable tales. The villainess in *Strathmore* has a partiality for French novels: 'Lady Vavasour was lying back in a dormeuse, glancing through George Sand's last novel.'[28] But reviewers were always loyally ready, like Wilde, to snub her pretensions and to point out the gulf between the two novelists. M'Carthy, for instance, talks coldly of 'such accomplished artists in impurity as the lady who calls herself Ouida', and claims that George Sand is 'no more open to the charge [of indelicacy] than the authoress of *Romola*'.[29]

One of Wilde's witty reviews[30] in the *Pall Mall Gazette* in 1883 was of E. M. Caro's *George Sand*, a critical biography. He begins in fine style: 'This is the biography of a very great man from the pen of a very lady-like writer', and proceeds to show how ill-suited M. Caro, a professor at the Sorbonne, is to convey George Sand's quality and genius. 'He never gets at the secret of George Sand and never brings us near to her wonderful personality'; Wilde recalls that Arnold had said that it was imperative to get the spirit of George Sand to appreciate her, and this is what M. Caro, who 'can chatter charmingly about culture', never succeeds in doing. George Sand's faith in social regeneration is an essential constituent of it: 'Her spirit which he treats with such airy flippancy, is the very leaven of modern life. It is remoulding the world for us, and fashioning our age anew . . . If it is Utopian, then Utopia must be added to our geographies.'[31] To add to his sins, M. Caro says nothing of her delightful treatment of art and the artist's life. And 'yet how exquisitely does she analyse each separate art and present it to us in its relation to life!' And in the list which follows, as well as in the books which he has already quoted, Wilde shows just how very conversant he is with her works. For *Consuelo* is concerned with music, *Horace* with authorship, *Le Château des Désertes* with acting, *Les Maîtres Mosaïstes* with mosaic work, *Le Château de Pictordu* with portrait painting and *La Daniella* with landscape painting. 'What Mr Ruskin and Mr Browning have done for England, she did for France. She invented an art-literature.'

But too much cannot be deduced from this impressive field of reference, for in fact the list is identical with one compiled by F. W. H. Myers in his 1877 article on George Sand, in which he discussed the importance of different forms of art in her novels, and it is likely that here, as so often, Wilde is skilfully plagiarising. The omission of one of the novels, *Les Ailes de Courage*, which Myers mentions as an example of 'the art of bird-stuffing', simply shows that Wilde had considerably more risibility than Myers and knew, at least in this instance, where to stop. But that he did feel warmly about George Sand, however many of her less well-known novels he had read, is quite patent from the tone of the review, which ends with an onslaught on the translator, Gustave Masson, and a long list of his howlers. He points out, among other examples, that 'il faudra relâcher mes économies' does not mean 'I will have to draw upon my savings'; that 'qui pourra définir sa pensée' does not mean 'who can clearly despise her thought'; and that 'the stream excites itself by the declivity which it obeys' scarcely conveys the feeling of the original. This English version, he suggests, 'may be up to the requirements of the Harrow schoolboys' but is 'quite undeserved by the public. Nowadays even the public has its feelings.'

One early tale of George Sand's which may well have appealed in the nineties was her charming romance *La Marquise* (1832), in which the old lady recalls the one time in her life when she has really known what love was. She had admired from afar Lélio, an actor in the *Comedie Francaise*, and had very frequently gone to watch his performance in Corneille and Racine. One day she saw him in a café and could scarcely believe her eyes; here was no hero, just a commonplace, shabby, raucous, rather battered actor. But despite her disillusionment she sees him again in *Le Cid* as Rodrigue and falls so completely under his spell that she continues to attend the theatre, night after night, month after month. Lélio becomes conscious of her presence in the audience and, from the other side of the footlights, falls deeply in love with her. Before he leaves the country he begs to be allowed to meet her, and she consents reluctantly, for she knows what he is really like. But when they meet a miracle has happened; he has become transformed by his love for her; he has taken on his heroic image; the man has become, however briefly, the mask. It is a story which brings to mind aspects of *The Picture of Dorian Gray* but, even more markedly, Max Beerbohm's *The Happy Hypocrite*, that appealing *fin-de-siècle* tale of how Lord George Hell wears an angelic mask to cover his debauched features to woo a pure young girl and how, through his love for her, he eventually becomes his image.

Wilde must have been attracted not only to George Sand's treatment of art but to her socialism, her romanticism and her unorthodoxy. The greatest of the Last Romantics, Yeats, no doubt relished her unorthodoxy in a different sphere – in matters of religion and spiritual enquiry. In *Autobiographies*, he tells of his conversations with Madame Blavatsky between 1887 and 1891 when 'She spoke of Balzac whom she had seen but once, of Alfred de Musset whom she had known well enough to dislike for his morbidity and George Sand, whom she had known so well that they had dabbled in magic together of which "neither knew anything at all in those days".'[32]

Yeats, who was only eleven years old when George Sand died, could certainly have said, with more justification than Moore 'she was not of my time', but a letter of 1922 reveals that she still had something to offer him as a mature poet. Two of her novels helped to fill his summer at Coole Park:

> July 27, 1922. Did you ever read George Sand's *Consuelo* and its sequel? Lady Gregory has read them out to me – a chapter at a time – during the summer. They fill one with reverie – secret societies of the eighteenth century, all turmoil of an imagined wisdom from which came the barricades. George Sand is a child when she tries to philosophise, but seems to know everything while she rolls images before us as we see things in the fire. I am writing verse, a long poem (long for me) about Ballylee. Four parts of (say) two dozen lines each. I have written 3 of the parts and have also written a lyric about the civil war.[33]

I said, in my Introduction, that no reader who began George Sand with *La Comtesse de Rudolstadt* (the sequel to *Consuelo*) could expect to get very far. Yeats, however, was the exceptional reader; he was not concerned, like the Victorians, with the charming heroine, but with everything that Browning had dismissed as clap-trap. George Sand was as interested in the occult as she was in history. Her alienation from Catholicism did not mean indifference to spiritual matters and she was always on the look-out for signs which could be interpreted as the proof of another existence; she felt that one should study, and not deride, supernatural phenomena. Her recreation of eighteenth-century Europe, especially of Italy and Austria, before the French Revolution has, along with the sense of impending rebellion against tyranny and despotism, almost every sort of mysticism and crankiness to delight Yeats's heart: Hussites, secret masonic societies, political intrigue, metempsychosis, reincarnation, thought-transference, possession by spirits and catalepsy. Among her characters is an aristocrat, of long lineage, fighting for freedom, and a hunchback who, though crazed, is regarded as a saint by the peasants because of his innocence.

That Yeats should have made his way through this paraphernalia and summed it up as 'all turmoil of an imagined wisdom from which came the barricades' is a tribute to his ability to extract his own nourishment from an extremely rich and indigestible compound. But it is also a tribute to George Sand's image-making, which had the power to fill his mind and feed his imagination through the long summer days. It may well be that these images, which pass so easily and imperceptibly in her novels from familiar landscape to the magical and transcendental and back again had a further-reaching effect upon Yeats than the immediate poem he was writing. Joseph Hone is absolutely correct in saying that 'something of the feeling of *Consuelo* and its sequel found its way into the conclusion of 'Meditations in Time of Civil War.'[34] In fact, the indebtedness is even more specific. The section of *La Comtesse de Rudolstadt* which especially fascinated Yeats must have been the heroine's initiation to the mysterious rights of free-masonry and her appearance before the tribunal of the 'Invisibles', when she is exempted from several of the masonic stages, including 'le grade où le néophyte se prosterne sur le simulacre des cendres de Jaques Molay, le grand maître et le grande victime du temple'[35] – the grade of vengeance for the death of the last Grand Master of the Templars, who was burned alive in 1314. Yeats's notes to this seventh section of the poem indicate his awareness of the esoteric nature of his references, although he does not mention George Sand there.

> A puff of wind
> And those white glimmering fragments of the mist sweep by.
> Frenzies bewilder, reveries perturb the mind;
> Monstrous familiar images swim to the mind's eye.[36]
>
> 'Vengeance upon the murderers,' the cry goes up,
> 'Vengeance for Jacques Molay.' In cloud-pale rags, or in lace,
> The rage-driven, rage-tormented, and rage-hungry troop,
> Trooper belabouring trooper, biting at arm or at face,
> Plunges towards nothing, arms and fingers spreading wide
> For the embrace of nothing; and I, my wits astray

Because of all that senseless tumult, all but cried
For vengeance on the murderers of Jacques Molay.
('Meditations in Time of Civil War' VII.)

2

George Sand's death, in 1876, was the signal, as always at such a time, for re-appraisal of her achievement. There was no doubt at all in anyone's mind that the life that had just ended was that of a woman of eminence, and perhaps the most indisputable proof of this for English readers was the fact of an obituary in *The Times* – something which would scarcely have been considered likely forty years earlier. It ran as follows:

The Times, Friday, 9 June 1876

Madame George Sand died this morning at her country home at Nohant and will be buried there. She was a descendant on the paternal side from Marshal Saxe, her father being Maurice Dupin. She was born in 1804, married in 1822, M. Dudevant, by whom she had a son and daughter, separated from her husband and assumed male costume in order to move about Paris freely, especially at the theatres. Her first novel being written in concert with M. Jules Sandeau who dropped the second syllable of his name on the title page, Delatouche, the editor of the newspaper in which it appeared, gave her the pseudonym of George Sand, which she thereupon adopted altogether. Even to enumerate all her productions in the course of more than 40 years would be too long a task. Inclined when a girl to become a nun, she renounced Catholicism at an early age, but held fast to a belief in the future state.

With this official underwriting of Madame Sand's *bona fides*, in a more than usual literal sense, *The Times*'s tribute ended. Although there had been space to mention her fleeting thought of taking the veil at the age of sixteen and to recount (still erroneously) the history of her pseudonym, there was none to list even a few of her best-known novels. But this omission was rectified by the major journals, most of which assigned the task of writing articles on George Sand to reputable men-of-letters and gave them plenty of elbow room, so that these accounts are often lengthy surveys of her life and works, with some comparative discussion of the state of the novel in England and France, for good measure. The contributions of Arnold and of James are considered separately. But in addition to these, there were substantial estimates of her in, among others, the *Athenaeum*, the *Nineteenth Century*, the *Saturday Review*, the *Quarterly*, the *Atlantic Monthly* and the *Dublin University Magazine*. The *Edinburgh Review* was silent as was, surprisingly, the *Westminster Review*, which had defended her so often in the past.

As *Histoire de ma Vie* was re-published in four volumes in 1876 and was lying on reviewers' desks waiting for their attention when George Sand died, most of the obituary notices made considerable use of it for details of her childhood and youth. The *Saturday Review*'s offering is primarily a discussion of the autobiography and the writer, who begins imposingly 'Now that Posterity has begun . . . for the illustrious author of *Mauprat*', feels constrained to point out that her style is lamentably diffuse: 'She is never prosy for she writes too well; but she often inspires the feeling with which we listen to a good sermon after we begin to feel hungry. It is excellent but we wish it would stop.'[37] And, without acknowledgement, he echoes James's remark, 'This kind of easy writing makes proverbially hard reading.' Her foreignness is remarked – 'The virtues, too, as well as the failings of George Sand are thoroughly un-English. No English girl ever did feel, or could feel, ever could behave as she felt and behaved. It is therefore hard to do her justice.' – and while this has undoubtedly a *plus ça change* . . . quality about it, the appraisal does end in a very different way from the conclusions of early reviews, with the firm conviction that there was 'both in her life and in what she wrote a spirit of nobleness which if sometimes obscured, was never absent. She strove to think and act rightly . . .'

The *Athenaeum* followed up its stop-press announcement of 10 June – 'With great regret just as we are going to press, we hear by telegraph from Paris of the death of Madame George Sand' – with a full-scale obituary in its next issue. Chorley, who had so often temporised about her, was dead, and the tone of the discussion is much more positive. 'The death of Madame Sand brings to a close one of the most brilliant of literary careers . . . Her resources seemed inexhaustible and her activity was indefatigable.'[38] The stress throughout is much more on her as an artist, 'a poetess', than as a social thinker. She was 'one of the noblest converts to Radicalism' but 'this period fortunately was like a passing cloud. She had attempted to be a strong man, and she found that she was a woman and above all, an artist.' *Consuelo* was probably her best known work, though others bore fuller evidence of her genius. 'She will be remembered as a consummate artist who however frequently misunderstood, was true to the last moment, to the ideal of truth, goodness and beauty.' The writer points out the fictional nature of much of *Histoire de ma Vie*, but then concludes with a bland statement, which constitutes an astounding *volte-face*: 'The absence of an authentic biography is however scarcely to be regretted for the private life of an artist is, after all, but of secondary interest.'

T. S. Perry, Henry James's friend, argues a more hostile case in the *Atlantic Monthly*. He is well aware that even in the poorest novels there is always 'some valuable and delightful material' but he deplores her assumption that 'society should be constituted for the purpose of yielding to exceptional individuals.' It is 'her own weakness that created her sympathy for weak people.' He feels that she neglects duty and conscience, and the ending of the notice is severe: 'She left little untasted in her long life except perhaps the sweetness of self-denial. One cannot help wondering what was her final verdict concerning the worth of it all.'[39] The assessment, with its New England distrust of European hedonism, could have come from a Jamesian character – the verdict of Waymark on Madame de Vionnet, perhaps. Perry is sternly aware of her unsound nature while at the same time he is conscious of her good qualities and her dangerous power over the reader who 'is led to sympathise with all sorts of uncommendable things of which he cannot really approve'.

These are not the things on which Myers concentrates in his very long article[40] on her in the *Nineteenth Century* in the spring of 1877. This was by far the most ambitious literary appreciation of her to appear and, as we have seen, influenced Arnold in his own conclusions. Best remembered in literary anecdotage for his account of his solemn conversation with George Eliot in the Fellows' Garden at Trinity one summer evening on the topic of 'God, Immortality, Duty', Myers was an admirer of both novelists and here he praises 'the multitudinous writings of the most noteworthy woman, with perhaps one exception, who has appeared in literature since Sappho.' From start to finish his tone is one of serious tribute. 'A great spirit has passed from among us . . . It is distinctly as a force, an influence, a promulgation of real or supposed truths that these books deserve consideration . . . George Sand's fame continues to shine with a steady lustre.'

Myers mentions the different stages of her career as a novelist, and recalls the time when her novels of revolt made her name 'a word of fear in British households'. But what he feels is most important about her is that she has 'toujours été tourmentée des choses divines'. The things which she has led Myers to sympathise with are far from uncommendable, although also far from original – her belief in a God, inconceivable and unknowable, but approachable by prayer; progress, as the law both of the universe and of the soul, continued through infinite series of existences; and unselfish love as the best and most lasting of human experiences. It can be seen that whereas Perry was concerned with what he thought she practised, Myers is moved by what she preached.

In the course of his discussion Myers makes some pithy comments. She had always 'the instincts of a gentleman' though not perhaps 'the instincts of a lady'; she was rather like the Sphinx, steadfast, disdainful and serene, and had 'the power of living down everybody and every-thing – enemies, partisanships, scandals, love – whole schools of thought and whole generations of men'. He sets the account straight about her views on marriage, while confessing that she did have a very painful characteristic – a tendency to idealise people for a time and then to *cease* to idealise them: 'A feminine Goethe is more than mankind can endure and there is much that is like Goethe in the emotional history of George Sand.' She is unsurpassed in her fictional treatment of love – unlike English novelists, whose reticence has always been a stumbling-block. He mentions many of her novels praising a late novel, *Valvèdre*, in particular, but does not feel it 'necessary in this paper to analyse in detail works so well known as George Sand's'.

In Myers's final paragraphs, after he has made his point that George Sand was an *'Anima Naturaliter Christiana,* one of those who must be ranged along with Christians in any reckoning of the spiritual forces of the world' comes an allusion to Matthew Arnold. He does not mention his name but he is easily recognisable.

> Perhaps the loftiest and most impressive strain of ethical teaching which is to be heard in England now comes from one who invokes no celestial assistance and offers no ultimate recompense of reward. The Stoics are again among us; the stern disinterestedness of their 'counsels of perfection' is enchaining some of our noblest souls. But the moral elevation of any portion of mankind tends to the elevation of all . . . Few writers have dwelt on this prospect with a more sustained and humble aspiration than George Sand.[41]

The highminded nature of this association of him with George Sand must have appealed to Arnold. It is certainly a very striking assessment of a writer who had more than once in the past been described by the British press as a disgrace to her sex, but it must be remembered that the writer was an open-minded scholar, thirty-three years of age, contributing to an independent literary journal. What of George Sand's old enemies, with confirmed religious and political views – the *Dublin University Magazine, Blackwood's* and, above all, the *Quarterly*?

Up to a decade before, the *DUM* had been continuing to attack strongly, and had published an article on 'The Life, Eccentricities and Literature of George Sand' which had been largely insulting in tone. Even when a later novel, *Mont Revêche*, was admitted to be fairly harmless, 'Mrs Marsh or Mrs Oliphant or Mrs Ellis would feel little flattered by being mistaken as the authoress.'[42] But after her death there is no question of comparing her to her detriment with minor literary figures. The magazine refers to 'the recent death of this great writer', and the contributor makes a determined effort to give a conciliatory account of her, although he depends mainly upon a résumé of *Histoire de ma Vie* and a translation of a laudatory French obituary to achieve the effect. Even so he cannot resist slipping in a comment at the end to the effect that the French writer's belief that there was 'no immoral tendency in George Sand's works in their bearing on the sanctity of the marriage bond was scarcely one which would be accepted by the majority of English readers.'[43]

Blackwood's made amends for past harshness much less grudgingly than the *Dublin University Magazine*, with a full-length obituary by A. Innes Shand: 'Not many months have passed since the death of George Sand yet we fancy that not a few of her faithful readers begin to realise how greatly they miss her. It is nearly five-and-forty years since she somewhat tardily awakened to her veritable vocation, and charmed the world with a finished romance.' If Innes Shand had looked up the *Blackwood's* files he would have found that she had charmed George Street, Edinburgh, considerably less than she had the rest of the world. But now bygones were not only bygones; they were transformed. A very thorough job of white-washing begins with the strange comment that 'Notwithstanding the somewhat unfeminine irregularity of her habits, she gave her constitution fair play to the last.' The praise of *Jacques*, that 'marvellously clever book' is still fairly canny, for it is an 'ingenious perversion of all our old-fashioned moral notions', and Shand finds it a relief 'to turn to the fresh air from the *landes*, to the mountains and the scent of the heath and broom', where the praise of her country tales can be wholehearted. He voices the puzzlement of many a reader of George Sand when, having given the outline of one of her novels, he says that 'it sounds and is absurd enough' and yet 'such is the inimitable skill of the narrator that the book does not strike us as ridiculous in the telling.' And his final verdict must be that 'on the whole she deserves our admiration as a woman . . . Her warm heart was essentially sound, as her purposes were always pure and honest. She laboured, according to her lights, for the enlightenment of human nature.'[44] *Blackwood's* rehabilitation of George Sand was completed two years later in a survey of outstanding French novelists of the century, when, without a blush, they sum her up: 'Universally read, she was universally admired; and she pleased the fastidious as she entertained the many.'[45]

The *Quarterly*, which had paid scant attention to George Sand over the years, now devoted twenty-six pages[46] to her. Croker was long since dead and the appraisal was put in the civilised hands of Andrew Lang. He is conscious that he is attempting to give an estimate of a writer who was 'the most widely talked of woman in Europe in the '30's', whose death had 'removed a literary force not abated by extreme age'. What he is certain of is that her enduring fame will be as an artist in words, a painter of life and not as a critic of society, in which rôle he feels she early shot her bolt. He talks of her affinity with Sainte-Beuve, who also was tormented with things divine and her debt to Scott – although her peasants are 'reflective and serious creatures unconsciously filled with the secret meanings of natural beauty', unlike his shrewd and humorous Lowlanders. He singles out discerningly her descriptions of the sleeping flowers in the Canon's garden in *Consuelo*, the migration of swallows in *Mauprat* and the noises of the night in *Lettres d'un Voyageur*. Lang shows himself extremely well and widely read in her novels and responsive to the 'peculiar quality in which she is unapproached . . . her rendering of the beauty of landscape into words singularly appropriate . . . very like Chopin's music'. He is aware of the importance of the personal element in her work, but suggests that the glimpses we are given in the prefaces, the authorial comments in the novels and in the *Lettres* are not of the real George Sand but of the ideal George Sand of the moment – a half-imaginary being. He stresses her own personal lack of passion and finds instead a restless curiosity to examine the struggle between sentiment and duty: 'No one can read her biography and her novels and continue of the opinion that love as between man and woman was one of the most masterful forces in her nature.'

Repeatedly in the course of the lengthy examination Lang makes interesting and shrewd points. One of the finest passages has already been referred to in the chapter on George Eliot, in which he discusses the presence in almost every novel of 'a high souled being . . . The balance between the weak and worldly lover and the austere and maternal or paternal lover is constantly vibrating and its movements make the action of the story.' George Sand had had to wait a life-time for the *Quarterly* to give her recognition but at least when the post-humous tribute came it was one of some critical distinction.

12 'Dear Old George'

1

Henry James is the last of the great nineteenth-century admirers of George Sand and her influence on him has, particularly in four books[1] in the last fifty years, received a fair amount of attention and some admirable analysis and identification of source material. The two writers never met; he was not born till the year in which *Consuelo* was published and so read her worst, and latest, novels first, and by the time of her death he had already begun to disapprove of many aspects of her life and art and to turn to other models. But none the less it can be called a relationship, because she was a significant part of James's consciousness for over fifty years and he was still capable of writing on her with as much fascinated, affectionate, though more ironic, interest the year before he died as he had when a young man. He penned more pages and published more reviews and articles (ten all told) on her than on any other writer. In fact, his total number of printed words on George Sand would make another novel the length of (aptly enough) *The Europeans*.

In including James, I am aware that I may seem to be straying from Victorian England into the realm of her North American influence, which was very considerable and has not yet been fully analysed.[2] Emerson, Poe and Whitman are as much outside the sphere of this book as Dostoievsky or Heine. However, James is, as always, another matter. His Europeanism was bred in the family; Henry James senior forced Europe down his children's throat from their infancy – much as Philip Gosse forced God down young Edmund's – but, unlike his friend Gosse, James was not sated by the experience. Indeed it was the father who tired first and returned with relief to being a staunch American. The background and education of James fitted him to be receptive to all the French novelists and playwrights whom he was to read so voraciously – Balzac, Flaubert, Zola, Maupassant, Mérimée, Daudet, Dumas fils, Feuillet and so on – but the convictions of his father must have prepared the way for George Sand with peculiar ease. In fact the French novelist and the elder James shared a remarkable number of beliefs and anathemas, even to a strong distrust of art for art's sake. James's father was a disciple of both Swedenborg and Fourier; he had misgivings about private property; he felt marriage was 'not administered *livingly*' and wished to liberalise it by freer divorce ('It is not essential to the honor of marriage that two people should be compelled to live together when they hold the reciprocal relation of dog and cat') ;[3] and, finally, he had a rooted dislike of the Roman Catholic church, 'the most ecclesiastical of ecclesiasticism'. So that many of the features of George Sand's writing which came as a shock to other readers were familiar and indeed orthodox territory to the James boys.

It was when Henry James returned from France to America at the age of seventeen in 1860 that, feeling homesick for Europe, he began serious study of the *Revue des Deux Mondes*, to which his father subscribed. As an elderly man, James looked back to the 'fairly golden glow of romance' with which the mere act of perusal was invested; in fact, his memories of that time are all *couleur de rose*. The closet 'on the shelves of which the pink *Revues* sat with the air, row upon row, of a choir of breathing angels'[4] seemed to him a far shorter cut to the literary world than his place at Harvard. He became addicted to the journal just at the time that George Sand returned to its fold as a regular contributor, so that it was the unusual issue that did not have some instalment of a novel from her hand.

> Oh the repeated arrival, during those years, of the salmon-coloured volumes . . . The sense of the salmon-coloured distinctive of Madame Sand was to come back to me long years after . . . a kind of domestic loyalty would operate . . . to make us take the thick with the thin . . . When I say all indeed I doubtless have in mind especially my parents and myself, with my sister and our admirable aunt (in her times of presence) thrown in – to the extent of our subjection to the charm of such matters in particular as *La Famille de Germandre*, *La Ville Noire*, *Nanon* and *L'Homme de Neige*, round which last above all we sat ranged in united ecstacy . . .[5]

No doubt at the same time he was making himself familiar with the earlier and greater George Sand, for he talks of their embracing their mother with fond patronage 'for so sweetly not knowing about *Valentine* and *Jacques* and such like and having only begun at *La Mare au Diable*'.[6] But no one who, as a contemporary, had felt the impact of her novels of revolt could have taken those smooth-flowing romances so seriously. Arnold looked back to his days of *Lélia* – James to his days of *L'Homme de Neige*. In the list of novels mentioned by James, *Nanon* is a misfit, a later work, not surprisingly confused, even in James's amazing memory, with some other of the hundred or so volumes of George Sand.

As can be seen, George Sand was very much a family affair, although Dickens and George Eliot, in instalments, Thackeray in his yellow numbers and Trollope in the orange-coloured *Cornhill*, had all preceded her in the affections of the young Jameses. They all read her and enjoyed her, but none of them seems to have taken her so much to heart as Henry. Writing home from France in 1868, William James mentions that he had 'read several novels lately, some of the irrepressible George's . . . [who] babbles her improvisations on so that I never begin to believe a word of what she says'[7] and asks whether the review of *Mademoiselle Merquem*, which he had just read in the *Nation*, had been by Henry for 'the thoughts' had suggested his younger brother's very high – no doubt, in William's view, inordinately high – estimate of the genius of Madame Sand.

Even in George Sand's late 'bland period' there are many novels which are much better than *Mademoiselle Merquem*, and James begins the review by admitting that the novel has deficiencies but that as it 'has enjoyed the rare fortune of being translated' he will seize the chance to discuss George Sand's qualities as a novelist. What is immediately striking to us now in the review is the sense it gives of her as an already historic figure:

> The time was when Madame Sand's novels were translated as fast as they appeared, and circulated, half surreptitiously, as works delightful and intoxicating, but scandalous, dangerous, and seditious. To read George Sand in America was to be a socialist, a transcendentalist and an abolitionist.[8]

The last sentence is a fairly accurate description of his own father. The son's first encounter with George Sand had been, he tells us, through the pages of Thackeray's *Paris Sketch Book*, in which the author had sneered at *Spiridion*, but had undone his effect by translating a lengthy passage which had remained in James's memory long after the ridicule had faded. He praises the beauty of her style, the seriousness and passion of her convictions, the harmony existing between her imagination and utterance, all of which make him place her above Dickens, above Thackeray and in a totally different sphere from Balzac. Her immortality is assured; 'Madame Sand will die but not her imagination.'

None the less, although James is enchanted by these later tales, they are 'almost too limpid, too fluent, too liquid', and he must admit to a preference for the earlier works (a proviso which he was no doubt grateful later to have made, if he ever cast his mind back to some of the astounding critical judgements of this early review): 'To find a greater magician we must turn to a few supreme names in literature.' If it is true that she has 'celebrated but a single passion – love', in doing so 'she may be said to have pretty thoroughly explored the human soul.'[9]

As Cornelia Kelley long ago commented, this last point, his defence of the centrality of love in George Sand's novels, had been anticipated by his sense of the lack of passion in English fiction. His 1866 review of *Felix Holt* had contained an oblique reference to George Sand. 'There is another great novelist, who has often dealt with men and women moved by exceptional opinions' who, unlike George Eliot, was capable of bearing the reader 'rapidly along on the floods of feeling which rush through her pages'. Duty might be a moral imperative, but love as a force was not as easily controlled and subdued as English novelists appeared to think. 'There is, to our perception, but little genuine *passion* in George Eliot's men and women.'[10] And again, a month or two later, in a survey of all George Eliot's novels, although he doled out a great deal of judicious praise, he objected to the redemption of Arthur Donnithorne: 'Why not see things in their nakedness? the impatient reader is tempted to ask. Why not let passion and foibles play themselves out?'[11] He clearly finds George Sand's treatment of characters such as Raymon and Horace much more realistic, in that the end of the novel leaves them virtually unaffected by the suffering to others caused by their weakness and self-indulgence.

This first appreciation of George Sand was written when James was twenty-five, in the full flush of his enthusiasm for her. He punctuated the following years of 'elegant and fruitful vagabondage',[12] as Gosse called them, with periods in America, and it was not until 1875 that he settled in Paris and became for a year, if not a part of, at least an observer of, the literary circle there. He was on good terms with Flaubert, Turgenev and Daudet, all friends of George Sand, so that there is a sense of vicarious intimacy in his references to her. He listened to the malicious gossip of the de Goncourts about her appearance at the dinners at Magny's – 'an old woman dressed up in her "robe de satin fleur de pêcher" '[13] – and mentions, in her obituary, that he had seen a letter from her, written a few weeks before her death. His description of musical evenings at the Viardots, with charades thrown in for good measure, strikes a familiar note. For Pauline Viardot, Turgenev's friend, was none other than the original of Consuelo, who had had her training in hospitality at Nohant in the 1840s. Now a prima donna past her prime, 'as ugly as eyes in the side of her head and an interminable upper lip can make her, and yet also very handsome',[14] and a life-long devoted friend of George Sand, she gave parties which sound like a pale echo of the revels at Nohant, when Chopin sat at the piano improvising and all the young people dressed up and played charades and produced little plays on the spur of the moment, with a great deal of noise and laughter.[15] Bored but watchfully alert, James would stand through three hours of music and find it 'strange but sweet to see poor Turgenieff acting charades of the most extravagant description . . . at his age and with his glories'. He concluded that it was a 'striking example of that spontaneity which Europeans have and we have not'.[16] It was also yet another sign of the presence, at one remove, of George Sand in this Paris élite, for Turgenev also had played his part in Nohant evenings.

Within a month or two, however, George Sand was dead, and James recorded the event firstly in a very brief note to the *New York Tribune*, then a month later in a longer notice, and last in a full-scale assessment of her in 1877. There are three other reviews about this time: one, in January 1876, of two late novels of hers, *Flamarande* and *Les Deux Frères*; another on Taine's tribute to her: and a final review of her *Dernières Pages*. After this flurry of activity he wrote no more upon her directly and formally for twenty years, although there are often references to her in articles upon other writers. By the time she died he had, over a very long period, got from her fiction all the good she had to give him. Cornelia Kelley's observation[17] that in this year he bade farewell to George Sand should be qualified, and Albert Mordell's suggestion[18] that James was apathetic to her later should be rejected. James's own conclusion in his essay on Balzac sums up exactly the case in respect of her. 'The authors and books that have, as we say, done something for us . . . have been intellectually so swallowed, digested and assimilated that we . . . cease to be aware of them . . . But they have passed out of sight simply because they have passed into our lives.'[19] The marvel was not that he went on to other authors but that for so long he had found pleasure and stimulus in novels so different from the kind he was to write. And when he did become critical of her art, her personality, as Jeanne Delbaere-Garant has pointed out, continued to matter to him as a 'supreme case of the successful practice of life itself'.[20]

2

There is no doubt that by 1874 his sense of her primacy among contemporary novelists had faltered. In an essay on Mérimée's last tales, he comments drily that 'Madame Sand would have been none the worse for occasionally emulating his extraordinary conciseness',[21] and, early in 1876, he writes that she had become in her old age merely a story-teller, however perfect a one, still charming us by her technique and genius, like an old opera singer 'with a thread of a voice comparatively'.[22]

His account of her for the *New York Tribune* a month after her death is largely a work of piety, stressing the fact that, despite her early notoriety, she had, for thirty years, been 'the most shade-loving and retiring of celebrities . . . Her life, indeed, was almost entirely in her books, and it is there that one must look for it.' Quite obviously her indefatigable industry appealed to the New England side of James, and in quoting a story of Mérimée's about his former intimate, he shows little sympathy for the author of it. Mérimée had told how

> very early one cold Winter morning he perceived her, with a handkerchief on her head, lighting the fire to resume her literary tasks. He also, it appears, had nerves; the spectacle disturbed them – he himself was not thinking of getting about his labours yet awhile – and from that moment the intimacy ceased.[23]

James gives another version in 1897 of the story in which he not only adds the word 'bravely' to her kindling of the fire but glosses the incident as a symbol of the compulsive nature of her genius. 'She rose early because she was pressed to write, and she was pressed to write because she had the greatest instinct of expression ever conferred on a woman.'[24] At least half of the 1876 notice is taken up with references to her kindness, hospitality, love of nature – he quotes her words on her death-bed, 'laissez verdure' – the affection felt for her by the villagers, the tributes to her of great men, ending with Renan's to 'that sonorous soul which was, as it were, the Aeolian harp of our time.' James's rider is demure: 'I suspect that M. Renan has not perused any great number of Madame Sand's fictions, but this is none the less very finely said.'[25]

Then, as one who has not only read them all, but who has been trying with some difficulty to re-read, James allows himself a brief appreciation of her novels. He still feels that the whole corpus is one of the great literary achievements of our time. 'She was an *improvisatrice* raised to a very high power; she told stories as a nightingale sings.' Her style is incomparable and her great quality, from the first, 'the multiplicity of her interests and the activity of her sympathies'. He questions the truth of the aphorism which has been wittily applied to her – 'the style is the man' – for, although she may have been temporarily influenced by different men she took only what suited her and 'at bottom the man was always Madame Sand herself.' As a moralist she was on much less sure ground than as a romancer, and her novels, when compared with the realistic fiction of the last decades, are seen to lack important qualities.

This done, a little later in the same month he wrote to William of *Daniel Deronda*

> (Dan'l himself) is indeed a dead, though amiable failure. But the book is a large affair; I shall write an article of some sort about it. All desire is dead within me to produce something on George Sand;

though perhaps I shall, all the same, mercenarily and mechanically –
though only if I am forced.[26]

Despite some shortcomings, George Eliot had now become a much
larger affair and very much more relevant to what he himself was
proposing to do with the novel than George Sand. He is as disinclined
to tackle a full-scale assessment of the latter as is Arnold, at about the
same time, to submit himself to the ordeal of a critical survey of his
former idol: in each case, the engine grows warm by turning, and
something of the earlier enthusiasm is sparked off. James, however,
writes not only as a former devotee but as a fellow novelist. When he
passes moral judgements upon her it is not simply that he has heard
too much gossip about her, but because of his sense of the responsibility
of the novelist to his art. It is an essay that has worn well, and when
Cornelia Kelley describes it as 'not a homage at all . . . at times
condescending, at others vehemently condemnatory', I think she is
overstating the case in the interests of her thesis that George Sand 'like
Balzac, was now shoved on the top shelf'[27] while James went on his way
with Turgenev and George Eliot as his mentors. The leave-taking was
less brutal than she implies, and the new allegiance less unequivocal.
James's praise is still generous, while many of the qualifications had
been in his mind for a long time and were well-deserved and
penetrating.

Like Taine, James stresses the clash in the novelist's picturesque
pedigree between the Bohemian strain and that of 'official' respectability. Though charmed by her complacent grace, he is sternly aware
of her 'peculiar want of veracity';[28] this is really her worst fault, and
he has been gradually coming round to the discussion of it. Her genius
may be masculine in its liberality and quantity, but in its quality it is
feminine, and in her habit of using truth for her own ends she is not
only 'a woman but a Frenchwoman'. The chauvinist, masculine note
here may be regrettable, but James is expressing honestly the unease
which even the most loyal George Sandist feels at times, and once he
has voiced it, it is a reservation which he never withdraws. The false
note of self-justification is more evident in her later work, but even in
her earlier, more frankly and honestly passionate tales, in which there
is not the later tendency to represent love as a sort of 'having one's cake
and eating it', he feels that there is a certain want of moral taste; an
'arranging' of the situations. And yet – how much that was new and
valuable George Sand had contributed to the novel, and what a great
service she had rendered her sex in the exercise of her extraordinary
talent.

In the course of his article, by qualifying his praise, James emerges
in more creditable critical colours than in his rapturous eulogy of 1868,

but his tribute is still warm and he does justice to many of George Sand's most remarkable features. 'In her expenditure of passion, reflection and curiosity there is something quite unprecedented . . . Balzac was a far superior artist; but he was incapable of a lucid reflection.' None the less Balzac had *form*, which was much more important than style – even than a style as 'loose, fluid and iridescent' as hers and language which 'had to the end an odour of the hawthorn and the wild honeysuckle'. Balzac would last longer; posterity would not carry much of George Sand's fiction in its baggage, even though her treatment of passion had shown up the reluctance of English novelists – Scott, Jane Austen, Dickens, Thackeray and George Eliot – to ' "go into" the matter' satisfactorily:

> Few persons would resort to English prose fiction for any information concerning the ardent forces of the heart – for any ideas upon them. It is George Sand's merit that she has given us ideas upon them – that she has enlarged the novel reader's conception of them and proved herself in all that relates to them an authority. This is a great deal.[29]

And yet, once again, this 'amatory disquisition' which is always present in George Sand's novels is 'sometimes very noble and sometimes very disagreeable'. She seems at times incapable of distinguishing between virtuous and vicious love. 'In her view love is always love' and excuses everything. As James ends his essay on a note of discriminating rebuke there is a certain reminiscence of Arnold's reproach to the Romantics for not *knowing* enough. James could not say that George Sand '*knew* human nature but that she felt it'. She was a sentimentalist not a moralist, an optimist more than an idealist, had wisdom not weight. Had Turner written his landscapes they would have been like a George Sand novel, for she leaves an impression of 'largeness, luminosity and liberality': 'But we suspect that something even better in a novelist is that tender appreciation of actuality which makes even the application of a single coat of rose-colour seem an act of violence.'[30]

In this analysis there is much that is revealing of James's maturing attitude to fiction. His consciousness of the alternative conception of fiction offered by George Eliot is even more fully manifested in the article which he had told William he was going to write on *Daniel Deronda* – which appeared in the *Atlantic Monthly* as '*Daniel Deronda*: A Conversation' three months later, in December 1876. Just as he juxtaposed the two Georges in his letter to William, so he treated them together in the 'Conversation'. George Sand's presence in the 'Conversation' is not discussed by Cornelia Kelley, who first pointed out the significance of it as a link between *Daniel Deronda* and *Portrait of a Lady*, and it is ignored by F. R. Leavis,[31] who is predominantly concerned

with his thesis of the great English tradition and James's indebtednes
to George Eliot. While both critics, like everyone else, accept Constan
tius as spokesman for James's views, Leavis's partiality for Theodora'
opinions is harder to justify; I agree with Oscar Cargill[32] that Jame
meant neither Theodora nor Pulcheria to be wholly right. They both
can be wildly off the mark or absolutely to the point; it is left to
Constantius to be the arbiter. The 'Conversation' gave James an
admirable chance to clarify his views on George Sand, George Eliot,
Turgenev and on fiction in general. It is something which he must have
very much enjoyed writing, for it licensed him to have it all ways and
to turn and turn again, so that all three characters are made to express
sentiments which James himself had felt the truth of, if not simultaneously, at least at successive times.

He is clearly determined to keep all his options open. There can be
no question, of course, of how much the feat of Gwendolen has
impressed him but he uses Pulcheria (the name an echo of *Lélia*'s
Pulchérie), who 'likes Balzac, and George Sand and other impure
writers', to voice his reservations about the strong certainties and
weighty moral judgements of George Eliot. Pulcheria refuses to be
pinned down as a devotee of only French novels; she admires Jane
Austen and Thackeray and above all Turgenev. It is Constantius who
points out that the later episodes of *Deronda* are like bad George
Sand – but 'George Sand would have carried it off with a lighter
hand' – and this allows both women to dissent in their different ways:

Theodora: Oh Constantius, how can you compare George Eliot's
novels to that woman's? It is sunlight and moonshine.

Pulcheria: I really think the two writers are very much alike. They
are both very voluble, both addicted to moralizing and philo-
sophizing *à tout bout de champ*, both inartistic.

Constantius: I see what you mean. But George Eliot is solid and
George Sand is liquid. When occasionally George Eliot liquefies –
as in the history of Deronda's birth, and in that of Mirah . . . It is
arranged, it is artificial, *ancien jeu*, quite in the George Sand
manner. But George Sand would have done it better. The false
note would have remained, but it would have been more
persuasive. It would have been a fib but the fib would have been
neater.

Theodora: I don't think fibbing neatly a merit, and I don't see what
is to be gained by such comparisons. George Eliot is pure and
George Sand is impure; how can you compare them?[33]

Here the perverse Pulcheria, who has clearly enjoyed George Sand in the past, seems much nearer to James's present views than Theodora, in her obtuse dismissal, for it is clear that he is still deriving benefit from comparing the two writers. On the other hand, Theodora is being made to utter puritanical sentiments which James would have blushed to express as Constantius, but with which he may well have had sympathy. What does come over clearly in the interchange is something of James's growing impatience with 'feminine minds'; this discussion of the volubility and moralising of the two celebrated women gives added force to the simple statement which follows it, 'Tourgenieff is my man'. And when he adds 'Tourgenieff is a magician, which I don't think I should call George Eliot', it is impossible to forget that this is how he has praised George Sand – 'a great magician'. The difference now is that he feels he can see through too many of her tricks, that however neat her fibs they are still detectable as fibs; whereas when he reads Turgenev he feels that 'It is life itself . . . and not this or that or the other story-teller's more or less clever "arrangement of life".'

3

Probably George Sand is much less in the forefront of James's consciousness in the 1880s than at any other time in his life, although he still carries her along with him easily as a constant point of reference. When he writes of Turgenev in 1884,[34] he talks of the latter's great regard for George Sand, as a woman rather than a novelist; when he discusses Cross's *Life of George Eliot* in 1885 he again compares the two writers and has, no doubt, George Sand in mind when he says: 'It would be too much to say that George Eliot had not the courage of the situation she had embraced, but she had, at least, not the levity, the indifference. If her relations with the world had been easier her books would have been less difficult.'[35]

When he writes in 1893 of Flaubert's correspondence with George Sand, he is especially interested in the extraordinary relationship between two people so divided by temper and so united in affection. Indeed, James is so moved by it that he indulges in an uncharacteristically sentimental image whose 'want of tact' would have aroused Pulcheria's scorn and amusement.

She offered her breast to his aggressive pessimism, had motherly, reasoning, coaxing hands for it, made in short such sacrifices that she often came to Paris to go to brawling Magny dinners to meet him and wear, to please him, as I have heard one of the diners say, unaccustomed peach-blossom dresses.[36]

This is a long way – almost twenty years, in fact, and even more, in tone – from the malicious de Goncourt story which had had the implication of an old woman setting her cap at the young novelist, but James is obviously deeply touched, as any sensitive reader is, by the 'large' relationship which the letters have revealed,[37] and he concludes that it is 'honourable that he [Flaubert] should have been able to read and enjoy so freely a writer so fluid; and it also reminds us that imagination is, after all, for the heart the safest quality.'

The Life of George Eliot had been met with more animosity by James's sister Alice, who recorded memorably her reactions to its portentous revelations:

> But the possession of what genius and what knowledge could reconcile one to the supreme boredom of having to take oneself with that superlative solemnity! What a contrast to George Sand who, whatever her failings never committed that unpardonable sin! It even makes her greasy men of the moment less repulsive.[38]

And Alice's mixture of admiration and distaste for the French woman is very much present in James's discussion in 1897 of the Sand-Musset correspondence which gave him the chance, which he took eagerly, of holding forth yet once again, and at length, on Madame Sand and of trying to solve the riddle of the sphinx – 'sphinx bon enfant', as she once described herself. He was fascinated to find that the ashes of his early ardour were so capable of being stirred. He has now got to the point of nostalgia at which Arnold had found himself – at exactly the same age, fifty-four – looking back to the days of his youth when she was 'a high clear figure, a great familiar magician'.

> One reads and wonders and enjoys again, just for the sake of the renewal. The small fry of the hour submit to further shrinkage, and we revert with a sigh of relief to the free genius and large life of one of the greatest of all masters of expression. Do people still handle the works of this master – people other than young ladies studying French with 'La Mare au Diable' and a dictionary? Are there persons still capable of losing themselves in 'Mauprat'? Has 'André' the exquisite, dropped out of knowledge, and is anyone left who remembers 'Teverino'? I ask these questions for the mere sweet sound of them, without the least expectation of an answer.[39]

But whether they do or not – and he suspects not – we can still 'read' George Sand, for we must look for her secret not in her books but in her life. He does not mention, or perhaps remember, that twenty years earlier he had said the exact opposite, but he has now come to think differently. Her correspondence with de Musset raises the interesting question, which James had already broached in his essay on Flaubert's letters, of the relation between literature and life and of how far the public is entitled to know what is none of its business: 'The lovers are naked in the market-place, and perform for the benefit of society.'[40]

The 'posthumous laideurs' are real enough, and yet are transformed by 'the rare personality' of Madame Sand and stubbornly refuse to come home, 'at least to the imagination of the fond quinquagenarian', with the crudity of contemporary things. As James reads her letters he feels their 'admirable ease, breadth and generosity; they are the clear quiet overflow of a very full cup.' She arranges the facts as they suit her best and 'is never left awkwardly straddling on the sandbank of fact'. In moral matters he finds it much easier to accept her behaviour if he thinks of her as he would of Goethe or Byron or Napoleon; on the other hand, she is more interesting in that, as she is a woman, she has constantly to prove herself not only in the right but virtuous. And this she does with 'immense plausibility'. Her case is prodigiously discouraging to the usual view that in life one has to pay for everything: 'She positively got off from paying – and in a cloud of fluency and dignity, benevolence, competence, intelligence.' This spectacle of 'our author's peculiar air of having eaten her cake and had it' was one which never failed to delight him.

Two years later, in 'dear old Venice', even as he wonders fastidiously why he finds that 'everything about this extraordinary woman is interesting', he jumps at the chance of being shown, by three ladies who know it well, the house to which 'dear old George' went after de Musset left. Till now he had followed the lovers no further than the Danielli: 'As an old Sandist – not exactly indeed of the *première heure*, but of the fine high noon and golden afternoon of the great career – I had been, though I confess too inactively, curious as to a few points in the topography of the eminent adventure to which I here allude.'[41]

In the same year, he welcomed the first two large volumes of Wladimir Karénine's extraordinarily detailed biography of her.[42] While deploring its diffuseness and its 'injudicious analyses of forgotten fictions', he was grateful for the copious documentation of 'one of the most remarkable of human creatures'.

Although James gets much satisfaction from *knowing* more about the early years of 'the wonderful young person growing up at Nohant', his 1899 review article does not add substantially to the considerable insights he had already attained. However, he seized eagerly on a letter from Balzac to Mme Hanska in which he analyses George Sand after a three-day visit and long fireside talks with her: 'He implies that though judged as a woman she may be puzzling enough she hangs together perfectly if judged as a man.' It was a point that James himself had frequently made but now, backed by Balzac's authority, he takes it even more seriously and finds that it reconciles for him 'her distinction and her vulgarity' – for it is vulgar to have 'so much experience reduced only to the terms of so many more or less greasy males' (in his choice of epithets he is at one with his sister, Alice). But it is vulgar only for a woman; for a man 'of the dressing-gown and slippers order', everything is quite different. If we can imagine a Bohemian, industrious and wise, we have the clue to George Sand: 'Madame Sand's abiding value will probably be in her having given to her sex, for its new evolution and transformation, the real standard and measure of change . . .' The difference between women so far and George Sand is that they have on the whole aimed to challenge the ordinary male only: 'George Sand's service is that she planted the flag much higher – her own approximation at least was to the extra-ordinary.'[43]

A long time was to elapse before Mme Karénine's third volume came out – and Henry James never saw the last. His main confidante about 'dear old George' was Edith Wharton, with whom he had visited Nohant in 1907, and his comments to her on Volume 3 when it came out eventually in 1912 have the familiar ring of fascinated horror, admiration and incredulity. He savours the extraordinary 'glibness' of her letters like a connoisseur:

> And what a value it all gets from our memory of that wondrous day when we explored the very scene where they pigged so thrillingly together. What a crew, what *moeurs*, what habits, what conditions and relations every way – and what an altogether mighty and marvellous George! not diminished by all the greasiness and smelliness in which she made herself (and so many other persons!) at home. Poor gentlemanly crucified Chop! – not naturally at home in grease – but having been originally pulled – and floundering there at last to extinction . . . It will be a joy when we can next converse on these and cognate themes – I know of no such links of true interchange as a community of interest in dear old George.[44]

The letter to Edith Wharton ends with a mention of contemporary events and 'window-smashing women' – the suffragettes were at large – and he says that he cannot understand why feminists do not make much more of George Sand. They seem blind to her precedent of dealing with life exactly like a man. 'Resignedly and triumphantly voteless', she found it easy to 'stretch forth her hand and take'.[45] . . . 'Her great value . . . is that she gives us the vision' – not so much of an extension to the feminine nature as a richness added to the masculine. For she is not concerned with woman's lot but with the relations, in the widest sense, of men and women.

James does full justice to the 'laideurs' once more, revealed in Volume 3 in the 'hysteric pitch of family life'; the 'multiplied lacerations' of Chopin; the 'hideous perversity and depravity of Solange and her husband'. And yet, in these 'highest tides of private embarrassment' and humiliation, sorrow and violence we see 'our heroine's genius – her genius for keeping her head in deep seas morally and reflectively above water'. Eloquent and, in the end, fortified by her sense of her ability to cope, accept and convert evil into a positive good, she was capable of carrying off every situation and eventually of transfiguring it imaginatively. James finds much to deplore, but the final impression given by his last essay on her is that now, more than ever, she is capable of making defect perfection by her art. These biographies have revealed many more ugly 'facts' about her than James can ever have conjectured, when long ago he had weighed her moral sense against that of George Eliot and found it sadly wanting. But now it seems to matter much less than it did!

> We absolutely believe . . . as we read – there is the prodigious part . . . If we put ourselves questions we yet wave away doubts, and with whatever remnants of prejudice the writer's last word may often have to clash, our own is that there is nothing for grand final rightness like a sufficiently general humanity – when a beautiful voice happens to serve it.[46]

This is James's last word of formal criticism on George Sand. The final allusion to her in correspondence – though many more may yet be revealed by Leon Edel – occurs in a letter to Gosse about the latter's article on the effect of the 1870 war on French literature. The year in which it was written, 1914, when the lights were going out all over Europe, makes it a poignant reference: 'Had I been at your elbow I should have suggested a touch or two about dear old George Sand, holding out through the darkness at Nohant, but even there giving out some lights that are caught up in her letters of the moment . . .'[47]

The note of affection recalls the point that Emile Faguet once made about the emotions that George Sand inspired in the reader. Faguet wrote 'Le goût que l'on prend d'elle est une sorte de sympathie. Son style nous devient un ami. On se détache plus facilement d'un enchantement que d'une amitié.'[48] It may well be that the reason that James found it impossible to get free of George Sand all his life was that for him her 'style' had always been both 'un enchantement' and 'une amitié'.

4

When Cornelia Kelley discussed the indebtedness of Henry James in his early fiction to European writers and stressed his 'long laborious apprenticeship to the masters of his craft',[49] she was a pioneer in such research. Almost half a century later, as Jeanne Delbaere-Garant has pointed out,[50] her parallels have all been fully absorbed by critics, and much more work has been done on James's debt to Balzac, Mérimée, Turgenev, Zola and George Sand. Even though the last has had much less full treatment than the others, the connections between her fiction and James's early tales have been very well made and I shall not spend long on familiar ground.

Cornelia Kelley had no doubt at all of George Sand's importance as an influence on James's early fiction. In fact she makes the point that 'George Sand at one time so strongly affected James that there was danger of his following her lead'[51] and becoming merely a successful imitator instead of a creator. She selected a few of the tales written between 1864 and 1874 which she felt most clearly indicated his discipleship: 'My Friend Bingham', 'Poor Richard', 'De Grey', 'Master Eustace' and, above all, 'Gabrielle de Bergerac'. For the most part she thought that James's chief debt lay in his treatment of passion, though often 'the entire story-conception, material, atmosphere and execution' bore her mark.

On the whole, I think that Miss Kelley came to almost all the right conclusions, but often by using evidence which does not stand much sceptical scrutiny. Certainly she equates passion with George Sand in much too facile a manner; she puts her thumb into a James short story, picks out the plum of passion and calls it a Sandian fruit, although she is well aware that James was reading other writers – like Balzac or Mérimée or Stendhal – in whose works passion, whether of love, greed, hate or ambition, plays a large part. And sometimes her examples are very weak. It is difficult for instance to see what 'My Friend Bingham' owes to George Sand – a story in which what little passion there is has to be vouched for by the narrator. And in 'De Grey' the presence of a doting mother, a young companion and a hero killed by being thrown from his horse scarcely make the tale, as she claims, 'decidedly French'. It is true that Maurice Sand met his end in that way, but then so did Sir Robert Peel. None the less, it would be very easy to supply much more convincing chapter and verse to support the case she is making, and when it comes to 'Gabrielle de Bergerac' there can, of course, be no question of James's indebtedness.

This romance, set in eighteenth-century France, is a story of the love which grows between Gabrielle and her young brother's tutor, Coquelin, despite the heroine's engagement to a Vicomte and the opposition of her family to a liaison with an *homme du peuple*. The theme is very close to that of *Valentine* which is also, as Miss Kelley points out, an out-of-doors tale through which 'the summer breezes blow . . . Gabrielle has the independence of spirit, the intensity of passion of a George Sand heroine.'[52] Miss Kelley cites several minor parallels, and there are many more she does not mention: the use of the 'pavillon' in the grounds for the meeting-place of the lovers – the ubiquitous *pavillon* of romance which not only turns up in *Valentine* and in countless other stories, but also in George Sand's real-life romances at Nohant; the narrator, once the young brother, now the old man, looking far back over the years, like Bernard de Mauprat, to this romance of his youth; the description of the night, which is in perfect George Sand style: 'Somewhere close at hand, out of an enchanted tree, a nightingale raved and called in delirious music.' It is a sentence which recalls that enchanting evocation, of which James was so fond, of an evening at Nohant: 'Jamais je n'ai vu autant de fleurs et d'oiseaux dans mon jardin. Liszt jouait du piano au rez-de-chaussée, et les rossignols, enivrés de musique et de soleil, s'égosillaient avec rage sur les lilas environnants.'[53]

While Jeanne Delbaere-Garant agrees that 'Gabrielle de Bergerac' owes much to George Sand, she feels that Coquelin, the lover, although lowly born like Benedict in *Valentine*, is a much more solitary figure, unsupported by other characters of his class: 'He stands above social distinctions and national frontiers, he is a Citizen of the World, convinced that personal merit is the only criterion by which a man is to be judged.'[54] But the point seems to me of little significance for, in addition to Benedict, George Sand has a seemingly endless supply of independent *hommes du peuple* who are convinced of their merit and fall in love with rich young women above their station. The whole story is so derivative of George Sand that I cannot see much to support the claim that 'under their French disguises Gabrielle and Coquelin have the moral complexity of his [James's] American characters.' If this had been the case James would not have been so discontented with it and would not have felt it was 'humbug' and Gabrielle 'thin and watery'.[55] He was too severe with a charming tale, but he was well aware that it was pastiche.

In these early stories there is a rustle of George Sand every few pages. Just as the very first piece of writing James ever offered for publication was connected with her – a review[56] of a performance of *Fanchon the Cricket* (a dramatisation of *La Petite Fadette*) which was put on in Boston in 1864 – so his very first tale of the same year, 'A Tragedy of Error', has a dénouement which recalls that of 'Léone Leoni'. In both stories of an illicit love-affair, the wrong man is killed by mistake, and the last scene by the sea-shore, in one case, and on the lagoon, in the other, strikes an ironic and startling note. In 'Travelling Companions' (1870) the setting is Venice, and the hero (who stays at the Danielli) observes that he is reading 'two or three of George Sand's novels. Do you know *La Dernière Aldini*? I fancy a romance in every palace.'[57]

By the time we reach 'Eugene Pickering', in 1874, James is sufficiently distanced from his former idol to use several of her traits in the
character of the amoral Madame Anastasia Blumenthal. She certainly
did not *look* like George Sand:

> She had a charming gray eye and a good deal of blond hair, disposed
> in picturesque disorder; and though her features were meagre and
> her complexion faded, she gave one a sense of sentimental artificial
> gracefulness. She was dressed in white muslin very much puffed and
> frilled, but a trifle the worse for wear . . .[58]

And James takes pains to stress her nationality as German, and to
describe this 'friend of poets, a correspondent of Philosophers, a muse,
a priestess of aesthetics' as 'something in the way of a Bettina, a Rahel'.
But having thus discreetly covered himself and, in addition, emphasised
the difference between the genuine article and Madame Blumenthal by
mentioning that the 'authoress of *Cleopatra* had written a novel with her
views on matrimony in the George Sand manner but really out-
Heroding Herod', James felt free to make use of quite a number of the
features that had intrigued him in George Sand: her ability to make
the sordid seem 'harmonious and beautiful'; her 'taste for spinning fine
phrases'; her 'unlimited cameraderie with scribblers and daubers,
Hegelian philosophers and Hungarian pianists waiting for engage-
ments'. The narrator watches her from afar as she sits in her theatre
box, with her young admirer Pickering – as so many English observers
had gazed at George Sand – and listens to gossip about her from an
acquaintance for, even though she is 'embalmed for duration in a
certain dilution of respectability', society is wary of this wonderfully
clever woman, the well-born daughter of a Gräfin who is a 'fierce
democrat . . . a revolutionist' and is never without 'some eligible youth
hovering about'. The anecdote which his acquaintance tells him of her
lover looking on in irritation while his 'inky goddess' scribbled away
indefatigably at her novel is certainly James's adaptation of Mérimée's
tale of George Sand; and although Madame Blumenthal's grand
gesture of throwing her manuscript of *Clorinda* into the fire to shame him
and later quietly retrieving it and publishing it as *Sophronia* has no basis
in fact, it may well have been suggested by George Sand's preface to
Pauline, in which she says that she had begun the novel in 1832 in her
attic in Paris but that the manuscript had gone astray and she thought
she must have thrown it into the fire by mistake, until it turned up
again almost ten years later.

This story, as James tells it, not only takes off all the eponymous
heroines of George Sand – Indiana, Valentine, Lélia, Consuelo,
Jeanne, and so on – but does convey something of the quality of having

the best of both worlds, which was then beginning to come home to James as one of the French writer's distinctive features. As the story progresses, the baffling and interesting element in Madame Blumenthal becomes subsumed in the hard ruthlessness of the adventuress but, for a brief space, in her characterisation James has put to good creative use his sense of George Sand's complexity.

The early novels, similarly, yield quite a number of instances of direct parallels with George Sand. Oscar Cargill detects her as a much more substantial influence upon *Watch and Ward* (1870) than does Cornelia Kelley, who tends once again to restrict the debt to 'passion'. After proposing the relationship of the twenty-eight-year-old Germain to the sixteen-year-old Marie in *La Mare au Diable* as a hint to James for the attachment of Roger Lawrence to Nora, Cargill moves on to what I think is very much surer ground in his suggestion of a Sir Ralph Brown-Indiana connection.[59] Ralph not only resembles Roger in that he is rich, introverted, modest and inarticulate, but just as Indiana underrates her relative and turns to the more fascinating Raymon, so Nora is dazzled by Hubert; Ralph acts as a mixture of father, cousin, brother, and lover to the little Indiana – the sort of anomalous relationship which George Sand was so fond of, and which Roger, too, appropriates in James's first novel. The botanical imagery is identical: both Roger and Ralph were 'cultivating young plants' with patience, devotion and total absorption in the hope of one day making their wards their wives. Even the male-female ratio is the same – three men to one woman – and James is well launched in this, his first novel, on the centrality of the heroine.

F. W. Dupee's suspicion that James was unaware of the erotic imagery in the novel is rightly scoffed at by Cargill, who reminds us that James had read every word of George Sand, 'the prime historian of "erotic sentiment" in the nineteenth century', and was certainly well aware of what he is doing – although it is a novel, as James himself came to feel, which is short on passion.

The hope of a reviewer of James's early tales that 'by and by no doubt he will write of something besides love' was partially fulfilled in *Roderick Hudson*, in which he attempts to 'do' Northampton, Massachusetts, as well as the art circles in Florence, to place the centre of interest in Rowland Mallet's consciousness and to trace and watch Roderick's disintegration as an artist through his passion for Christina Light. By this time James had matured so much as a writer that particular instances of indebtedness in character or incident take on a much more academic, much less vital interest, unless the whole complex web of possible influences is considered. But it is certainly of significance, as Cargill points out, that Rowland's death in the Alps is reminiscent of that of George Sand's Jacques on a glacier, for such a parallel takes away the ambiguity surrounding the death and supports the case that James intended it as a suicide:

> It was this sensational Frenchwoman, rather than Hawthorne (as has been supposed) who influenced this particular novel by providing Henry James with its climactic episode. In her novel *Jacques* (1834) the husband generously hurls himself into an Alpine crevasse, making his death appear as an accident, in order that his wife may continue happily her affair with a younger lover. The impulsive Roderick . . . similarly disposes of himself.[60]

This seems to me an illuminating comparison, unlike Cornelia Kelley's explanation of the relationship between the Marquise and her elder son in *The American* as the result of James's long brooding over George Sand: she had suggested to him that 'mothers were often proud and domineering, that men might be haughty and cold and villainous, that one might in fact make characters what one chose to.'[61] It is difficult to take such a comment seriously when we think of all the other novelists whom James had read who treated such familiar material. I warm much more to her claim that in this novel it was George Sand's example which 'led him unwittingly to go too far': 'When he was searching for a supreme test for Newman's character, she saw her chance and whispered of a château in the country, falling to ruin, gloomy, dismal, and then of the murder which had been committed there by the Marquise, the knowledge of which might be Newman's to use or not to use.'[62] George Sand did indeed have a disconcerting habit of switching the ambiance of a novel from realism to the trappings of romance in just this way.

I have no intention of going systematically through one James novel after another, discussing features which might have originated in the pages of George Sand but could equally have been met with in Balzac or Stendhal, Feuillet or Dumas fils. But some of the situations do seem deserving of brief comment. As Cargill says, George Sand's novels 'bristle with suggestions that James may have found usable'; she was the 'great improvisatrice' and her 'fertility brought him often to her . . . in his search for creative ideas.' The relationship between Indiana and Sir Ralph, in which he has to stand by as a pained and loving observer while his cousin makes her mistakes, may well have been still in James's mind when he created Isabel Archer and Ralph; and equally significant is Indiana's decision to return freely to her husband when she has escaped from her imprisonment in his house and gone to her lover. She is disillusioned with both Raymon's passion and her husband's tyrannical jealousy, and all that matters to her at this point is her own will-power: 'I went in order to breathe the air of freedom and to show you that morally you are not my master and that I am dependent on no one in the world. While I was walking, I reflected that it was my duty and I owed it to my conscience to come back and place myself once more in your charge. I did it of my own free will.'[63] This could well be the voice of Isabel Archer on her return to Rome.

One need not restrict oneself either, as most critics have, to the early fiction of James. In *The Ambassadors*, for instance, the famous scene between Little Bilham and Strether in which the latter advises the young artist to 'Live all you can; it's a mistake not to . . . Live, live!' was identified firmly by James as the 'grain of suggestion dropped by W. D. Howells[64] from which the whole grew.' But James's sources are never simple. Cargill suggests that Howells's remarks may have 'triggered off an idea long in gestation' and alludes to the earlier comment made by Louis Leverett in a James short story, 'A Bundle of Letters' (1879).[65] I would go even further back, to the character of Stephen Morin in *Mademoiselle Merquem* (1868), which James had early reviewed and pondered. For Stephen has something in him of Little Bilham – he is an unsuccessful artist – and rather more of Sam Single-ton, the patient, humble painter in *Roderick Hudson*; but also in his sense of having missed out on life – mechanically painting to kill time, aware that he has nothing to give to art, although he knows all the 'ficelles' – and in his middle-aged loneliness, there are hints of Strether. The young hero, Armand, decides that he knows what is wrong: 'What he lacked was the sense of being someone in his own right, of having a personality, of living. He had made his own existence into a sterile, tiresome task, a martyrdom. He worked too hard; he was forgetting to live, he was in a rut, he was ossifying.'[66] Armand feels that anything would do – a love-affair, a holiday, even debauchery – to release Stephen's captive personality from 'ce régime admirablement sain, égal et irréprochable qui le détruisait', but he starts by making Stephen come alive through friendship, through a sense of involvement in the lives of others. And, by the end of the book, Stephen has decided to give up his painting temporarily, in order to live. It is an important enough issue for George Sand to give it the concluding paragraph of the novel. Stephen tells Armand, as he sets out on his ocean voyage, that his hint has gone home to him: 'I was in an impasse. I was not aware that it is life which makes art and should not be swallowed up by it. I want to live at first hand, to feel, to understand . . .'[67]

Stephen is totally lacking in Strether's subtlety of mind, but there is enough resemblance in the situation of the two men – the unsuccessful painter with no sense of having an individuality and the editor of the Woollet journal, who was 'Lambert Strether because he was on the cover' – to justify considering the novel a fruitful memory for James.

There are so many resemblances, so many suggestions, that it would be tedious to attempt to catalogue them all; it is obvious that George Sand had indeed, like Balzac, passed into James's life, so that if he appears to echo her he is merely drawing upon experience he had made his own. But what we can do with advantage is to discuss in more general terms the nature of his debt. There seems to me to be four principal ways in which she contributed to his art: the first lies in her stress upon passion and her unwearying analysis of emotions and states of consciousness; the second in the important part which questions of art play in her novels; the third in the prefaces which she wrote to the collected edition of her works; and the fourth, and not least important, in the character of the novelist herself.

5

Passion is not the first thing that comes to mind when James is discussed; in fact, a case could be made out – as it was by Gide – that it is the last. But although 'all the weight of the flesh is absent, all the shaggy tangled undergrowth, all the wild darkness', there is never any question, as in George Eliot, of passion being under-rated and treated as something manageable, entirely within the control of the will. We are never dragged into the undergrowth, nor do we roll in the bluebells, but we have no doubt at all as to the reality of the passion of Roderick Hudson for Christina Light, of Madame de Vionnet for Chad or of Charlotte Stant for the Prince. In each case, the distance which James retains between author and characters increases our sense of the dangerous nature of the passions which have been aroused. He is never too familiar with the victims, and treats them with compassion and understanding. His respect for passion was undoubtedly encouraged by his reading of George Sand; his technique in conveying it was entirely his own. The best example of a Sandian passionate moment which comes readily to mind is James's description of Caspar Goodwood's embrace at the end of *Portrait of a Lady*, which shows well what he could do in this line – the rushing torrent, the kiss like a flash of white lightning. But he turned away from it, and this earlier scene compares interestingly with the one kiss in *The Golden Bowl*, a sexual pledge of astounding intensity, bare of all romantic imagery.

When it comes to the question of analysis, however, his debt to George Sand is more straightforward. She was certainly not the first author to analyse emotions – her own familiarity with Richardson is testified to by the number of times she mentions Lovelace in her novels and letters – but as far as James was concerned, I think we may take it that she was the formative influence. Certainly his brother William had no doubt of the source of Henry's tendency to analyse, and disapproved of it. Of *Roderick Hudson* he wrote: 'I am again struck unfavourably by the tendency of the personages to reflect on themselves and give an acute critical scientific introspective classification on their own natures and states of mind à la George Sand.'[68] Miss Kelley, too, comments on James's indebtedness several times, not always with enthusiasm; she felt that it was as well that Mérimée counteracted 'James's tendency to analyse and to follow the expansive effusiveness, the copiously gushing narrative of George Sand'.[69] But Cargill wisely sees it as an unmitigated good: 'What a blight would have been put upon Henry's genius had he taken seriously his brother's animadversions on this Sandian influence!'[70] He suggests that George Sand provides the 'real clue to James's analytical method', and says that anyone who looks at *Jacques* with its minute and prolonged dissection of emotions will see what William meant. Any novel, or even the personal correspondence of George Sand, would do almost as well, for her interest in analysing a situation or character never flagged – but *Jacques* is an extreme case, since it is almost wholly given over to introspection.

It is easy to justify James's objection that although George Sand 'illuminates and glorifies the divine passion' she also 'handles it too much; she lets it too little alone', exhibiting 'a sort of benevolent, an almost conscientious disposition to sit down as it were, and "talk over" the whole matter.'[71] But *Jacques* contains many examples of prolonged, sensitive character-analysis, detached yet involved, unsparing yet compassionate, which are totally different from anything in Balzac or Flaubert, but which often remind us of the approach of both James and George Eliot. Sometimes the character is looking at his own situation, like Jacques alone in the mountains before taking his life (or like Isabel Archer in the drawing room in the early hours, or Dorothea in her midnight vigil); sometimes the analysis is of another person, as in the narrator's account of Horace in the novel of that name, a careful psychological study of a charmer, egotistical, vain, snobbish yet attractive and not devoid of conscience, which can compare with James's discussion of Madame Merle or George Eliot's of Gwendolen Harleth. What intrusions are made by the narrator or author are normally on the side of humanity, in softening the outlines.

Indeed, George Sand then very often goes on to waste all her minute analysis by blurring the image of her characters in trying to present them in the most favourable light. Here James's enormous superiority in conveying a sense of the autonomy of his characters as well as his own authoritative intimacy with them becomes very obvious. Especially in George Sand's later novels, the reader experiences the odd sensation of having lost his grip on what has seemed to be the characters' rationale, when the author tires of keeping her distance and begins to speak in her own voice through them; her own ego cannot be subdued for very long.

When both F. W. H. Myers and Wilde drew attention to 'George Sand's delightful treatment of art and the artist's life' in her novels, they were stressing something which, indeed, formed a most significant part of her fiction. From first to last, art and the artist provided her with material to draw upon and questions to raise. The sub-title of the first novel she ever wrote, along with Jean Sandeau, was *The Actress and the Nun*; and her very last, unfinished novel, *Albine*, has as its heroine a dancer, who is the daughter of an actor. She was always fascinated by the stage, although, like James, she might have done better to resist its lure, as far as writing plays went. In well over a score of her novels and tales she creates characters whose authenticity in their different artistic callings is a remarkable tribute not only to the width of her interest but to her ability to 'get up' a subject at short notice. Bohemianism, as well as ascetic dedication, the sense of belonging to a coterie as well as the essential solitariness of the professional, the unworldliness and the ambition, the splendid appearance and the sordid realities, the generosity and the jealousy, creative fulfilment and popular success – all the paradoxes of the artist's life stimulate her interest.

Many of the questions raised by George Sand are, inevitably, such as will always arise whenever the question of the artist in society comes up. How different a being is he? Should he be judged by different standards from ordinary people? To what extent should appreciation and tolerance and understanding go? Is there a gulf between the actor and society? Is marriage demeaning for a member of 'official society', and is it inhibiting to the career of the artist? These are considered in a number of her novels and tales, among them *La Marquise, Pauline, La Dernière Aldini, Consuelo* and *Teverino*; they are also dealt with by Henry James in several of his short stories and in, especially, *Roderick Hudson, The Tragic Muse* and *The Ambassadors*. Cargill suggests Mrs Humphrey Ward's *Miss Bretherton* as an unacknowledged source of *The Tragic Muse*, and there seems to me little doubt that it started James off on that specific novel. But although Mrs Ward's own immediate inspiration was the actress Mary Anderson, just as Geraldine Jewsbury's had been Charlotte Cushman for *The Half-Sisters*, both these minor novelists were *afficianados* of George Sand and no doubt received their literary stimulus to tackle the problems of the actress in society from that same vital source. James is vague about the origin and growth of *The Tragic Muse*; there is no particular 'sharp impression or concussion' which he can bring to mind. Instead

What I make out from furthest back is that I must have had from still further back, must in fact practically always have had the happy thought of some dramatic picture of the 'artist-life' and of the difficult terms on which it is best secured and enjoyed, the general question of its having to be not altogether easily paid for. To 'do something about art' – art, that is, as a human complication and a social stumbling block – must have been for me early a good deal of a nursed intention, the conflict between art and 'the world' striking me thus betimes as one of the half-dozen great primary motives.[72]

The conflict between art and 'the world' had not, however, been treated to such an extent by anyone else in the nineteenth century in France, America or England as by George Sand, not even by Browning, so that James's conception of it as one of the 'half-dozen great primary motives' must certainly have been coloured by his reading of her. His 'original perception of its value was quite lost in the mists of youth', he confesses later in the preface, and when we remember the part played by George Sand in that youth it seems only fair to allow her some credit in his decision to 'do something about art'. I would put the claim no more strongly. As a dedicated writer he knew enough about art as 'a human complication and social stumbling block' to draw in all other respects on his own experience and material.

The debt of Jamesians to George Sand is even further increased if, as has been suggested,[73] James got the idea of his prefaces from her. It is a very feasible proposition. Scott had written prefaces to his collected novels, so that she was not first in the field, but what is particularly interesting about her prefaces is the personal note they strike and her attempt to recapture the mood, the origin, the occasion of her writing of that particular story. Looking back ten years, she writes in her 1842 Preface to *Indiana*, for instance, that she feels she is now detached enough about her work to say that all her early novels were based on 'la même donnée – le rapport mal établi entre les deux sexes'. The prefaces vary in weight and interest so that, in a way, if they did give James the idea of writing his own, it was because he felt how much better use he could have put them to – while still retaining their particular charm of taking the reader into the confidence of the author. He comments:

> To the cheap edition of her novels, published in 1852–53, she prefixed a series of short prefaces in which she relates the origin of each tale – the state of mind and the circumstances in which it was written. These prefaces are charming; they almost justify the publisher's declaration that they form the 'most beautiful examination that a great mind has ever made of itself'. But they all commemorate the writer's extraordinary facility and spontaneity.[2] . . .

These proofs of spontaneity were very far from being the exhaustive critical discussions for which James was really hankering; in fact he reproached George Sand for writing so little in the course of her long life about her own art:

> During the five and forty years of her literary career, she had something to say about most things in the universe; but the thing about which she had least to say was the writer's, the inventor's, the romancer's art. She possessed it by the gift of God, but she seems never to have felt the temptation to examine the pulse of the machine.[74]

None the less, he much appreciated George Sand's recapturing of the atmosphere of the place in which the novels were written – Rome, Paris, Venice, the Chartreuse de Valdemosa – and followed her habit in his own prefaces. Even more, however, he enjoyed being told her *donnée*: not just a social or philosophical attitude, like the conception from which *Indiana* sprang, but the fleeting incident or anecdote which got her imagination going. 'A hint – a mere starting point was enough for her,' he wrote admiringly. The chatter of her maid and sempstress in the next room in Venice which reminded her of the local gossip at Berry; the contrast between a Holbein engraving and a labourer in the field; the sea wind howling round the windows of the vast, dusky room in which she was sitting alone in the Nasi palace; a brief anecdote of mosaic workers told her by a priest; each a recovered moment, an identified 'particle of suggestion', to use James's phrase.

Just occasionally, as in the Preface to *François le Champi*, she gets down to more solid fare and tackles the question of dialect and how best to represent the inarticulate peasant without falsifying him. She even evaluates retrospectively – which is something much more typical of James – the novel *Jeanne*, which she feels has failed by making the reader too much aware of the disparity between Jeanne's peasant simplicity and the elevated claims made for her. There is quite enough meat in this discussion to have shown James some of the possibilities of turning the preface into a leisurely, full-scale critical feast.

And last of all – and perhaps most important – is George Sand's own personality as an influence upon James. No one who has read all his comments on the novelist, made over fifty years, could fail to see her as a continuing and significant part of his consciousness. Professor Kelley's suggestion[75] that the Countess in James's early short story 'Benvolio' can be equated with her is an over-simplification in the interests of her argument. She sees her as standing for Romance, abandoned by the hero for the serious young woman Scholastica (George Eliot) representing Realism. But features of her character continued to fascinate and trouble him, and his later fiction is full of realistic European charmers who exemplify aspects of the mature George Sand.

Before looking at them, however, I should like to draw attention for the last time to the characteristics of 'the wonderful young person growing up at Nohant' which delighted him and to which he returned many times. He admired greatly her courage and independence, her ability to call the tune and to take life on her own terms, and was imaginatively stirred by the daring of her gesture in leaving the shelter of the country house and betaking herself to Paris. He wrote sympathetically of her

> deepening sense . . . that outside of the quiet meadows of Nohant there was a vast affair called *life*, with which she had a capacity for making acquaintance at first hand. This making acquaintance with life at first hand is, roughly speaking, the great thing that as a woman, Madame Sand achieved; and she was predestined to achieve it . . .[76]

James wrote this of George Sand in 1876. Three years later he started the 'large building' of *The Portrait of a Lady* with, as he tells us in his Preface, only one 'single corner stone . . . the conception of a certain young woman, affronting her destiny' – that, and nothing else. It would clearly be ridiculous to attempt any sort of comparison between the characters of James's best-known American girl and Aurore Dudevant; no two complex young women could be more unlike. But is well to remember that it was in this Preface that James quoted the familiar words of Turgenev on sources of inspiration:

> As for the origin of one's wind-blown germs themselves, who shall say, as you ask, where *they* come from? We have to go too far behind to say. Isn't it all we can say that they come from every quarter of heaven, that they are there almost any turn of the road? They accumulate, and we are always picking them over, selecting among them.[77]

Long ago, James had read *Indiana*, in which George Sand speaks through her heroine, 'heurtant son front aveugle contre tous les obstacles de la civilisation'.[78] And for many years he had marvelled at the audacity and resolution with which George Sand had 'addressed herself to life', an acquaintance she was 'predestined to achieve', so that when he began building *The Portrait of a Lady* with 'the conception of a certain young woman, affronting her destiny' it is difficult to believe that one or two 'particles of suggestion' did not drift to him from the Nohant quarter of heaven to assist in the conception, though not in the character, of Isabel Archer. And it is also worth remembering that the other independent American girl in the novel, Henrietta Stackpole, found Isabel's determined plunge into the unknown quite foreign to her upbringing and background and, when she expressed the romantic notion that happiness was 'a swift carriage of a dark night, rattling with four horses over roads that one can't see', accused her of speaking 'like the heroine of an immoral novel'.[79] As immoral novels were always French in the vocabulary of any American girl, there is just an indication here of cross-fertilisation in the creation of Isabel.

But, of course, it is in the maturer European women who are found in plenty in James's novels that the real effect of George Sand's personality can be seen. Characters as different from each other as, for instance, Madame Merle in *The Portrait of a Lady*, Baroness Munster in *The Europeans*, and the Comtesse de Vionnet in *The Ambassadors*, reveal facets of 'the great familiar magician'. They all, like the Baronne Dudevant, are women of rank – or appear to be so. Madame Merle *looked* like 'a countess, a princess'. Oscar Cargill ingeniously links the name of Madame Merle with George Sand:

> Serena Merle's name had, however, a greater significance for Henry James, with his thorough familiarity with the affair between George Sand and Alfred de Musset, than it has, regrettably, for most of his modern readers; to him it suggested the ambiguous 'white blackbird' – Madame Merle is very fair – of de Musset's once famous portrait, 'Histoire d'un merle blanc'.[80]

But, with less virtuosity, one can detect in that lady's remarkable poise, her ability to 'arrange' facts so that they appear in the best possible light, her manipulation of people and her wonderful resilience, the sort of qualities that James both marvelled at and deplored in George Sand. James is at pains to give all three – Eugenia and Madeleine de Vionnet, as well as Madame Merle – somewhat disreputable or lurid histories, involving separation from unsuitable husbands. In fact, the account which Maria Gostrey gives Strether of Madame de Vionnet's past seems strangely out of keeping with the woman we meet in the course of the novel, and strikes the reader as fitting into a preconceived formula. It is interesting, too, that in each case James refers to a relationship with a younger man. The Baroness is not above baiting her trap for the young cub, Clifford, and although the entanglement is played on a comic level and Clifford is immune to the temptations of the 'very amusing old woman', Felix's uneasiness about his sister's intentions touches an ominous chord. Even the witty and clear-sighted Ralph has, in his youth, fallen victim to Madame Merle's charms, while the difference in age between Madame de Vionnet and Chad is obsessively stressed; George Sand's attraction for younger men, her 'nurslings', had always interested James. However different these ladies are from each other – and in many ways Madame Merle is at the other end of the spectrum from Madame de Vionnet – they all are, or have been, irresistible and intelligent, and are represented as pursuing their own interests with courage, resource and ruthlessness. For even Madame de Vionnet has no scruples where her love is concerned. And, most important, each has the ability which James detected in George Sand and which he considered typical of the fact that she was 'a woman and a Frenchwoman' to 'fib neatly':

> Women we are told do not value the truth for its own sake, but only for some personal use they make of it. My present criticism involves an assent to this somewhat cynical dogma. Add to this that woman, if she happens to be French has an extraordinary taste for investing objects with a graceful drapery of her own contrivance, and it will be found that George Sand's cast of mind includes both the generic and the specific idiosyncrasy.[81]

The fibs of James's characters vary greatly in importance. Madame Merle's whole life is a lie and brings tragedy upon others, whereas the Baroness Munster, when caught out in a fib, realises simply that she has 'struck a false note' and feels irritation with 'these people to whom fibbing is not pleasing'.[82] And Madame de Vionnet's evasion of the truth, though symbolised at first only by the wavering course of the boat and the absence of a shawl on her shoulders in the evening air, is pinned down sorrowfully by Strether in the small hours:

> He kept making of it that there had been simply a *lie* in the charming affair – a lie on which one could now, detached and deliberate, perfectly put one's finger. It was with the lie that they had eaten and drunk and talked and laughed . . . It had been a performance, Madame de Vionnet's manner, and though it had to that degree faltered toward the end . . . a performance it had none the less quite handsomely remained . . .[83]

'The graceful drapery of her own contrivance' with which Madame de Vionnet has so long invested her relationship with Chad has at last fallen and exposed the truth.

What, I suppose, can be said with no fear of contradiction is that however much James learned from other writers and from his own experience of life, George Sand contributed in no small measure to his sense of women, that 'to deal with them was to walk on water'.[84] Jeanne Delbaere-Garant has remarked that, in his age as in his youth, James associated George Sand with France: 'He was still trying to penetrate the secret of the French art of living and looking for the answer in George Sand's own life as representative of French manner and genius. From the beginning to the end of his long career she was with him.'[85] While this is true, I think James went further and associated George Sand not only with France but with Europe. Many of James's Europeans owe something to his knowledge of her works, her life and her personality. Some, like her, try not to 'allow facts to make them uncomfortable'; others make their own 'arrangement of life'; most are eager to have their cake and eat it, to get away without paying. That they do, in the end, all pay is largely due to James's strong moral sense. He was aware that in her own life George Sand presented 'a case prodigiously discouraging to the usual view – the view that there is no surrender to "unconsecrated passion" that we escape paying for in one way or another . . . She positively got off from paying.'[86] But he was not prepared, as a realistic novelist, to allow his characters a similar good fortune. Transferred to fiction, George Sand's escape from retribution would have savoured too much of an impossible probability; as a fact, James was content to consider it the final illusion created by the 'great fluent artist' of total mastery over life.

Notes

INTRODUCTION

1 Marguerite Iknayan, *The Idea of the Novel in France: The Critical Reaction 1815–48* (Paris, 1961) p. 29.

2 e.g. W. E. Houghton, *The Victorian Frame of Mind* (New Haven, 1959) p. 564 n. 'A general study of her reputation and influence among Victorians has still to be written. I have the impression that she was the most widely read of all foreign authors except perhaps Goethe.' and Georges Lubin, Vol. IX, *George Sand, Correspondance* (Paris, 1972) p. 437 n. '. . . les recherches sur la fortune de George Sand en Angleterre n'ont paru tenter jusqu' à ce jour ou un chercheur britannique ou français'. One work, however, which came to my attention only after I had completed my research is P. G. Blount's 'Reputation of George Sand in Victorian England, 1832–1886' [unpublished dissertation, 1961] (University Microfilms, 1970).

3 George Sand, *Indiana*, ed. P. Salomon (Paris, 1962) 1832 Préface, p. 9. '. . . a type; she is Woman, the frail being whose mission it is to represent the *passions*, repressed, or if you prefer it, suppressed, by the *Law*; she is will at odds with necessity; she is love, dashing her head blindly against all the obstacles of civilisation.'

4 Quoted by Bernard Guyon in *La Pensée Politique et Sociale de Balzac* (Paris, 1967) p. 582.

5 George Sand, *Histoire de ma Vie* in *Oeuvres Autobiographiques*, ed. G. Lubin (Paris, 1970) II p. 164.

6 Ibid., II p. 322.

7 C. A. Sainte-Beuve, *Causeries du Lundi* (Paris, n.d.) I p. 354.

8 Wladimir Karénine, *George Sand* (Paris, 1912) Vol. III p. 21.

9 *Causeries du Lundi*, I p. 353.

10 George Sand, *La Mare au Diable* (Paris, 1962) Préface by P. Salomon and J. Mallion, p. vii.

11 *The Letters of Robert Browning and Elizabeth Barret Browning*, ed. Elvan Kintner, 2 vols (Cambridge, Mass., 1969) II pp. 652–3.

12 *The Letters of Henry James*, ed. Percy Lubbock (London, 1920) II pp. 401–2.

13 George Saintsbury, *History of the French Novel* (London, 1919) II p. 191.

14 Matthew Arnold, *Mixed Essays* (London, 1880) p. 319.

1. GEORGE SAND AND ENGLISH REVIEWERS

1 *Athenaeum* (Feb 1833) 74.

2 Ibid. (Mar 1833) 163.

3 Ibid. (Sep 1833) 646.

4 Ibid. (Dec 1834) 883.

5 *Foreign Quarterly Review*, 14 (Dec 1834) 271–97.

6 *Monthly Magazine*, 17 (Mar 1834) 283–93; see pp. 283–4.

7 *Blackwood's Magazine*, 34 (Dec 1833) 902–28.

8 *Edinburgh Review*, 57 (July 1833) 357.

9 *Blackwood's Magazine*, 37 (Jan 1836) 76.

10 *Blackwood's Magazine*, 37 (Mar 1836) 516.

11 'Des Jugemens sur notre Littérature Contemporaine à l'Etranger', *Revue des Deux Mondes*, 4e Serie, 6 (June 1836) 751.

12 *Quarterly Review*, 56 (Apr 1836) 65–131; see p. 66.

13 Marcel Moraud, *Le Romantisme Français en Angleterre de 1814 à 1848* (Paris, 1933) Chapter VI.

14 *Dublin University Magazine*, 36 (Sep 1850) 351.

15 *Examiner*, 24 April 1836.

16 *Westminster Review*, 25 (July 1836) 300.

17 *Athenaeum* (June 1837) 424–6.

18 Attributed to Francis Burdett in W. F. Poole's *Index to Periodical Literature*.

19 *Westminster Review*, 29 (Apr 1838) 73–98; see p. 82.

20 Ibid., 22 (Apr 1835) 314–21.

21 *Dublin University Magazine*, 12 (July 1838) 35.

22 L. A. Marchand, *The Athenaeum: A Mirror of Victorian Culture* (Chapel Hill, North Carolina, 1941).

23 *British and Foreign Review*, 8 (Apr 1839) 360–90. See also 'French Romances', *Fraser's Magazine*, 27 (Feb 1843) 184–94, in which *Spiridion* is said to reveal 'the helmless hopelessness' of her 'drifting' mind (p. 186).

24 *Monthly Chronicle*, 4 (July 1839) 23–40; see pp. 23–4.

25 H. L. Bulwer, *The Monarchy of the Middle Classes* (London, 1836) I p. 47.

26 Frances Trollope, *Paris and the Parisians in 1835*, 2 vols (London, 1836) II pp. 258–69.

27 G. W. M. Reynolds, *The Modern Literature of France*, 2 vols (London, 1839) I pp. 1–25.

28 W. M. Thackeray, *The Paris Sketch Book* (London, 1900) 211–36; see p. 218.

29 *Foreign Quarterly Review*, 27 (Apr 1841) 118–41; see p. 132.

30 *Foreign Quarterly Review*, 30 (Jan 1843) 414–28.

31 *Athenaeum* (Aug 1843) 766–8; see p. 768.

32 *Dublin Review*, 9 (Nov 1840) 353–96.

33 Moraud gives figures taken from the *New Monthly Magazine* which show that in the early 1830s England brought in 400,000 French books annually (1:53 inhabitants), whereas France imported only 80,000 (1:400).

34 *Foreign and Colonial Quarterly Review*, 1 (Apr 1843) 478–508; see p. 507.

35 *Foreign Quarterly Review*, 33 (July 1844) 265–98; see p. 298.

36 *Monthly Magazine* (May 1842) 578–91.

37 *Edinburgh Review*, 79 (Jan 1844) 157–88.

38 *Foreign Quarterly Review*, 37 (Apr 1846) 21–36; see p. 25. There is a similar reference in a review article by Lewes in *Fraser's Magazine*, 36 (Dec 1847) 686–95.

39 *Westminster Review*, 47 (Apr 1847) 236–7; see p. 236.

40 The novels translated were: *The Last Aldini*; *Simon*; *André*; *The Mosaic*

Masters; Fanchette; Mauprat; The Companion of the Tour de France; The Miller of Angibault; Letters of a Traveller.

41 *Quarterly Review*, 81 (Sep 1849) 533. Edmund Larkin was rebuked by Archbishop Whateley for his involvement in the enterprise, in a letter in which he enlarges upon the 'anti-Christian and profligate character of that woman's writings . . . A strict regard for the principles of morality and religion, and for delicacy, may be fairly expected at least from clergymen and ladies, if anywhere.' *The Life and Correspondence of Richard Whateley DD*, ed. E. J. Whateley (London, 1875) pp. 253–4.

42 He was the engraver, described by Carlyle as 'one Linton, a noisy worshipper of George Sand': see *New Letters of Thomas Carlyle*, ed. A. Carlyle (London, 1904) II p. 90. According to his own account, when he was in Paris in 1848 he met George Sand and secured from her the authority to translate her novels, but made no use of it.

43 *People's Journal*, I (1846) 12.

44 *Howitt's Journal*, I and II (1847) 98.

45 *George Sand, Correspondance*, ed. Georges Lubin (Paris, 1971) VIII p. 119: 'I am all the rage at the moment on the other side of the Channel'.

46 *People's Journal*, III (1847) 130–4; see p. 134.

47 *Howitt's Journal*, I and II (1847) 128–9.

48 *Fraser's Magazine*, 39 (1849) 423.

49 *Blackwood's Magazine*, 64 (Nov 1848) 557–72.

50 Ibid., 66 (Nov 1849) 607–19; see p. 607.

51 *Athenaeum* (May 1848) 502–3; see p. 502.

52 *Westminster Review*, n.s.2 (July 1852) 129–41; see p. 133.

2. 'GEORGE SANDISM' IN CHEYNE ROW

1 *Jane Welsh Carlyle: Letters to her Family 1839–1863*, ed. L. Huxley (London, 1924) p. 7.

2 *Jane Welsh Carlyle: A New Selection of her Letters*, ed. Trudy Bliss (London, 1950) p. 19.

3 *Letters*, ed. Huxley, p. 348.

4 *Letters*, ed. Bliss, p. 233.

5 *Letters*, ed. Huxley, p. 152.

6 Ibid., pp. 80–1.

7 Ibid., p. 234.

8 Ibid., p. 172.

9 Francis Espinasse, *Literary Recollections* (London, 1893) p. 277.

10 *Letters*, ed. Huxley, p. 38.

11 Thomas Carlyle, *Latter Day Pamphlets* (London, 1872) pp. 68–70.

12 Espinasse, pp. 223–4.

13 Ibid., p. 171.

14 *The Correspondence of Emerson and Carlyle*, ed. Joseph Slater (Columbia University Press, 1964) p. 410.

15 Ibid., p. 428.

16 *Letters*, ed. Bliss, p. 250.

17 *Selections from the Letters of Geraldine Endsor Jewsbury to Jane Welsh Carlyle*, ed. Mrs Alex. Ireland (London, 1892) p. viii.

18   *Letters*, ed. Huxley, p. 91.
19   *Letters*, ed. Ireland, p. 12.
20   Ibid., p. 154.
21   Ibid., p. 212.
22   Ibid., p. vii.
23   Susanne Howe, *The Life and Times of Geraldine Jewsbury* (London, 1935) p. 76.
24   *Letters*, ed. Ireland, p. 140.
25   *Letters and Memorials of Jane Welsh Carlyle*, ed. J. A. Froude, 2 vols (London, 1883) I p. 321.
26   Ibid., p. 55.
27   Espinasse, p. 153. Harriet Martineau also smoked cigars; obviously the habit was not unknown among respectable women at this time.
28   *The Correspondence of Arthur Hugh Clough*, ed. F. L. Mulhauser (Oxford, 1937) I pp. 237–8.
29   *Letters*, ed. Huxley, p. 241.
30   Discussed by V. E. A. Bowley in 'George Sand and Geraldine Jewsbury: An Unpublished Letter', *Revue de Littérature Comparée*, xxx, 3. 396–8. See also *George Sand, Correspondance*, ed. Georges Lubin (Paris, 1969) VI pp. 845–6.
31   *Letters*, ed. Froude, I p. 215.
32   Ibid., I p. 2.
33   A. T. Kitchel, *George Lewes and George Eliot* (New York, 1933) pp. 38–9.
34   John Stuart Mill, *The Subjection of Women* (London, 1960) Ch. 3, p. 509.
35   *Letters*, ed. Huxley, p. 204.
36   Introduction by Mazzini to *Letters of a Traveller*, tr. E. A. Ashurst (London, 1847) passim.
37   *People's Journal*, II (1847) 132.
38   *Mazzini's Letters*, tr. Alice de Rosen Jarvis (London and Toronto, 1930) (Letter to George Sand, 7 October 1848) p. 125.
39   *Letters*, ed. Froude, II p. 13.
40   Quoted by Elizabeth Schermerhorn, *The Seven Strings of the Lyre* (London, 1927) p. 214.
41   *Letters*, ed. Froude, p. 248.
42   *Letters*, ed. Huxley, p. 300.
43   *George Sand, Correspondance*, ed. Lubin, VIII pp. 639–40.
44   Ibid., VIII p. 716.
45   *George Sand, Correspondance*, ed. Lubin, IX p. 242.
46   Ibid., VIII p. 437.
47   H. F. Chorley, *Music and Manners in France and Germany*, 3 vols (London, 1841) III pp. 7–10.
48   Anne Thackeray Ritchie, *Chapters from Some Memoirs* (London, 1894) p. 166.
49   Ibid., p. 211.
50   Ibid., p. 211.
51   *George Sand, Correspondance*, ed. Lubin, VI p. 783.
52   *Diaries of W. C. Macready*, ed. William Toynbee, 2 vols (London, 1912) p. 357.

53 *George Sand, Correspondance*, ed. Lubin, VII p. 60.
54 Quoted by B. Juden and J. Richer, in 'Macready and George Sand', *Revue des Lettres Modernes* (1962–3) 48–58.
55 *Diaries of W. C. Macready*, II p. 344.
56 Edgar Johnson, *Charles Dickens, His Tragedy and Triumph* (Boston, 1952) II p. 851.
57 Ibid., II p. 859.
58 *Letters*, ed. Huxley, p. 304.
59 *George Sand, Correspondance*, ed. Lubin, v p. 284.
60 James Pope-Hennessy, *Monckton Milnes: The Years of Promise* (London, 1949) p. 20.
61 Ibid., 283–6. See also *George Sand, Correspondance*, ed. Lubin, VIII pp. 590–1.
62 *George Sand, Correspondance*, ed. Lubin, VIII pp. 590–1.
63 James Pope-Hennessy, *Monckton Milnes: The Flight of Youth* (London, 1951) p. 188.
64 G. S. Haight, *George Eliot and John Chapman* (Yale University Press, 1969) pp. 42–3.
65 Eliza Lynn Linton, *Reminiscences* (London, 1899) p. 31.
66 See above, Chapter 1, p. 24 (note).
67 Kitchel, Ch. 4.

3. 'THROUGH THE PRISON BARS . . .'
1 *The Letters of Robert Browning and Elizabeth Barrett Browning*, ed. Elvan Kintner, 2 vols (Cambridge, Mass., 1969) I p. 160.
2 *Elizabeth Barrett to Miss Mitford*, ed. Betty Miller (London, 1954) p. 50.
3 Miller, p. 47.
4 Ibid., p. 144.
5 Ibid., pp. 144–5.
6 Ibid., p. 145.
7 Ibid., p. 146.
8 Ibid.
9 Ibid., p. 147.
10 Ibid., p. 156.
11 Ibid., p. 155.
12 Ibid., p. 232.
13 Ibid., p. 156.
14 Ibid.
15 Ibid., p. 158.
16 *Aurora Leigh*, Book I 845–52.
17 Miller, p. 226.
18 The tribute was Renan's: see *Oeuvres Complètes de Ernest Renan*, ed. H. Psichari (Paris, 1947) II p. 1105.
19 See *Oeuvres Autobiographiques*, ed. Georges Lubin, II p. 939.
20 Miller, p. 225.
21 *The Letters of Elizabeth Barrett Browning*, ed. F. G. Kenyon, 2 vols (London, 1897) I p. 233.
22 Miller, p. 225.

23   Ibid., pp. 226–7.
24   *Letters of M. R. Mitford*, ed. H. F. Chorley, 2 vols (London, 1872) II p. 128.
25   Op. cit., Kenyon, I p. 363.
26   Miller, pp. 227–8.
27   Op. cit., Kintner, I pp. 113–14.
28   Ibid., I p. 150.
29   Ibid., I pp. 157–8.
30   Ibid., I p. 159.
31   Ibid., II pp. 652–3.
32   Ibid., II p. 657.
33   Op. cit., Kenyon, I p. 357.
34   Ibid., II p. 26.
35   Ibid., II p. 50.
36   Ibid., II pp. 39–40.
37   Ibid., II p. 50.
38   Ibid., II p. 55.
39   Ibid., II pp. 56–7.
40   Ibid., II pp. 59–60.
41   Ibid., II p. 62.
42   Ibid., II pp. 63–4.
43   Ibid., II p. 222.
44   See Dedication of *Aurora Leigh*.
45   Kintner, I p. 31.
46   Alethea Hayter, *Mrs. Browning* (London, 1962) Ch. 12.
47   Op. cit., Hayter, p. 159.
48   Martha H. Shackford, *E. B. Browning, R. H. Horne; two studies* (Wellesley Press, Mass., 1935) p. 23.
49   Ellen Moers, *Literary Women: The Great Writers* (New York, 1976) p. 176.
50   *Harriet Hosmer, Letters and Memories*, ed. Cornelia Carr (London, 1913) p. 99.
51   George Sand, *Consuelo*, ed. Léon Cellier and Léon Guichard (Paris, 1959) Introduction, p. xv.
52   Miller, p. 260.
53   Ibid., p. 212.
54   Ibid., p. 260.
55   George Sand, *Histoire de ma Vie*, in *Oeuvres Autobiographiques*, II p. 296.

4.   'ANOTHER BALE OF FRENCH BOOKS' AT HAWORTH

1   Emily Brontë, *Wuthering Heights* (London, 1920), Preface by Mrs Humphrey Ward, p. xvii.
2   Charlotte Brontë, *Jane Eyre* (London, 1920) Preface, p. xvii.
3   Ibid., p. xxxviii.
4   Ibid., p. xxxv.
5   *The Shakespeare Head Brontë*, ed. T. J. Wise and J. A. Symington: *The Life and Letters*, 4 vols (Oxford, 1932) I p. 107.
6   *Letters*, I p. 215.
7   *Jane Eyre*, Ch. 15 p. 175.
8   *Letters*, I p. 276.

9 Ibid., I p. 80. She no doubt read *Consuelo* in 1843. Cf. a letter from Mary Taylor to Ellen Nussey in that year:

> I have read a French novel called Consuelo which I admire exceedingly was that the one you spoke of? if so you would not have given yourself too much trouble if you had learned French for the express purpose of reading it. I have spoken first of this because it is the thing that has interested me most in the last month.

See *Mary Taylor. Letters from New Zealand and Elsewhere*, ed. Joan Stevens (Auckland and Oxford, 1974) p. 49.

10 *Letters*, II p. 180.

11 *Letters*, III pp. 172–3.

12 *The Letters of George Eliot*, ed. G. S. Haight (New Haven, 1959) II p. 91.

13 *Westminster Review*, n.s. 3 (1853) 490.

14 The *Cornhill* (Dec 1877). Quoted in *Charlotte Brontë: the Critical Heritage*, ed. Miriam Allott (London, 1974) p. 415.

15 *Daily News*, 3 February 1853.

16 Winifred Gérin, *Charlotte Brontë* (Oxford, 1967) p. 167.

17 *Letters*, VI p. 206.

18 *Letters*, VI p. 221.

19 George Sand, *Lélia*, ed. P. Reboul (Paris, 1960) p. 227.

20 *Dublin University Magazine*, XXI (May 1848) 614.

21 'Vanity Fair, *Jane Eyre* and the Governesses' Benevolent Association', *Quarterly Review*, 84 (Dec 1848) 174.

22 *Letters*, IV p. 17.

23 George Sand, *La Mare au Diable*, ed. P. Salomon and J. Mallion (Paris, 1962) p. 12.

24 George Sand, *Lettres d'un Voyageur* (Letter 4) in *Oeuvres Autobiographiques* ed. G. Lubin (Paris, 1970) II p. 757. 'Is it a crime to show all one's grief, one's ennui? Does virtue consist in concealing it? It may perhaps be a virtue to stay silent – but to lie! . . .'

25 Charlotte Brontë, *Villette* (London, 1920) Ch. 38 p. 538.

26 Ibid., Ch. 57 p. 577.

27 Ibid., Ch. 51 p. 588.

28 Charlotte Brontë, *Shirley* (London, 1889) Ch. 40 p. 195.

29 Charlotte Brontë, *The Professor* (London, 1924) Ch. 25 p. 361.

30 *Lélia*, p. 90.

31 *The Professor*, Ch. 25 p. 360.

32 George Sand, *Indiana*, ed. P. Salomon (Paris, 1962) Ch. 21 p. 225.

33 *The Professor*, Ch. 22 pp. 318–19.

34 George Sand, *Lettres à Marcie* in *Les Sept Cordes de la Lyre* (Paris, 1869) p. 272 and *passim*.

35 *Shirley*, Ch. 10 p. 157.

36 *Shirley*, Ch. 12 pp. 193, 202.

37 *Letters*, III pp. 104–5.

38 Jean Baelen, *Le Vie de Flora Tristan* (Paris, 1972) p. 184.

39 *Shirley*, Ch. 31 p. 491.

40 Ellen Moers, *Literary Women* (New York, 1976) p. 178.

41 Mrs Humphrey Ward, Preface to *Shirley*, p. xxiv.

42   Ibid., p. xxv.

43   *Lettres à Marcie*, p. 230.

44   *Shirley*, Ch. 6 p. 83.

45   George Sand, *Jacques* (Paris, n.d.) Letter 8 p. 45.

46   G. Sand, *Rose et Blanche*, 2 vols (Bruxelles, 1837) II pp. 70–1. (Cf. *The Professor*, Ch. 10):

> And then at last to make your way towards the sound of youthful, joyous laughter . . . to enter a classroom! To see around you a harem of maidens who blush, are abashed, hide behind each other, gain confidence, get bolder . . . to have the right to scold them, to be their supervisor, their master and not to dare to go any further; to be always under the watchful eye of a mistress . . . whose presence chills and petrifies; to affect calm and indifference . . . for these mocking and mischievous girls want to make you laugh . . . heedless and unkind, they are coquettish with you.

47   Ibid., II p. 59.

48   Ibid., II pp. 137–8.

49   George Sand, *Hiver à Majorque* (Paris, n.d.) p. 8.

50   *Shirley*, Ch. 32 p. 505.

51   Ibid., Ch. 33 p. 521.

52   A. C. Swinburne, *Charlotte Brontë, a Note*, quoted in *Critical Heritage*, op. cit., p. 406.

53   *Jane Eyre*, Ch. 23 p. 300.

54   *Oeuvres Autobiographiques* (Letter 1) II pp. 653, 9:

> The countryside was not yet in its full splendour . . . But almond trees and peach trees in blossom here and there broke up the dark masses of cypress with their pink and white garlands. A semi-circle of fertile hills formed a first frame to the picture; and snow-covered mountains, glittering in the first rays of the sun, made, farther away, a second vast frame, which stood out like silver fretwork from the solid blue of the sky. . . . From those distant peaks, I said to myself, my golden dreams have come; they have flown to me, like a flock of passenger birds.

55   *Jane Eyre*, Ch. 26 p. 360.

56   *Lélia*, p. 53: 'Let the child grow and live, do not nip the flower in the bud. Do not blow with your icy breath upon his beautiful days of sunshine and springtime.'

57   *Oeuvres Autobiographiques* (Letter 5) II p. 777:

> Winter spreads out its grey cloak over the melancholy earth, the cold whistles and laments about our roof-tops . . . branches stand out black in the white frost laden air . . . Cold, night, death are here. This last glance of the sun through my windowpanes, is my last hope gleaming . . . The winter of my soul has come, an eternal winter! There was a time when I did not look at the sky or the flowers, when I did not worry about the absence of the sun and did not pity the sparrows, benumbed on their branch . . . Now . . . my soul is bereft.

58   *Villette*, Ch. 15 p. 186.

59   *Lélia*, p. 129:

> Alas, how many worlds I have traversed in these journeys of the soul!

I have crossed the whitened steppes of icy regions. I have cast my swift
glance over the perfumed savannas where the moon rises so white and
beautiful. I have skimmed on the wings of sleep over these vast seas,
whose immensity is terrifying to contemplate . . .

60   Virginia Woolf, *The Common Reader* (London, 1925) p. 199.

5.   'WUTHERING HEIGHTS' AND 'MAUPRAT'

 1   See, in particular, J. Hewish, *Emily Brontë* (London, 1969) pp. 118–35. He
     discusses, among others, Scott, Shakespeare, Byron and Hoffmann.
 2   J. V. Arnold, 'George Sand's *Mauprat* and Emily Brontë's *Wuthering
     Heights*', *Revue de Littérature Comparée*, 46 (1972) 209–18.
 3   Winifred Gérin, *Emily Brontë* (Oxford, 1971) p. 124.
 4   *The Shakespeare Head Brontë*, ed. Wise and Symington: *The Life and Letters*,
     I p. 261.
 5   *Wuthering Heights* (London, 1920) p. liv.
 6   Henry James, *French Poets & Novelists* (London, 1919) p. 181.
 7   George Sand, *Mauprat*, ed. Claude Sicard (Paris, 1969) Préface, p. 21.
 8   *Mauprat*, Ch. 7 p. 100: 'When I was alone I longed to roar like a caged
     lion, and at night I had dreams in which the woodland moss, the screen
     of forest trees and even the gloomy battlements of Roche-Mauprat seemed
     to me like an earthly paradise.'
 9   *Wuthering Heights*, Ch. 13 p. 60.
10   *Mauprat*, Ch. 11 p. 142.
11   Ibid., Ch. 10 p. 123:
     I went into the garden and strode frantically up and down the walks
     . . . I went blindly and leant against a gloomy wall, and burying my
     face in my hands, I burst into hopeless sobbing. My sturdy breast felt
     as if it would burst and I got no relief from my tears; I longed to roar
     aloud and I had to bite my handkerchief to keep myself from yielding
     to the temptation.
12   Ibid., Ch. 29 p. 309:
     All right! Since you want to know the truth, yes, I love him! It's as you
     say – I have fallen in love with him. It's not my fault; why should I
     blush for it? I can't help it; it has been the work of fate. I have never
     loved M. de la Marche; I feel only friendship for him. As for Bernard,
     my feeling is very different – a feeling so strong, so variable, so full of
     unrest, of hatred, of fear, of anger, of pity, and of tenderness that it is
     quite beyond me and I no longer try to comprehend it . . . I know that
     Bernard is a bear, a badger . . . a savage, a boor and anything else you
     like. There's nothing more shaggy, more bristly, more cunning, more
     vicious than Bernard. He is a brute who scarcely knows how to sign his
     name . . .
     The worst of it is – I love him. Look at the symptoms: I think of no
     one else, I see no one else and I could not eat any dinner tonight because
     he had not come back. I find him handsomer than any man in the
     world. When he says he loves me, I see, I feel that it is true; it shocks
     and delights me at the same time. M. de la Marche seems insipid and

affected since I have known Bernard. Only Bernard seems as proud, as passionate, as bold as I am – and as weak as I am; for he cries like a child when I vex him and here am I crying too as I think of him.

13 *Wuthering Heights*, Ch. 9 p. 84.

14 *Mauprat*, Ch. 20 p. 241.

15 Ibid., Ch. 13 p. 175:

I understand only that I love you madly and will claw out the heart of any man who tries to take you from me. I know that I shall force you to love me and that if I don't succeed I will at any rate not let you belong to anyone else while I am alive. He will have to walk over my wounded body, bleeding from every pore, to put the wedding ring on your finger and with my last breath I shall dishonour you by saying you are my mistress, in order to mar the joy of the man who has triumphed over me; and if, as I die, I can stab you I will do it, so that in the tomb at least you may be my wife.

16 Ibid., Ch. 21 pp. 244–5:

but . . . I fear that I should love you dead with as much passion and tenacity as if you were alive. I am afraid of being restrained, governed, dominated by your image, as I am by your person; and besides there is no means by which a man can kill the being whom he loves and fears. When she has ceased to live on earth she will live on within him. It is the lover's soul which serves as a coffin for his mistress . . . As I write to you, Edmée, the sky is full of clouds that are darker and heavier than lead; the thunder is rumbling and anguished ghosts of purgatory seem to be floating in the glare of the lightning. The weight of the storm lies on my soul, my troubled mind vacillates like these wavering lights which flare up on the horizon. I feel as if my whole being were going to explode like the storm.

17 Ibid., Ch. 17 p. 210:

I arrived at Roche-Mauprat one foggy evening, in the early days of autumn; the sun was hidden, and nature was hushed in silence and mist; the plains were deserted; the air alone seemed full, with the noise and movement of great flocks of birds of passage; cranes were drawing huge triangles in the sky, and storks, passing immeasurably high overhead were filling the clouds with mournful cries, which hovered over the saddened country like the dirge of summer.

6. ARNOLD'S 'DAYS OF "LÉLIA" '

1 Matthew Arnold, *Mixed Essays* (London, 1880) p. 318.

2 Ibid., pp. 322–3. I have not come across the actual phrase 'days of *Corinne*', but have always assumed that Arnold was referring to the passage in *Lettres d'un Voyageur* (Letter 7): 'Heureux temps! ô ma Vallée Noire! ô Corinne! ô Bernardin de Saint-Pierre! ô l'Iliade . . . ô ma jeunesse écoulée!'

3 Ibid., pp. 318–19.

4 *Letters of Matthew Arnold*, ed. G. W. E. Russell, 2 vols (London, 1895) II p. 131.

5 Ibid., I p. 106.
6 *Mixed Essays*, p. 320.
7 *The Notebooks of Matthew Arnold*, ed. H. F. Lowry, K. Young and W. H. Dunn (London, 1952) p. 277.
8 *Mixed Essays*, pp. 328–9.
9 Ibid., pp. 346–7.
10 Mary A. Ward, *A Writer's Recollections* (London, 1918) p. 12.
11 *The Correspondence of Arthur Hugh Clough*, ed. F. L. Mulhauser, 2 vols (Oxford, 1957) I pp. 178–9.
12 *Letters of Matthew Arnold to Arthur Hugh Clough*, ed. H. F. Lowry (London, 1932) pp. 58–9.
13 George Sand, *Jacques* (Paris, 1854) Letter 29, p. 132:
> She has not been formed, like you, with a body and soul of iron; she has been talked to about prudence and reason, about certain contrivances to avoid certain misfortunes and about certain considerations to arrive at a certain state of well-being which society permits women under certain conditions. No one has said to her as to you, 'The sun is fierce and the wind is rough; man is made to brave the storm on the sea, woman to tend the herds, in the burning heat on the mountains. In winter, when the snow and ice come, you will still go there and will try to warm yourself at a fire which you will kindle with dry branches from the forest; if you don't want to do that you will just have to put up with the cold. These are the realities – the mountain, the sea, the sun. The sun scorches, the sea devours, the mountain exhausts. It can happen that wild beasts carry off the flocks and the child who is tending them; you will live in the midst of all this as best you can; if you are good and brave, you will be given shoes so that you can dress up on Sunday.'
14 *The Poems of Matthew Arnold*, ed. Kenneth Allott (London, 1965) p. 163.
15 *Letters*, II p. 137.
16 *Letters of Arnold to Clough*, pp. 132–3.
17 *The Complete Prose Works of Matthew Arnold*, ed. R. H. Super (Michigan, 1972) Vol. 8 p. 434.
18 Iris Sells, *Matthew Arnold and France* (Cambridge, 1935) p. 36.
19 Louis Bonnerot, *Matthew Arnold, Poète* (Paris, 1949) p. 39.
20 George Sand, *Lélia*, ed. Pierre Réboul (Paris, 1960) p. 540.
21 Ibid., p. 111: 'Man has the powerlessness of the mollusc with the appetites of the tiger; he is imprisoned like the tortoise, in a shell of misery and necessity.'
22 Ibid., p. 330.
23 *Poems*, ed. Allott, p. 129.
24 F. J. W. Harding, *Matthew Arnold: The Critic and France* (Geneva, 1964) p. 61.
25 George Sand, *Lettres d'un Voyageur*, in *Oeuvres Autobiographiques*, ed. Lubin, II p. 651.
26 Etienne Pivert de Senancour, *Obermann* (Paris, n.d.) p. 28.
27 Bonnerot, p. 189.
28 *Poems*, p. 22.

29 *A Writer's Recollections*, p. 45.
30 Bonnerot, p. 190.
31 *Lélia*, pp. 44, 49.
32 Ibid., p. 113: 'Some memories which come to light are accompanied by a sense of melancholy which might be said to have been acquired in the tomb, for perhaps man leaves the chill of the coffin to return to the warmth of the cradle.'
33 Ibid., p. 70: 'The last feather has not yet fallen from your wing.'
34 Ibid., pp. 52–3: 'Do you realise how many centuries you are apart from him?'
35 *Poems*, p. 34: 'You still have some memories of the past.'
36 Ibid., pp. 34–5.
37 *Lélia*, p. 140:
    The façades and the courtyards of the villa sparkled with lights, but the gardens were lit only by reflections from the rooms. As one moved further away one was engulfed in a soft, mysterious darkness and could rest from the bustle and noise in the depth of these shadows, where the strains of the orchestra came sweetly and gently, often interrupted by gusts of a scented breeze.
38 Ibid., pp. 217–20.
39 Ibid., pp. 241–8.
40 Bonnerot, p. 380.
41 *Poems*, p. 175.
42 Ibid., p. 171.
43 *Obermann*, p. 160: 'Call a halt to your desires, limit these too avid needs.'
44 *Lélia*, p. 150: 'I have not asked more of life than it can give me. I have confined all my ambitions to knowing how to enjoy what there is.'
45 Ibid., pp. 67–8: 'Alas, Trenmor, where have we got to? What has the age come to? The scholar denies everything, the priest doubts. Let us see if the poet still exists. Sténio, take your harp and sing for me the verses of Faust or else open your books and tell me again of the sufferings of Obermann, the ecstasies of Saint-Preux.'
46 Ibid., p. 379.
47 *Lélia*, p. 380.
48 Ibid., p. 16.
49 Ibid., p. 109.
50 Ibid., pp. 37–9:
    The lake was calm that night; as calm as in the last days of autumn when the winter's wind does not yet dare to stir the silent waves and the pink sword-lilies on the bank scarcely sleep, rocked by the gentle rising and falling. Gradually the sharp outlines of the mountains were eaten away by the pale mists which, falling on the waters, seemed to draw the horizon so far back as to make it totally disappear. Then the surface of the lake appeared to become as vast as that of the sea . . . The sense of reverie became solemn and profound, as indefinite as the misty lake, as immense as the boundless sky. Nothing was left in Nature but the heavens and man, the soul and doubt . . . 'Calm!' said Trenmor, as he looked up at the heavens with a gaze of sublimity; 'Calm is God's

greatest boon, it is the prospect towards which the immortal soul is always reaching, it is beatitude! Calm is the Divinity.'

51 Ibid., p. 98: 'My eyes are drier than the sandy deserts where the dew never falls and my heart even more dry . . . for me, everything is spent, everything has evaporated.'

52 *The New Zealand Letters of Thomas Arnold the Younger*, ed. James Bertram (Auckland, 1966) pp. 216–17.

53 *Lélia*, p. 220.

54 Ibid., pp. 55–7:

We refuse to worship God . . . Instead we transfer our adoration to a frail, imperfect being, who becomes the god of our idolatrous creed . . . And when the veil of divinity slips and behind the clouds of incense and the halo of adoration, the flawed and paltry creature is seen for what it is, we are shocked out of our illusion, we blush for it, we overthrow the idol and trample it underfoot.

And then we seek another! for we must love someone . . .

55 Bonnerot, p. 104.

56 *Jacques*, pp. 127–8: 'Love is the sole happiness of life – it governs all things and has been well called the soul of the world . . . but when it dies real life reappears in all its starkness.'

57 *Letters to Clough*, p. 126.

58 *Lélia*, p. 45.

59 *Jacques*, p. 347.

60 Ibid., p. 541: 'I have sought everything, suffered everything, believed everything, accepted everything . . . Of love I have asked its joys, of faith its mysteries, of pain its merits . . . Truth! Truth! you have not revealed yourself to me, for ten thousand years I have sought you and I have not found you.'

61 *Letters*, I p. 52.

62 Ibid., II pp. 82–3.

63 *Notebooks*, p. 121.

64 *Mixed Essays*, p. 315.

65 *Notebooks*, pp. 10–11.

66 *Letters*, p. 131.

67 Ibid., p. 137.

68 *Notebooks*, p. 290.

69 George Sand, *Valvèdre* (Paris, 1861) p. 141. In George Sand's later novels, as in her life, the patient observation and collection of data outside the self rather than creation takes over as the heroic occupation. Entomologists, geologists, naturalists and minerologists abound – though her artists are more memorable than her field-workers. Cf. her youthful remark to her entomologist friend, in *Lettres d'un Voyageur* (IV): 'Hélas! si je pouvais comme toi me passionner pour un insecte!'

70 Lionel Trilling, *Matthew Arnold* (London, 1939) p. 381.

71 *Notebooks*, p. 307: 'Nothing will ever again come right in the world without reason and justice, patience, knowledge, dedication and modesty.'

72 Ibid., p. 255: 'In everything, needless to say, one must so arrange matters as to have them in perspective.'

73 Ibid., p. 322: 'The most precious thing he taught me was to get to know myself and to meditate upon my impressions.'
74 *Westminster Review*, xxxix (Feb 1843) 274.
75 W. M. Thackeray, *The Paris Sketch Book* (London, 1900) p. 229.
76 *Monthly Review*, n.s. 3 (Nov 1842) 359.
77 *Quarterly Review*, cxxxxiii (Apr 1877) 423–49.
78 *Notebooks*, p. 601.
79 George Sand, *Mauprat*, ed. Claude Sicard (Paris, 1969) p. 32: 'In the impression she made upon me something so comforting mingled with something so wholesome for the spirit . . .'

7. 'CITIZEN CLOUGH'

1 Paul Veyriras, *Arthur Hugh Clough* (Paris, 1964) p. 225.
2 W. H. Dunn, *James Anthony Froude 1818–1856* (Oxford, 1961) p. 96.
3 *The New Zealand Letters of Thomas Arnold the Younger*, ed. James Bertram (Auckland, 1966) pp. 216–17.
4 *The Correspondence of Arthur Hugh Clough*, ed. F. L. Mulhauser, 2 vols (Oxford, 1957) II p. 503.
5 Ibid., p. 150.
6 Ibid., p. 152.
7 Ibid.
8 *Selection from the Letters of Geraldine Endsor Jewsbury to Jane Welsh Carlyle*, ed. Mrs Alex Ireland (London, 1892) p. 333.
9 *Correspondence of Clough*, I p. 159.
10 George Sand, *Valentine* (Paris, 1852) Ch. XIV pp. 116–17: 'Valentine . . . sat on, under that spell whose electrical charge at her age and Benedict's . . . has so much magical power! They did not say anything, they did not dare exchange a smile or word. Valentine was as if transfixed, Benedict lost all consciousness of himself in his sense of violent happiness.'
11 See, for instance, 'Nature', in R. W. Emerson, *Essays*, 2nd series (1844) no. 18; R. W. Chambers, *Vestiges of Creation* (1844). Veyriras discusses Clough's indebtedness, pp. 206–8. See also W. E. Houghton, *The Poetry of Clough: An Essay in Revaluation* (New Haven, 1963) pp. 53–5, for an excellent analysis of the poem.
12 Quoted by Biswas, p. 245.
13 Bodleian MS. Eng. Misc. d. 512. fols 1–6. (I am indebted, for helpful discussion of this MS., to Stephen Medcalf and the Rev. Bertie Moore.)
14 *Correspondence of Clough*, II pp. 417–18.
15 George Sand, *Jeanne* (Paris, 1892) Ch. 15 pp. 209–10.
16 *Correspondence of Clough*, I p. 159.
17 Biswas, p. 384.
18 *Correspondence of Clough*, I p. 182.
19 Ibid., I p. 172.
20 Ibid., I p. 228.
21 Ibid., I p. 156.
22 Ibid., I p. 301.
23 *Letters of Matthew Arnold to Arthur Hugh Clough*, ed. H. F. Lowry (London, 1932) p. 77.

24 *Correspondence of Clough,* i p. 206.
25 Ibid., i pp. 210–11.
26 Ibid., i p. 216.
27 Ibid., i p. 213.
28 Quoted in R. L. Rusk, *The Life of Ralph Waldo Emerson* (New York and London, 1947) p. 347.
29 *Correspondence of Clough,* i p. 232.
30 *Jeanne,* Prologue p. 8:
   . . . another treasure is needed to get it out.
   'Yes, capital!' said Marsillat.
   'And peasants!' added Guillaume. 'This district is depopulated.'
   'Men and then men,' replied the Englishman.
   'Don't understand,' said Guillaume, smiling, to Marsillat.
   'Not masters and slaves; men and men,' Sir Arthur said again, astonished at not having been understood – he who thought he spoke clearly.
   'Are there slaves in France?' cried Marsillat, shrugging his shoulders.
   'Yes, and in England too,' the Englishman responded, unruffled.
   'Philosophy bores me,' Marsillat murmured to his young compatriot, 'your Englishman would put me off being liberal.'
31 Biswas, p. 267.
32 *Jeanne,* Ch. xiv p. 196: ' "Ho!" said M. Harley, with the indefinable accent of phlegmatic surprise, with which Englishmen can imbue that exclamation.'
33 Ibid., Ch. xix p. 252.
34 Ibid., Ch. xviii pp. 246–7:
   . . . proprietor of a good farm in the Marche or Berry district, living, just as he pleased, as a good countryman far from the world he was tired of; getting in his harvests himself, doing a man's work, along with his small holders, bringing prosperity to his husbandmen, seeing to the welfare of his parish and tasting himself the greatest happiness alongside his beautiful, sturdy companion. That's the life I've always dreamed of, he thought . . . Arthur, his forehead bathed in sweat, and his eyes gleaming with hope, exchanged with Jeanne, affectionate glances, playful words and huge forkfuls of hay . . .

8. 'GEORGY SANDON'

1 George Sand, *Correspondence,* ed. Georges Lubin (Paris, 1970) vii p. 321.
2 Ibid. (1971) viii p. 119.
3 'The State Murder, A Tale', *Fraser's Magazine* (Oct–Nov 1844) 394–412; 563–71.
4 Francis Espinasse, *Literary Recollections* (London, 1893) p. 278.
5 G. H. Lewes, *Rose, Blanche & Violet,* 3 vols (London, 1848) Prologue.
6 E. W. Hirshberg, *George Henry Lewes* (New York, 1970) p. 48.
7 *Jane Welsh Carlyle, Letters to her Family,* ed. L. Huxley (London, 1924) p. 66.
8 Ibid., p. 189.
9 Ibid., p. 194.
10 Espinasse, p. 136.
11 Geraldine Jewsbury, *Zoë,* 3 vols (London, 1848) ii p. 202.

12   Ibid., II pp. 260–1.
13   See Lewes on Charlotte Brontë's heroes in the *Leader* (12 Feb 1853) 163–4: 'They are the Mirabeaux of romance, and the idolatory of a nation follows the great gifts of a Mirabeau, let "Propriety" look never so shocked.'
Mirabeau's career had long been a talking-point and much was written on him about this time; but Geraldine Jewsbury's interest may have been aroused by Carlyle's picture of him in *The French Revolution* (1837). However, 'Geraldine's Mirabeau' was also a talking-point, and Charlotte Brontë would almost certainly have read *Zoë*. See her letter to Lewes: 'You mention Mrs. Gaskell and Miss Jewsbury. I regard as an honour any expression of interest from those ladies. The latter I once had the pleasure of meeting.'
14   *Zoë*, III p. 223.
15   Ibid., III p. 226.
16   *Letters*, ed. Huxley, p. 236.
17   Ibid., p. 234.
18   Susanne Howe, *The Life and Times of Geraldine Jewsbury* (London, 1935) p. 110.
19   Geraldine Jewsbury, *The Half-Sisters*, 2 vols (London, 1848) II pp. 15–32.
20   Ibid., II p. 243.
21   Ibid., II p. 246.
22   Ibid., II p. 81.
23   *Athenaeum* (18 Mar 1848) 288–90.
24   E. Lynn Linton, *Reminiscences* (London, 1899) p. 31.
25   L. P. Stebbins, *A Victorian Album* (London, 1946) p. 9.
26   *Reminiscences*, p. 17.
27   E. Lynn, *Amymone, a Romance of the Days of Pericles*, 3 vols (London, 1848) II p. 88.
28   Ibid., III p. 106.
29   G. H. Lewes, 'The Lady Novelists', *Westminster Review* (July 1852) 141.
30   *Selections from the Letters of Geraldine Endsor Jewsbury to Jane Welsh Carlyle*, ed. Mrs Alex Ireland (London, 1892) p. 405.
31   G. S. Haight, *George Eliot and John Chapman* (New Haven, 1961) p. 119.
32   Eliza Lynn Linton, 'George Eliot', in *Women Novelists of Queen Victoria's Reign* (London, 1897) p. 114.
33   Eliza Lynn Linton, *My Literary Life* (London, 1899) pp. 99–100.
34   J. A. Froude, *The Nemesis of Faith* (London, 1903) Foreword by Moncur D. Conway.
35   Elie Halévy, *Victorian Years (1841–95)* (London, 1962) p. 400.
36   *Nemesis of Faith*, p. 113.
37   Ibid., p. 147.
38   *The George Eliot Letters*, ed. G. S. Haight (New Haven, 1885) I p. 279 n.
39   Ashford Owen, *A Lost Love* (London, 1890) Foreword.
40   Browning recommended the book highly to Hale White (Mark Rutherford) who, when it was re-published in 1883, also recommended it to a friend – and yet again, to another, in 1911, when at the age of eighty he was re-reading it with great approval.
41   *A Lost Love*, p. 173.

9. THE TWO GEORGES
1 *Fortnightly Review*, n.s. 20 (Nov 1876) 614.
2 Francis Espinasse, *Literary Recollections* (London, 1893) p. 297.
3 *The George Eliot Letters*, ed. G. S. Haight (New Haven, 1955) v pp. 8–9, 464.
4 Edmund Gosse, *Aspects and Impressions* (London, 1922) p. 4.
5 *Letters*, I p. 267.
6 Ibid., I p. 275.
7 Ibid., I pp. 277–8.
8 Ibid., I pp. 250–1:

Joy and Grief course	Joy makes us glad,
From the same source –	Grief makes us sad –
In that, they don't vary.	In that, they're contrary.

'Are you aware that everything is said before God and man when the unfortunate man asks for a reckoning of his troubles and receives this reply? What more is there to say? Nothing.'
9 Ibid., I p. 274.
10 Ibid., I p. 250.
11 Ibid., I p. 278.
12 Ibid., I p. 251.
13 Ibid., I p. 261.
14 Ibid., I p. 270.
15 Ibid., I p. 275.
16 Marcel Moraud, *Le Romantisme Français en Angleterre, 1818–48* (Paris, 1933) p. 406.
17 L. Feuerbach, *Essence of Christianity*, tr. Marian Evans (New York, 1957) p. 48.
18 *Letters*, II p. 171.
19 *Athenaeum* (28 Nov 1885) 702.
20 E. V. Lucas, *The Colvins and their Friends* (New York, 1928) p. 97.
21 *Quarterly Review*, 143 (Apr 1877) 477.
22 Leslie Stephen, *George Eliot* (London, 1907) p. 111.
23 Virginia Woolf, *The Common Reader* (London, 1925) p. 213.
24 *Revue des Deux Mondes* (Dec 1894) 847–72.
25 *Letters*, p. 18.
26 George Sand, *Oeuvres Autobiographiques*, ed. Lubin, I p. 954. 'I saw a huge, vast, boundless path open up before me; I longed to rush onto it.'
27 Ibid., I p. 965: 'I was literally consumed with ardour like Saint Theresa ... I inflicted on myself penances which were pointless because there was nothing left for me to sacrifice, to change or to immolate.'
28 Ibid., I p. 1039: 'What is this thing or that to thee? Follow thou me ... Forsake thyself and thou shalt find me ... Thou must give all for all ... Thy heart shall be free and thou shalt no longer walk in darkness ... Forsake thyself, renounce thyself.'
29 George Eliot, *The Mill on the Floss*, 2 vols (Edinburgh and London, n.d.) Bk I Ch. 3 *passim*.
30 Ibid., Bk v Ch. 1 and Ch. 3.
31 Henry James, *French Poets and Novelists* (London, 1919) p. 182.
32 Bertha Thomas, *George Sand* (London, 1883) p. 183.

33   See Ellen Moers, *Literary Women* (New York, 1976) p. 190.
34   *Saturday Review* (14 Apr 1860) 470–1.
35   James, *French Poets and Novelists*, p. 172.
36   *The Nation*, 316 (Aug 1866) 128.
37   *The Mill on the Floss*, Bk vi Ch. 6 and Ch. 10.
38   Ibid., Bk vi Ch. 11 p. 281.
39   Ibid., Bk vi Ch. 13 pp. 309–11.
40   George Sand, *Consuelo*, ed. Léon Cellier and Léon Guichard, 2 vols (Paris, 1959) ii pp. 78–84:

> Consuelo left the drawing room and went into the garden . . . She was trembling, as if she had felt her courage desert her in the most perilous crisis of her life and she was aware that she had lost for the first time that instinctive integrity, that saint-like trust in her own intentions which had always sustained her in her trials. She had left the drawing room in order to escape from the fascination which Anzoleto was exerting upon her and at the same time had felt a vague longing to have him follow her . . . and, poised for flight, not daring to return, she stayed rooted to the spot as if spell-bound . . . She felt as if she were falling down a precipice, trying to break her fall by snatching at spindly branches which snapped off one after another, and as she gazed, appalled, down at the bottom of the abyss, her head was whirling . . . Anzoleto stood beside her . . . he took her hands and held them in his own for a second but in that swift, burning pressure was concentrated the sensual delight of an entire age. Unseen, he spoke words which suffocate, he cast devouring glances at her. . . .
>
> And always this sense of insurmountable falsehood and duplicity troubled her thoughts and set her heart at odds with her conscience. Never before had she felt so wretched, so vulnerable, so alone in the world.

41   Quoted by G. S. Haight, *George Eliot: A Biography* (Oxford, 1968) p. 335.
42   *Consuelo*, i p. 250.
43   Ibid., ii p. 77: 'a lover so bold, dangerous and eager in pursuit'.
44   Ibid., ii p. 96: 'She is pure; she wants to love me. She is aware that my love is true and my faith unshakeable.'
45   Ibid., i p. 33: 'As for causing me sorrow, that is not in your power Consuelo. I have not been nurtured on illusions; I have grown accustomed to the most grievous sorrow; I know that my life is doomed to the most bitter sacrifices . . . But one glance at you is enough to give my spirit new life and to send it soaring to the heavens like a hymn of gratitude and an incense of purification.'
46   *The Mill on the Floss*, Bk vii Ch. 3 pp. 371–2.
47   *Consuelo*, ii p. 527: 'I believed you had abandoned me and I let despair seize me; . . . but I am now in my right mind . . . I knew in the end that you had kept your vow, Consuelo; that you had done your best to love me; that you had shown me true love for several hours.'
48   *Mill on the Floss*, Bk vii Ch. 3 p. 370.
49   F. R. Leavis, *The Great Tradition* (London, 1948) p. 39. One has only to look at the essay in Marian Evans' school notebook [Haight, p. 553] and

to read some of her letters to Miss Lewis to recognise the difference between the emotional self-sacrifice of Maggie Tulliver and the sanctimonious puritanism of her creator, in her own adolescence.

50 George Eliot, *Scenes of Clerical Life*, 2 vols (Edinburgh and London, 1858) II Ch. 20 p. 33.

51 George Eliot, *Daniel Deronda*, 3 vols (Edinburgh and London, n.d.) Bk I Ch. 5 p. 68.

52 *Consuelo*, I pp. 242–3: 'She realised at last that she knew nothing and that perhaps she would never be able to learn anything.'

53 *Daniel Deronda*, Bk III Ch. 23 p. 382.

54 Ibid., Bk VII Ch. 51 p. 131.

55 George Eliot, *Middlemarch*, 3 vols (Edinburgh and London, n.d.) I Ch. 7 p. 96.

56 George Sand, *Lettres d'un Voyageur*, Letter 10, in *Oeuvres Autobiographiques*, ed. Lubin, II p. 914.

57 George Sand, *Jacques* (Paris, 1852) Letter 29, p. 127.

58 Quoted by André Maurois in *Lélia*, tr. G. Hopkins (London, 1953) p. 132.

59 *Jacques*, Letter 93, p. 132 (see Ch. 6 note 13): '. . . No one had the wisdom to tell her this: life is arid and terrible, repose is a dream, prudence is useless; mere reason serves simply to dry up the heart; there is but one virtue, the eternal sacrifice of oneself.'

60 *Middlemarch*, I Ch. 20 pp. 298–9.

61 Ibid., III Ch. 64 p. 181.

62 George Eliot, *Felix Holt*, 2 vols (Edinburgh and London, n.d.) I Ch. 10 p. 186.

63 *Letters*, V p. 107.

64 *Jacques*, Letter 93, p. 337: 'He's got room in his life for other things than love; solitude, travel, study, meditation – he loves all that; but we only love each other.'

65 *Middlemarch*, I Ch. 16 p. 251.

66 *Jacques*, Letter 29, p. 134: 'It's neither her fault nor mine.'

67 George Sand, *Indiana*, ed. Pierre Salomon (Paris, 1962) pp. 200–1: 'A wife who was no more than a child had made him unhappy like this! . . . To tell the truth, I don't know which of the two was the more miserable.'

68 Ibid., p. 272: 'a consuming need for happiness'.

69 Ibid., p. 50. The day he made this easy conquest, he returned home dismayed by his victory and, striking his brow, said to himself 'Let us hope she doesn't love me!'

70 Ibid., p. 191: 'From that moment he loved her no longer. She had wounded his self-esteem; she had cheated him of one of his triumphs, frustrated him of one of his pleasures . . . His love had already reached the last stage of aversion – tedium . . . He swore that even if it were only for a day he would be her master, and then he would throw her over.'

71 Ibid., p. 214: '. . . Indiana felt afraid. A good angel spread its wings over that tremulous, troubled soul . . .'

72 Ibid., p. 227. 'When he woke up he was filled with a sense of well-being . . . he had foreseen for a long time that a moment would come when he would find himself at odds with feminine love, when he would have to defend his

freedom against the demands of romantic passion and he had fortified himself to combat such claims . . . He felt he had at last regained his liberty and he gave himself up totally to blissful contemplation of this precious state.'

73 George Eliot, *Romola* (Edinburgh and London, n.d.) Ch. 48 pp. 429–30, 432.

74 George Sand, *Valvèdre* (Paris, 1861) p. 203: 'There are moments in the most irrevocable destinies when Providence offers us a sheet-anchor and seems to say, "Take it or you are lost." '

75 *Romola*, ɪ Ch. 22 p. 230.

76 *Nineteenth Century*, 17 (Mar 1885) 464–85. Quoted in *A Century of George Eliot Criticism*, ed. G. S. Haight (London, 1966) p. 156.

77 *Letters*, ɪɪɪ p. 382.

78 Mathilde Blind, *George Eliot* (London, 1883) p. 147.

79 'Amos Barton' in *Scenes of Clerical Life*, ɪ Ch. v p. 67.

80 N. C. Knoepflmacher, *George Eliot's Early Novels* (Berkeley, 1968) p. 110.

81 *Letters*, ɪɪɪ p. 155.

82 *Felix Holt*, ɪɪ Ch. 27 p. 39.

83 Stephen, *George Eliot*, p. 197.

84 *The Essays of George Eliot*, ed. T. Pinney (London, 1963) p. 55.

85 *Fortnightly Review*, n.s. 20 (Nov 1876) 612.

86 Quoted in R. Doumic, *George Sand* (Paris, 1922) p. 332.

87 James, *French Poets and Novelists*, p. 181.

88 Preface by John Oliver Hobbes to *Mauprat*, ed. E. Gosse (London, 1904) p. xi.

89 Haight, p. 472.

10. WESSEX AND 'LA VALLÉE NOIRE'

1 *Thomas Hardy, Personal Writings*, ed. H. Orel (London and Melbourne, 1967) p. 148. (The quotation is from *André*, Ch. 3.)

2 *The Letters of Henry James*, ed. P. Lubbock (London, 1920) ɪɪ p. 363.

3 *The Life and Letters of Leslie Stephen*, ed. F. W. Maitland (London, 1906) pp. 266–7.

4 Carl Weber, *Hardy of Wessex* (New York, 1940) p. 12.

5 *The Poems of Thomas Hardy*, ed. T. R. M. Creighton (London, 1974) p. 240.

6 *Personal Writings*, p. 140.

7 *Westminster Review*, n.s. cxɪx (Apr 1883) lxiii, 334–64.

8 Quoted in *Thomas Hardy and his Readers*, ed. L. Lerner and J. Holstrom (New York, 1968) p. 17.

9 *Life and Letters of Leslie Stephen*, p. 290.

10 F. E. Hardy, *The Early Life of Thomas Hardy* (London, 1908) Ch. 14 p. 113.

11 Donald Davidson, 'The Traditional Basis of Hardy's Fiction', in *Hardy*, ed. A. J. Guérard (Englewood Cliffs, N.J., 1963) p. 10.

12 For the best evidence of this see George Sand's glowing account of her country childhood in *Histoire de ma Vie*, in which the apocryphal element is lacking (*Oeuvres Autobiographiques*, ed. Lubin, especially pp. 830–9). It brings out well her knowledge of the peasant life, its poverty in the midst of the beauty of the changing seasons.

13 G. S. Haight, *George Eliot* (Oxford, 1968) pp. 3–4.

14 *Early Life*, p. 129.

15 Thomas Hardy, *Tess of the D'Urbervilles* (London, 1908) Ch. 14 p. 111.

16 George Sand, *Jeanne* (Paris, 1892) Prologue, pp. 19–20:
The native of these mountains, attached as he is to a barren land and inured to sober parsimony, has a sharper eye for profit than anyone in the world. He is active and hard-working like all those whom Nature, that hard-hearted mother, puts under the yoke of Necessity. He loves this thankless soil which does not sustain him, and when, in his youth, he has earned his living as horse-dealer or itinerant mason, he comes back to die of an ague under his own thatched roof.

17 George Sand, *Le Compagnon du Tour de France* (Paris, 1852) Preface, p. 9:
'You have the desire and the ability to paint man as he is . . . Well and good . . . I, on the other hand, feel moved to portray him as I hope he is, as I believe he should be.'

18 George Sand, *La Mare au Diable*, ed. P. Salomon and J. Mallion (Paris, 1962) p. 25: '. . . as straightforward and as unadorned as the furrow he was tracing with his plough.'

19 *Tess of the D'Urbervilles*, Ch. 18 p. 152.

20 *La Mare au Diable*, p. 77: 'You are going to live far from your own folk, where the land is bad – all marshes and heath – where you'll catch fevers in the autumn and where the sheep don't thrive, which is always vexing for a shepherdess who's conscientious.'

21 Thomas Hardy, *The Return of the Native* (London, 1949) Ch. 1 pp. 6–7.

22 *Jeanne*, Ch. 1 pp. 27–8:
It is a magnificent prospect, but one which it is impossible to stand for long. The sense of infinite space makes for giddiness . . . It seems to me that, always standing on the top of those isolated summits, gazing like this at the whole circle of the horizon, one has the most vivid sense of the globe's roundness and of being rapidly carried along by that headlong force which impells it in its eternal rotation. One feels oneself swept into this ineluctable race across the abysses of the sky and looks up in vain for a branch to hold on to.

23 Thomas Hardy, *Far from the Madding Crowd* (London, 1914) Ch. 2 pp. 9–10.

24 *The Return of the Native*, Ch. VI p. 61.

25 Ibid., Bk 4 Ch. 2 p. 296.

26 Thomas Hardy, *The Mayor of Casterbridge* (London, 1924) Ch. 13 p. 99.

27 *Tess of the D'Urbervilles*, Ch. 43 p. 372.

28 Thomas Hardy, *The Woodlanders* (London, 1929) Ch. 8 p. 76.

29 *Le Mare au Diable*, p. 46: '. . . anxious, snuffing the breeze, her mouth full of grass, which she no longer thought of eating.'

30 C. A. Sainte-Beuve, *Causeries du Lundi* (Paris, n.d.) I p. 356: 'This is no amateur painter who has walked across the fields to find a prospect; the artist is a native, has lived here for years; he is familiar with everything and knows it to the core.'

31 *Jeanne*, Ch. 21 p. 284: '. . . the little sounds of nature . . . The insect of the fields and the frog of the marshland scarcely paused in their prayerful intoning and as soon as she was past they began again with new fervour that mysterious psalmody to which the night inspires them.'

32   *La Mare au Diable*, pp. 138–9:

> The fruit has not yet been gathered and thousands of unusual cracking sounds make the trees seem like live beings; a branch creaks under a weight which quite suddenly can grow no greater; or else an apple detaches itself and falls with a thud at your feet on the damp ground. Then you hear the rustle of branches and grass which marks the retreat of some invisible creature; it is the peasant's dog, this inquisitive, restless rover, cowardly and impudent at the same time, who skulks everywhere, who never sleeps, who is always looking for something, who, hidden in the underbrush, spies on you and takes flight at the noise of the fallen apple, thinking that you have thrown a stone at him.

33   *Tess of the D'Urbervilles*, Ch. 4 p. 35.

34   George Sand, *André* (Paris, 1852) Ch. 7 pp. 128–30:

> Isn't it extraordinary to look at all these thousands of worlds and to think that beside them ours is simply a speck of light in space?
>
> Do you really not know that all these lights, as you call them, are worlds and suns?
>
> Yes, I believe that our world is only a testing-place which we pass through and that amongst all those that you see in the sky there is a better world, in which kindred spirits can reunite and belong to each other . . . I don't know where God has hidden the happiness he makes men hope for.

35   *Valentine*, Ch. 15 p. 125.

36   *Tess of the D'Urbervilles*, Ch. 23 p. 188.

37   *Jeanne*, Prologue, p. 5.

38   Ibid., p. 6.

39   Ibid., Ch. 1 p. 27.

40   Cf. extract from *Jeanne*, p. 126, and Hardy's observation in *Tess*, Ch. 16:

> 'Let the truth be told – women do as a rule live through such experiences, and again look about them with an interested eye. While there's life there's hope is a conviction not so entirely unknown to the "betrayed" as some amiable theorists would have us believe.'

41   H. de Balzac, *Lettres à l'Etrangère* (Paris, 1906) ii p. 125.

42   George Sand, *Spiridion* (Paris, 1837).

11.   THE LATE MADAME SAND

1   *Westminster Review*, n.s. 26 (July 1864) 40.

2   *Galaxy* (1870); reprinted as appendix to translation of George Sand's *Antonia* (Boston, 1870).

3   See Zola's essay on George Sand in *Messager de l'Europe, Documents Littéraires*, Vol 44 (July 1876) 185.

4   Quoted by J. P. Couch in *George Eliot and France* (Chapel Hill, 1967) p. 186.

5   *Westminster Review*, n.s. 26 (July 1864) p. 35.

6   Ellen Terry, *The Story of My Life* (London, 1908) p. 87.

7   *Life of Edward Bulwer Lytton, First Lord Lytton*, 2 vols (London, 1913) ii pp. 392–4.

8   *The Diaries of John Ruskin*, ed. Joan Evans and J. H. Whitehouse (Oxford, 1958) II p. 521.

9   *George Eliot, The Critical Heritage*, ed. David Carroll (London, 1971) p. 167.

10   *A Century of George Eliot Criticism*, ed. G. S. Haight (London, 1966) p. 126.

11   *Early Life and Letters of John Morley*, ed. F. W. Hirst, 2 vols (London, 1927) pp. 220–1.

12   *The Letters of John Addington Symonds*, ed. H. M. Schneller and R. L. Peters (Detroit, 1967) I p. 201.

13   Ibid., p. 251. Cf. also Hale White who, in 1892, was 'reading *Consuelo* again, for the second or third time, and this time in French. So much is left out in the English translation, and some of the best things are omitted. What a book it is!' *Letters to Three Friends* (London, 1924) p. 61.

14   Ibid., p. 647.

15   *Letters of Anne Thackeray Ritchie*, ed. Hester Ritchie (London, 1924) p. 256.

16   Lady Ritchie, *Blackstick Papers* (London, 1908) p. 80.

17   *Letters*, ed. Ritchie, pp. 171–2.

18   Ibid., p. 166.

19   *Blackstick Papers*, p. 103.

20   *The Swinburne Letters*, ed. Cecil Y. Lang, 6 vols (New Haven, 1962) I p. 76.

21   Ibid., III p. 291.

22   Ibid., V pp. 35–6.

23   *The Letters of Robert Louis Stevenson*, ed. Sir Sidney Colvin, 3 vols (London, 1926) I p. 116.

24   Quoted by Jacob Korg in *George Gissing, A Critical Biography* (London, 1965) p. 100.

25   *George Moore in Transition*, ed. H. E. Geiler (Detroit, 1968) p. 125.

26   Walter Pater, *Appreciations* (London, 1918) p. 52.

27   *The Artist as Critic*, in *Critical Writings of Oscar Wilde*, ed. Richard Ellmann (London, 1970) p. 141.

28   Ouida, *Strathmore* (London, 1865) I p. 156.

29   *Antonia*, appendix.

30   *The Artist as Critic*, ed. Ellmann, pp. 86–9.

31   Ibid., p. 87.

32   W. B. Yeats, *Autobiographies* (London, 1955) p. 177.

33   *Letters of W. B. Yeats*, ed. Allan Wade (London, 1954) pp. 687–8.

34   Joseph Hone, *W. B. Yeats (1865–1939)* (London, 1947) p. 347.

35   George Sand, *La Comtesse de Rudolstadt*, ed. Léon Cellier and Léon Guichard (Paris, 1959) Ch. 38 p. 455.

36   Ibid., Ch. 41 p. 481. George Sand's vision of the eighteenth century as a period of extraordinary polarity, out of which was to come the revolution: ce logogriphe immense, cette brillante nébuleuse, où tant de lâcheté s'oppose à tant de grandeur . . . tant de barbarie à tant de civilisation . . . laboratoire effrayant, où tant de formes hétérogènes ont été jetées dans le creuset, qu'elles ont vomi, dans leur monstrueuse ébullition, un torrent de fumée, où nous marchous encore enveloppés de ténèbres et d'images confuses.

37   *Saturday Review*, 42 (21 Oct 1876) 510–12.

38   *Athenaeum* (June 1876) 830.

39 *Atlantic Monthly*, 38 (Oct 1876) 444.
40 *Nineteenth Century* (Apr 1877) 221–40.
41 Ibid., 240.
42 *Dublin University Magazine* (Feb 1863) 233.
43 Ibid. (Aug 1876) 368.
44 *Blackwood's Magazine* (Jan 1877) 70.
45 Ibid. (June 1879) 690.
46 *Quarterly Review*, 143 (Apr 1877) 423–49.

12. 'DEAR OLD GEORGE'
1   Marie-Reine Garnier, *Henry James et la France* (Paris, 1927); Cornelia P.
    Kelley, *The Early Development of Henry James* (University of Illinois Press,
    1965); Oscar Cargill, *The Novels of Henry James* (New York, 1961); Jeanne
    Delbaere-Garant, *Henry James. The Vision of France* (Paris, 1970).
2   See e.g. C. M. Lombard, 'The American Attitude towards the French
    Romantics, 1800–1861', in *Revue de Littérature Comparée*, 39 (1965) 358–71;
    and 'George Sand's Image in America, 1837–76', in *Revue de Littérature
    Comparée*, 40 (1966) 177–86.
3   C. Hartley Gratton, *The Three Jameses* (New York, 1932) p. 64.
4   Henry James, *Autobiography*, ed. F. W. Dupee (London, 1956) p. 413.
5   Ibid., pp. 404–6.
6   Ibid., p. 406.
7   Ibid., p. 502.
8   Henry James, *Literary Reviews and Essays*, ed. Albert Mordell (New York,
    1957) p. 122.
9   Ibid., pp. 122–8.
10 *George Eliot: The Critical Heritage*, ed. David Carroll (London, 1971)
    pp. 273–7, especially p. 275.
11 Henry James, *Views and Reviews*, ed. Le Roy Philip (New York, 1908:1969)
    p. 24.
12 Edmund Gosse, *Aspects and Impressions* (London, 1922) p. 21.
13 *Autobiography*, p. 404.
14 Leon Edel, *Henry James: The Conquest of London 1870–1831* (London, 1962)
    p. 212.
15 Wladimir Karénine, *George Sand* (Paris, 1912) III p. 509.
16 *The Letters of Henry James*, ed. Percy Lubbock, 2 vols (London, 1920) I
    p. 46.
17 Kelley, p. 250.
18 *Literary Reviews*, p. 367.
19 *Notes on Novelists*, p. 86.
20 Delbaere-Garant, p. 125.
21 *Literary Reviews*, pp. 169–70.
22 *The Nation*, 22 (13 Jan 1876) 34.
23 *Literary Reviews*, p. 131.
24 *Notes on Novelists*, p. 130.
25 *Literary Reviews*, p. 133.
26 *Letters*, I p. 51.

27 Kelley, pp. 247–55.
28 Henry James, *French Poets and Novelists* (London, 1878) pp. 149–85, especially p. 155.
29 Ibid., p. 172.
30 Ibid., p. 185.
31 F. R. Leavis, *The Great Tradition* (London, 1948) p. 86.
32 Cargill, p. 82.
33 Henry James, '*Daniel Deronda*: A Conversation', in *The Atlantic Monthly*, 38 (Dec 1876) 684–94.
34 Henry James, *Partial Portraits* (London, 1905) p. 301.
35 Ibid., p. 46.
36 Henry James, *Essays in London and Elsewhere* (London, 1893) p. 140.
37 One such reader was Virginia Woolf who, in 1906, was re-reading the letters and commented:
   I think no letters I have read interest me more or seem more beautiful and more suggestive ... She brings out all his peculiar qualities so finely that no autobiography could tell so much as he tells almost unconsciously. I have read none of her novels: but only the autobiography. It is an immense lucid kind of mind, something like a natural force – with no effort or consciousness about it ... I sink into her and am engulphed! *The Flight of the Mind: The Letters of Virginia Woolf*, ed. Nigel Nicolson, Vol. 1: 1888–1912 (London, 1975) p. 229.
38 *The Diary of Alice James*, ed. Leon Edel (New York, 1934) p. 42.
39 *Notes on Novelists*, p. 127.
40 Ibid., p. 136.
41 Henry James, *Italian Hours* (London, 1909) p. 71.
42 *Notes on Novelists*, pp. 148–68.
43 Ibid., p. 162.
44 *Letters*, II pp. 235–6.
45 *Notes on Novelists*, pp. 168–93.
46 Ibid., p. 193.
47 *Letters*, II p. 426.
48 Emile Faguet, *Dix-Neuvième Siècle: Etudes Littéraires* (Paris, 1887) p. 408: 'When one takes to her it is with a sort of sympathy. Her style becomes a friend. It is easier to get free of enchantment than friendship.'
49 Kelley, p. 13.
50 Delbaere-Garant, p. iii.
51 Kelley, p. 14.
52 Ibid., p. 90.
53 George Sand, *Les Maîtres Mosaïstes* (Paris, 1837) Preface: 'Never before have I seen so many flowers and birds in my garden. Liszt was playing the piano on the ground floor and the nightingales, intoxicated with music and sunshine, were frenziedly singing themselves hoarse on the near-by lilacs.'
54 Delbaere-Garant, p. 234.
55 Edel, p. 304.
56 Ibid., p. 202.
57 *Complete Tales of Henry James*, ed. Leon Edel (New York, 1962) I p. 194.

58 Ibid., III p. 301.
59 Cargill, p. 8.
60 Cargill, p. 24.
61 Kelley, pp. 242–3.
62 Ibid., p. 243.
63 *Indiana*, Ch. 21 p. 226.
64 Henry James, *The Art of the Novel*, ed. R. P. Blackmur (New York, 1934) p. 307.
65 Cargill, p. 304.
66 George Sand, *Mlle Merquem* (Paris, 1868) p. 229.
67 Ibid., p. 309.
68 Cargill, p. 24: quoting from R. B. Perry, *The Thought and Character of William James*, 2 vols (Boston, 1935) I p. 313.
69 Kelley, p. 158.
70 Cargill, p. 24.
71 *French Poets and Novelists*, pp. 175–6.
72 *Art of the Novel*, p. 79.
73 See Albert Mordell, *Literary Reviews and Essays* (New York, 1957) and E. L. Volpe, 'Prefaces of George Sand and Henry James', *Modern Language Notes*, 70 (Feb 1955) 107–8.
74 *French Poets and Novelists*, p. 163.
75 Kelley, p. 233.
76 *French Poets and Novelists*, p. 160.
77 *The Art of the Novel*, p. 43.
78 *Indiana*, Preface.
79 Henry James, *The Portrait of a Lady*, 2 vols (New York, 1908) Ch. 17 p. 235.
80 Cargill, p. 91.
81 *French Poets and Novelists*, p. 155.
82 *The Europeans*, Ch. 6 p. 92.
83 Henry James, *The Ambassadors* (New York, 1909) II Bk XI pp. 262–3.
84 Ibid., II Bk XII p. 284.
85 Delbaere-Garant, p. 124.
86 *Notes on Novelists*, p. 143.

Bibliography

As all the books from which I have quoted in the text are fully documented in the notes, there has seemed little point in inflicting on the reader a vast bibliography of the books and articles which I have consulted in the course of my research but whose relevance might not be easily apparent. I have instead restricted this section to a chronology of George Sand's works and a note of translations to be found in the British Museum, the Library of Congress, the London Library and the Cambridge University Library. The most exhaustive account of George Sand's output will be found in George Lubin's *Chronologie* in his *Oeuvres Autobiographiques*. I cite most of the novels and any short stories which have been of use for this study or were mentioned by Victorian readers; her steady stream of articles, prefaces, criticism, short stories, plays and her Niagara correspondence I have allowed to flow past unrecorded here.

It will be seen that many of the translations were published in Boston or New York although some of the earliest were the work of English translators. So much scorn was poured on their efforts, which were indeed often very bad, that it is small wonder that they seem to have got discouraged. It is interesting that one of the finest of George Sand's works, *Lettres d'un Voyageur*, has to this day not had another attempt made upon it since Eliza Ashurst squared up to it manfully in 1847; a sensitive rendering of it is long overdue. Where the translator is known I have given the name; when the place of publication is not London I have in each case given the reference.

Chronology of Works by George Sand

1831	Rose et Blanche (J. Sand)
1832	*Indiana*
	Valentine
	La Marquise
1833	*Lélia*
	Lavinia
1834	*Le Sécretaire Intime*
	Jacques
	Leone Leoni
1834–7	*Lettres d'un Voyageur*
1835	*André*
1836	*Simon*

1837   *Mauprat*
       Lettres à Marcie
       Les Maîtres Mosaïstes
1838   *L'Uscoque*
       La Dernière Aldini
1838–9 *Spiridion*
1839   *Les Sept Cordes de la Lyre*
1840   *Le Compagnon du Tour de France*
1841   *Un Hiver au midi de l'Europe* (later *Un Hiver à Majorque*)
1841–2 *Horace*
1842–3 *Consuelo*
1843   *La Comtesse de Rudolstadt*
1844   *Jeanne*
1845   *Le Meunier d'Angibault*
       Le Péché de M. Antoine
       Teverino
1845–6 *La Mare au Diable*
1846–7 *Lucrezia Floriani*
1847   *Le Piccinino*
1847–8 *François le Champi*
1848   *Lettres au Peuple*
1848–9 *La Petite Fadette*
1851   *Claudie*
       Le Château des Désertes
1852   *Mont-Revêche*
1853   *La Filleule*
       Les Maîtres Sonneurs
1854–5 *Histoire de ma Vie*
1855   *Le Diable aux Champs*
1857   *La Daniella*
1858   *Les Beaux Messieurs de Bois-Doré*
1859   *Elle et Lui*
       L'Homme de Neige
       Les Dames Vertes
       Promenades autour d'un Village
1860   *Jean de la Roche*
       Constance Verrier
1861   *La Ville Noire*
       Le Marquis de Villemer
       Valvèdre
       La Famille de Germandre
1862   *Souvenirs et Impressions Littéraires*
       Tamaris
1863   *Mademoiselle la Quintinie*
1865   *Laura*
       La Confession d'une Jeune Fille
1866   *Monsieur Sylvestre*
1867   *Le Dernier Amour*

1867   *Cadio*
        Mademoiselle Merquem
1869   *Pierre Qui Roule*
        Le Beau Laurence
1870   *Malgrétout*
1871   *Césarine Dietrich*
        Journal d'un Voyageur Pendant la Guerre
1872   *Francia*
        Nanon
1873   *Impressions et Souvenirs*
        Contes d'une Grand-mère
1874   *Ma Soeur Jeanne*
1875   *Flamarande*
        Les Deux Frères
1876   *La Tour de Percemont* & *Marianne*
        Contes d'une Grand-mère (2e série)
1877   *Dernières Pages*
1878   *Questions d'Art et de Littérature*
        Questions politiques et sociales

Translations

1842   *Spiridion*
1844   *The Mosaic Workers*, trans. E. A. Ashurst; 1845, another trans.
        (Philadelphia); 1895, *The Master Mosaic Workers*, trans. C. C.
        Johnstone (Boston); 1899.
1846   *Consuelo*, trans. F. G. Shaw (Boston) [1850]; 1847, another trans.
        (Parlour Library); 1851, trans. F. Robinson (New York) [1870; 1882;
        1894]; 1889, trans. F. H. Potter (New York); 1876; 1891 (New York);
        1893 (Oxford Library).
1847   *The Works of George Sand* (ed. M. M. Hays): Vol. I *The Last Aldini*,
        Simon; II *André*, trans. E. A. Ashurst, *The Mosaic Masters, Fanchette*;
        III *Mauprat*, trans. M. M. Hays; IV *The Companion of the Tour of
        France*, trans. M. M. Hays; V *The Miller of Angibault*, trans. Rev.
        E. R. Larkin; VI *Letters of a Traveller*, trans. E. A. Ashurst.
1847   *The Miller of Angibault* (Parlour Library); 1871, trans. M. E. Dewey
        (Boston); 1892.
1847   *Jacques*, trans. A. Blackwell (New York).
1847   *The Countess of Rudolstadt*, trans. F. G. Shaw (Boston); 1851, another
        trans. (Parlour Library); 1862 (Shilling Readable Novels); 1870,
        trans. F. Robinson (Philadelphia) [1883; 1893 (Oxford Library);
        1895]; 1891, trans. F. H. Potter (New York); 1906 (Everyman)
        [1912].
1847   *The Journeyman Joiner*, trans. F. G. Shaw (New York) [1849 (Dublin)].
1848   *The Haunted Marsh* (Parlour Library) [1884]; 1850, *The Enchanted
        Lake*, trans. F. G. Shaw (Boston); 1861, *The Devil's Pool*; 1890, *The
        Devil's Pool*, trans. F. H. Potter (New York); 1892, *Germaine's*

Marriage; 1894, *The Devil's Pool*, trans. J. M. and E. Sedgwick (New York) [1901, Boston]; 1897, *The Devil's Pool*; 1906, 1911, 1930, *The Devil's Pool* (Everyman); 1966, *The Devil's Pool*, trans. Antonia Cowan.

1850   *Little Fadette*, trans. J. Mazzini; 1851, *Fadette*; 1863, *Fanchon the Cricket. A Tale* [1864 (New York); 1891 (Philadelphia)]; 1878, *Little Cricket* (play), trans. J. Mortimer; 1885, *Fanchon the Cricket* (play); 1893, *Fadette*, trans. J. M. Sedgwick (New York) [1895; 1899]; 1896, *Fadette*, trans. Mrs J. M. Lancaster (New York); 1967, *Little Fadette*, trans. Eva Figes.

1850   *The Uscoque*, trans. J. Bauer (New York); 1851.

1850   *Indiana*, trans. by 'one of the best French scholars in this country, a member of the Philadelphia bar' (Philadelphia); 1881, *Indiana. A Love Story*.

1855   *Teverino*, trans. by 'a lady' (New York); *Jealousy or Teverino*, trans. O. S. Leland (Philadelphia and New York).

1868   *Mademoiselle Merquem* (New York).

1870   *Antonia*, trans. V. Vaughan (Boston), with an essay on George Sand by Justin McCarthy.

1870   *M. Sylvestre*, trans. F. G. Shaw (Boston).

1870   *Mauprat*, trans. V. Vaughan (Boston) [1883]; 1891, trans. H. E. Miller (Chicago); 1901, trans. S. Young, with an introduction by John Oliver Hobbes.

1871   *Césarine Dietrich*, trans. E. Stanwood (Boston).

1871   *The Snow Man*, trans. V. Vaughan (Boston) [1898].

1871   *A Rolling Stone*, trans. Carrill Owen (Boston).

1874   *Recollections by George Sand*, trans. R. H. Stoddard; 1877, *Impressions and Souvenirs*, trans. H. K. Adams (Boston).

1874   *My Sister Jeannie*, trans. S. R. Crocker (Boston).

1877   *The Last Aldini* (New York, Seaside Library).

1877   *The Tower of Percemont* (New York); 1880, *The Tower of Percemont* and *Marianne* (Popular French Novels) [1883].

1878   *George Sand's Novels* (*The Miller of Angibault*; *The Comtesse of Rudolstadt*; *Mauprat*; *Little Fadette*).

1884   *The Wings of Courage*, trans. Mrs Corkran etc. [1911; 1915]; 1931, trans. M. V. Chadwyck-Healey; 1931, trans. B. B. Lifschultz (Chicago).

1884   *The Castle of Pictordu*, trans. G. S. Grahame (Edinburgh).

1884   *Lady Blake's Love-Letters* (George Sand's *Lavinia*) trans. Page McCarty (New York).

1886   *Letters of George Sand*, 3 vols, trans. R. Ledos de Beaufort.

1889   *Francis the Waif*, trans. G. Masson; 1894, trans. J. M. Sedgwick (New York); 1906 (Everyman).

1890   *The Bagpipers*, trans. K. P. Wormeley (Boston).

1890   *The Gallant Lords of Bois-Doré*, trans. Steven Clovis (New York).

1892   *The Naiad: A Ghost Story*, trans. K. Berry di Zéréga (New York).

1893   *Convent Life of George Sand* (from *Histoire de ma Vie*), trans. M. E. Mackaye (Boston).

1900–2   *The Masterpieces of George Sand* (limited subscribed edition) 20 vols, trans. G. Burnham Ives: *Indiana*; *Consuelo*; *The Sin of M. Antoine*; *Leone Leoni*; *The Piccinino*; *The Last of the Aldinis*; *Les Beaux Messieurs de Bois-Doré*; *The Snow Man*; *Antonia*; *Nanon*; *A Rolling Stone*; *Handsome Laurence*; *The Germandre Family*; *The Marquis of Villemer*; *Valentine*; *Mauprat*; *He and She*; *Lavinia* (New York).

1911   *George Sand: Thoughts and Aphorisms from her Works*, arr. A. H. Hyatt.

1922   *The George Sand–Gustave Flaubert Letters*, trans. A. L. McKenzie (New York).

1929   *Intimate Journal*, trans. M. J. Howe (New York).

1928–30 *The Select Novels and Tales of George Sand* (3 vols): 1928, *Little Fadette*, trans. H. Miles; 1929, *The Devil's Pool*, trans. H. Miles; 1930, *The Country Waif*, trans. Eirene Collis, and *The Castle of Pictordu*, trans. P. H. Watson.

1930   *Tales of a Grandmother*, trans. Margaret Bloom (Philadelphia and London).

1930   *Letters of George Sand*, selected and trans. by V. Lucas, Introduction by E. Drew.

1956   *Winter in Majorca*, trans. R. Graves.

Index

Page numbers in bold type indicate a series of entries relating the subject to George Sand.

By the same author:

The Victorian Heroine: A Changing Ideal

GEORGE SAND AND THE VICTORIANS